D1383708

DATE DUE

FEB 1 7 2015	
JAN 3 1 2017	

ARAB & ARAB AMERICAN FEMINISMS

Gender, Culture, and Politics in the Middle East

miriam cooke, Simona Sharoni, and Suad Joseph, *Series Editors*

ARAB & ARAB AMERICAN

Feminisms

GENDER, VIOLENCE, & BELONGING

Edited by Rabab Abdulhadi,
Evelyn Alsultany, and Nadine Naber

SYRACUSE UNIVERSITY PRESS

Cover art by Christina Dennaoui. *Seeing Yourself in Fragments* is the final piece of the "Rendering the Arab Woman Visible: Constructing the Self in a Cultural Diaspora" series. The series addresses the complex relationship between culture, transnationalism, and positionality through the repetition of a central figure, an Arab Muslim woman, situated in various visual contexts, each differentiated by the use of cartographical imagery.

Parts of this volume first appeared in *The MIT Electronic Journal of Middle East Studies*, Vol. 5, Spring 2005, © The MIT Electronic Journal of Middle East Studies (MIT-EJMES). They are reprinted here with permission.

∞ The paper used in this publication meets the minimum requirements of the American National Standard for Information Sciences—Permanence of Paper for Printed Library Materials, ANSI Z39.48-1992.

For a listing of books published and distributed by Syracuse University Press, visit our Web site at SyracuseUniversityPress.syr.edu.

ISBN: 978-0-8156-3223-8

Library of Congress Cataloging-in-Publication Data

Arab and Arab American feminisms : gender, violence, and belonging / edited by Rabab Abdulhadi, Evelyn Alsultany, and Nadine Naber.
       p. cm. — (Gender, culture, and politics in the Middle East)
    Includes bibliographical references and index.
    ISBN 978-0-8156-3223-8 (cloth : alk. paper)
   1. Women, Arab—Social conditions.   2. Arab American women—Social conditions.
3. Feminist theory.   I. Abdulhadi, Rabab.   II. Alsultany, Evelyn.   III. Naber, Nadine Christine.
    HQ1729.5.A73 2010
    305.48'8927—dc22   2010051388

Manufactured in the United States of America

Contents

Acknowledgments

Arab and Arab American Feminisms has been a collaborative journey that began in 2002. It came together through ongoing conversations with colleagues, mentors, friends, and loved ones. We are indebted to everyone who has been there for us along this journey. As members of the American Studies Association's (ASA) annual meetings organizing committee of 2003, Amy Kaplan and Melani McAlister enthusiastically supported two roundtable discussions we organized that helped to spark this book project. Maha Yahya invited us to edit a special issue of the MIT *Electronic Journal of Middle East Studies,* following the ASA meeting, at a time when area studies journals were not as interested in transnational discussions, let alone gendered transnational frameworks. The special *MIT-EJMES* issue on Arab and Arab American feminisms (spring 2005) was instrumental to the development of this book. We are indebted to Maha for her patience, support, the extensive time and energy she put into the journal's special issue, as well as her unwavering commitment to the project of Arab and Arab American feminist knowledges as a valuable, legitimate, and necessary scholarship.

We recognize our colleagues who participated in the roundtable discussion or the special *MIT-EJMES* issue who were unable for one reason or another to contribute to this book. In this respect, we acknowledge the important contributions of Hala Nassar, Amal Abdelrazek, Alia Malek, Lara Deeb, Nathalie Handal, and Rosina Hassoun to conversations on Arab and Arab American feminisms in the earlier stages of this project.

This project would not have been possible without the love, support, and sisterhood of every contributor in this book. We would like to thank Deena Al-Adeeb, Anan Ameri, Amal Amireh, Janaan Attia, Emanne Bayoumi, Moulouk Berry, Youmna Chlala, Susan Darraj, Christina Dennaoui, Mona El-Ghobashy, Nada Elia, Noura Erakat, Amal Hassan Fadlalla, Suheir Hammad, Mervat F. Hatem, Happy/L. A. Hyder, Huda Jadallah, Amira Jarmakani, Randa Jarrar, Joe Kadi, Mohja Kahf, Lisa Suhair Majaj, Dunya Mikhail, Therese Saliba, Sherene

Seikaly, Ella Habiba Shohat, Ameena Sultan, Kyla Wazana Tompkins, Kathy Wazana, Imani Yatouma, and Zeina Zaatari.

We thank LeAnn Fields at University of Michigan Press who offered us feedback from anonymous reviewers and who encouraged us to develop the journal issue into a book manuscript.

Mary Selden Evans, Marcia Hough, Lisa Renee Kuerbis, Kelly Lynne Balenske, and Kay Steinmetz at Syracuse University Press provided us with untiring assistance and support. We are appreciative of Mary Selden Evans's steadfast dedication to emerging scholarship in the fields of Arab and Arab American studies. Working with an editor who was deeply sensitive to the historical and political issues that framed our book was not only a pleasure but also an essential ingredient in turning the idea of this book into a concrete reality.

We are especially grateful to our students Andrew McBride, Kenny Garcia, Vanessa Saldivar, Sriya Shrestha, and Lee Ann Wang. Their remarkable assistance in logistical work, editing, proofreading, and formatting the journal issue and book manuscript was truly invaluable. We are also grateful to Rabia Belt for proofreading and for developing our index. We enjoyed working with these emerging scholars and learning from their insights.

Each of us gives thanks to the mentorship, comradeship, and support of exceptional feminist scholars and activists with whom we have had the privilege to work over the years. We would like to acknowledge Ella Shohat, Suad Joseph, Cherríe Moraga, Jacqui Alexander, Drucilla Cornell, Penelope Eckert, Sondra Hale, Neferti Tadiar, Chandra Talpade Mohanty, Ruthie Gilmore, Barbara Harlow, Rosalind Petchesky, and Kent Ono, who have been instrumental in our lives.

We would also like to acknowledge the organizations and movements that have contributed to the shaping of our political consciousness over the years: the African and Caribbean People's Resource Center; American Arab Anti-Discrimination Committee, San Francisco Chapter; Association of Arab American University Graduates (AAUG); Arab American Resource Center; Arab Movement of Women Arising for Justice; Arab Women's Solidarity Association; Center for Political Education; Center for Women's Development, Medgar Evers College; Committee for a Democratic Palestine; El Centro Puerto Ricaño at Hunter College; Feminist Arab American Network; General Union of Palestine Students; General Union of Palestinian Women; INCITE! Women of Color Against Violence; Organization of Asian Women; Palestine Solidarity Committee; Patrice Lumumba Coalition; Radical Arab Women's Activist Network; South West Asian North African Bay Area Queers; Union of Palestinian Women's Associations in

North America; Women of Color Resource Center; and Women's Studies Center, Bir Zeit University.

We are fortunate to be surrounded by supportive friends and colleagues: Ziad Abbas, Suheir Abbasi, Nahla Abdo, Sawsan Abdulrahim, Mireille Abelin, Tom Abowd, Dina Abu Lughod, Catherine Acey, Fahd Ahmed, Fadwa Al-Labadi, Nisreen Alami, Mona Al-Ali, Deborah Alkamano, Tomas Almaguer, Allam Al-Qadah, Sam Anderson, Barbara Aswad, Kathryn Babayan, Myrna Baine, Falu Bakrania, Elif Bali, Omar Barghouti, Somaya Barghouti, Suha Barghouti, Riham Barghouti, Magdalena Barrera, Linda Basch, Hatem Bazian, Susanne Begeron, Rawia Bishara, Maylei Blackwell, Michael Bobbitt, Lillian Boctor, Jane Bower, Elombe Brath, Dorothy Duff Brown, Jeanne Butterfield, Louise Cainkar, Amy Carroll, Linda Carty, Christianne Cejas, Lauren Chew, Erskine Childers, Cathy Cohen, Ebony Coletu, Vivia Costalas, Maria Cotera, Renda Dabit, Lara Deeb, Deirdre de la Cruz, Tina Delisle, Philip Deloria, Nacisse Demeksa, Eman Desouky, Vicente Diaz, Carolyn Dinshaw, Gregory Dowd, Lisa Duggan, Maurice and Najwa El-Qare, Catriona Esquibel, Amal Hassan Fadlalla, Laila Farah, Jason Ferreira, Alia Gabra, Josh Gamson, Leonor Garcia, Melissa Garcia, Jess Ghannam, Simmi Ghandi, Rita Giacaman, Reem Gibriel, Dena Goodman, Catherine Groves, Christine Guivernau, Sandra Gunning, Beverly Guy-Sheftall, George Habib, Elaine Hagopian, Nuhad Hamad, Khader Hamide and Julia Mongai Hamide, Rema Hammemi, Kathy Hanna, Sandra Hanna, Mary Harb, Mona Harb, Rebecca Hardin, Barbara Harlow, Lily Haskell, Salah D. Hassan, Rima Hassouneh, Lolita Hernandez, Elana Herrada, Monadel Hirzallah, Nubar Hovsepian, Anya Hurwitz, Adnan Husain, Shazia Iftkhar, Islah Jad, Maha Jarad, Penny Johnson, Darrel Jordan, Reena Karni, Nadera Shalhoub Kevorkian, Aneb Kgositsile, Senan Khairi, Mona and Rashid Khalidi, Osman Khan, Maha and Riad Khoury, Emily Katz Kishawi, Eyad Kishawi, Scott Kurashige, Eileen Kuttab, Lawrence LaFountain-Stokes, Jayati Lal, Emily Lawsin, Maureen Linker, Alex Lubin, Barbara Lubin, Sunaina Maira, Sana' Malhees, Samori Marksman, Esperanza Martell, Mai Masri and Jean Chamoun, Florencia Masri, Jorge Matos, Khaled Mattawa, Rosemari Meely, Chandra Mohanty, Ken Monteiro, Mira Nabulsi, Susan Najita, Lamis Abu Nahleh, Maha Nassar, Marisol Negrón, Heba Nimr, Hilton Obenzinger, Camilia Odeh, Jack O'Dell, Rupal Oza, Julia Paley, Damani Partridge, Rosalind Petchesky, Dahlia Petrus, Douglas Pineda, Lavinia Pinto, Vanessa Primiani, Osama Qasem, Fadia Rafeedie Khoury, Ramiz Rafeedie, Omneya Ragab, Elizabeth Roberts, Gilda Rodriguez, Paola Rojas, Lauren Rosenthal, Naila Sabra, Steven Salaita, Rosemary Sayigh, Helen Schaub, Sarita See, May Seikaly, Jack Shaheen, Abla Shamieh, Jamal and Wafa Shamieh, Simona

Sharoni, Nadia Sheikh, Shahid Siddiqui, Andy Smith, Deborah Smith-Pollard, Amy Sueyoshi, Lisa Taraki, Miriam Ticktin, Valerie Traub, Ruth Tsoffar, Shouleh Vatanabadi, Penny Von Eschen, Alan Wald, and Michelle Zamora.

Our deepest thanks go to our loved ones for their unyielding patience, love, and support: Atef and Kinan Said; Benefo, Nubian, Zeeza, and Monaluna Ofosu-Benefo; Jaime Veve; Mrs. Alida Veve and the Veve family; Samiha Khalil; Ibrahim and Rafee'a, and Reem, Samir, Saad, Nasser, Amer Abdulhadi, and their families; the Ofosu-Benefo family; Maggie, Kamal, and Fabian Alsultany; Fatima and Raul Chavez; Maria Jimemez, Martha Jaramillo, and Steven Cuevas; and the Naber family.

Contributors

Rabab Abdulhadi is an Associate Professor of Ethnic Studies/Race and Resistance Studies and Senior Scholar in the Arab and Muslim Ethnicities and Diasporas Initiative, College of Ethnic Studies, San Francisco State University. She is the coauthor of *Mobilizing Democracy: Changing U.S. Policy in the Middle East*. Her work has appeared in *Gender and Society, Radical History Review, Peace Review, Journal of Women's History, Taiba, Women and Cultural Discourses, Cuadernos Metodologicos: Estudio de Casos, This Bridge We Call Home, New World Coming: The 1960s and the Shaping of Global Consciousness, Local Actions: Cultural Activism, Power and Public Life in America, The Guardian, Al-Fajr, Womanews, Palestine Focus, Voice of Palestinian Women*, and several Arabic-language publications.

Dena Al-Adeeb is an Iraqi visual artist, educator, writer, and activist-organizer living in San Francisco. She worked in the multimedia and e-learning industries as a graphic designer, illustrator, publisher, and user-interface architect and taught at Expression College for Digital Arts. Her work has been presented and exhibited nationally and internationally at the Arab American National Museum in Michigan, SomaArts Gallery in San Francisco, Mashrabia Gallery in Cairo, Karim Francis Gallery in Cairo, and Falaki Gallery in Cairo, among others. Dena has also been published in *Alif: Journal of Comparative Poetics* and the *Color of Violence: The INCITE! Anthology*, among others.

Evelyn Alsultany is an Assistant Professor in the Program in American Culture at the University of Michigan. She is currently completing a book manuscript, tentatively entitled, "Arabs and Muslims in the U.S. Media Post-9/11." She is coeditor (with Ella Shohat) of the forthcoming volume *The Cultural Politics of the Middle East in the Americas*. She is the guest curator of an exhibit, "DisORIENTation: Arabs and Arab Americans in the U.S. Popular Imagination" at the Arab American National Museum. She has published in *American Quarterly, Race and Arab Americans Before and After 9/11, The Arab Diaspora, This Bridge We Call Home*, and *Mixing It Up*.

Anan Ameri is the Founding Director of the Arab American National Museum in Dearborn, Michigan. She has been with ACCESS since 1997 as the Director of the Cultural Arts Program, which led the project plans for the museum. She has more than thirty years of experience working with Arab American communities and is the author of several books and articles.

Amal Amireh is an Associate Professor of English at George Mason University. She is the author of *The Factory Girl and the Seamstress: Imagining Gender and Class in Nineteenth-Century American Fiction* and coeditor (with Lisa Suhair Majaj) of *Going Global: The Transnational Reception of Third World Women Writers* and *Etel Adnan: Critical Essays on the Arab-American Writer and Artist*. Her essay "Between Complicity and Subversion: Body Politics in Palestinian National Narrative" won the Florence Howe Award for best essay from a feminist perspective.

Janaan Attia is an Egyptian Copt raised in Los Angeles and is currently living in Oakland, California. She is a registered nurse dedicated to working in community health with elders of color. She has been involved in grassroots organizing since high school and has worked on issues ranging from violence in the home to teaching social justice education in high schools. She served as a member of the organizing committee for the Arab Movement of Women Arising for Justice, a historic conference of Arab and Arab American women in 2006.

Emanne Bayoumi is a cultural activist, performance artist, and DJ. Oakland is her home, and Egypt is her homeland.

Moulouk Berry is an Assistant Professor of Modern and Classical Languages in the Department of Language, Communication, and Culture at the University of Michigan–Dearborn. She served as the interim director for the first and only Center for Arab American Studies in the United States and is currently directing the Arabic-language program at the University of Michigan–Dearborn. Her publications include "Rethinking Notions of Sexuality: Muslim Legal Writings," "Teaching Scriptural Texts in the Classroom: The Question of Gender," "The Women's Right to Occupy Position of Judge in Muslim Shi'i Law," and "Lebanon," a chapter in the *WorldMark Encyclopedia of Religious Practices*. In addition to her academic work, Berry writes fiction and poetry in English and Arabic.

Youmna Chlala is a writer and an artist, born in Beirut and currently based in California. She was the founding editor of the *Eleven Eleven [1111] Journal of Literature and Art*. Nominated for a Ruth Lilly Poetry Prize, she has published her work in the *MIT Journal for Middle Eastern Studies* and *XCP: Journal of Cross Cultural Poetics*. She has exhibited and performed in the United States, Lebanon,

Egypt, Spain, Canada, and France, as well as at the San Jose Museum of Art, Berkeley Art Museum, National Arab American Museum, and Yerba Buena Center for the Arts.

Susan Muaddi Darraj is an Associate Professor of English at Harford Community College in Bel Air, Maryland, and a Lecturer at Johns Hopkins University. Her book of short fiction, *The Inheritance of Exile*, was published in 2007 and won the *ForeWord Magazine* Book of the Year Award for Short Stories. She is Senior Editor of the *Baltimore Review*, a literary journal of fiction, poetry, and essays.

Christina Dennaoui is an independent artist and musician living and working in Chicago. She works in the field of digital media and Web analytics. Her work can be viewed at http://www.cdennaoui.com.

Mona El-Ghobashy is an Assistant Professor of Political Science at Barnard College. Her work on Egyptian politics has appeared in the *International Journal of Middle East Studies, Middle East Report*, and *American Behavioral Scientist*.

Nada Elia is the author of *Trances, Dances, and Vociferations: Agency and Resistance in Africana Women's Narratives*, and has guest edited a special issue of *Radical Philosophy Review* devoted to the Second Intifada.

Noura Erakat is currently a human rights attorney and writer. Upon graduating from Berkeley Law School in 2005, Noura received a New Voices Fellowship to serve as the National Grassroots Organizer and Legal Advocate at the U.S. Campaign to End the Israeli Occupation. She then served as Legal Counsel to a congressional subcommittee in the House of Representatives before beginning to teach at Georgetown University as an Adjunct Professor.

Amal Hassan Fadlalla is an Assistant Professor of Women's Studies and African Studies at the University of Michigan. She is the author of *Embodying Honor: Fertility, Foreignness, and Regeneration in Eastern Sudan* and coeditor of *Gendered Insecurities: Health and Development in Africa*. Her articles include "The Neoliberalization of Compassion: Darfur and the Mediation of American Faith, Fear and Terror," "Modest Women, Deceptive Jinn: Identity, Alterity, and Disease in Eastern Sudan," and "State of Vulnerability and Humanitarian Visibility: Lubna's Pants and Sudanese Trans-Politics of Rights and Dissent."

Suheir Hammad is the author of *Breaking Poems* as well as *ZaatarDiva; Born Palestinian, Born Black;* and *Drops of This Story*. Her award-winning work has appeared in numerous anthologies and journals. She was an original writer and performer in the Tony Award–winning *Russell Simmons Presents Def Poetry Jam on Broadway*. Suheir appears in the 2008 Cannes Film Festival Official Selection *Salt of This Sea* and has read her work throughout the world on stage, radio, and screen.

Mervat F. Hatem is a Professor of Political Science at Howard University. She has published more than fifty journal articles and book chapters on the study of gender and politics in the Middle East and the role of gender in Arab American politics. Most recently, she served as president of the Middle East Studies Association in North America (2007–9).

Happy/L. A. Hyder is a fine artist working in color photography, mixed-media constructions, and large-scale installations. She has been instrumental in bringing art by women and by lesbians to a large audience through her work with Vida Gallery and LVA: Lesbians in the Visual Arts. View her intricately compelling photographs at http://www.lahyderphotography.com.

Huda Jadallah is a Palestinian lesbian born and raised in the San Francisco Bay Area. She and her partner of eighteen years, Deanna Karraa, were finally able to get legally married in Oakland, California, on June 16, 2008. They have three children (Omar, Hady, and Hind). Huda has been an activist for more than twenty years working for social justice in many communities, including queer Arab and Arab American communities. Currently, she is active in the movement for welcoming and inclusive schools and the marriage equality movement.

Amira Jarmakani is an Assistant Professor of Women's Studies at Georgia State University. Recent publications include her book *Imagining Arab Womanhood: The Cultural Mythology of Veils, Harems, and Belly Dancers in the U.S.*, which was awarded the Gloria E. Anzaldúa Book Prize from the National Women's Studies Association. Currently, she is at work on a project about the popularity of the "sheikh" hero in mass-market romance novels.

Randa Jarrar is the award-winning author of the critically acclaimed novel *A Map of Home*, as well as numerous short stories.

Joe Kadi is the editor of *Food for Our Grandmothers: Writings by Arab-American and Arab-Canadian Feminists* and author of *Thinking Class: Sketches from a Cultural Worker*. Both these books were published under the name Joanna Kadi. Kadi, a transgender/genderqueer female-to-male (FTM), is now going by Joe.

Mohja Kahf is an Associate Professor of Comparative Literature at the University of Arkansas in Fayetteville. Her books include a poetry book, *E-mails from Scheherazad*; scholarship, *Western Representations of the Muslim Woman*; and a novel, *The Girl in the Tangerine Scarf*, which was a Booklist Reading Group favorite in 2007 and Bloomington, Indiana's Art Council Book of the Year in 2008. Her poetry, which won an Arkansas Arts Award, has been projected on the facade of the New York Public Library as installment art and published more conventionally in *Mizna*, *Banipal*, the *Paris Review*, and the *Atlanta Review*. Kahf's work is anthologized in *Enduring Ties: Poems of Family Relationships*, *Shattering the Stereotypes: Muslim Women Speak Out*, *Inclined to Speak: Contemporary Arab American Poetry*, and *Face to Face: Women Writers on Faith*.

Lisa Suhair Majaj, a Palestinian American writer and scholar, is the author of the poetry collection *Geographies of Light* (winner of the 2007 Del Sol Press Poetry Prize) and of two poetry chapbooks. She also writes on Arab American literature and is coeditor of three collections of critical essays: *Going Global: The Transnational Reception of Third World Women Writers*, *Etel Adnan: Critical Essays on the Arab-American Writer and Artist*, and *Intersections: Gender, Nation, and Community in Arab Women's Novels*.

Dunya Mikhail is an Iraqi American poet. She has published five books in Arabic and two in English. The Arabic titles include *The Psalms of Absence* and *Almost Music*. Her first book in English, *The War Works Hard*, won the PEN Translation Award, was shortlisted for the Griffin Prize, and was named one of the twenty-five best books of 2005 by the New York Public Library. Her latest, *Diary of a Wave Outside the Sea*, won the Arab American Book Award. In 2001, she was awarded the UN Human Rights Award for Freedom of Writing.

Nadine Naber is an Assistant Professor in the Program in American Culture and the Department of Women's Studies at the University of Michigan. She is the author of *Articulating Arabness* (New York University Press). She is coeditor (with Amaney Jamal) of *Race and Arab Americans Before and After 9/11: From Invisible Citizens to Visible Subjects* (Syracuse University Press) and coeditor of *The Color of Violence: The Incite! Anthology* (South End Press). She has published articles in the *Journal of Asian American Studies*, *Journal of Ethnic Studies*, *Journal of Cultural Dynamics*, *Journal of Feminist Studies*, and *Meridians: Feminism, Race, Transnationalism*.

Therese Saliba is Faculty of Third World Feminist Studies at Evergreen State College, Washington, and former Fulbright Scholar in Palestine. She is coeditor of two collections, *Gender, Politics, and Islam* and *Intersections: Gender, Nation, and Community in Arab Women's Novels*. Her essays on Arab and Palestinian feminisms, postcolonial literature, media representations, and Arab American experience have appeared in numerous journals and collections. Saliba is currently associate editor of the online *Brill Encyclopedia of Women and Islamic Cultures* and a board member of the Rachel Corrie Foundation for Peace and Justice.

Sherene Seikaly is an Assistant Professor of History at the American University in Cairo and Fellow in the Europe in the Middle East—The Middle East in Europe program at the Wissenschaftskolleg zu Berlin. She is coeditor of the *Arab Studies Journal*.

Ella Habiba Shohat is a Professor of Cultural Studies in the Departments of Art and Public Policy and Middle Eastern Studies at New York University. Her books include *Taboo Memories, Diasporic Voices; Talking Visions: Multicultural Feminism in a Transnational Age; Israeli Cinema: East/West and the Politics of Representation*; and (with Robert Stam) *Flagging Patriotism: Crises of Narcissism and Anti-Americanism* and the award-winning *Unthinking Eurocentrism*. Over the past three decades, Shohat has also produced an influential scholarly work concerning the question of Arab-Jewish identity in the context of Israel and Palestine.

Ameena Sultan is a human rights lawyer in Toronto. She is a founding director of the Arab Canadian Lawyers' Association and cofounder of the Toronto Just Peace Seder Community.

Kyla Wazana Tompkins is an Assistant Professor of Gender and Women's Studies at Pomona College. She is a former journalist and food writer and is finishing her first book.

Kathy Wazana is a Toronto-based peace activist currently working on a historical documentary that explores the relationship between Arabs and Jews in Morocco. She is a coauthor (with Reem Bahdi and Audrey Macklin) of *Speaking Through Walls*, a report of the Canadian Jewish and Palestinian Women's fact-finding mission in Israel-Palestine (2003). She is cofounder of the Toronto Just Peace Seder Community.

Imani Yatouma is a freelance writer who has lived in Montreal, Madrid, and Beirut. She calls Boston her home. She is working on a novel.

Zeina Zaatari is the Senior Program Officer for the Middle East and North Africa at the Global Fund for Women in San Francisco. She is the author of "The Culture of Motherhood: An Avenue for Women's Civil Participation," "In the Belly of the Beast: Struggling for Non-violent Belonging," "Lebanese Country Report," and a report on advancing women's rights in conflict zones in the Arab world. In addition, Zeina is a Core Group member of the Arab Families Working Group, conducting research on families and youth in television programs. She is one of the producers for *Voices of the Middle East and North Africa* on KPFA in Berkeley. In addition, Zaatari is one of the founders of the National Council of Arab Americans, the Radical Arab Women's Activist Network, and Sunbula: Arab Feminists for Change in the Bay Area.

Arab and Arab American Feminisms

An Introduction

RABAB ABDULHADI, EVELYN ALSULTANY, AND NADINE NABER

Episode 1: November 22, 2002

In Brooklyn, Yusra Awawdeh, a sixteen-year-old Arab American student at Franklin D. Roosevelt High School, wore a "Free Palestine" T-shirt, a Palestinian flag pin, and a *kufiya* (checkered Palestinian scarf) to school. A security guard removed her from class and took her to the dean's office, where a female school safety officer patted her down and told her to remove her shoes and socks while the dean looked on. The guard told Yusra to empty her pockets and then checked to see if she was hiding anything around her abdomen. "I was really embarrassed," said Yusra. "They made me feel like I was a terrorist with weapons." After the search, the dean told Yusra that she could no longer wear her scarf or flag pin. "The only flag I can represent at the school is the American flag," said Yusra, who was born and raised in Brooklyn. "I am American but I also want to represent my heritage. I felt like they were trying to take something away from me. They never said I broke any rules."[1]

Episode 2: June 16, 2008

At a Detroit rally for Barack Obama's presidential campaign, volunteers removed two Arab American Muslim women from behind the stage where Obama was to hold his speech to prevent their appearance in photographs and television frames with the candidate. In a statement released to the *New York Times*, the two women, Shimaa Abdelfadeel and Hebba Aref, explained that the campaign volunteers told them that they were not allowed to sit in that area because of the *hijab* each wore on her head. Koussan, Hebba's friend who also attended the rally, said that the Obama volunteer told her that it was "not good for her to be seen on TV or associated with Obama" because "of the political climate and what's going on in the world and with Muslim Americans." Obama released a public apology following the incident, stating that "the actions of these volunteers were unacceptable and in no way reflect any policy of my campaign. I will continue to fight against discrimination against people of any religious group or background."[2]

Episode 3: January 5, 2009

"Get the F*** out of the USA . . . NOW!!!" wrote a Mark Redlich, responding to a statement issued by California Scholars for Academic Freedom that denounced the Israeli war on Gaza. In one of several hate e-mails the group received, a Keith Weinman accused the Arab media of lying and referred to what he claimed to be a prototypical Arab woman who appeared repeatedly in different contexts: "One fat arab cow has appeared in 3 different photos bewailing the loss of a home in Gaza, children in Baghdad, and a husband somewhere else and under three different names."

◆   ◆   ◆

Why do we begin with these three episodes, and what do they tell us about the subject of this book: gender, violence, and belonging and the relevance of these concepts to the lives of Arab and Arab American feminists in the United States today? Conventional analysis might suggest that the three episodes are isolated incidents that do not constitute a pattern especially now, in a country such as the United States that purports to be "postracial," as evidenced by the election of a Black man as president. We insist that the three episodes are anything but isolated and that, in fact, they represent a pattern of rising xenophobia against Arabs and Muslims in the post–September 11, 2001, United States. Backlash against persons perceived to be "Arab or Muslim or both" has become an increasingly widespread consequence of the construction of the "Arab and Muslim" as an Other in the dominant "American" imaginary, revealing how long-term trends of racial exclusion intensify during moments of crisis and war.[3] Episode 1 demonstrates how a dominant U.S. imperialist ideology inscribes meanings of anti-Americanness, foreignness, and treason upon certain symbols, such as the Palestinian flag and *kufiya*. New York City continually reinforces liberal multicultural notions of "diversity" in multiple ways within restaurants, theater productions, art installations, fashion exhibits, and so on. New York City is home to countless holidays, parades, and festivals—the Chinese New Year Celebration, St. Patrick's Day Parade, Arab American Day Parade, Puerto Rican Day Parade, Lesbian and Gay Pride March, Sweden Day, African American Day Parade, West Indian–American Day Parade, and Pagan Pride Day. These events are not seen as threats, or instruments meant to undermine the "Americanness" of the city or its patriotism. They are, rather, cited as proof of the diversity New York City embraces. Yusra's case, however, reminds us of the clear limitations of multiculturalism when tested at this particular moment in history. Indeed, Yusra's experience illuminates the tenuous sense of belonging for diasporic communities while the U.S. government wages war on their homelands. But if Yusra's experience exemplifies tensions around nationness and belonging, how gender specific is it?

We part ways with conventional women's studies approaches that attribute any victimization of women, regardless of the cause, to gender inequality, we argue that what happened to Yusra could have just as easily, if not more violently, happened to someone perceived to be an Arab male, a queer Arab, or a transgender Arab. This episode calls for an analysis of gender oppression in relationship to collective engagements with racial oppression.

In Episode 2, the removal of the two Arab American Muslim women from the backdrop of Obama's rally is a variation on the long-standing vilification of Arabs and Muslims in the United States that has resurfaced with a vengeance in the post-9/11/2001 climate. Just as Zionist sympathizers have sought to equate Palestinian the flag and *kufiya* with "terrorist" symbols, so has Islamophobia marked the *hijab* as negative and threatening. Although we are troubled by this incident, we do not share its interpretation as evidence that Obama's campaign actively sought to exclude Arabs and Muslims. We suggest that the subtext of the removal of the young women resonates with the persistent construction of Obama not as a qualified Black candidate but as a qualified candidate who happens to be Black. In other words, in removing the young women from the backdrop, Obama volunteers merely translated what they understood to be the message of the campaign, namely, that Arabs and Muslims were welcomed to the ranks of Obama's diverse and broad-based campaign as long as they did not bring along telltale signs of who they were.[4] This "postracial society" notion is problematic on two levels: First, it inaccurately equates the election of a Black president with the disappearance of the wide gap between whites and people of color in all facets of life. Second, if Arabs and Muslims (or even Obama himself) must normalize themselves into hegemonic whiteness as the price of acceptance into the American imaginary, while the same is not expected of dominant white ethnic groups, we would infer that Arabs and Muslims would be welcome as long as they accept remaining in their marginalized place and do not demand more prominence.[5]

Supporters of the Republican presidential nominee, John McCain, sought to discredit Obama by labeling him as an Arab or a Muslim. This action demonstrates how Arabness and Muslimness have been seen as irreconcilably different from and opposed to anything remotely resembling normalized Americanness. It speaks to an "America" that might be ready for a president who "happens to be Black" but not for a "Black president" or a president who "might 'happen to be Muslim.'" McCain's defense of Obama by announcing that the latter was not an Arab but in fact a "decent family man," and Obama's thanks to McCain for defending him against such libel, further indicates the extent of anti-Arab and anti-Muslim consensus in U.S. public discourses today. Obama's apology for his volunteers' removing the young women, which demonstrates the candidate's familiarity with the depth of anti-Muslim bigotry, is welcomed. His avoidance, however, of any mention of widespread anti-Arab and anti-Muslim bigotry—a topic that was a consistent staple of his stump speech before he started his presidential campaign—underlines the heavy price he must have felt that he had to pay in an environment in which there is a relative ease with which anti-Arab racist statements and actions could be made without fear of retribution or accusations of hate speech.

In Episode 3, four scholars received e-mails that attacked them and challenged the political stance of their group, the California Scholars for Academic Freedom; offensive and foul language, however, was reserved for the one scholar whose last name sounded as if she were an Arab or a Muslim.[6] These hate e-mails worked with and through racist and Orientalist U.S. discourses that dehumanize Arab women and further claim not only that Israeli violations of Palestinian human rights are fabricated but that they are not legitimate concerns for the U.S. population or the U.S. academy.

Each of the three episodes points to the intensification of ethnic profiling and rising xenophobia toward Arabs and Muslims in the post-9/11/2001 United States. Does this focus then mean that racial profiling against other communities of color has disappeared, that Arabs and Muslims are the most persecuted communities, or that we have a monopoly on oppression? We do not think so: we are not claiming an Arab or a Muslim exceptionality, but we do argue that historical and contextual factors related to the imperialist relationship between the United States and the Arab world have produced distinct forms of racism against and criminalization of individuals and communities perceived to be Arab or Muslim, especially in the aftermath of September 11, 2001. Our analysis is based on a historically specific approach toward gendered racialization that assumes that racial logics are flexible and mutable to accommodate imperialist power in different temporal and spatial contexts.[7]

The three episodes above, then, reflect the historically specific logic underpinning *anti-Arab* and *anti-Muslim racism*. We locate this logic within the histories of U.S.-led military, political, and economic expansion in the Arab world and other Muslim-majority countries such as Pakistan, Afghanistan, and Iran. These histories are constituted by a racialized, Orientalist mind-set that constructs Arabs and Muslims as enemies of the "West." Such mind-set is but a continuation of centuries of Orientalism, or what Edward Said defines as the assumption of a "basic distinction between East and West as the starting point for elaborate theories, epics, novels, social descriptions, and political accounts concerning the Orient, its people, customs, 'mind,' destiny, and so on" that facilitate settling, ruling, and having authority over it. Combined with the Orientalist imaginary, normative American Judeo-Christian concepts of culture or civilization exclude Islam (and other religious beliefs) and enable the construction of Arabs and Muslims as backward, barbaric, misogynist, sexually savage, and sexually repressive.[8]

In the United States, an Orientalist mind-set, coupled with a Judeo-Christian normative outlook, intersects with xenophobia and an imperialist foreign policy. These imperatives constitute the positioning of an imagined Arab or Muslim enemy as inherently foreign and outside the boundaries of U.S. nationness. This dominant U.S. discourse conflates the categories "Arab" and "Muslim" and assumes that all Arabs are Muslim, all Muslims are Arab, and all Muslim Arabs are the same.[9] It obscures the existence of Arabs who are not Muslim (including, but not limited to, Christians and Jews) and Muslims who are not Arab (including Indonesians, Malaysians, Chinese, South Asians, Africans, African Americans, and Latinos/as). It also erases the historic and vast ethnic communities who are neither Arab nor Muslim but who live amid and interact with a majority of Arabs or Muslims (such as Greeks in Egypt; Armenians in Palestine; Roma in Jordan; Kurds in Iraq, Turkey, and Iran; and Imazighen in North Africa, to name a few).

The rising xenophobia against immigrants of color and the fact that many Arabs and Muslims come from countries at which the United States is at war further contribute to the normalization of anti-Arab and anti-Muslim violence. Recent geopolitical developments have further enabled the vilification of Arabs and Muslims. The collapse of the Soviet Union and the socialist camp in 1989 eliminated the threat of what then U.S. president Ronald Reagan called "the evil empire." Out of this historical moment, the U.S. power elite constructed an alternative "viable" threat that has worked to justify weapons production amid increasing popular demand for a peaceful economy.[10] Twenty years later, former U.S. president George W. Bush and his speechwriters constructed another threat that they named "the axis of evil. The centrality of Israel to U.S. foreign policy, reflected in the U.S.-Israeli strategic government alliance coupled with the powerful role of the Israeli lobby in Washington, exacerbates the location of the Arab or Muslim in dominant U.S. discourses. This alliance places Arabs and Muslims at the core of U.S. policy and denies them the benign neglect with which the U.S. government responds to the needs of the majority of the people of the world in Asia, Africa, and Latin America. Unlike Arab and Muslim communities for whom Palestine lies at the center of political concerns, Palestinians in dominant U.S. and western European discourses are portrayed as villains who seek to destroy the "only safe haven" for the Jewish people.

♦   ♦   ♦

In this book, we use the term "Arab" to refer to people whose primary language is Arabic and who come from the twenty-two member nations of the Arab League: Algeria, Bahrain, Comoros, Djibouti, Egypt, Iraq, Jordan, Kuwait, Lebanon, Libya, Mauritania, Morocco, Oman, Palestine, Qatar, Saudi Arabia, Somalia, Sudan, Syria, Tunisia, the United Arab Emirates, and Yemen. At the same time, our use of the terms "Arab" and "Muslim" has been particularly challenging. We find ourselves obliged to clarify the overlapping as well as the distinctiveness of both terms primarily because of the ways in which Arabs and Muslims were lumped together by the "war on terror" during the eight years of the Bush administration. A similar logic has facilitated the racial profiling and the criminalization of diverse communities of Arabs and Muslims. This logic makes it imperative that we deal with individuals and communities perceived to be Arab or Muslim when we refer to anti-Arab racism, despite the many ways in which these categories do not perfectly fit onto one another.

In this book, Arab and Arab American women, queer, and transgender writers, scholars, creative writers, and activists express a multiplicity of experiences, identities, and social locations. We refer in the book title to "Arab" and "Arab American" to signal our rejection of categories that box persons or experiences within an either-or formula. While we were developing this book, most of us were living in the United States.[11] Yet whereas some contributors were born and raised in the United States, others were born and raised in the Arab world and other Arab diasporas. Most of us imagine home to exist on a continuum of "here" and "there" and consider both as the "here" of their/our belonging. Several of us, whether we were born in the United States or hold U.S. citizenship or not, do not comfortably identify as "American" because of the implication of patriotism, genocide, and colonization such hegemonic identification implies. The contributors to this book highlight how developments "back home" as well as the ways that our homelands are imagined and remembered within and between our immigrant communities in the United States are just as significant to our lives as what happens "here." In this sense, the interplay between homeland and diaspora, the

Arab context and the United States, shapes our identities, experiences, loyalties, and affiliations.

Race, Gender, and Nation

Returning to the three episodes with which we started and our discussion of gender, we propose that although markers of Arab womanhood might have inspired the attackers, the targets of the attacks were not gender specific: In Yusra's case, a male high school student wearing the Palestinian head scarf could have as easily been targeted. In Shimaa and Hebba's story, the Obama volunteers would just as soon have removed a Muslim or an Arab male had his dress code hinted at his background—for example, by wearing a *sirwal kameez*, *kufiya*, or an untrimmed beard. At the same time, we doubt that a Jew wearing a yarmulke or a Christian nun in her habit would have been removed in the current context. And in the e-mail over the Israeli war on Gaza, attempts to invalidate the suffering of Palestinians are not unique to women; all who speak in defense of Palestinians regardless of gender or ethnic background are at risk of being attacked, harassed, and charged with supporting terrorism and anti-Semitism. If gender is understood as a useful analytical category and a structural hierarchy, we can no longer continue equating "gender" with women.[12] The episodes are works of gender, but how do we understand them in light of our argument and the range of power structures at play?

This book builds on radical U.S. women of color's visions of the world that argue that the experiences of U.S. women of color should not be subsumed within the conventional dichotomies of *either* racism *or* sexism but must be seen as simultaneous, overlapping, and constitutive of each other. We agree with Kimberlé Williams Crenshaw that racism and sexism intersect in the lives of all women in ways that cannot be captured by looking at either the racial or the gendered dimensions of those experiences separately. This book also draws on critiques by radical queers of color that call feminists to task for reifying heteronormative visions of liberation.[13] We share the postcolonial feminist critiques of the "sisterhood is global" model. This critique contends that there is no universal woman's experience and that "the category of women is constructed in a variety of political contexts that often exist simultaneously and overlaid on top of one another."[14] Consistent with Mohanty's argument, this book offers historicized perspectives on gender, sexuality, and Arab and Arab American women, queer, and transgender experiences that are situated within multiple overlapping and intersecting structures of power and privilege.

We use the words "gender" and "nation" broadly and conceptually, not in terms of belonging to a singular monolithic national body. We are interested in how gender and sexuality shape negotiations over belonging and nonbelonging within the context of multiple imagined communities that intersect and overlap, such as the ones produced by the workings of race, nation, and spiritualities. We take interest in how Arab and Arab American women, queer, and transgender writers make, remake, and transgress normative communal boundaries and the ways that we negotiate the relationship between concepts of Arabness and Americanness in the process. The writings in this book illustrate how boundaries of belonging and nonbelonging are often entangled within U.S. imperialist projects in Arab countries and within Arab experiences of displacement, immigration, and racialization to and within the United States. Many contributors prioritize the themes of displacement and diaspora and their negotiations over belonging and nonbelonging to the United States and the homeland. Emanne Bayoumi highlights a yearning for home, safety, and belonging as she narrates the life of a queer working-class Arab woman in the United States far from her family in the homelands. Randa Jarrar illustrates the diasporic conditions through which communities traumatized by displacement often hold on to idealized fixed meanings of what practices they deem representative of an "authentic" Arab homeland, lest they lose who they are. For Jarrar, idealized notions that imagine a singular "Arab culture" as fixed, rigid, and in opposition to an imagined "American culture" are gendered in that they disproportionately pressure daughters into conformity more than they do sons. Youmna Chlala's poems also address Arab identity as dislocated during political crises and concomitant tensions between the individual and the collective. As well, Christina Dennaoui's cover art, *Seeing Yourself in Fragments*, represents a transnational sense of displacement as the figure of the Arab woman is positioned in relation to cartographic imagery that questions the location of home and belonging.

Several contributors describe how assumptions that "real" Americans do not place their loyalties elsewhere make suspect their affinities to homelands outside the United States. The USA PATRIOT Act, signed into law by President George W. Bush on October 26, 2001, intensified the pressure on immigrant communities to keep their identification with the homelands of their ancestors underground. The USA PATRIOT Act expanded the reach of the government and law enforcement agencies under the guise of fighting terrorism. In this context, *belonging* to "America" becomes a site of intensified contradiction for Arab diasporas in the United States. Reflecting on this contradiction, Rabab Abdulhadi compares the post-9/11/2001 moment in New York City in which Arabs became suspect to how the Israeli security services treat Palestinians as potential terrorists. This heightened sense of insecurity impacts her everyday experiences as she anticipates being targeted, searched, and harassed. Within this context, she questions where home as a safe haven might be, given the escalating criminalization of Arabs, Muslims, and Palestinians that further disturbs her sense of belonging to the United States as a home. Dena Al-Adeeb contemplates similar questions as she speaks of the multiple displacements she has experienced: displaced from Iraq for being Shia of Iranian descent, displaced from Kuwait because of the Iraqi invasion in 1990, and later choosing to move from the United States to Cairo. She outlines the ways in which violence impacted her ability to belong and subsequently inspired her involvement in political activism.

Violence emerges as a central theme in the experiences of many contributors. Dunya Mikhail writes of watching the war on Iraq from afar:

I search you on the Internet.
I distinguish you
Grave by grave,
Skull by skull,
Bone by bone.

Zeina Zaatari contrasts her growing up in war-torn Lebanon with her academic experiences in Iowa and California. She demonstrates the pervasive violence of war, in the racialization of Arabs in the United States and in the silencing of the Palestinian struggle for human rights and self-determination, which collude into a diasporic struggle over belonging and nonbelonging. Suheir Hammad responds to images of torture at Abu Ghraib prison and the impact of militarized "patriotism" resulting from the U.S. invasion of Iraq. She comments on her loss of words that would adequately express such horrors. Amal Hassan Fadlalla responds to the crushing violence with which communities live and die with a poem that expresses a longing for hope and freedom. For our contributors, gender cannot but be entangled with a range of power structures in the context of multiple transnational tensions, connections, and contradictions.

A Collaborative Journey

This book emerges out of a collaboration that began in 2002 to make critical Arab and Arab American feminist interventions at the academic conferences in which we participate, such as the American Studies Association, Middle East Studies Association, American Anthropological Association, and American Sociological Association. Not only were our voices rarely heard at these academic gatherings, but our collective perspectives were virtually absent from the very intellectual fields and their intersections such as American studies,

Middle East studies, U.S. ethnic studies, and gender studies. We brought together a collective of Arab and Arab American feminists with critical perspectives and located themselves not in an either-or Arab or American dichotomy but in a positionality from which they and we could conceptualize ideas and experiences for which conventional area studies fell short of accounting. This volume, then, argues against the limitations of academic boundaries and presents, analyzes, and reflects upon personal and collective experiences that are inflicted with gender, violence, and belonging.

It was a year after September 11, 2001, that the three of us sat at New Orleans's Café du Monde to discuss the challenges facing Arab and Arab American activist scholars at this historic moment that was characterized by rising xenophobia, racism, and the silencing of dissent in political and intellectual spaces. We noted with alarm the rise of McCarthyist-type groups such as Campus Watch that have launched smear campaigns against critics of U.S. and Israeli government policies and labeled them anti-Semitic, anti-American, and terror supporters. We were equally concerned that liberal multicultural diversity initiatives had inadvertently reinforced the crackdown on public dissent by funding nongovernmental tolerance projects and criticizing individual hate crimes while ignoring the intensification of systemic state violence—such as the targeting of immigrants under the USA PATRIOT Act and the massive killing in Iraq and Afghanistan. Opposition to the war in Iraq, the detention and deportation of Arab immigrants, and U.S. support for Israel's war against the Palestinian people had been deemed unpatriotic, undemocratic, and anti-American.

As contributors and editors, we were exasperated by the countless times we had received invitations to speak on "the veil," cliterodectomy, and suicide bombings.[15] Although none of us was in principle opposed to discussing these issues, the ways in which these issues were framed greatly hindered our abilities to offer critical and thoughtful analysis of Arab and Muslim women's condition without feeling suffocated. We were repeatedly forced to fit the varied, rich, and complex lives of Arab and Muslim women into limited stereotypical boxes. These stereotypes take "women's oppression" out of context and reinforce imperialist discourses that reduce Arab and Muslim social practices to misogyny, violence, and sexual repression and have the effect of justifying anti-Arab and anti-Muslim violence at home and occupation and colonization in the homelands.

We shared an urgent need to highlight a plurality of Arab and Arab American perspectives within and beyond the walls of the academy. Thus, we came together to organize a roundtable discussion at the 2003 meeting of the American Studies Association. Our roundtable was a response to the conference title,

"Violence and Belonging." In our invitation, we asked participants to address the following questions:

1. How have you experienced being racially marked in the U.S.? In the class-room? In academic and intellectual circles?

2. What are some of the struggles/tensions around issues of homophobia, sexism, and racism that you have experienced in the different communities to which you belong?

3. What have been your experiences with feminisms in the U.S.? What does women-of-color-feminism mean to you? (Or are there other feminist spaces that have meaning to you?)

4. When you hear "violence and belonging" what do these terms evoke for you?

5. What are some of the resources/spaces that have been relatively safer (if any) for you?

Out of the enthusiastic responses to our invitation, we organized two back-to-back roundtable discussions with twelve participants at the American Studies Association meeting, followed by the special issue of the MIT *Electronic Journal of Middle East Studies* (spring 2005) that we coedited.[16] This book builds on and expands this project. It includes several revised essays that were originally pub-lished in *MIT-EJMES*, along with many new contributions. This book presents our readers with a slice of the complex regimes of power that have circumscribed and shaped our lives. As our contributors show, despite the many points of unity that bring us together, there is no single site of Arab and Arab American femi-nist struggle.

Experiences and Epistemologies

Our commitment to the production of knowledge that is drawn from individual and collective experiences informed our invitation to each contributor to take his or her own history and experiences as a point of departure. As valuable starting points, experiences allow us to identify, analyze, and understand structures of power and privilege that shape our lives. Not all contributors were equally will-ing to share what they saw as their personal experiences. Several participants at the original ASA roundtables feared what they saw as the potential trivialization of their individual experiences had they submitted such reflections to ink; oth-ers felt that focusing on personal experiences would classify them as theoretical lightweights in the eyes of their peers. In this volume, Kyla Wazana Tompkins muses on the problem of experiential narration because of the way first-person narratives by women of color are often used in women's studies classrooms as "the instrumental performance of suffering toward the end of bearing witness to diversity." Women of color, Tompkins argues, bear the unfair burden of realism in their personal narratives that often result in their marginalization in academic spaces, especially when personal narratives are rendered as illegitimate sites for knowledge production. Writing of Arab Jewish identifications that are often misunderstood and misrepresented, she calls for strategic narration instead of confessionals or positivist testimonies. Our intention in this volume, then, is not to "valorize the experience of oppression as the alleged ground of truth or politics, but [rather to] investigate how we might transform lived experiences of discontent into critical knowledge and political consciousness [since] narration [is] key in the transformation of experience into useful knowledge."[17] By centering the project on experience-based knowledge production, we hope to illuminate the structural forces that influence our lives as Arab and Arab American women, queer, and transgender writers.

Earlier writings of Arab American women, such as *Food for Our Grandmothers* edited by Joe Kadi in 1994 (who previously identified as Joanna Kadi) and *Bint Arab: Arab and Arab American Women in the United States* by the late Evelyn Shakir in 1997, opened the door for collections such as this one.[18] Our volume belongs to the tradition of Arab and Arab American knowledge production, and further engages in a "theory in the flesh" or knowledge derived from narrating lived experiences and producing critical lenses through which we see and analyze the social and political world.[19] Agreeing with Shari Stone-Mediatore, we resist the formulation that assumes that personal narrative and theoretical analysis are mutually exclusive and antithetical: "When writers use narration strategically to publicize obscured experiences, they enrich not only language practices but experience itself, for they provide a new lens through which we can organize our everyday experience and historical world. Neither empirical reporting nor discourse analysis has this effect on our experience of our identity and history."[20]

From this standpoint, we decided not to separate essays that might be grouped under the rubric of social sciences as "factual" from those essays that might be considered "fiction." We consider this volume of knowledge production from personal experiences an act of strategic narration. This methodology allows us to record Arab and Arab American feminist knowledge productions, the histories through which they have emerged, and their convergence and divergence with a range of U.S. feminist frameworks and practices.

We attempted to incorporate multiple genres of writing: poetry, short stories, interviews, and essays by poets, creative writers, artists, activists, and academics. We sought to include authors from multiple geographical sites, religious commitments, occupations, sexualities, class backgrounds, and generations. Nonetheless, this volume does not include writings or writers from every single Arab or Arab American community, nor does it include the full range of views that span the political spectrum. We do not subscribe to the liberal notion that defines diversity as the inclusion of each and every group irrespective of the content or purpose of such inclusion. In recognizing the historical and political realities of our communities, certain concerns become more visible, certain voices louder, and certain demands more pressing at any given moment or context. Ours is not an "add-and-stir" approach that merely represents contributors from every Arab country or every Arab American diasporic location. This volume also goes beyond liberal multicultural notions of *adding* Arab and Arab American feminist perspectives to the landscape of existing models of U.S. feminisms.[21] We agree with Andrea Smith as we shift the question from "how can we *include* Arab American women, queer, and transgender perspectives" to "what would analyses of race, gender, sexuality, and nation look like if we were to center Arab and Arab American women, queer, and transgender experiences?"[22]

This book centers upon lived experiences, emphasizing how contributors' essays articulate Arab and Arab American feminist agendas and the resulting themes that emerge: the post-9/11/2001 climate of intensified racism and violence; the resulting pressure on Arab and Muslim women to accept the Orientalist and racist notion that Arab society is inherently violent, misogynist, and sexually repressive; the linkage between these pressures and hegemonic U.S. feminisms; the impact of such a hostile environment on the struggles Arab and Arab American feminists wage within and outside our communities for gender and sexual liberation; the displacement of the experiences of Arab Jews from conventional Arab and Arab American narratives and their relocation instead in Israeli- and Zionist-centric narratives and discourses; the targeting and smearing of Arab and Arab Americans feminists (along with other Arab Americans) who publicly support justice for Palestine; the racial ambiguity of Arab American identities between their official classification as white and our own identification (and treatment) as communities of color; the centrality of homophobia to anti-Arab racism, exemplified by the torture in Abu Ghraib and our commitment to struggle against homophobia and the marginalization of queer and transgender people within dominant Arab and Arab American spaces and discourses; and the unsettled (and often violent) experiences of exclusion from home and homeland.

The Centrality of Palestine

The recurring themes in this volume reflect issues that are most pressing to our contributors. The number of submissions focusing on Palestine reflects the centrality of the liberation of Palestine to Arabs and Arab Americans. Palestine appears in different forms in specific essays focusing on topics such as exile and displacement, the effects of the Israeli occupation, U.S.-Israeli relations, as well as Palestine-centered activism in the United States.

Why is Palestine so central? There are several historical reasons. First, Palestine's vast diaspora exceeds the size of the Palestinian population of the West Bank, Gaza, and Israel combined. From this vast diaspora emerge Arab and Arab American imaginaries of longing, belonging, and exile. In her essay, Sherene Seikaly, a Palestinian who grew up in Lebanon and the United States, explores the disparities between the Palestine of her imagination and the Palestine to which she returns as a young adult, a doctoral candidate researching material for her dissertation. Seikaly calls for rethinking history as she takes up the challenge of archival research. She turns to her grandmothers' memories to document history in resistance to "the fragmentation of Palestine" and the "continuous process of removal and distancing—distancing people from one another, their land, and their history."

Second, Palestine lies at the center of the dominant U.S. and Israeli alliance that enlists the tragic events of September 11, 2001, to reinforce the campaign to vilify Palestinians, labeling their resistance against occupation as terrorism, while presenting Israeli colonial state violence against Palestinians as self-defense. Increasingly, after 9/11 the terrorist label has been extended to all persons perceived to be Arab or Muslim. In her essay on Rachel Corrie, the white student activist from the United States who was killed by an Israeli military bulldozer as she tried to prevent a Palestinian home from demolition, Therese Saliba reflects on the ways in which Corrie has been constituted as a violent person because of her association with Palestinians. Saliba further discusses how racial discourses that exclude Arabs by denying their racial marginalization simultaneously deny the racialized victimization of Palestinians by Israeli government policies and minimize the extent of their oppression.

Third, much like McCarthyism, anti-Arab racism is used to delegitimate those persons demanding justice for the Palestinians and to legitimate Zionist perspectives that enable Israel to maintain its denial of Palestinian rights.[23] Dominant U.S. and Israeli state discourses strategically conflate criticism of Israel with anti-Semitism. Such discourses are sometimes reproduced in U.S. civil society and social movements. This conflation, coupled with the association of Arabs with violence and terrorism, often serves to stifle criticism of Israeli government and military policies and strategies. As an activist and law student at the University of California–Berkeley's Law School, Noura Erakat recounts how her progressive peers of color were silenced by a Jewish group that equated support for Palestinian self-determination with anti-Semitism. Nada Elia concurs with Erakat in how pro-Palestinian activism becomes silenced even in peace and justice circles. As she moves from one progressive circle to the next, she repeatedly confronts hostility for asserting that Zionism is a form of racism. Erakat's and Elia's experiences were not exceptional. At the World Conference Against Racism in Durban, South Africa, in 2001, the U.S. government used its opposition to the proposal that Zionism was equated with racism as a pretext to justify its withdrawal in order to avoid the very pressing issues of reparations and the legacy of slavery and genocide that mar its history. The United States banded with the Israeli government and the Zionist movement to accuse Palestinians of "hijacking" the conference to divert attention from issues raised by antiracist grassroots groups.

Palestine, however, is experienced differently by our contributors. Several challenge the framing of the Israeli-Palestinian conflict as a problem between Arabs and Jews, convincingly arguing instead for defining it as a colonial context in which the colonized wage a struggle for liberation, thus problematizing this binary configuration of Arabs versus Jews that in addition to other damaging consequences denies the existence of Arab Jews. As Ella Habiba Shohat argues, the experiences of Iraqi (Arab) Jews should not be reduced to such a binary: "My parents used to say: 'In Iraq we were Jews, and in Israel we are Arabs.' Our Arab culture was taboo in Israel. Yet, even if we tried, we could not easily escape the mark of otherness. It was written all over our bodies, our looks, our accents. . . . If in the Arab world the Jewishness of Arabs gradually came to be associated with Zionism, and therefore was subjected to surveillance, in Israel their Arab culture was under watchful eyes, disciplined and punished."

Reinforcing the notion that Arabness and Jewishness are not mutually exclusive categories, the Toronto Just Peace Seder Community rewrites in this volume the traditional Jewish seder into a peace seder for the Passover holiday. Composed of Arab Muslims, Christians, and Jews, as well as Ashkenazi Jews, the peace seder rescripts the ritual from a perspective of narration of "the Jewish ethos of fear of persecution and exile" to an acknowledgment of how "Jewish freedom" in the dominant Israeli discourse has been constituted and enabled by the denial of Palestinian freedom.

Whiteness, Race, and Identifications

Some contributors criticize the contradictory positioning of Arabs and Arab Americans within dominant U.S. racial schemas as different from and inferior to whites or, more generally, as potential foreigners, enemies, criminals, or terrorists, made evident in the portrayal by corporate media and the U.S. government, especially during the eight years of the presidency of George W. Bush. At the same time, the U.S. Census classifies Arab Americans as white/Caucasian. Scholars have theorized the racial positioning of Arabs in the United States as "not-quite white," "not-quite people of color," or "between Arab and white."[24] Some contributors (Majaj, Erakat, Elia) reflect on how this ambiguous positionality operates to obscure Arab and Arab American critiques and experiences of racism and further impacts their relationships to other communities of color, especially to activist organizations of women of color.

Some contributors who may pass as white, or non-Arab, stress that "passing" is not always as simple as it might seem. Although they may pass because of the way they look, they are nonetheless targeted as non-white/Arab/Other because of other markers such as an accent or an Arab- or a Muslim-sounding name. Lisa Suhair Majaj's poem ironically offers her Arab and Arab American reader "guidelines" for navigating the ambiguous terrain of U.S. racial categories. She advises:

If they ask you if you're white, say it depends.
Say no. Say maybe. If appropriate, inquire casually,
Have you always been white, or is it recent?

Several contributors tackle these questions, sharing experiences of exclusion from debates on race and racism or experiences where others perceived them as Latinas, Greeks, Italians, South Asians, or African Americans depending on the context or on assumptions about race, ethnicity, and skin color.

Some contributors illuminate the ways in which Muslims have come to be visualized and racialized. Mona El-Ghobashy's and Evelyn Alsultany's pieces reflect opposite sides of the same coin. El-Ghobashy recounts her experiences as a Muslim woman who wears the *hijab*, while Alsultany recounts her experiences as a Muslim woman who is unidentifiable because she does not wear the *hijab*. Both explore the assumptions projected on them in their daily lives while raising questions around the rigid assumptions of who they are. Both face a variety of reactions depending on the context. El-Ghobashy recounts a range of reactions, including what seemed to her as surprisingly pleasant interactions on New York City subways or the curiously bizarre encounters at an academic lecture where she is called upon to speak on behalf of "the Muslim woman," even though it was not remotely the topic of her talk. Meanwhile, Alsultany finds herself challenged by some white Americans who insist that it is not possible to be both a Muslim and a feminist and by some devout Muslims who insist that she is not a "real" Muslim because she does not wear the *hijab*. The two contributors bring up questions of how Islam and Muslims are imagined and politically identified.

Some authors speak to the ways in which progressive U.S. politics have taken the problem of anti-Arab and anti-Muslim racism more seriously than ever before in the aftermath of the events of September 11, 2001. As the U.S. war machine continues to be fueled by an anti-Arab and anti-Muslim discourse, some contributors—including Hammad, Hyder, Ameri, Attia, and Toronto Just Peace Seder—underline the urgent need to continue struggling against racism, empire, and war and to envision a world without violence.

Whose Feminism?

This book coalesces around a specific political vision broadly shared by our contributors that excludes homophobic, prowar, and racist perspectives. Recognizing that no single book can be inclusive of all the voices that share the editors' vision, the writings here specifically tackle the (discursive, epistemic, and materialist) themes of violence and belonging. We imagine a radical feminist politics that insists on the simultaneity of racial justice, gender justice, economic justice, and self-determination for colonized women, men, queer, and transgender people "over here" and "over there." This transnational feminist vision inspires us to imagine a world without oppression and think about alternatives to exclusionary heteromasculinist and xenophobic politics. We hope that this book will contribute to efforts aimed at alliance building between Arab and Arab American feminists, on the one hand, and Native feminists, U.S. feminists of color, diasporic feminists from the global South, and feminists in other parts of the world who struggle for justice and peace, on the other.

Although this volume is about Arab and Arab American feminist perspectives, many of us do not comfortably identify with the term "feminism." We use the term "feminism" as a shorthand for a commitment to gender justice, including an end to gender inequality, homophobia, and transphobia.[25] We further note that not all struggles for gender justice are the same: some tend to be hierarchical; some privilege struggles against sexism over struggles for feminist, queer, and transgender justice; others position gender justice in tension with and opposition to other forms of justice. As editors, we share a commitment to the necessity of resistance against hegemonic liberal U.S. feminisms that reinforce Orientalist and racist discourses on Arab and Muslim women. These feminist frameworks call for an end to what they define as inherent "cultural" or "religious" practices that they take out of historical and political contexts while ignoring historical and political realities. Several contributors engage feminists who view the category "Arab feminism" as an oxymoron—as if Arabness or Muslimness were incompatible with feminism or as if Arabs were "inherently" or genetically incapable of understanding, advocating, or fighting for an end to gender and sexual oppression.

Several authors speak of the limitations they find in mainstream feminist agendas that confine Arab feminist concerns to issues liberal feminists view as the purview of Arab feminists, such as "the veil," "the harem," or "female circumcision," and rely on these issues as symbols of a backward and misogynist culture. Amira Jarmakani writes that Arab American feminists often find themselves trapped by the image of the veil, which dominant U.S. discourses presume to be the most urgent issue facing Muslim women—constantly having to respond to it and correct stereotypes about it. This constant forced engagement with the veil, she argues, displaces other struggles in which Arab American feminists are engaged. Jarmakani calls this process "the politics of invisibility" and suggests that it silences Arab American feminists "by the very categories that claim to give them voice."

In her essay, Amal Amireh criticizes Western feminist discourses for misrepresenting the experiences of Palestinian women by locating suicide bombers within cultural gender oppression rather than the violence of the Israeli military occupation. Amireh demonstrates how feminist writings, such as those works of Robin Morgan and the late Andrea Dworkin, extract the experiences of Palestinian women from the historical and political context of Israeli occupation and place them exclusively in a cultural context in which "Palestinian women are seen as victims of an abusive patriarchal Arab culture that drives them to destroy themselves and others. Thus, their violent political act is transformed into yet another example of the ways Arab culture inevitably kills its women."

While some contributors highlight the ways in which U.S. mainstream feminism has co-opted and defined feminist agendas in ways that exclude Arab and Arab American women, other contributors articulate their own feminist visions. Anan Ameri, for example, argues that there is no singular feminist agenda, since priorities are different for different women. Providing the example of women living in war zones, Ameri suggests that their priority might be securing food for their children and physical safety from rape, whereas for low income women in the United States, it might be affordable housing and health care. Ameri stresses that she ascribes to a feminism that is based on ending all forms of discrimination. Meanwhile, Joe Kadi places sustainable environment at the center of his feminism, incorporating yet another layer of social justice demands to this definition. As the keynote speaker at the 2004 San Francisco Dyke March, Happy/L. A. Hyder connects the dots among anti-Arab racism, the destruction of the Palestinian people and Iraqi civilization, and struggles for racial and sexual justice.

Arab and Arab American women's commitment to the eradication of multiple forms of oppression has meant addressing the theme of political resistance, activism, and organizing. Janaan Attia, a youth organizer and activist, illustrates the arduous process of coalition building. She explains the predicament of U.S. activism that often forces activists to choose one struggle over another. Colonialism, racism, and sexism, the struggle against which remains incomplete if homophobia is not viewed as an essential structure of inequality that affects our lives, privilege heteronormativity and binary understandings of gender, disenfranches queerness and transgender people. Imani Yatouma juxtaposes her experiences with childhood sexual abuse with family pressure to enter into a heterosexual marriage and have children. As she narrates her experience, Yatouma speaks of her struggles to embrace a queer identity as she recovers from multiple traumas.

Huda Jadallah calls for transgressing the simplistic binary that men and women have distinct experiences with discrimination. A common discourse in Arab and Arab American feminist writings reinforces a gender binary that associates masculinity with male bodies and femininity with female bodies. This framework neglects people whose bodies do not fit into this gender binary. In her discussion of anti-Arab racism, Jadallah makes clear that there are more than two genders. As a woman who might be perceived as a male, Jadallah does not experience being stereotyped into a submissive Arab woman, but she is rather seen as a violent Arab man. As a result, she calls for a more complex feminist analysis that accounts for the intersections of racism and gender nonconformity.

Beyond the "Internal-Communal" and "External-Political" Binary Divide

Some contributors focus on tensions that emerge within and between Arab American communities. Several authors (Jarrar, Yatouma, Berry, Hatem) reflect on the sense of being caught between pressures by their communities and dominant U.S. assumptions on the role of women in Muslim or Arab communities. Mohja Kahf, for example, writes about the challenges of being a Muslim woman writer in the West, where success is predicated on producing narratives that place the victimization of women at the center, focusing narratives on the experiences of either the victim or the escapee. She also discusses the pressure she faces from some Muslims to refrain from what they perceive as airing dirty laundry in public.

Mervat F. Hatem tackles the ways in which gender permeates the racialization of Islam and how racialization by the dominant society shapes polarizations within Arab American communities. In this context, *al-Muhajjabat* (those who wear the *hijab*), according to Hatem, claim their legitimate rights and interests by participating in this debate. However, some Muslim, Christian, and Jewish members of the community have tended to look down on this group, defining its members as "socially backward," thus feeding into Orientalist stereotyping, and refusing to deal with *al-Muhajjabat* as equals when debating women's rights.

Moulouk Berry illustrates how fixed and rigid perceptions of Islam emerge not only from external U.S. sources but also within and between Arab and Arab American communities. She relates her experience of teaching a course on the Quran to predominantly Arab American Muslim students. Assigning her students to read a woman's challenges to different Islamic texts and understand the contexts in which they were codified, Berry finds some of her students threatened, as they assume that knowledge of the sacred text rests with Muslim male clerics but not with women, and thus perceiving Berry's feminist stance as an attack on established traditional and patriarchal interpretations of the text.

Susan Muaddi Darraj argues that the popular feminist slogans "The personal is political" and "The political is personal" are inapplicable to Arab American women in the same way as they are to other women in the United States. She argues that Arab American women fight two separate battles—one at home against sexism that is personal and one in society against racism that is political. Nadine Naber expands on this notion by exploring the ways in which the Arab American communities where she lives and works mark certain issues as "cultural" and "private" and therefore distinct from "political" and "public" issues. Sexism and homophobia become "cultural," while U.S. racism and imperialism become "political." Naber calls for a new movement that resists the choice between racism and imperialism, on the one hand, and sexism and homophobia, on the other.

Inspiration

We draw our inspiration from the many Arab and Arab American feminist activists in North America who have come before us: from the Arab immigrant women's magazine *Al Hoda* in the early 1900s and the Syrian Ladies' Aid Society of Boston, founded in 1917, to the Union of Palestinian Women's Associations in North America (1980s); Feminist Arab American Network (1983); Palestine Aid Society/Al-Najda (1983); Arab Women's Solidarity Association, AWSA, North America (1999); Radical Arab Women's Activist Network, RAWAN (2003); and Arab Movement of Women Arising for Justice, AMWAJ (2004).

This collection of essays would not have been possible were it not for the cumulative contributions of Arab and Arab American feminist scholars and activists who have set the stage for our work. The contributions by activists whose stories remain unwritten have had a particularly profound effect on us. We are humbled by Camilia Odeh, Rawia Bishara, Ahla Shounich, Somaia Barghouti, Hala Maksoud, Mona Khalidi, Nabiha Ghandour, Abla Shamieh, Maha Khoury, Fadia Salfiti, Fatima Zeidane, Maha Jarad, Suheir Abbasi, Nabila Mango, Mary Harb, Helen Samhan, and many others.

For us, Arab and Arab American feminisms are ongoing processes that build on the cumulative struggles of those persons who have preceded us. We therefore offer no conclusions. We hope that this volume will debunk the notion of the "monolithic Arab woman"; will make clear how the geographic boundaries between Arab homelands and diasporas are fluid and overlapping; will articulately, theoretically, and experientially reflect our ideas, desires, emotions, and strategies for survival; and will affirm that Arab and Arab American feminist discourses and practices have existed, on multiple fronts, simultaneously, within our families and communities, in struggles against racism and colonialism, in debates over spirituality and the divine, within progressive and feminist and queer spaces, in academia, and among each other.

1 LIVING WITH/IN EMPIRE

Grounded Subjectivities

1

Beyond Words

SUHEIR HAMMAD

Photos out of Abu Ghraib were being circulated on the Internet, as the Israeli Defense Forces entered and nearly destroyed the Gaza Strip town of Rafah. There must have been a saturation point, what with the constant stream of images from Iraq, Afghanistan, the Congo. The poem accepts Suheir Hammad's inherent weakness, her dependency on language for expression. If there is redemption, it is indeed beyond words, which have been twisted into justifications for so long. Hammad read this poem in front of many government officials one night. That was a trip.

1.

Where has my language gone?
The poet searches for words to wrap around these times
Make them sense Make them pretty Make them useful

Words from the past haunt our conversations
Empire and Crusade
Plans and Centuries
All these words cleared understanding before
Fall heavy now
And weightless into this abyss of bad news

I have seen the photographs
Again words Prison Torture

Desperate for words I can write
That are not profane That are objective Read as rational
So people will not stop reading this self-conscious poem
So my parents will not be embarrassed
So Americans will demand the return of their own

3

Desperate for words I can write
So I can keep from becoming something hard and unforgiving

Language has failed me

I am told to believe nothing I read
Then everything I read
I am given my own face to be wary of
I am told to fear colors as alerts
I am told over and over
Iraq is not Palestine
Kabul is not New York

The photos
Women Raped
Posed as girls gone wild
This is entertainment This is staged This is recorded
Men Chained
Do words such as humiliation and torture
Truly fit the immensity of these acts?
What happens to those who survive?
What happens to those responsible?

Haiti is not Chechnya
Chiapas is not East L.A.
Iraq is not Palestine
Over and over I am told

I am given a vantage point and a lens and instructed
Do not move Do not look up Do not look down

I am falling

2.

No connections here
No illuminated parallels
Two different histories and two different peoples
Make no links
Do not confuse the issues

Only confuse the people

For 56 years Israel has legitimized
This type of behavior
Sanctioned violence in the name of a god
Who does not have enough love for us all
A god who chooses sides
A god who has favorites and chosen ones.
A god who cuts deals and shuffles souls
The type of god who does not answer prayers
Who understands only one language
A god who does not worry his beautiful mind with
Such ugliness
I am told this is America's god

The photos from Rafah Palestine
It is 1948 and 2004 in the same frame
Their eyes say to the camera
What will you do with this pain?
Where will you take it?
Can you take it from me?

This space between the lens and the subjects
Is concentrated with pleas for witness
With promises of cycles unbroken
With children's bicycles under the rubble of once were homes

Another level of exile is being constructed

And I am falling

Aaagghh, ya Phalesteen
What is it about us they hate so much?
This face? These eyes? This obstinate refusal to die?
How much trauma can one nation endure with the world staring?
Some mouths open in shock
Others silent and sneering
While women scream at a frequency the living cannot hear
Again? Again ya Phalesteen?

3.

How fucked up is it that I have to choose between ending
One occupation or another?
Partition my time and portion my information

I have to make Nice Play Fair and Polite
When I want to tear open my chest to void it of this emptiness
This ache has eaten into my head and wears down my dreams
My friends worry I am not eating enough
Am taking too much on Too much in
I find nowhere to rest this responsibility

If I say nothing I am complicit
If I say something I am isolated as extreme
As a theorist in conspiracy
As if war is ever a coincidence
As if genocide simply happens

This is about oil and land and water
This is about illusion and the taking on of airs
The poor once again the munitions in rich men's cannons

This is about light and dark
There is no black and white in humanity

I am told
Venezuela is not Cuba
Rwanda is not Kurdistan

I am not the woman kneeling
In front of soldiers and their cameras and their weapons
I am not the child shot in the head by the Israeli Defense Forces
I am not the starving AIDS inflicted mother
Praying I live longer than my children
So they will not be orphaned and sick and have to bury me
I am not the child who watched
Her family chopped to death in Lebanon in Sudan in Nicaragua
I am not the father who leaves his children so as not to hear their
empty Bellies call out Baba, where is the bread?

I am the woman whose taxes outfitted this tragedy
The American the Authority does not speak for
The Arab the Arab leaders do not speak for
The woman whose shouts of Not in My Name
Were spit back at me as a slogan of the misguided at best
I am the girl from Brooklyn told to mind her business
I am the poet in search of new words
And a new world Not Mars

4.

We use antiquated terms that cannot stretch enough to touch this
truth
We have not learned from the past enough to not repeat it

I am told it has always been this way
War and Pillage
Rape is older than prostitution
And prostitution is the oldest politic
The way the world has always been
The pimps and those they pimp

The human race has always left
Those who fall behind

If I am to survive then
I learn from the present
From the future promised

We learn to live with madness
One cannot be healthy in a sick world
Only navigate illnesses Only medicate wounds
Pray you are not contagious
Try to hurt no one

My elders say dissent has always been watched
Radical ideas have always been recorded
But even those who have lived on the margins admit
Under breath It has never been this bad

Not everyone is suffering True
Most thirst
A few swim in pools that fake connection to seas
Most starve
I throw away meals I have no appetite for
You can shop from your couch and eat food fast
And never think about anything other than your credit card debt
And the next hour's purchases
Shop and stop asking questions
I have envied this stupor
Even knowing it is the least honorable suicide
Even knowing its apathy is another kind of murder

5.

Sometimes all you can do is inhale and exhale
Life a shallow version of its potential
Sometimes all you can do is search for life where you are
In the city A flash of yellow on the basketball court
The divine geometry in the pattern of a girl's hijab

For a week I have been cleaning and knifing enough
Parsley for tabbouleh to feed hundreds
I pray over the green
That what I make will feed those in need of a meal

There is still love in us
The proof is that we are watching it die
There is still hope in us
Hope is there in my sisters' eyes
There is still enough resistance in us
To create a world where there is no
Your people or my people
But our people
Our people who kill Our people who are killed

I somehow know love will save us
The proof is in the stories not broadcast
The poems not published

The truth between the lies
The stories whispered in the dusk of this day

I know somehow love will save us
Though I can't find the passion or desire in my body to make it

There is still a source for peace deeply embedded in this chaos

I know love will save us
Though words fail to point out how

Amazingly I still pray
To a god I envision to be larger than any nation Any religion

And I still hunt for language to gather into a poem
That I pray will feed those like me
In need of proof they are not alone

2

The Political and Cultural Representations of Arabs, Arab Americans, and Arab American Feminisms after September 11, 2001

MERVAT F. HATEM

In this chapter, Mervat Hatem reflects on the impact that September 11 had on her own writings, specifically the study of the changing political and cultural representations of Arabs, Arab Americans, and Arab American feminisms in the United States. Historically, our understandings of these international and national actors influenced the general locations of Arab American men and women and the debate on gender in their communities. The post–September 11 representations show how the definition of the transnational loyalties and identities associated with a global world continues to be rooted in national communities and agendas. It has affected the national history of Arab American organizing in the United States and how it combined international and national issues and agendas that shaped their political relations with the African and Jewish American communities before and after September 11. Finally, the ethnic and political tensions that surfaced in the Arab American communities in the post–September 11 period have had feminist and gendered implications.

September 11 Through Arab American and Feminist Eyes

The events of September 11, 2001, presented complex challenges to American society and its citizens. These challenges were deeply felt in Arab American communities that found themselves in a unique position. Like the larger American community, Arab Americans were horrified by the massive loss of civilian lives

Evelyn Alsultany, Rabab Abdulhadi, and Amaney Jamal have read different versions of this paper and offered valuable suggestions for revisions. The responsibility for the views expressed here, however, is mine.

that resulted from the use of airplanes as weapons to attack the World Trade Center and the Pentagon as symbols of American economic and military power. At the same time, many members of Arab American communities were keenly aware and critical of the general contempt for Arabs as outsiders and insiders in U.S. society. Cultural prejudice against Arab culture and American foreign policy in the Middle East, especially its support of conservative authoritarian Arab governments and Israeli repression of the Palestinian struggle for national self-determination in the occupied West Bank and Gaza, was a major source of discontent. This position as outsiders and insiders in the U.S. national community made Arab Americans critical of the national and international U.S. policies isolating them from other Americans who closed ranks and became unified in the demand for retaliation against the national and international groups associated with the perpetrators.

The fact that the September 11 attacks were led by Arab Muslim men from Saudi Arabia, Egypt, Lebanon, and the United Arab Emirates led to the general suspicions of Arabs and Arab and Muslim Americans, who were seen by the larger public as homogeneously complicit in these horrific events. As a result, members of these distinct but overlapping communities (especially women in Islamic dress) bore the brunt of the early attacks by an angry American public. It is worth noting here that Arabs and Arab Americans trace their national roots to the twenty-two member states of the League of Arab States: Egypt, Sudan, Jordan, Syria, Lebanon, Iraq, Saudi Arabia, Kuwait, Bahrain, Qatar, United Arab Emirates, Oman, Yemen, Djibouti, Somalia, Eritrea, Libya, Tunisia, Algeria, Comoros, Morocco, and Mauritania. Religiously, they include Muslims (Sunnis, Shiites, Alawites, and Ismailis), Christians (Protestants, Catholics, members of the Greek Orthodox Church, as well as member of regional churches like the Copts, Caldeans and Assyrians, and Maronites), and Jews.

American Muslims represent a much larger diverse national group that includes Arabs, Africans (from East, West, and southern Africa), South Asians (from India, Pakistan, and Bangladesh), Indonesians, Turks, Iranians, and African Americans speaking many languages and representing many histories and cultural traditions. Whereas the size of the Arab American community is estimated to be between 2.5 and 3 million, the American Muslim community is estimated to be about 7 million. According to one recent source, South Asians represent 32 percent of the community, Arabs 26 percent, and African Americans 20 percent, with the remaining numbers coming from other countries.[1]

The religious, cultural, and linguistic diversity of Arab Americans and American Muslims was not appreciated by the larger public, especially those individuals who committed hate crimes against members of these communities leading to indiscriminate assaults on Arab Muslims and Christians, but also South Asian non-Muslims like the Sikh. In fact, the first victim of anti-Muslim attacks was a Sikh whose turban was mistakenly taken as a Muslim article of clothing.

Next, private and governmental U.S. groups began a sustained attack on the major institutions of Arab and Muslim American communities, including their schools, charitable organizations, and mosques, as breeding grounds for terrorism and terrorists. This action paved the way for the broad violation of the civil and citizenship rights of Arab and American Muslims.[2] The precariousness of the civil status of members of these overlapping communities was brought home to me when a highly skilled family member whose name revealed his Arab Muslim ancestry was consistently denied employment during this period, adding a personal dimension to the feeling of a "community under attack."

The passage of the USA PATRIOT Act, the massive random imprisonment of Arab Americans and American Muslims, and their maltreatment in captivity provided other examples of the increasing violation of the civil rights of these groups. In response, one's political energy was both consciously and unconsciously channeled into the defense of the community. Intellectually, I switched my research focus from the primary study of gender and politics in the Middle East and in the United States to a primary preoccupation with the U.S. policies on the war on terrorism and homeland security and how they generated new representations of Arabs and Arab and Muslim Americans as external and internal enemies.[3] A major preoccupation became the systematic critique of the official U.S. government discourses as well as the conventional academic ones, which treated these populations, their cultures, and their national and social projects as homogeneously suspect, providing justifications for continued attacks (for example, the clash of civilizations thesis, the new mushrooming literature on Islamic terrorism, and the literature on Islamic fundamentalism). The new powerful representation of being indiscriminate "terrorists" served to classify them as antisocial, pathological, fanatical criminals whose motives and actions did not deserve historical or political analyses.

Because U.S. policies and discourses on the war on terrorism and homeland security pitted an abstract "good" Western civilization against an "evil" Islamic one, I found it important to counter these constructions with a discussion of how September 11 was part of an expanded political challenge that the Palestinians and the Islamist movements in the Middle East mounted against Israel, Arab authoritarian governments, and American support of both. Because the discourse on the war on terrorism objectified Arab and Muslim women as victims in Islamic societies that needed the United States to liberate them, it was important to couple the critique of these condescending constructions with parallel critiques of the regional secular nationalist discourses that also attacked Islam and Islamists as the causes of the backwardness of Arab and Islamic societies and their gender roles, along with Islamist discourses that attacked the failures of postcolonial societies, offering what they argued were more "authentic" conservative definitions of gender roles and relations. Because U.S., Arab nationalist, and Islamist discourses used the discussions of women and their roles to settle political scores with each other, students of gender relations needed to simultaneously critique these complicit discourses.

Here, I found myself partially agreeing with Fouad Ajami, the neoconservative Arab political theorist, in rejecting what he often described as "Arab victimology" with its simplified analysis of U.S. global dominance as the only source of problems facing the region, its populations, and its women. Unlike him, I do not limit my analysis of the problems facing Arab societies and their women to national actors like Arab states and Islamist groups, but add to the discussion the role played by international actors, like the U.S. government and American feminists who are also engaged in the production of degraded representations of Arab societies, Islam, and women to give their projects political legitimacy.[4] The goal was to deconstruct and neutralize the negative political effects on these discourses, creating an independent intellectual space where Arab and Arab American men and women can develop voices that are clear about the challenges within and without.

While the above reading continued to give importance to gender in the discussion of U.S., Arab nationalist, and Islamist policies and discourses, coupling it with the study of the war on terror and homeland security, which generated new conflicts and unexpected alliances, a feminist journal that reviewed a conference paper I submitted on the U.S. war on terrorism that dealt with the Arab, Muslim, and gendered "other" suggested that I cut the sections that dealt with the Arab and Muslim components, focusing only on how Muslim American women were affected! This recommendation indicated continuing feminist suspicions of male nationalist perspectives of theorists, like Frantz Fanon, who underlined the importance of locating gender issues and debates in a national context, avoiding its colonial use to divide the community.[5]

This view leads one to revisit the following old question: must the attempt to juggle the understanding of the impact that powerful government policies have on the Arab and Arab and Muslim American communities be necessarily seen as an abandonment of the feminist agenda and acquiescence to a nationalist standpoint? Conversely, can women simultaneously rise to the defense of the community without betraying their gender interests? I have to confess that I remain suspicious of the binary definitions of the multilayered identities and concerns of women that give credence to past and present nationalist arguments that continue to be popular in the Arab world and in the United States, charging feminism with dividing the national community and conversely viewing national communities as irretrievably less woman friendly. I do not see any reason Arab and Arab and Muslim American feminists should not also embrace the role of being national speakers or representatives of the community without betraying their gender interests. In this new role, one can expect them to combine an understanding of the international and national challenges facing their communities with an appreciation of their distinct gender implications. At the present historical and national moment, it is crucial that Arab and Arab and Muslim American feminist theorists have intellectual room to freely articulate the different constructions of the intersection of the national and international with the gendered.

Those individuals who argue that, in view of the global context of the war on terrorism, transnational identities and concerns have superseded national ones ignore how the former continue to be rooted in national agendas. For example, the U.S. response to the war on terrorism, which was defined as a war without borders, has been largely focused on homeland security.[6] U.S. national interests have clearly guided the war on terrorism and have superseded the interests of other partner nation-states in that military effort. The U.S. definitions of its enemies within and without have also been national. They have reinforced the national bonds that tie Arab American communities in the United States with their Arab counterparts in the Middle East and opposed them to the United States and its national agendas.

The Changing International and National Challenges Facing Arab Americans Before September 11

As Arab Americans politically organize to defend themselves against the attacks that use the war on terrorism and homeland security as justifications, it is important to appreciate how the intersection of international and national policies underlined their representations in the United States before and after September 11, 2001. In this section, I will begin with a discussion of how the centenary celebrations of Ralph Bunche's birthday have led me to consider how U.S. foreign policy toward the region in the post–World War II period and the decolonization of the region produced representations of Arabs as international actors with complex relations to African and Jewish Americans. These U.S. representations of Arabs and Muslims provide historical and political depth to the understanding of how the location of Arab Americans in the U.S. national cultural and political landscapes has changed over time.

Ralph Bunche, the Arab Israeli Conflict, and Early Political
Representations of Arabs as International Actors

Ralph Bunche, a distinguished African American political scientist who founded the Political Science Department at Howard University, of which I am a present member, developed an interest in the study of North Africa when he worked for the Office of Strategic Services (the precursor of the Central Intelligence Agency) during the Second World War, producing a manual titled *A Guide to North Africa* that was designed to educate American soldiers about those countries where U.S. forces were to be stationed after 1941. Bunche went on to play an active role in the founding of the United Nations, the new international organization established in 1945, whose early history was identified with the rise of the United States and the Soviet Union as new superpowers that eclipsed Great Britain and France as the old colonial powers.

One of Bunche's earliest assignments at the new international organization was to facilitate the work of the UN Special Commission on Palestine (UNSCOP). Great Britain, which had been given the contradictory mandate of preparing Palestinians for self-government and establishing a national homeland for Jews in Palestine at the end of World War I, referred the escalating conflict between Palestinian and Jewish national aspirations to the UN in 1947. Bunche was one of the few diplomats on that committee who had any knowledge of the region. UNSCOP eventually recommended the partition of Palestine,[7] leading to the outbreak of the first Arab-Israeli War in the wake of the withdrawal of British forces and the establishment of the state of Israel in 1948.

From this experience, Bunche noted that a general lack of U.S. knowledge and understanding of the region coupled with early popular references to "Ayrabs" reflected a tinge of racism. This analysis emerged as a serious criticism of U.S. foreign policy in some of his public writings. The following represents the clearest articulation of his views:

> We have first of all a vast job of self-education to undertake. Cultural under-
> standing is something, which must properly begin at home. We need to realign
> our human relations' sights in the most basic way, in order that we may come to
> think of peoples in the Near East, the Far East, the Caribbean and Africa with

regards to their abilities and to be able to treat them as such in our policies and actions in a convincing way. That, I think, is one of the most imperative jobs that we in this country have to do in meeting the new responsibilities which have come to us as a result of the role of leadership assumed by this country since the end of the last war.[8]

The statement suggests that Bunche made connections between the peoples of North Africa and Southwest Asia, who were Arabs, with those peoples of the rest of the African and Asian continents, the Caribbean, and the U.S. diaspora. He also acknowledged that the new leadership role of the United States entailed new responsibilities that included learning about these different regions. As a political scientist by training and a diplomat by profession, he worked over the years to increase his knowledge of the Middle East as a region with which he was preoccupied. He worked with Count Folke Bernadotte, the UN special mediator in Palestine, to stop the fighting that broke out after the establishment of the state of Israel in 1948. When Bernadotte was assassinated by Jewish extremists and terrorists, Bunche replaced him as acting mediator, successfully negotiating the armistice agreements between Israel and the Arab states. For that achievement, he was awarded the Nobel Peace Prize in 1950, highlighting both his individual diplomatic skills and the success of U.S. diplomacy in this part of the world. Following the conclusion of the 1956 Suez War, he embarked on the development and annual supervision of the peacekeeping forces placed on the Egyptian-Israeli border.

Although Bunche avoided for the most part any public discussion of U.S. foreign policy and how it intersected with his UN work, he connected his experiences as an African American academic and a former state functionary in a racially segregated U.S. government in the 1940s and the 1950s with his views of the Palestinian-Israeli conflict. He acknowledged that the UN partition of Palestine was not an ideal solution but the only one realistically possible under the circumstances. He suggested that the Palestinians paid the price of this resolution dictated by new power relations[9] and the asymmetry of the political resources available to Palestinians and the Jews in Palestine, the United States, and the world community.[10]

As part of this view, he recognized two cornerstones of an emerging U.S. foreign policy following the Second World War. With the United States and the Soviet Union as the first two states to recognize Israel in 1948, he was clearly aware of how these two new powers were determined to spread their influence to the territories that were abandoned by the former colonial powers. In addition to containment of Soviet influence, U.S. support of Israel demonstrated the emergence of a Judeo-Christian alliance that influenced American foreign policy in the Middle East, which, through the use of a dominant political discourse, identified Palestine as the Holy Land,[11] giving Israel a source of national and religious support that Arabs and Muslims lacked.

Finally, Bunche's experience and knowledge of the African American struggles in the United States mediated his views of the Israelis and the Arabs in other ways. His sympathy for Jewish aspirations in Palestine was shaped by the long history of discrimination against them in the United States and the alliances between them and African Americans as representatives of visible minority groups allied in the struggle for civil rights during that period.[12]

His views of the Arabs were equally complex. Given his interest in African national struggles, he sympathized with the regional plight of the Arabs as people going through the difficult decolonization process. He also noted how American political discourses produced racist representations of the Arabs, reflecting a general ignorance of their history and culture,[13] treating them as another minority group that suffered from the discrimination of the majority.

The Nexus Between International Political and National Cultural Representations of Arabs and Muslims in the 1950s and the 1960s

While the Palestinian-Israeli conflict provided a powerful grid for representing Arabs as outside international actors, U.S. pursuit of its economic and political interests in this strategic part of the world added new representations of its peoples and leaders. In the 1950s, the United States began a record of active intervention in the affairs of Middle Eastern states, especially those countries that produced oil. The Arab and non-Arab populations of the region emerged as "objects" of U.S. national interests. The newly created Central Intelligence Agency played a prominent role in overthrowing the regime of Mohammed Mossadegh, who attempted to nationalize the Iranian oil industry in 1953.[14] The support of the shah of Iran and the conservative governments of the oil-producing Arab Gulf states against national and regional challengers became a pillar of U.S. policy. This new economic dimension to U.S. foreign policy in the region complemented the goal of Soviet containment in the region.

The 1956 Suez War provided a good example of the increasing importance of the area for U.S. international agendas. The United States and the Soviet Union jointly condemned the tripartite aggression by Great Britain, France, and Israel against Egypt, which nationalized the British- and French-owned International Suez Canal Company. This rare display of superpower agreement was designed to attract regional allies to their competing camps. More important, the war presented a rare international occasion whereby the new superpowers used the UN to punish and humiliate the old colonial powers for ignoring the new international realities in which the interests of the former now overshadowed the interests of the latter.

The withdrawal of British and French forces from Egypt and the end of Israeli occupation of Sinai in 1956 led to the stationing of UN Emergency Forces, as representatives of the first successful international peacekeeping operation, keeping the Egyptian-Israeli border peaceful for eleven years. The region remained far from stable, however, with the United States landing its troops in Lebanon in 1958 in an attempt to influence the outcome of the first Lebanese Civil War and also meddling in Syrian and Jordanian policies at the time.

In response, some Arab states chose to embrace the policy of nonalignment with either the United States or the USSR to maximize their desire to protect the hard-won goal of political independence and to play the superpowers against each other in the quest to increase economic resources that would serve their development. The leaders of this movement were Gamal Abdel Nasser of Egypt, Kwame Nkrumah of Ghana, Jawaharlal Nehru of India, and Jozip Broz Tito of Yugoslavia. Arab support of nonalignment was considered by the foreign policy establishment to be anti-American, reinforcing the negative perceptions of them as an alien group.

Paradoxically, the close Egyptian and Ghanaian connection in the quest of nonalignment and African unity contributed to the production of positive cultural representations of Arabs among African Americans as advocates of anticolonialism and a new world order that challenged white supremacy. Up until then, there was only strong positive support within that community of the creation of the state of Israel as a demonstration of the religious narrative in which Jewish exodus from Egypt signified the end of slavery and the successful realization of the goal of statehood.[15]

The cultural and political rise of the Nation of Islam during this period contributed to new positive forms of cultural representations of Islam within the African American community. Although the Nation of Islam had its own distinct history and religious traditions, it presented Islam as an alternative source of spirituality whose transnational connections brought Africa, the Middle East, and African America together. It provided African Americans with a basis of cultural and political autonomy not offered by the civil rights movement, whose explicit goal was integration into U.S. culture and policies.[16] These new positive definitions of Islam in a minority context coexisted with the negative majority views of Islam as inferior to both Christianity and Judaism.

Israeli Militarism and the Development of Arab
and Arab American Voices in the 1970s and 1980s

The war of 1967 transformed the Palestinian-Israeli national conflict into a regional conflict, with Israel occupying territories that belonged to Egypt (Sinai), Syria (the Golan Heights), and what was left of Palestine before the 1948 war (the West Bank and Gaza) and emerging as a victorious military power at a time when the United States was struggling militarily and politically in the Vietnam War. Given the popular and the liberal critiques of the war as an example of failed U.S. imperial politics, neoconservatives used Israel as a successful military model that provided an acceptable alternative to what they characterized as appeasement.[17]

In this liberal-versus-conservative polemics, Arab Americans found political and intellectual spaces where the Arab territorial, political, and nationalist concerns coupled with attacks against Arab Americans in the United States during and after the 1967 war could be articulated. The civil rights struggles of the 1960s also had the effect of encouraging them to form their first national organization: the Association of the Arab American University Graduates (AAUG) in 1967. It was to represent the pooling of the intellectual resources of the community for the "purpose of warding off the intense and often indiscriminate attacks against [the community] and against the old homeland."[18] Even though the AAUG was a middle-class professional organization, it acquired dual Arab and American nationalist credentials through its commitment to the "goal of producing first-rate literature on the Arab world [in the United States] and in this way challeng[ing] the Zionist [representation of the Arabs and the Arab-Israeli conflict]."[19] This task was made more pressing because Palestinian activism in the 1970s, through a series of dramatic incidents designed to educate the world about their concerns, led to another negative representation of Arabs and Palestinians as terrorists who were a moral foil for a triumphant Israel.[20]

As a result, some of the members of the Arab and Jewish American communities became engaged in a battle to inform American public audiences about their diametrically opposed nationalist perspectives of the issues involved in the Arab-Israeli conflict. As an expression of the dominant nationalist dynamic within the Arab American community, many other associations proliferated in the 1970s and 1980s, reflecting the varied needs. In 1972, the National Association for Arab Americans emerged as a political lobbying group, the American-Arab Anti-Discrimination Committee (ADC) followed in 1980 to fight against the prevalent public defamation of Arab Americans in the United States, and, finally, the Arab American Institute was established in 1985 to increase Arab American participation in electoral politics.[21]

In the 1980s, Arab Americans' increased interest in electoral politics contributed to the building of new alliances and the intensification of old political rivalries. The attempt on the part of some Arab Americans to maximize their leverage within the Democratic Party contributed to a significant alliance with African Americans who supported Jesse Jackson's presidential campaigns in 1984 and 1988. The alliance with Arab Americans challenged those people within the Democratic Party who questioned African American interest in international issues and conflicts, like the Palestinian conflict, where race was not the central issue. The alliance with African Americans gave Arab Americans greater visibility, allowing them to engage in a deeper discussion of intifada and the goal of Palestinian statehood in the Democratic Party platform in July 1988. It also contributed to the development of triangular tense relations with Jewish Americans: relations between political segments of African and Jewish Americans became strained, and relations between organized Arab and Jewish Americans within the Democratic Party became more competitive.

Equally significant, the important gains made in this party convention reflected improved Arab American grassroots organizing, signaling a new political balance between national and international interests and concerns.[22] In fact, the AAUG and ADC during the late 1980s and the 1990s witnessed a realignment in the definition of Arab American agendas, stressing the American national agendas of the community that focused on the needs of women and the younger sections of the community and the deepening of civil rights.[23] Reinforcing that new development, some Arab American and American Muslim groups became publicly critical of the way Palestinian or international issues or both were used to define the community and its concerns.

In view of the rise of Iran's Islamic republic in 1979 and the emergence of political Islam as a dominant oppositional movement that challenged U.S. interests in the Arab world, the representation of Arabs and Arab Americans in the United States focused on Islam as the primary cultural signifier of the community. Even though there were many Muslims who were not Arabs, like Iranians, Turks, and South Asians, there were also many Arabs who were not Muslims but were members of the Christian and Jewish faiths. This new representation created new sources of confusion and tensions among the larger U.S. public. It also began to slowly eclipse the Arab agenda of the community.

The Political Challenges in the Post–September 11 World

September 11, 2001, represented the intensification of these developments. It had a negative effect on the process of political integration that sought to give a greater emphasis to the national agendas of the community. It contributed to a return to the prominence of international concerns, especially the war on terrorism, in the definition of the citizenship rights of Arab Americans. Not only did this turn affect existing political rivalries with some Jewish Americans, but it also affected the alliance between Arab and African Americans. In this hostile political climate, the categories "Arab" or "Arab American" were submerged into the larger and more diffuse categories of "Muslim" or "Muslim American," leading to the widespread and gross violation of civil rights. Paradoxically, the new climate also offered potential opportunities for coalition building.

Whereas the collapse of the Oslo Accords in the summer of 2000 contributed to a greater polarization between some Arab and Jewish American groups, September 11 added fuel to that process. The Israeli government was successful in presenting the second Palestinian intifada as a continuation of the terror that was inflicted on the United States on September 11, 2001. The result was the negative reinforcement of the connection among Arabs, their interest in Palestinian rights, and terrorism.

Next, some conservative American Jewish groups began a coordinated attack on the alliance between Arab and African Americans, by which Arab Americans sought to strengthen their concerns with the attacks on their civil rights after 9/11. In 2002, a conflicted triangular relationship developed among the politicized segments of African, Jewish, and Arab Americans, with Arab and Jewish Americans supporting different African American congressional candidates for the same seats in some parts of the South. A good example of one such political race was the one occupied by Representative Cynthia McKinney, a black congresswoman from Georgia who had emerged as a vocal critic of the Bush administration's policies after September 11 and a supporter of the protection of Arab American civil rights. Whereas some Arab American groups financially supported her reelection bid, other Jewish Americans supported her African American opponent, who eventually unseated her. The result contributed to complicated divisions within and among the politicized segments of these three minority groups.

Racial politics represented another challenge to potential alliances between Arab Americans and other minority groups on civil rights issues. Before

September 11 major Arab American organizations paid limited attention to the extensive use of racial profiling against African and Latino Americans. When Arab Americans became the latest victims of the practice, some of the previous African and Latino American victims reported a temporary sense of relief from the harassment of law enforcement agencies. The expanded use of this practice in the post–September 11 period against Arab and Muslim Americans made it a potent civil rights issue that could potentially unite the members of the Arab, African, and Latino American communities who remain its main victims.

Finally, the influx of Muslim immigrants from different parts of the Arab world in the 1970s and the 1980s contributed to the further diversification of the political voices within the community. The secular Arab nationalist discourse that dominated the discussions of community issues, including the Arab-Israeli conflict during the 1960s and the 1970s, fractured in the wake of the Camp David Accords in 1979. Nowhere was this made clearer than on the many university campuses where the different branches of Arab students' organizations, which used to bring Arab students together irrespective of nationality, were gradually replaced by smaller national organizations that appealed to students of the same nationalities. The only large organizations that emerged to fill the vacuum left by the demise of Arab nationalism represented by the old Arab students' organizations were the Muslim Students Associations, which appealed to students' faith irrespective of national divisions. They brought together Muslims from the Arab world with American Muslims, whether African, African American, or South Asian.[24]

Whereas some of the new immigrant Muslim voices tended to be socially conservative, some were not. The result was power struggles between the old secular voices and the new religious ones and between the conservative and liberal voices within the Muslim and Christian Arab communities. Within the larger American Muslim community, there were also power struggles between the representatives of African American Islam who identified themselves as the indigenous Muslims versus immigrant Muslims from the Middle East and South Asia (India, Pakistan, and Bangladesh). Some African American Muslims went so far as describing these immigrant Muslims as "white" in their privileged socioeconomic status and definition of community and political agendas. They viewed immigrant coreligionists as socially backward and unfair to women, reinforcing the prejudicial majority view of Muslims. They also accused them of ignoring African American Islamic history and not acknowledging the contributions made by African American Muslims to the religion.[25]

Last but not least, there were tensions that divided Muslim immigrants from South Asia and their Arab counterparts. South Asian Muslims considered those individuals who come from some parts of the Middle East, especially the Gulf region, to be more socially "backward" and resented the imposition of the question of Palestine, as a contentious political issue, on the Muslim agenda.[26] Conversely, Arab Muslims thought of Southeast Asian Muslims as representatives of the Muslim periphery. In short, religion, nationality, and national origin have contributed to the fragmentation of Arabs and Muslims as transnational groups within the United States. The potential for building bridges among these different groups remains at the moment largely unrealized.

September 11 and the Contested Definitions of Feminism

Before September 11, the concern with Arab nationalism overshadowed the development of a clearly defined Arab American feminism. There were several attempts to form networks of women to articulate a feminist agenda, but they never went beyond critiquing the degraded definitions of Arab and Muslim women produced by American feminists in the academy. It was not surprising, therefore, that the important attempts to define feminism came from a new source.

Immediately after September 11, Muslim women emerged as the earliest targets of anti-Muslim and anti-Arab violence and were the first to successfully organize against it. They used their Muslim attire, which gave them away, as a means of educating Americans in general about their experiences and their religion. The initial response to the attacks in the United States came from some Muslim scholars, who issued edicts that justified the taking off of the *hijab*,[27] the modest Islamic mode of dress, including the head covering, as an implementation of the religious principle that instructed the believers that matters of necessity should supersede those matters that were religiously forbidden.

This stance was shocking to some Muslim women, who felt that their dress was once again used by Muslim and non-Muslim men in the service of politics. As American Muslims, they believed that their *hijab* was legitimately part of the American cultural landscape. The paternalist religious recommendation that women take off the *hijab* ignored the religious feelings of some Muslim women, who considered this expression of their faith to be much more important than self-protection. For some, the *hijab* acquired more importance after 9/11 as an expression of their pride in a religion that was increasingly maligned in the United States. It also served to affirm the rights of American Muslim women to exercise their freedom through dress.[28]

In response to these attacks, Muslim college women embraced *Hijab* Days as a way of promoting solidarity with the group during this difficult period.[29] On the University of Michigan campus, a coalition of peace activists and Muslim women declared Fridays to be days in which Muslim women would give away *hijabs* at a central part of campus to anyone who wanted to put them on as an expression of solidarity that effectively confused the people who were targeting them. No one was turned away, and this act of solidarity provided a means of communication between Muslim and non-Muslim women about their dress and their experiences after 9/11. In these exchanges some lesbian women articulated their sympathy for Muslim women who were attacked, because they too were frequently attacked because of the way they dressed and looked. For other non-Muslim women who put on the *hijab,* it served as an eye-opening experience of how Muslim women were viewed and treated by other Americans just because of how they were dressed.

One of the organizers of *Hijab* Days at the University of Michigan explained how the event was not without its challenges from outside and within the community. The following was her description of these challenges:

> Some of the critics were self-identified Arab feminists who saw the veil as a symbol of the oppression and misogyny in the Middle East [that was] used to repress women. They were adamantly opposed to the event and the irresponsible use of the symbols we were promoting. A number of non-Arab, non-Muslim feminists objected as well.
>
> Some men asked if they could wear the veil, which we did not permit explaining that it would be seen as making a mockery of the Muslim community as opposed to the purpose of the event that was to show solidarity to it in this difficult time. We provided wristbands for them instead.
>
> Finally, some Muslims, both men and women, raised concerns about the Islamic and legal use of hijab [which is a form of worship] as a political symbol. I explained that in Islamic history, non-Muslim women had worn the hijab, that promoting modesty was a general Islamic ethic and that all over the world non-Muslim women, particularly in the countryside, cover their hair as do nuns and that this was not seen as some kind of blasphemous act.
>
> These arguments were augmented by the authority of the local imams, who agreed that there was nothing inappropriate about this and who were consulted early in the process.[30]

The above showed an interesting convergence of opposition to the *hijab* from within and outside the community in the United States. Arab Muslim and non-Muslim American secular feminists rejected it as an unacceptable symbol of political solidarity. Both clung to the old Orientalist definition of the Islamic mode of dress as a symbol of oppression, imposed on women and denying them active participation in society. For American Muslim college women, who chose to wear the *hijab*, this Orientalist view of their dress did not represent who they were. As active women in their communities and society, the continued devaluation of their dress by Arab secular Muslims and American non-Muslim women reflected the political agendas of these groups who were incapable of thinking of difference as other than subordination. The continued condemnation of the *hijab* served to silence this religiously observant minority that behaved in ways that contradicted widely held assumptions about Muslim women.

Finally, this group of Muslim women responded confidently to conservative critics within their community who were opposed to their political activism. These critics advocated a very narrow definition of women's dress as a religious duty and opposed its appropriation by activist women as a symbol of pride and a means of forming coalitions with non-Muslim women. The activist women were, in turn, not willing to cheapen this religious symbol by having men put it on. At the same time, they showed themselves to be politically savvy in successfully channeling male solidarity through an alternative symbol, namely, wristbands. Finally, this group of women worked successfully with the representative of religious authorities in their community, getting their approval, enjoying their support, and making responsible decisions regarding the particulars of that event. All of it suggests that this group of American Muslim women emerged as active members of their community, challenging the very dated views and assumptions that Muslims and non-Muslims alike made about devout women.

As a result, it is fair to say that Arab American and American Muslim communities are witnessing a new power struggle between the representatives of a secular and an Islamic feminism. Up until now, Arab, American, and Arab American secular feminists have dominated the limited debate on women's rights. More recently, religious Muslim women (*al-Muhajjabat*, or those women who wear the *hijab* and Islamic mode of dress) have claimed their legitimate right and interest to participate in this debate. Unfortunately, some Muslim, Christian, and Jewish members of the community look down on this group, view them as socially backward, and refuse to deal with them as equals in the debate on women's rights. I find this refusal to be an alarming development that reflects the internalization of Orientalist views of Islam and Muslim women within large segments of the community, including Muslim ones. When did Arab or Muslim women start believing that their observant counterparts were less critical or liberated? Should not Arab women in general, whether they are secular or religiously observant, have the right to choose their politics? The a priori *assumptions* that religious

Muslim women are conservative and backward and that only secular ones are liberal and progressive lay at the heart of the split between Western versus Oriental and Muslim versus Christian. For some Arab Muslim women to internalize these assumptions about their more religious counterparts is alarming and may explain that what one is dealing with is not a religious division but rather a political and intellectual one that should be addressed.

Here, I want to share personal experiences I had a couple of years ago, which made the politics of these attitudes simultaneously personal and intellectual. I fell sick in 2002 and lost all my hair. Wearing a wig was not something I was comfortable with, so I ended up wearing a beret or scarves. The experience was an eye-opener about my own response to being perceived as a *muhajjaba*, that is, someone who is religiously observant and adheres to the Islamic mode of dress that instructs women to cover their hair and bodies (in other words, to dress modestly or conservatively) and how it influenced the attitudes of people I encountered in the professional and academic arenas. As I prepared to present a paper at the World Bank, I found myself thinking about whether I could tolerate people thinking that I was becoming more religiously observant or if I should tell them about my illness as an explanation of why I was covering my hair. The assumption that I was making was that becoming more observant was automatically a reflection of political and social conservatism and that I needed to deny that charge! Although I ended up sharing my illness with an Iranian scholar who was also a good friend, I left all others wondering about the meaning of my beret and then scarf. Initially, the World Bank professionals, both Arab Muslims and non-Muslims, seemed puzzled about my beret and its political symbolism. Only after I delivered my paper could I see the equivalent of a sigh of relief on their faces.

This experience was augmented by another encounter that I had with a Jordanian Ph.D. candidate who asked to see me. She e-mailed me saying that she used my work in her dissertation and was in town and asked if I would take the time to see her. We agreed to meet at a Starbucks near my house. When I walked in with a scarf on my head, she immediately identified me, even though we had never met. This reaction, of course, indicated the extent to which the Islamic mode of dress had become widespread among women in the region. As we chatted away, she told me that she was a Christian. We spent more than an hour talking about shared interests and views. Yet during most of that time her eyes remained transfixed on my scarf. I debated while we sat there if I should say something about my scarf, but I did not, hoping that our nice meeting and the ability to easily exchange views about different issues and ideas would be more important in determining how she felt. Was my scarf a disappointment? I like to believe that she walked away thinking that it was possible for a Christian woman and a *muhajjaba* to share positive encounters and that religious differences do not have to be an obstacle that prevent either from sharing similar views or extending support to the other.

Finally, I gave a draft of this chapter to an Egyptian colleague, Dr. Omaima Abou-Bakr, who is a professor of English at Cairo University and a good friend who is a *muhajjaba* and whose work on Islamic feminism promises to change our understanding of both Islam and feminism.[31] I wanted to see what her response would be to the thoughts that I have expressed about my unease at being identified as a *muhajjaba*. She was not surprised by my discomfort and reported that she experienced similar discomfort to that which I felt whenever she appeared in secular gatherings that automatically treated her with suspicion, with people attributing to her conservative and illiberal views because of her mode of dress. Islamic dress, though, did not necessarily make her more comfortable in Islamic circles. Their views did not correspond to hers, and they too assumed that just because she was *muhajjaba* she would denounce feminism and take a more apologist position on Islam and women.

She also reported feeling equally uneasy about women *munaqabat*, who in addition to covering their hair and bodies choose to cover their faces, leaving only their eyes uncovered. In her view, their conservatism went beyond what was required. She also suspected that they discounted her *hijab* as a chic fashion statement that was not truly Islamic.

This whole discussion has made me aware of the connection between dress and a modern definition of femininity. In addition to dress as a means of self-definition, I am reminded of John Berger's suggestion that when women look at themselves, they are also conscious of the way men and the larger society see them.[32] As representatives of minority women in the United States, Muslim women know that men and other women judge them by the way they represent themselves through dressing their bodies without really knowing much about them as individuals. Rather than use different modes of dress to reproduce power relations that exist within society at large, I have tried to destabilize them, encouraging the women I encounter to tolerate others whose self-definition and self-image are different from theirs and to fight the powerful urge to make them into clichéd others.

◆　　◆　　◆

I have attempted to offer my own take on the important international and national challenges facing Arab American communities and their women. My research interests and professional training as a political scientist have shaped my perspective. There is an urgent need to openly articulate, discuss, and theorize about the representations of religious, political, gender, and national differences that distinguish segments of Arab and Arab American communities from others with the goal of building bridges across them. Similarly, there is an equally urgent need to form coalitions with other minority groups whose histories and experiences are different but who share our concern for civil rights in the post–September 11 political system.

One can choose to accept or critique the clichéd representations of national, religious, class, sexual, ethnic, and gender differences within and between communities leading to sources of division or strength. The binary Orientalist categories that counterpose the presumedly oppressed and conservative *muhajjabat* versus the presumedly assertive and independent feminist Arab, American, or Arab American need to be questioned. This examination should be part of an ongoing debate about the impact that these constructions have on the community and whose interests they serve at a time when the collective mobilization of important human resources is needed to meet the serious national and international challenges that September 11 produced.

3

Palestinian Women's Disappearing Act

The Suicide Bomber Through Western Feminist Eyes

AMAL AMIREH

This chapter critiques some Western feminist representations of the female suicide bombers of the second Palestinian Intifada. It argues that Palestinian women suicide bombers posed a challenge to the Orientalist view of Arab and Muslim women's bodies as demure and passive. By looking at the way this figure is deployed in the works of three writers, Andrea Dworkin, Robin Morgan, and Barbara Victor, the essay points out the different ways these writers use a "death by culture" paradigm that erases the political and replaces it with the cultural to explain the motivations of the women's violent acts. In the resulting imperial "feminist" discourse, Palestinian women are seen as victims, not of war or occupation, which are factored out of their lives, but of a killer culture that always abuses and victimizes them. The chapter concludes by underscoring the damaging effects this kind of discourse has on transnational feminist solidarity.

My interest in writing this essay was sparked by an encounter I had in the spring of 2004 with a British reporter who called my office to interview me about Palestinian women suicide bombers. After introducing herself and the topic on which she was working, she asked her first question: "Can you please talk about the treatment of Palestinian women?" When I started to talk about the hardships Palestinian women experience living under occupation, she interrupted me. "I meant for you to talk about how Palestinian society treats its women," she explained. "But the occupation . . . ," I stammered. "Well, the occupation is really another topic for another article." At that point, I asked the reporter how she knew there was a connection between the way women were treated by their society and suicide bombings. From her answers, it became clear to me that she had no evidence to support that connection, but rather an assumption, which I, the Palestinian feminist native informant, was being called upon to validate. For the rest of the conversation, I questioned that assumption and insisted that she consider the occupation as a relevant issue for her piece. The rest of this essay is specifically an extended questioning of the connection the reporter assumed between suicide bombings and culture. More broadly, it is also a critique of some problematic paradigms in Western feminist writings about gender and Palestinian nationalism.

Mistranslating Gender

To illustrate some of these problematic paradigms, let me begin with two examples of gender-related mistranslations from Arabic into English. In an article about Arab women's war-writing in her book *Gendering War Talk*, and in a section devoted to a discussion of the first Palestinian uprising, miriam cooke translates the Arabic word "intifada" for her readers by writing: "It is worth noting that *intifada* is a domestic term referring to the shaking out of the dustcloths and carpets that illustrates so brilliantly the process of these women's almost twenty-five-year-old insurrection." Cooke maintains, "The naming changed the nature of the war."[1]

The second example is from a recent book called *Army of Roses: Inside the World of Palestinian Women Suicide Bombers*, by Barbara Victor. Early in the book, Victor focuses on a 2002 speech by the president of the Palestinian Authority, Yāsir 'Arafāt, to a crowd of Palestinian women who came to his bombed-out quarters in a show of support. In this speech, 'Arafāt reportedly uttered a phrase that, according to Victor, "changed forever the nature of the Palestinian-Israeli conflict" and "would become his mantra in the weeks and months ahead." What was this amazing phrase? According to Victor, 'Arafāt said "*Shahida* all the way to Jerusalem," thus "coining on the spot the feminized version of the Arab word for martyr, *shahide*, which previously existed only in the masculine form."[2]

In the first case, cooke's statement is a mistranslation because "intifada" is not a domestic term. It is true that one of the uses of the root verb *nafad* may be to shake up the carpets, but it can also mean to shake hands, cigarette ashes, a part of the body, or anything else. To select that one possible use and generalize it as the main meaning of the word to underscore the domestic or feminized nature of the intifada is a stretch. It is to ignore that, after all, "intifada" also comes from the verb "intafada," which is an intransitive verb meaning to shake off, often the body or part of it. According to this meaning, "intifada" describes the Palestinian rebellion in the West Bank and Gaza as a shaking off of the chains of Israeli occupation and of Palestinian inertia by the collective Palestinian national body that includes men and women, adults and children. This definition is the generally accepted meaning of the word "intifada." Although it is true that the first intifada witnessed a more visible role for women (one of the icons of that intifada is the Palestinian woman deploying her body between Israeli soldiers and Palestinian youth to prevent the latter's arrest), it is an exaggeration to say that it was a women's uprising or that, to use cooke's words, it was "the most explicitly feminized of all postmodern wars."[3] It is significant that at the very moment Palestinian women were assuming a more visibly public political role (as opposed to their more traditional private political role), their actions are mistranslated into a language that emphasizes their domesticity. This domesticating language is the effect of a Western feminist paradigm that, in the name of politicizing the personal, ends up domesticating the political in third world women's lives. In the process of this domestication, the dichotomy between the political and the personal, the public and the private, is upheld.

The second example is also an attempt to draw attention to the role of Palestinian women but this time in the second intifada. Victor takes one of 'Arafāt's familiar statements, "Shahada hatta al Quds" (which literally translates to "Martyrdom till Jerusalem," a variation on, "Shahada hatta al nasr," or "Martyrdom till victory"), and transforms it into *shaheeda*, meaning female martyr (both have the regular feminized ending, but they are different words). Moreover, she claims that the feminine form *shaheeda* did not exist before and was invented by 'Arafāt on that wintry morning. As anyone who is familiar with the Arabic language knows, *shaheeda*, the feminine form of *shaheede*, preexists both 'Arafāt and Victor. It is the regular feminine form of a regular noun. Victor goes even further by arguing that on that same day, and after that explosive speech, a woman called Wafa Idris exploded a bomb and herself in Jerusalem, becoming the first Palestinian *shaheeda*. So not only did 'Arafāt invent a new word for the Arabic language, but he also invented a new woman for the Palestinian people. Like the sorcerer of *A Thousand and One Nights*, 'Arafāt used his magical words to conjure up the Palestinian woman suicide bomber. Victor mentions his amazing feat on page 20 and goes on to write three hundred more pages on the basis of this mistranslation. Ignorant of the existence of the word, she erases the hundreds of women martyrs in Palestinian history through an act of mistranslation.

Gendering Suicide Bombers

These mistranslations are symptomatic of a deeper problem relating to discussions of gender and nationalism. Whereas recent feminist scholarship has drawn attention to the relevance of gender to the study of nationalism, the specific ways by which gender and nationalism inform each other remain undertheorized and captive to certain feminist paradigms that are limited in their relevance and application.[4] When Western feminists, for instance, address gender and nationalism in relation to Palestinian women, they privilege sexual politics to the exclusion of all else, such as history, class, war, and occupation. The result is a privatization of the political instead of a politicization of the private. One important consequence of this privatization is the disappearance of women as national agents. This fact is nowhere more evident than in the Western feminist discourse on Palestinian women suicide bombers.

Since September 11th, a whole industry has evolved to explain the motive of the suicide bomber. Much ink has been spilled in an attempt to develop a profile for the male suicide bomber. The more serious studies tend to emphasize a complexity of motives and thus the elusiveness of a fixed profile, whereas the more ideological ones focus on psychological aspects, with special emphasis on pathology.[5] Sex has figured prominently, with U.S. and Israeli media advancing the *hour el 'ain* theory of suicide bombing, according to which men become suicide bombers because they are promised seventy-two virgins in paradise.[6] One thing that can be discerned from most of these studies is that the image of the male suicide bomber could fit easily into the preexisting dominant discourse about Muslim and Arab men as violent and licentious others. The female suicide bombers, however, have posed more of a challenge.

The female suicide bomber challenges the image of Muslim and Arab women as docile bodies that is dominant in the Western context. Although this image of docility has its roots in the long history of Orientalist stereotypes of Muslim women, it has become more visible in recent years. Certainly, in the aftermath of September 11th, the image of the veiled and beaten body of the Afghan woman under the Taliban was deployed on a massive scale and came to stand for Muslim and Arab women generally. U.S. feminists played a key role in disseminating this profile, when the Feminist Majority, a prominent U.S. feminist organization, joined forces with the Bush administration to "liberate" the bodies of the downtrodden women of Afghanistan. The oppressed body of the Muslim woman was inserted into debates about American national security and was offered as an important reason to justify a war. In contrast to this image, the female suicide bomber's body is far from dormant or inactive, passively waiting for outside help. It is purposeful, lethal, and literally explosive. Sometimes veiled, sometimes in "Western" dress, this body moves away from home, crosses borders, and infiltrates the other's territory. It is a protean body in motion and, therefore, needs a translation.

Another reason the woman suicide bomber poses a challenge to feminists in particular is the ambivalent view feminists have concerning women's relationship to nationalism. Despite recent scholarship that attempts to provide a nuanced analysis of women's connection to national institutions, the dominant view continues to see women of the third world as victims of nationalism, simultaneously embodied by their governments, countries, and cultures. While U.S. feminists may acknowledge that American women have a complex relation to their country and its patriarchal institutions (such as the military), they often deny that same kind of relationship to Arab and Muslim women, who are usually seen as a monolithic group always tainted with victimhood. As a result, the nationalist Arab and Muslim woman, with the suicide bomber as her most sensational embodiment, urgently needs an explanation.

To make this incomprehensible woman figure accessible to a Western readership, some U.S. feminists have deployed what Uma Narayan has called, in the context of her critique of Western feminist discourse on *sati*, a "death by culture" paradigm.[7] This paradigm abstracts Palestinian women suicide bombers from any historical and political context and places them exclusively in a cultural one. Culture is opposed to politics and is seen as "natural," "organic," "essential," and therefore unchanging.[8] Doomed to this cultural context, Palestinian women are seen as victims of an abusive patriarchal Arab culture that drives them to destroy themselves and others.[9] Thus, their violent political act is transformed into yet another example of the ways Arab culture inevitably kills its women.[10]

Going Back to Basics; or, One Step Forward, Two Steps Back

The uncontested spokeswoman for this paradigm has been Andrea Dworkin, who wrote an essay for the online feminist magazine *Feminista!* called "The Women Suicide Bombers." When I first read Dworkin's essay, I was simply irritated by it, regretting that with such publications feminist solidarity between first and third world women takes a step backward. But when I reread it through my graduate students' eyes, I was angered. At the time the essay came out, I was teaching a seminar on postcolonial fiction and theory. Since one of the sections dealt with postcolonial feminist theory, I thought Dworkin's essay would be a good example of problematic Western feminist writings about third world women, an easy exercise for the students to analyze using the feminist theory they had been reading. I e-mailed the essay to my nineteen students (seventeen of whom were women) without comment, just asking them to read it and post their responses to the rest of the class.

Their responses shocked me. The two self-identified feminists among my students admired the essay greatly. The others agreed. None of them questioned Dworkin's racist characterization of Palestinian women and their society. On the contrary, those claims were assumed to be correct. The one dissenting post came from the Arab American student in the class. But her response was delayed, making me suspect that she was intimidated by the consensus. I then e-mailed the class a letter to the editor responding to Dworkin's essay written by Monica Tarazi, an Arab American woman who was once a student of mine at Birzeit University. Unfortunately, Tarazi was attacked for her lack of sources, something the students never demanded of Dworkin. More ironically, she was chastised for daring to speak about women she did not know.

As I stood in front of my students the next class, I could not hide my distress and spent some time explaining it. I spoke as a Palestinian, a feminist, and a teacher. Although there were several uncomfortable moments, I could tell that my students heard me, and that, by the end of the day, we all had learned something: They learned to be more alert to their unexamined preconceptions about women of "other" cultures, particularly Arab and Muslim women, and not to let their misconceptions undermine their critical faculties. I learned that as sophisticated as postcolonial feminist theory has become, it might still fail, as it did in this case, in shaking deep-rooted assumptions about Arab women and their culture. The following critique of Dworkin's essay is an attempt to go back to basics, that is, to a critical examination of these faulty feminist assumptions that continue to undermine the efforts to consolidate a transnational feminist movement.

Death by Culture as Racist Discourse: Andrea Dworkin

Dworkin confidently gives her readers three reasons there are Palestinian women suicide bombers. The first reason is sexual abuse. She states that Palestinian women are raped "often by men in their own families," and since they will be killed by their families, they "trade in the lowly status of the raped woman for the higher status of a martyr." Although one cannot deny that Palestinian women, like women everywhere, are subject to sexual assault and that so-called honor killing does exist in Palestinian society, the second part of Dworkin's statement is baseless. Dworkin offers no evidence whatsoever to support a link between sexual abuse and suicide bombing. The only evidence she provides to support her claim is that Palestinian and Israeli feminists have worked together in rape crisis centers to repair torn hymens of Palestinian women. That no one else has uncovered the truth of the suicide bomber as sexual abuse victim "has to do with the invisibility of women in general and the necessary silence of injured victims." Indeed, an American feminist is needed to expose these women for the sexual abuse victims they really are.

It is fascinating that despite the loud explosions, Dworkin can hear only the "silence of injured victims." Blind to the hundreds of Palestinian women whose bodies have been torn to shreds by Israeli missiles and bullets during the intifada years, she can shed tears only for the torn hymens between Palestinian women's legs. According to Dworkin's logic, Palestinian suicide bombers are really victims of their culture, a culture that systematically rapes them and then punishes them for the act. The only context that matters in understanding their action is a reified cultural one that completely supersedes all historical and political contexts.

The other two reasons Dworkin gives illustrate that not only abused women but also the "best and brightest" die by culture. She claims that the suicide bombers are Palestinian women who are trying to "rise up in a land where women are lower than the animals." Their societies are so oppressive and demeaning that these women are left only with the option of exploding their bodies to advance the cause of women in their societies: "The more women want to prove their worth, the more women suicide bombers there will be" is Dworkin's ominous prediction. She does not explain whether these women are recruited by Palestinian feminist organizations or are free feminist agents working on their own.[11] But worried that she may have assigned too much agency to them, she does remind us that they are really just dupes of nationalism. To seal her argument, she invokes what has become the scarecrow of Arab women nationalists, the "Algerian woman," who heroically fought for her country but was "pushed back down" after liberation.

Not only are Palestinian women dupes of nationalism, but they are also dupes of their families, according to Dworkin. "The best and the brightest are motivated to stand up for their families," who, Dworkin begrudgingly admits, suffer from Israeli occupation. Whereas Palestinian women's violence against Israel is highlighted at the beginning of the essay and even given a "long history," this reference is the first time that Dworkin mentions the occupation and its violence against Palestinians. This violence, however, is reduced to "beaten fathers," "destroyed homes," and "angry mothers." There is a tentative mention of "the brothers," but before one thinks that the brothers too must be suffering from Israeli aggression, Dworkin adds, "who are civilly superior to them [their sisters]." In other words, Palestinian women are acting on behalf of brothers, fathers, and mothers who, as we were told earlier, abuse and kill them. At no point in her article does Dworkin consider that Palestinian women themselves can be subject to Israeli violence.[12]

On the contrary, Dworkin works hard on suppressing Israeli violence against Palestinian women. At some point she quotes an unnamed Palestinian woman as saying: "It is as if we were in a big prison, and the only thing we really have to lose is that. Imagine what it is like to be me, a proud, well-educated woman who has traveled to many countries. Then see what it is like to be an insect, for that is what the Israeli soldiers call us—cockroaches, dogs, insects." This testimony undermines Dworkin's main argument: the Palestinian woman here is not speaking as a victim of her patriarchal society; she is educated and proud. She, like others, is imprisoned and treated like "less than animals" not by the culture but by Israeli soldiers. She sees herself in unity with, and not in opposition to, Palestinian men, who, like her, are oppressed by the racism and injustice of the occupation.

Dworkin, however, turns a blind eye to all of it. She quotes this woman to prove that "the best and the brightest" are dupes who find it easier to blame "the Israelis for women's suffering than to blame the men who both sexually abuse and then kill them according to honor society rules." This woman's complaint about Israeli oppression is, according to Dworkin, misplaced. Dworkin, the American feminist who has not spent one day in her life living under occupation, clearly knows what is oppressing Palestinian women better than the women themselves. She can only shake her head in disbelief that a woman who is treated like a cockroach by her Israeli occupier is directing her anger at him and not at the men of her culture, who, after all, can only be rapists and murderers. Dworkin's imperial and racist discourse regarding Palestinian women blinds and deafens her to their suffering for which she can allow only one reason—culture.[13]

Robin Morgan's Demons

The racism of Dworkin's essay is so blatant that it is tempting to dismiss her argument as an exception. But, unfortunately, the "death by culture" paradigm seeps into the discourse of feminists who have expressed more sympathy toward women of the third world and who have worked hard to build bridges among women globally. One such feminist is Robin Morgan, founder of the Sisterhood Is Global Institute, editor of the landmark *Sisterhood Is Global* anthology, and former editor in chief of *Ms.* Morgan entered the fray when she wrote an article in *Ms.* explaining the phenomenon of the Palestinian female suicide bombers. In this article, Morgan extends to them the argument she made in her 1989 book, *The Demon Lover: The Roots of Terrorism,* a new edition of which was issued after September 11th. According to Morgan, these women are "token terrorists"; they are "invariably involved because of . . . the demon lover syndrome, their love for a particular man: a fraternal or paternal connection but more commonly a romantic or marital bond." Whereas men, according to Morgan, "become involved because of the politics," the women "become involved because of the men." To support her point, she mentions that two of the women had fathers or brothers or both who had been tortured while in custody of the Israeli army. Morgan undermines the women's political motivation by privatizing their political agency. She ignores all the signs that framed their action as a political one: that the would-be bomber publicly declares her allegiance to a political group (by leaving a videotaped message in the hand of that group, by allowing her picture to be used on their posters, and by inscribing their slogans on her body); that she declares in a read statement her motivation to be nationalist, not personal; that she commits the violent act in a public place for all to see (restaurant, supermarket, checkpoint, street)—all these facts are ignored, and Morgan can see this woman's action only in "private" terms.

Moreover, Morgan belittles the women's political agency by casting the "demon lover" syndrome as a form of false female consciousness that women should transcend. Here is another version of the "they are duped" argument that Dworkin propagates. But this time, Palestinian women are dupes because they are adopting a male form of political expression. While the Palestinian woman has engaged in nonviolent resistance, Morgan maintains that such a woman discovered that "to be taken seriously—by her men, her culture, her adversary, and even eventually herself—she must act through male modes, preferably violent ones." By "acting through male modes," she is not really exercising her full agency or will; she is under the spell of the "demon lover." Only nonviolent activities can be accepted as genuine expressions of women's will since, according to Morgan, women are essentially nonviolent.[14]

To be fair to Morgan, her essentialism has a universal sweep and does not target specific cultures. Still, Palestinian culture as a source of the suicide bomber's motivation does creep into her argument. After mentioning the two women who fit the diagnoses of the "demon-lover syndrome," Morgan refers to a third suicide bomber, one who "was reported to be depressed about [her] impending arranged marriage." Although this example obviously does not fit Morgan's theory, the "demon lover" explanation slips in nevertheless. In this case, the violent act is seen as an expression of female agency, but this agency is allowed only because it is to "escape" the woman's oppressive culture, metonymized by the "arranged marriage." We are back, then, to the formulation of "death by culture." The woman destroys herself and others in order to escape a traditional oppressive patriarchal culture, the root cause of her violent act.

Morgan has written about Palestinian women's relation to their culture in more detail in a chapter in *The Demon Lover* titled "What Do Men Know about Life? The Middle East," in which she relates her encounters with Palestinian women in the West Bank and Gaza in the late 1980s. Morgan is eager in this chapter to dispel stereotypes of the Palestinian woman as either "a grenade-laden Leila Khaled" or "an illiterate refugee willingly producing sons for the revolution." She acknowledges the Palestinian women doctors, nurses, dentists, midwives,

social workers, educators, researchers, professors, architects, engineers, and lawyers whom she meets. Still, she admits that the "focus of this journey was the
women in the refugee camps, who suffer from the sexuality of terrorism with
every breath they inhale." Although Morgan does not explain what "sexuality of
terrorism" is, the meaning of the phrase becomes clearer as she proceeds in her
narrative. It becomes evident, for instance, that "sexuality of terrorism" cannot
be referring to the Israeli military occupation, for even though Morgan mentions
it as a factor in refugee women's lives, she minimizes its effects (for example, she
calls the houses the Israeli army demolishes "shelters"). Soon we realize that the
one issue that seems to plague refugee women's lives and terrorize them is multiple
pregnancies. In fact, the body of the Palestinian mother haunts Morgan, and by
the end of her journey, it assumes demonic proportions. Ironically, it is this image
with which she concludes her chapter in solidarity with Palestinian women: "The
form is also grossly misshapen. This specter has a protruding belly, and balances a
bucket on the head. Dark, cheap cloth shrouds the body, and smaller forms cling
leechlike to every limb like growths on the flesh—children at the hip, thigh,
calf, waist, breast, back, and neck. She is trying to refuse the job he requires of
her. She is almost dying, almost surviving."[15] What we have in the above image
is a description of the body of the Palestinian woman as an "other." Hers is a
nonhuman body, a "grossly misshapen form," a "specter," made up of disjointed
body parts, such as a "protruding belly," a head, a hip, thigh, calf, waist, breast,
back, and neck. It is a zombielike body, wearing a shroud, and invaded by alien,
nonhuman "smaller forms" that "cling leechlike . . . like growths on the flesh."
This deformed, diseased, silent body of the Palestinian mother can only put her in
the range of our condescending pity, rendering Morgan's profession of empathy in
the chapter's concluding words, "she is ourselves," completely hollow. Morgan can
express solidarity only with women abstracted from men, country, and history;
she certainly has little sympathy for real women of flesh and blood and is almost
terrified by those women with children.

The horror that permeates Morgan's description of Palestinian women's bodies echoes the racist Israeli anxieties about the high birthrate among Palestinian
women. Morgan's reference to diseaselike growth brings to mind those Israeli officials who always saw the Arab presence as a "cancer" in the body of the Jewish
state. Morgan's feminist rhetoric, then, coincides with the colonialist racist discourse about Palestinian women's bodies. With this view of Palestinian women's
bodies, it is not surprising that any explanation of their political involvement
would be seen as an example of their subservient bodies and minds to their demon
lovers or as a desperate attempt to escape from their repressive culture.

Barbara Victor's Sensational Designs

But if the discourse of death by culture is implied in Morgan's narrative, it is the structuring principle in Barbara Victor's *Army of Roses: Inside the World of Palestinian Women Suicide Bombers.* Although Victor is not a feminist theoretician and activist, as Dworkin and Morgan are, she does employ a feminist language in addressing her general reader. Using investigative reporting to construct a profile for the first four women suicide bombers, Victor discovers that "all four who died, plus the others who had tried and failed to die a martyr's death, had personal problems that made their lives untenable within their own culture and society." Victor offers a parable that "tells the story of four women who died for reasons that go beyond the liberation of Palestine," a feminist morality tale that serves "as an example of the exploitation of women taken to a cynical and lethal extreme." Political motives are allowed only in relation to the men. Thus we are told, without any evidence, that 'Arafāt "shifted the emphasis on his military operations onto a very special kind of suicide bomber" because he failed to find any men who would do the job.[16] Then he sent out his men to "seduce" the women. When it comes to the women's motives, politics is jostled to the background by seedy narratives of sex and seduction. Victor writes a book full of egregious factual errors, unsubstantiated claims, distortions, and suspicious evidence to prove that culture, not politics, is indeed the main factor behind these women's violent actions.

The erasure of politics is evident even when Victor mentions the role women played in the first Palestinian Intifada. She writes that the Palestinian woman became a symbol "who for the first time in the history of her culture was involved in and indicted for acts of subversion and sabotage and jailed in Israeli prisons." This statement erases a long history of women's political involvement and foregrounds culture by using the curious phrase "history of her culture." It reflects the reductive view that Palestinian women's history has always to be a cultural history, because their lives are mostly shaped by culture even when they are asserting their political wills. Not surprisingly, women's political involvement, according to Victor, takes the form of them "shorten[ing] their skirts, wear[ing] trousers, and leav[ing] their heads uncovered."[17]

The erasure of Palestinian women's history of victimization by, and resistance to, the occupation is glaring when Victor declares Wafa Idris the first *shaheeda.* In Victor's hands, *shaheeda*, meaning female martyr, becomes a synonym for "suicide bomber." This "mistranslation" ends up writing off hundreds of Palestinian women martyrs and makes incomprehensible statements such as "the whole question of the religious legitimacy of martyrs in general prompted debate within the Muslim community."[18] According to Victor, suicide bombing marks the beginning of Palestinian women's history. But, of course, martyrdom, defined as dying for one's country or faith or both, has the highest national and religious values ascribed to it, and, contrary to Victor's claim, at no point has it been a subject of debate in the Palestinian or Muslim community. What has been debated are suicide attacks (*al 'amaleyyat al intihareya*) against Israeli civilians, which the Palestinians prefer to call *al 'amaleyyat al isteshhadeya*. The man or woman who undertakes such an act is referred to as *Isteshhadi* and *Istishhadeya*, respectively, which can be translated as "that who seeks martyrdom." This word distinguishes him or her from the regular "martyr," whether a member of an armed militia or a civilian bystander, by underscoring the individual will and purposefulness behind the act.

So perhaps Victor intended to say that Idris was the first Palestinian woman *istishhadeya*. Even this statement, however, is not totally accurate. Both Palestinian and Israeli sources raise questions about her being an *istishhadeya*/suicide bomber and speculate that it is likely she was a carrier of a bomb that may have gone off prematurely. Victor herself quotes an Israeli eyewitness, for instance, saying that Idris's backpack was caught up in the door of the store on her way out, which may have led to the explosion. Others point out the fact that unlike in every other case of a suicide bombing, no taped or written statement was found left behind from Idris. Such evidence should alert us to the possibility that Idris's *isteshhadeya* identity was constructed by both the Palestinians and the Israelis after her death. Nevertheless, Victor ignores this evidence and takes Idris's *isteshhadeya* status for granted and then goes on to focus on the motives that drove her to suicide.

In exposing the motives of the female suicide bombers, Victor constructs a fictional narrative that casts the women as always victims of their culture. According to this narrative, Wafa Idris and Hiba Daraghmeh may seem confident and independent on the surface but are in fact brutalized by their culture, one as a divorced and barren woman and the other as a rape victim. Darine Abu Aisheh is a "brilliant" student and an ambitious "feminist" who is thwarted by a culture that values only defeated women. Shireen Rabiya, "a beautiful, long-legged girl with all the attributes and grace of a fashion model," is demoralized by a culture that teases its "too attractive" women. A ubiquitous Arab "honor code" is invoked to explain the actions of some: thus, Ahlam al Tamimi (a.k.a. Zina), for example, was pushed by her family to become a suicide bomber to redeem the family honor after becoming pregnant out of wedlock, while Ayat al Akhras sacrificed herself to redeem the honor of a father accused of collaboration with

Israel. And when the woman has "no sensational story," and Victor is unable to conjure up any scandal to explain her motivation, as in the case of Andaleeb Takatka, we are told that she wanted so much to be a "superstar" and suicide bombing was her only route to stardom (the evidence for this claim is that as a teenager she had pictures of Arab entertainers on her bedroom wall).[19] In other words, marginalized, talented, and ordinary Palestinian women are all persecuted by their culture in one way or another and therefore are viable candidates to carry out suicide bombings.

Noncultural reasons that may explain the women's actions do appear in Victor's book, but only to be subtly dismissed or transformed into cultural effects. Thus, Victor reports the stories about how Idris was moved by the injuries of children that she witnessed as a volunteer paramedic, that she herself was shot twice, that Ayat al Akhras was shaken by witnessing the killing of a neighbor, that Abu Aisheh was humiliated at a checkpoint by Israeli soldiers who unveiled her in public and forced a cousin to kiss her on the mouth. These reasons, however, along with the women's public political activism (as in the case of Abu Aisheh and Daraghmeh), invariably recede into the background once Victor uncovers the "secret" reason that supersedes all others and becomes the basis for her psychoanalysis of dead women she has never met. As a result, Victor's narrative predictably dwells on Idris's marital problems, on al Akhras's "disgrace," on Abu Aisheh's desire to escape a marriage, and on Daraghmeh's alleged rape. Even when a certain "cultural" practice is not relevant to her story, Victor still uses it the way a prosecutor prejudices the jury with immaterial yet tainting evidence. An example of this strategy is her going on about "wife beating" as a practice in Muslim society only to conclude that Idris's husband did *not* beat her.[20]

However, the nature of the evidence Victor uncovers and her way of uncovering it are both problematic. Her sensational information usually comes in the form of gossip whispered to Victor by a friend or relative of the dead woman or a "confession" of some juicy detail that hitherto has been kept secret. An example of the first kind of revelation is the statement by Abu Aisheh's friend that Darine "told me she would rather die" than marry.[21] Victor uses this statement to construct a profile for Abu Aisheh as a desperate feminist rebelling against her culture. There is no other evidence to support this conclusion, and Abu Aisheh's public political commitments as a student activist at An Najah University are eclipsed by this friendly revelation.

More sensational are the "confessions" Victor receives from, for instance, Hiba Daraghmeh's mother and the woman she calls "Zina." In the first case, the mother tells Victor that her daughter was raped by a mentally retarded uncle, and in the second, Zina, who was indicted for aiding a suicide bomber, reveals that she had a child out of wedlock. These confessions are problematic because Victor does not explain why these women would trust her with information that was not revealed to anyone else. Why would Hiba Daraghmeh's mother allegedly reveal to Victor, a foreign reporter she is meeting for the first time in her life, a much guarded secret about her daughter, now celebrated as an *istishhadeya*, that would tarnish the family's name? In Zina's case, Victor claims that at the request of the woman's family she gives her an alias. But this attempt at protecting her identity is not convincing because the moment we read that "Zina" is the woman who helped transport Izz el Deen al Masri, the bomber of the restaurant Sbarro's, her real identity as Ahlam al Tamimi is revealed. Al Tamimi is well known; in fact, her posters are all over the walls in the West Bank, and her defiant words in court after her sentencing are quoted all over the Internet. Why would a woman who has the status of a national celebrity, whose story is common knowledge, make such a gothic confession of secrets she and her family supposedly guarded for years? And if we assume that Victor is not really slandering al Tamimi in this underhanded way and is truly ignorant of her public image, how could she justify such ignorance when she supposedly researched the minutest detail of this woman's life? It does not help matters that Victor does not explain how she conducted her interviews: How did she introduce herself to her subjects? What language did she use in interviewing them? Were these "confessions" made in front of an interpreter as well? Were the people aware that she was researching a book and that she would be making the intimate details of their lives public?

The veracity of Victor's "evidence" is further undermined by the many factual errors that riddle her narrative. According to her, the late Syrian president Hafez al Asad is a Christian Alawi (no such thing exists; he is a Muslim *alaway*); Birzeit University is Christian and its student council was Christian before it was over taken by Islamists (both the university and the council are secular; different political groups, including the Islamists, run for the council's elections); the color of mourning in Palestinian culture is white (it is black); and Darine Abu Aisheh is Hamas's first female suicide bomber (a simple Google search would reveal that Reem al Reyashi was, whereas Abu Aisheh was claimed by Al Aqsa Martyr's Brigades, who prepared her for her mission after Hamas refused to).[22] In addition, Victor either gets the names of her interviewees wrong (Wafa Idris's mother, Wasfeyeh, is renamed Mabrook, a male name) or consistently misspells them beyond recognition (I counted twenty-two such instances). The accumulative effect of the egregious factual errors, the misspellings, and the mistranslations should undermine Victor's authority as someone reporting from "inside the world of Palestinian suicide bombers," as her subtitle claims. But while reviewers of her other books, such as her biography of Madonna, point to Victor's love for sleaziness and her penchant for unnamed sources,[23] none of the reviewers of her book on Palestinian women seems to be bothered by the sloppiness of her evidence and her, at best, questionable relationship to her Palestinian informants.[24]

The Consuming Gaze: The Woman Suicide Bomber as an Object of Desire

In Victor's narrative, Palestinian female suicide bombers, and Palestinian women generally, are objectified through a voyeuristic Western perspective that can see them only as sexual beings violated by their culture. When Victor meets Idris for the first time, she presents her as an object of Western desire: she lingers on Idris's attractive physical features, and then concludes: "It was not surprising, given her cheerful personality and good looks, that I later learned that several Western journalists had asked her out, although, as a good Muslim woman, she had refused their advances." Then there is the odd description of Idris's body after the explosion: "I rushed over to see it, and while the entire scene was horrifying, the sign of Wafa's body lying in the middle of Jaffa Road in Jerusalem, covered haphazardly with a rubber sheet, was stunning. Even more shocking was the image of an arm, her right arm, which had been ripped from her body, lying bloody and torn several inches away."[25] The choice of the word "stunning" (synonyms: "beautiful," "gorgeous," "lovely," "irresistible," "breathtaking," "awesome") in this context shows how Victor's gaze is fixated on sexualizing and objectifying Idris's body, even in death.[26] Victor's voyeurism is not unique. Mainstream Western media have referred to Palestinian female suicide bombers as "lipstick martyrs," who are "dressed to kill." Writing for the *Observer*, Kevin Toolis could not hide the sexual undertones in his description of Hiba Daraghmeh's poster: "On the walls of Jenin she stares out from her poster like a vengeful nun. Her eyes are defiant, her pupils enlarged, and her eyebrows are plucked." This is the same Toolis who offers the following sexually loaded mistranslation of Hanadi Jaradat's will. According to him, Jaradat declared in her videotaped statement: "By the will of God I decided to be the sixth martyr who makes her body full with splinters in order to enter every Zionist heart who occupied our country."[27] It is a statement that is, in Toolis's words, "suffused with sexuality." But in fact Jaradat did not say what Toolis attributes to her. A more accurate translation of her Arabic words is: "I do not have but this body, which I will make into splinters to uproot anyone who had tried to uproot us from our homeland." By using the word "uproot," Jaradat is employing a familiar national metaphor used by the Palestinians to describe their experience of displacement and exile. The sexual connotations that Toolis reads in Jaradat's words are but a figment of his overheated imagination—an imagination more interested in the woman's "plucked eyebrows" and "ruby lips" than in the causes and consequences of their act.

Early in her book, Victor recalls an encounter she had with a Palestinian woman in the Shatila refugee camp in Lebanon right after the Phalangist militia, with Israeli complicity, massacred hundreds of Palestinian men, women, and children. Sitting in the midst of a scene of carnage and destruction, cradling a dead child in her arms, this survivor confronts Victor, whom she recognizes as an American: "You American women talk constantly of equality. Well, you can take a lesson from us Palestinian women. We die in equal numbers to the men." Victor chooses to understand this woman's bitter and ironic statement as an expression of a "tragic concept of women's liberation," that is, Palestinian women cannot be equal in their society except through death.[28] By ignoring the context of the encounter, Victor misses the obvious—that the woman is condemning the hypocrisy of Western feminists who clamor for women's rights but turn a deaf ear to Palestinian women suffering at the hands of Israeli soldiers and their friends. Victor's blindness to the context in which this woman is speaking—the scene of death and devastation around her, the dead child in her arms—is astounding. She is so fixated on seeing the woman as a victim of her culture that even when the woman's loss and suffering, as a result of political violence against her and her family and neighbors, is staring Victor in the face, she is blind to it.

This Western feminist discourse on Arab women has a chilling effect particularly on the relationship between Arab and Arab American feminists, on the one hand, and their American counterparts, on the other. Arab American feminists and activists have long shouldered a double burden: not only do they work against sexism and patriarchy in their communities, but they also have to contend with the harmful stereotypes propagated about them and their Arab culture in the mass media. Because of their hard work and their forming of important alliances with other women of color in the United States, who also had to struggle against the racism and classism of mainstream white feminists, their voices have made some impact and better channels of communication have been opened. However, since the tragic events of September 11th, these small gains in feminist solidarity seem to have been eroded in the face of the mobilizing of U.S. feminists in the service of nationalism and militarism. The discourse on Palestinian women suicide bombers, just like the one on Afghan women, is bound to widen the gap separating Arab Americans from feminists like Dworkin, Morgan, and Victor.

But beyond feminist solidarity, invoking the "death by culture" paradigm to understand why some women become suicide bombers leads to a dead end, for this understanding implies a Kurtzian "exterminate all the brutes" solution, the "brutes" in this case being all those persons who are made by Arab or Palestinian culture. For anyone who does not believe this solution is a viable one, it is crucial to acknowledge that suicide bombings by women, just like the ones by men, are, first and foremost, forms of political violence. The culture that is implicated in this phenomenon is not a fetishized, oppressive "Arab culture," but rather a culture of militarization whose effects are by no means limited to Palestinian society. The recognition of suicide bombing as a political form of violence neither trivializes nor idealizes the suicide bomber/*istishhadeya*. On the contrary, seeing her as a political agent is a first and necessary step for launching a feminist critique of women, militarization, and nationalism that goes beyond casting Palestinian women as demons, angels, or victims of a killer culture.

4

Arab Jews, Diasporas, and Multicultural Feminism

An Interview with Ella Shohat

EVELYN ALSULTANY

In this interview, Ella Shohat discusses her family's multiple displacements from Iraq to Israel and to the United States. She articulates the relevance of the question of Arab Jews to the Israeli-Palestinian conflict as well as to the Middle Eastern–American diaspora. Shohat discusses the fraught position of Arab Jews in a historical context in which "Arab versus Jew" became the operating framework for identities with the emergence of Zionism. In addition to discussing the dislocation from Iraq to Israel of her own family, Shohat also addresses her scholarly work on the question of Arab Jews, as part of her broader work on postcolonial displacements. She addresses her writing on multicultural feminism within her broader work on the critique of Eurocentrism—for example, the tendency of Eurocentric feminism to frame the debate within the rescue fantasy of saving brown women from brown men. Shohat concludes this interview by discussing the potential of multiculturalism as an epistemological project for critical thinking and social change.

Evelyn Alsultany: Your writing often highlights the paradoxes of exile and home. I wanted to begin with your own Arab Jewish background and your family's history in Iraq, Israel, and then the U.S. What was your family's experience of coming to Israel from Iraq?

Ella Shohat: I was born into a situation of displacement. In the early 1950s, my parents had to depart from Iraq, and went to Israel via Cyprus. My grandparents, uncles, aunts, and different members of the larger family arrived, dispersed and separately, to the point that it took a good while for them to locate each other. My parents carried only a suitcase and their baby—my sister—as they descended from the plane in the airport of Lod, in Hebrew and in Arabic, Lydda. Some of my relatives were sprayed with DDT because it was assumed that they were disease ridden. The Iraqi Jews descended into a whole new world, a world that had its own lexicon and cultural repertoires, and that aggressively shaped a new collective identity, which Arab Jews were supposed to join. The first period in Israel was full of rude shocks for our family and for most families like ours. Within a few months of our arrival, the authorities at the Ma'abara [transit camp] removed my sister from the baby-care center [where parents were obliged to leave their babies under the care of state workers] without my parents' knowledge and on false pretenses. In a combination of luck and help, my parents were able to locate my sister in another city, in a hospital in Haifa. But my grandmother was less fortunate. She gave birth to her last child in Israel, and was told that the baby died, and yet she was never given a body or issued a death certificate. Later we learned that such experiences had been common, and that many babies—some say in the thousands—had been taken away by the authorities and sold for adoption. The assumption was that one group—us—was having too many children, while another group needed children and could offer a better life than the biological parents, seen as primitive breeders. Activists claim that the payments went to the state, which obviously hasn't been eager to investigate itself. The scandal, which is still a major unresolved sore point, is known as the case of the "kidnapped Yemeni and Sephardi-Mizrahi babies."

In Israel, partly because of racism and partially because theirs was the culture of the Arab enemy, my family felt out of place. My parents used to say: "In Iraq we were Jews, and in Israel we are Arabs." Our Arab culture was taboo in Israel. Yet, even if we tried, we could not easily escape the mark of otherness. It was written all over our bodies, our looks, our accents. My parents didn't dare put my Arabic name, Habiba, from my maternal grandmother who passed away soon after their arrival to Israel, on my birth certificate.

If in the Arab world the Jewishness of Arabs gradually came to be associated with Zionism, and therefore was subjected to surveillance, in Israel their Arab culture was under watchful eyes, disciplined and punished. Ben-Gurion, the first prime minister of Israel, referred to Levantine Jews as "savages," and many scholars during that period wrote about the need to civilize the "backward" Sephardim and "cleanse" them of their Orientalness. The new context obliged Arab Jews to redefine themselves in relation to new ideological paradigms and an overwhelming new polarity: Arab versus Jew.

I was raised among people who, due to the sudden dislocation and disorientation, felt an immense sense of loss; today it would probably be diagnosed as a state of posttraumatic stress. And in many ways I think I lived and internalized my parents' and grandparents' pain. To an extent, I believe that my writing about the subject was also a mode of translation: translating their pain into words; giving voice to their sense of loss. Their powerlessness in Israel only added to their sense of alienation. Although such experiences are in some ways typical of refugee and even immigrant communities, what was rather anomalous about this situation, I think, was that we Arab Jews were expected to define this exilic condition as a "coming home." I described this feeling of lamentation by inverting the famous biblical phrase about remembering Zion: "By the waters of the Zion, we laid down and wept when we remembered Babylon."

EA: In your work you have offered a different take on what you call "the rupture."[1] For those who are unfamiliar with this history: how in your view did Arab Jews in general, and Iraqi Jews in particular, end up in Israel?

ES: The violence generated in the wake of colonial partitions (Israel-Palestine, Pakistan-India) led to the uprooting, virtually overnight, of venerable communities. What such abstract terms as "the Arab-Israeli conflict" and "population exchange" concretely meant for my family was the abandonment of Baghdad, Iraq, Mesopotamia, where Jews had lived and often prospered for millennia. The displacement of Iraqi Jews was not the result of a decision made simply by Arab Jews themselves, though this is how it is often narrated. Even if some Arab Jews expressed a desire to go to Israel upon its creation in 1948, the displacement for most Arab Jews was the product of complex circumstances that forced their departure. There were the efforts of the Zionist underground in Iraq to undermine the authority of traditional Jewish religious leaders, and also to place a "wedge" between the Jewish and Muslim communities in order to generate anti-Arab panic on the part of Jews.

At the same time, just because we criticize Zionism doesn't mean that we should not also take a critical look at the fragile place of minorities in the Arab world. It's not about equating Zionism and Arab nationalism. But it is about offering a complex understanding of tensions and contradictions that made such a rupture possible. In the case of Iraq, the anti-Jewish propaganda, especially as channeled through the Istiqlal, or Independence Party, also played a role in the insecurity and fear sensed by Iraqi Jews. As the Israeli-Palestinian conflict escalated, with the Palestinians violently scattered and dispossessed, the distinction on the ground between Jews and Zionists was gradually eroding in Arab countries. In my various essays I have examined the complexity of this issue in terms of when and where such a distinction was maintained, but also in what ways it was not always maintained. In Arab countries, as the conflict in Palestine was accelerating, Arab Jews were gradually regarded more and more as simply "the

Jews," and ended up bearing the brunt of the anger about what Zionism, in the name of presumably all Jews, was doing to the Palestinians. As a result, even when the distinction between Jews and Zionists was asserted in theory, it was not always lived as such. Ultimately, the erosion of such distinctions helped provoke the dislocation of Arab Jews, ending up with negative consequences for Palestinians as well. There was a failure to actively secure the place of Jews in the Arab world in spite of what was happening in Palestine. At the time the majority of Jews in Iraq were not Zionists. The word "Zion," or "Sion," in our Arabic pronunciation, was thoroughly associated with traditional biblical Jewish celebrations and lamentations, having little to do with a political nationalist project in Palestine. For the most part, Arab Jews at the time were not aware what settlements in Palestine had meant for Palestinians on the ground.

It is therefore not surprising that there were misconceptions on the part of many Arab Jews about the differences between their own religious identity and sentiments and the secular nation-state project of Zionism, which didn't have much to do with those sentiments. The Jews within Islam regarded themselves as Jews, but that Jewishness formed part of a larger Judeo-Islamic cultural fabric. Under pressure from Zionism, on the one hand, and Arab nationalism, on the other, that set of affiliations gradually changed. Arab Jews, to my mind, have come to occupy an ambivalent position vis-à-vis both movements. The explosive politics after the partition of Palestine, especially the establishment of the state of Israel and the arrival of Palestinian refugees to Arab countries, rendered Arab Jewish existence virtually impossible. Within this new context, Iraqi or Egyptian Jews came to be viewed as almost by definition "Zionist traitors." This history is full of ironic twists. In Iraq, the persecution of communists, among them Jews who actively opposed Zionism, created a paradoxical situation in which the only viable way to stay alive or avoid imprisonment for communist Jews was to leave for Israel. Another irony: despite pro-Palestinian posturing of Arab regimes, they collaborated in practice in what Israeli officials came to call "population exchange."

EA: What were then the Arab cultural aspects of your home, and given your own Iraqi-Israeli-American history, what is your sense of home? And to what extent does language play a role in this?

ES: As I reflect back, I think that Baghdad did not really disappear but continued to live in Israel, at home, in the neighborhoods. And today, you can even speak of a certain public renaissance among young Mizrahim, even if Arab culture is transformed and takes place within highly modified forms. But for the first decades in Israel, Arab culture for the newly arrived Jews and their children was an unofficial public culture; it was, as it were, collectively private. For my parents, it was as if time were frozen in 1940s Baghdad. My father played the *kamanja* [violin] in the *haflas*, or family gatherings. Even now, in New York, my parents listen to exactly the same songs of the Iraqis Nathum al-Ghazali and Salima Pasha or of the Egyptians Um-Kulthum and Mohamed Abdul Wahab. They are still faithfully dedicated to daily rituals of preparing of Iraqi dishes (*keba hamez-helu, ketchri, tbit,* and so on), even as elderly people living in their third country, the U.S. Their lack of openness to any other culture at times reflects a kind of Judeo-Baghdadi provincialism, experienced decades later and lived in several elsewheres. I read this kind of provincialism as a sign of refusal of an enforced cosmopolitanism that descended upon them. Years ago they came to visit me in Rio de Janeiro, where I was living. All they were looking for were some familiar spices and foods, and in no time we found ourselves in Rio's Middle Eastern Sahara neighborhood. Food, it seems to me, has become a kind of portable home where the repetitive act of cooking the same dishes becomes a way of maintaining a sense of stability given an unstable life, of home given that they are no longer at home in the world. Instead of George Steiner's "homeland as text," it's more like "homeland as cuisine." The obsessive repetition of listening to the same ol' music, viewing the same old films, or cooking the same old dishes, cannot be reduced to a simple melancholic nostalgia; it also represents an act of defiant survival in the face of a disappearing cultural geography.

For them, Arabic continues to be a vital language of reference, and to this day we still communicate at home largely in Judeo-Arabic. For me, being raised between Arabic and Hebrew was far from being a situation of happy bilingualism. It was an experience of conflict where my school language was at war with my home language, which those in authority expected us to forget and erase. Until they passed away, my grandparents, decades after their arrival, continued to speak only Baghdadi-Judeo-Arabic, never mastering Hebrew. For years I served as their everyday translator in Israel. With the passing away of my parents' and my own generation, the Judeo-Iraqi dialect will hardly be a living language. And the elegy you may hear sometimes in my tone is linked to this "last of the Mohicans" feeling.

This Hebrew-Arabic schism nourished my fantasies of an elsewhere. Israel may have been a land of diverse immigrants and dislocated people, but it was not a multicultural democracy. It was a centralized nation-state dominated by the ideology of modernization that favored Eurocentric narratives of belonging. In 1981, I moved to New York, where I found a place inhabited by various kinds of dislocated people. Here, belonging to multiple geographies was not out of the norm; it was almost a norm! Being at home for me could no longer be easily bounded by geography. Iraq was out of bounds, but at the same time, I insisted on reclaiming the part of my identity and history that was denied me: my Arabness. Therefore, my work on the notion of "Arab Jew" tried to offer a non-Eurocentric reading of the past, while suggesting potentialities beyond the impasses of Arab versus Jew. It was in New York that I could meet and befriend Iraqi Muslims and Christians. New York, in a strange way, afforded me a relief from a somewhat schizophrenic existence.

EA: Can you now address another dimension of your New York experience? How did your background in the Middle East affect your relationship to people of color in the U.S.? And what was the context for your scholarly work on race issues, and how is that related to your personal history?

ES: I grew up in a situation which I only later recognized as "racialized." In Israel, we were sometimes called "blacks" (in the negative sense), and we ended up actually reclaiming this term as a positive signifier. I learned about the American Black Panthers through the Israeli Black Panthers, which were named after and inspired by the American movement, and which generated a huge movement of Sephardi-Mizrahi protest in the early 1970s. Not simply gender but race and class left dramatic marks in my life. When I was six years old, my shyness at school was understood to be a sign of "retardation" by my Ashkenazi teacher, who wanted to send me to a "special school." Although I knew the material and the answers, I did not speak. A nuanced awareness of "cultural difference" was not part of my teacher's pedagogical understanding when she made her "diagnosis." But my mother fought the verdict successfully, because by that point she had become aware of what such a system of labeling and tracking meant. Later, I learned that it was a similar system that reproduced the "savage inequalities": the mechanisms, ideas, and attitudes toward minorities, especially Native Americans, blacks, and Latinos in the U.S. This is only one example from my life, to explain that sense of identification with racialized minorities that I felt when I came to the U.S. The American academy and New York afforded me an intellectual space from which to speak, alongside others with similar experiences and projects.

But, when I am asked where I am from, I can never give a simple answer. That my family is from Baghdad, and that they are also Jews, startles many Americans. Over and over, I have to go through the same detailed explanation about my origins. If I say I'm an Arab Jew, some people assume that I'm the product of a mixed marriage. Others, of a certain ideological inclination, become apoplectic at the very idea of an Arab Jew. In my work I have insisted on the hyphen, but the Arab-versus-Jew discourse has made it difficult for people to comprehend that not all Arabs are Muslims, that one can be culturally Arab and religiously Jewish.[2]

In my scholarly work on the subject, I wanted to create an intellectual and institutional space that would address various Arab-Jewish and Sephardi-Mizrahi perspectives on Zionism. I felt that even critical discourses, ironically, were falling inadvertently into the paradigms of Eurocentric historiography. My article published in *Social Text,* entitled "Sephardim in Israel: Zionism from the Standpoint of Its Jewish Victims," partially dialogued with Edward Said's article entitled "Zionism from the Standpoint of Its Victims."[3] Said focused on the Palestinian perspective on Zionism. While endorsing much of the Palestinian critique, I also proposed to deconstruct the idea or supposition of a homogeneous view of "Jewish history."

EA: How is your critique of the homogenizing view of "Jewish history" related to the question of Orientalism and Eurocentrism?

ES: It is very directly related, but in complex ways. On the one hand, Jews have been the victims of Orientalism and of anti-Semitism. On the other, Zionism itself has an Orientalist dimension, shaped within a sense of inferiority toward the West and superiority toward the East. Herzl's book *Altneuland* manifested obsessive competitiveness with Europe, demonstrating that Jews can generate utopian modernity. Within that framework, I have attempted to disentangle the complexities of the Mizrahi question by unsettling the conceptual borders erected by more than a century of Zionist discourse, with its Eurocentric binarisms of savagery versus civilization, tradition versus modernity, East versus West, and Arab versus Jew. I have argued that Zionist discourse, in a sense, has hijacked Jews from their Judeo-Islamic cultural geography and subordinated them into the European Jewish chronicle of shtetl and pogrom.

Zionist discourse, it seems to me, offers a schizophrenic master narrative, not unlike America's own settler-colonial narrative, which is why so many Americans find it so easy to identify with Israel. The U.S. combines elements of anticolonialist discourse vis-à-vis Britain with colonialist practices toward the indigenous peoples. It's interesting in this regard to think about the common trope about America and Palestine as "virgin lands."[4] In the case of Zionist discourse, it contains a redemptive nationalist narrative vis-à-vis Europe and anti-Semitism and a colonialist narrative vis-à-vis the Arab people who are portrayed as people who "happened" to reside in the place designated the Jewish homeland and therefore presumably have no claim over the land. But I also suggested that, unlike colonialism, Zionism constituted a response to oppression in Christian Europe, and in contradistinction to the classical colonial paradigm, it did not regard itself as having a "mother country." Zionist discourse partially repeats the *terra nullius* of conquest and discovery doctrines, with the difference that Jews, if only in part and distantly, have some claim (although not an exclusive one) to indigenous roots. And just to further complicate the analogy, within Zionist discourse the "East" is simultaneously the place of Judaic origins and the locus for implementing the "West." In other words, the "East" is associated with backwardness and underdevelopment, and also it is associated with oasis and solace, because it signifies a return to origins and the biblical past. Meanwhile, the West is also viewed ambivalently. It is the historic scene of the crime of anti-Semitism and the Shoah, or Holocaust, and yet is also an object of desire, as evoked in the "founding fathers'" desire to make Israel the "Switzerland of the Middle East." The paradox of Zionist discourse, in my view, is that despite the victimization of Jews by European anti-Semitism, it ended up in a Eurocentric journey, believing that the "West" should be the authoritative norm to be emulated in the "East."

EA: What has been the reception of your work? Have you encountered resistance? Political harassment? If so, what forms has it taken?

ES: I should begin by saying that although the childhood and familial experiences I described earlier are quite common to people of my background, I don't think that my perspective is necessarily representative of a large movement. I don't pretend to speak for all Sephardim or Mizrahim. And ironically, although in recent years I have not been terribly vocal on this topic, I continue, in large part, to be stigmatized. In Israel and the U.S. the harassment has taken different forms over the years, including public attacks (especially in the Israeli media), character assassination, words taken out of context, censorship, hate mail, blacklisting, the "uninviting" from conferences because of outside pressure, events canceled at the last minute, and so forth. In nonacademic contexts, articles that had been solicited were refused, when seen by the higher-ups. (I even "earned" a few kill fees over the years.) My work has been more or less excommunicated from fields related to Jewish studies. Those of us who have taken critical positions have been the objects of harassment, years before the establishment of Campus Watch.

My first book, *Israeli Cinema: East/West and the Politics of Representation*, was the object of extremely virulent attack in Israel. Some critics tried to delegitimize my academic credentials, as if symbolically to take away my Ph.D. A number of critics suggested that I never could have gotten a Ph.D. in Israel, which was probably true, at least then, if only for reasons of prejudice and political views. Another critic compared Edward Said and myself to the *kushi* [roughly the N-word], admiring the shiny buttons on the colonial general's coat;[5] we were seen as borrowing and mimicking theories of the West that have little to do with the Middle East. Panels were organized not to debate my work but to denounce it. Nor did this "banning" cease in the U.S. Whether here or there, students and scholars have told me that they have been warned against citing my work. A New York Jewish institute refused to lend MERIP [Middle East Research and Information Project] archival images of Arab Jews for an article I was writing without their prior reading and approval. Obliged to submit to their "politically correct" requirements, we have lost the right even to use the archive concerning our own lives to narrate our own experiences in our own voice. A young professor in an Israeli university was told that it would hurt her academic career to include in her CV that she is a translator of my work (from English to Hebrew). The institute for Sephardic studies in my previous home institution, in my decade of teaching there, never invited me to speak or have a discussion of my work. When at a reception I was introduced to the head of the center, she refused the collegial gesture of shaking my hand, reminding me that I "met with Palestinians," referring to my participation in the meeting between Palestinian and Sephardi intellectuals in Toledo, Spain, in 1989. This just a small sample of incidents, but I think you get the drift. But frankly, I don't feel like a victim, and overall I am quite happy with the reception of my work.

To be fair and give a well-rounded picture, the field has been changing for the better as critical Arab-Jewish/Mizrahi scholars, and scholars sympathetic to Mizrahi perspectives, have emerged. More recently, you can find courses that have also been inclusive of my work and of the work of other critical Arab-Jewish/Mizrahi intellectuals and activists. There are more critical Arab-Jewish/Mizrahi spaces now than there were decades ago when I began writing about this question, when also the words "Palestinian" and "Palestine" could hardly be uttered. There is a growing number of young scholars working on these issues of diverse backgrounds; many more dissertations are currently being written. I find this development truly exciting. For example, Shoshana Madmoni wrote a dissertation about the Israeli media representation of the Yemeni and Mizrahi baby kidnapping. And Sami Shalom Chetrit published a book about the history of the Mizrahi struggle. Also, over the years you cannot imagine how many sympathetic e-mails and letters I have received from Arabs who have fond memories of Jewish friends and neighbors from Baghdad, Cairo, Tunis, and Tangier. So, on the whole, it's decidedly a mixed bag.

EA: Your work has also dealt with the intersection of gender and race discourse, or with the imaginary of sexuality and empire. Can you elaborate more on the academic context in which you began your work on this intersection? What were you trying to accomplish in *Talking Visions,* and can you elaborate on the subtitle of the book, "Multicultural Feminism in a Transnational Age"?

ES: My academic background is in philosophy, literature, and cinema/media studies. In the humanities, when I began writing, the dominant feminist discourse then was feminist psychoanalysis. Such scholarship allowed little place for race, class, nation, and other forms of social stratification. When in the late '80s, I wrote my first explicit critique of Eurocentric feminist approaches, it was, in part, a response to feminist literary/film Theory, with a capital *T.*[6] The essays proposed alternative methods for feminist analysis. For example, I looked for a submerged racial presence in all-white films, or I examined tropes of empire—for example, Freud's notion of the "dark continent of female sexuality," which I contextualized within archaeological and geographical discourses of empire.

Talking Visions tried to provide a space for many constituencies and for many discourses concerning the intersection of race, gender, nation, and sexuality. The book came out of a conference that I organized at the New Museum in Soho, New York, a museum that in many ways represented a white urban art-world space. My goal was to "color" the museum and present alternative work and vision. However, the book is not an essentialist celebration of identity and difference with a Latina contributor speaking for "the Latina woman" or a black contributor speaking for "the black woman." We cannot reduce any community to one representative, speaking on its behalf. The book's purpose, in any case, wasn't simply to include representatives of different origins, but rather to orchestrate multiple voices and issues.

The subtitle calls attention to issues that tend to be segregated and not addressed in relation to each other: feminism in relation to both multiculturalism and transnationalism, and also transnationalism in relation to multiculturalism. It does not exalt one political concern (feminism and sexuality) over another (multiculturalism and transnationalism); rather, it highlights and reinforces the mutual embeddedness between these concerns. My hope was to tie these terms together, and thus refuse any assertion of a hierarchy within class-, racial-, national-, sexual-, and gender-based struggles. The essays taken together highlight the intersection of all these different axes of stratification. The term "multiculturalism" tends to be associated with issues of race addressed within the North American context, and too often fails to take into account transnational and cross-border perspectives. Meanwhile, "transnationalism" is associated with a debate about globalization, immigration, and displacement that is not usually associated with issues of race in the North American context. And both of these debates do not necessarily address issues of gender and sexuality. The hope, in *Talking Visions*, was to create a space for a multifaceted debate.

The subtitle also reflects my effort to go beyond the cartographic zoning of knowledges. The circulation of goods and ideas, of images and sounds, and of people is not a new phenomenon, but it has intensified over the past decades due to new technologies and new modes of capitalism. In *Talking Visions*, the assumption was that genders, sexualities, races, classes, nations, and even continents cannot be fenced off into hermetically sealed compartments. Here, I was picking up on the work that I did with Robert Stam in *Unthinking Eurocentrism*. Instead of segregating historical periods and geographical regions into neatly fenced-off areas of expertise, the goal was to highlight the multiplicity of community histories and perspectives, as well as the hybrid culture of all communities, especially in a world characterized by the "traveling" of images, sounds, goods, and people.

The notion of "multicultural feminism" for me was to take as a starting point the cultural consequences of the worldwide movement and dislocations of peoples associated with the development of "global" or "transnational" capital. National borders and disciplinary boundaries are in tension with such transnational movements. Even if the major point of reference in the book is the U.S.—since that is the context of the production of the book—the book isn't nationalist in intent and hopefully isn't provincial in scope. In fact, the introduction criticizes certain modes of multicultural and queer works that often have an implicit U.S. nationalist agenda, just as it critiques a certain tendency in transnational and post-colonial studies in the U.S. to detach itself from issues of race within the U.S. In this sense, *Talking Visions* attempts to place diverse gendered/sexed histories and geographies in dialogical relation in terms of the tensions and overlaps that take place "within" and "between" cultures, ethnicities, and nations.

Talking Visions was a book not about women of color but about multicultural feminism as a shared political, social, and epistemological project. At the same time, I suggested that it's not a coincidence that women of color largely produced multicultural feminism because their experiences at the intersection of oppressions have generated their pioneering work toward a different kind of knowledge. In a sense, multicultural feminism is an inclusive space, which is not to suggest that there are no contradictions. I was also hoping to articulate those contradictions. I wanted us to be more conscious of what's taking place and why it's so hard to actually do coalitionary work, since there are different interests at stake: different utopias, social desires, and political visions.

EA: How do you see feminism in this context? Can you elaborate on what you find to be the limits of feminism, particularly in the case of Middle Eastern women?

ES: It depends on how we narrate feminism. This is precisely why I find multicultural critique of Eurocentrism quite central to feminist studies. *Talking Visions* offers a critique of the linear master narrative of how feminism began, and it is usually a very Eurocentric narrative, which imagines women's fighting to empower themselves in the "West," with their ideas then spreading to the "backward" world. It's the usual diffusionist narrative. What are elided in this modernizing narrative are the "other" women around the world struggling in other battles, but who are disqualified as feminists because they did not label themselves as such. Take the anticolonialist movement in Algeria. How can one not understand it as a feminist struggle when Algerian women were fighting to empower themselves within the anticolonial movement? Should we not incorporate their perspective into feminist studies just because we have been using this word in a very narrow, Eurocentric sense? The antipatriarchal, and even, at times, antiheterosexist subversions within anticolonial struggles, remains marginal to the feminist canon, because, unfortunately, one strand of feminism generally exercises the power of naming and narrativizing. The book argues that we need to redefine what we mean by feminist studies, to broaden its significations to include a variety of battles.

From the perspective of multicultural and transnational feminists, it is important to view Muslim and Arab women not simply as victims. To reduce Muslim culture to one term, "fundamentalism," for example, is to miss a more complex picture. We need to analyze questions of agency: how women fighting for social change have exercised a modicum of power. Let's take the case of clitoridectomy. We all react very strongly to this practice because it denies women's pleasure, reinforces the ideology that women are impure, excludes women from marriage if they don't practice it, and so forth. Yet many women around the world practice it and initiate one another into that practice. How do we then think of the contradictions generated from a feminist perspective? When women participate in oppressive practices, how should we react as feminists? Such dilemmas become more complicated in relation to issues having to do with human rights and international immigration. The work of transnational feminism addresses the tensions generated when women or gays apply for asylum as refugees, claiming they are suffering gender or sexual oppression, but their application is premised on reinforcing the conception of the "barbaric" nature of their culture to the sympathetic "Western ears." We should worry about activism in the West that fights to rescue Arab and African women, but does so in a way that reproduces Eurocentric discourse about the Middle East and Africa. The work of transnational feminists on the subject is therefore really crucial. Writers such as Caren Kaplan, Inderpal Grewal, Chandra Talpade Mohanty, Jacqui Alexander, and Minoo Moallem and others have contributed significantly to the illumination of such dilemmas.

The problem, in other words, is not only the practice but also what narrative we deploy to resist such practices. The challenge is to avoid narcissistic rescue fantasies, which take us back to colonial narratives; but instead of white men rescuing brown women from brown men, it becomes white women, or even first world women of color, rescuing brown women from brown men. I am reminded of the film *Around the World in Eighty Days* where David Niven rescues an Indian princess, played by Shirley MacLaine, from *sati*, the burning of the widow. Yet, today, Eurocentric feminists also occupy the traditional position of the male rescuer in colonial narratives. They play the role of the heroine in the discourse of modernization. Implicit in this rescue narrative is the assumption that the "West" is free of gender oppression. Simply discussing cliterodectomy as barbaric erases the struggles of women in Kenya or Egypt who are against such practices and elides the complexity of African cultures, which cannot be reduced to this practice. It also erases the pathology of appearance in the West. My point is that the question for feminist studies is not simply whether we should or should not condemn a specific practice, but how to represent it, and in what context. Feminist analysis must situate practices within a complex local-global economic, social, political, and cultural context.

Another problem in the traditional feminist assumption concerning gender and colonialism is the claim that patriarchy and homophobia have existed everywhere at all times. I find such statements to be ahistorical. For instance, among some indigenous Americans there have been different traditions, which have not necessarily been homophobic, which have not necessarily been patriarchal, which have been marked by egalitarian structures, and where the question of gender identity has been very fluid. This is not romanticization. When colonizers arrived to the Americas, not only did they occupy indigenous land; they also imposed new structures that were patriarchal. The colonizers, for example, would not negotiate with indigenous women who had the right to represent their people. Native American women have addressed the consequences of such impositions.

EA: In your view, does the concept of multiculturalism provide us with theoretical and political tools to problematize dichotomies, including the local-global one?

ES: First of all, "multiculturalism" is just one of many legitimate terms that evoke decolonizing and antiracist movements. The idea of multiculturalism does not mean simply the fact of "many cultures." It is both a political and an epistemological project. Moreover, the concept of multiculturalism has to be defined in relation to Eurocentrism. I'm uncomfortable with the image of multiculturalism as just celebrating the many cultures of the world, all dancing around the maypole. For that, we can go to Disneyland. This is a caricature of multiculturalism. Especially in the 1990s, multiculturalism was attacked not only in the U.S. but also in Brazil and France. For example, in a widely circulated series of essays, French sociologists Pierre Bourdieu and Loic Wacquant argued that multiculturalism was a product of Anglo-American hegemony, a tool of globalization and of American imperialism. (they seemed not to be familiar with any of the actual work). Robert Stam and I are presently working on a book entitled *Culture Wars in Translation*, examining how issues of multiculturalism, postcolonialism, race, and globalization are articulated and translated across borders. We, too, criticize surreptitiously nationalistic versions of multiculturalism, but having said that, we need to be aware of how the attacks on critical multiculturalism and race studies by some leftist intellectuals serve to reproduce Eurocentric premises and power.[7]

Other critics of multiculturalism argue that it has nothing to do with the "real world," that it is restricted to the academy and the debates about curriculum innovation. What these critics do not realize is that these curricula are designed for a large number of people, and that it does matter how students will study history, geography, anthropology, and literature! Besides, if the academy is shown to have little impact on public debates, it might be because we, critical academics, are often pushed out of the public debates in the U.S. context by a corporate culture that limits access to the media for critical scholars. And if the academy is so irrelevant, why is it so often under fire? Pedagogy is very much part of the real world!

5

In the Belly of the Beast

Struggling for Nonviolent Belonging

Zeina Zaatari

Questions about belonging and nonbelonging, identities created and remade, spaces for empowerment and action, and feminist analysis impact our lived realities as Arabs and Muslims, in the United States or at least in a world dominated by U.S. hegemony. How does belonging to an imagined community inflict violence on those persons who do not belong, who refuse to belong, or who refashion belonging in their own image, in their own imagining? The following chapter is a critical narrative of Zeina Zaatari's belonging/nonbelonging, of growing up in South Lebanon during war times and thriving in the Belly of the Beast. The chapter takes the approach of "carrying history in my pocket" as an emblem to understanding subjectivities made and transformed, processes of feminist engagements by Arab and Arab Americans, and the violence of nonbelonging. Oppressed communities find it necessary at times to redefine the labels bestowed upon them by the imperial other by way of reclaiming, redefining, and entering the arena of public and political discourse as empowered subjects. Personal experience and writing, therefore, become powerful means of empowerment. Zaatari's understanding of herself as an Arab feminist is a product of personal struggles[1] and translations of national and public experiences. The following pages are reflections on experience and attempts at theorizing a journey and the struggle of an everyday life.

Foucault argues that subjectivity is created at the intersection of a number of dominant discourses and practices.[2] As an Arab residing in the United States, my experiences of racialization and discrimination are colored by my own experience of growing up in Lebanon (a country ravaged by war and grappling with its identity), the historical moments at which I entered the racial space in the United States, the various engagements with feminist activists and others on college campuses and beyond, and the political consciousness I bring to bear on it all. Eagerness not to fit the stereotype can translate into naive attempts to make the other see you as a human being, a willingness to be the token Arab or the token Muslim. Experience, social context (that is, the difference between living in the Midwest or in the West of the United States), historical changes, and political contexts (wars) transform one's consciousness, and a different engagement with the dominant racist society results. It is an engagement that, today, still attempts to dismantle the stereotypes for a better dialogue, but one that is politically aware and oftentimes angry. Here, I aim for a more in-depth exploration of these transformative processes through reflections on personal experiences (mine and others') and the different communities of Arabs and Arab Americans they produce. Racialization and discrimination may be most reflected in our marginalization, as we become the margins of the margins, in our invisibility as subjects, and in our denial of a space of self-determination. For many of us, violence is a daily reality that is experienced on multiple levels and oftentimes reminds us of our nonbelonging.

Silencing comes from a neocolonial, imperial, and paternal attitude on behalf of various members of society. Arabs and Arab Americans and Muslims and Muslim Americans are discriminated against, seen as lesser humans by the dominant society, thus denying us the right to even claim victimization, discrimination, or love and care. We cannot expect things like freedom of speech to cover our speech; it covers only the speech of our offenders. While we are denied access to a platform to speak about discrimination against Arabs and Muslims, racist discourses against us are deemed "sacred" by FOX News and a variety of media outlets. As community members and activists, we have come not to expect an administration (be it a government or a university) to protect our rights and to make us feel safe even when we are attacked on a daily basis. However, it is evident how administrations across this country are attempting to create safe environments for our oppressors, by eliminating us.[3] We do not "belong" to this nation, but our oppressors do.[4] If anything, it seems that the 2004 elections reaffirmed this nonbelonging. Whereas that fact seems obvious to many after four years of the Bush doctrine of wars, occupations, and detentions, it sadly seems less obvious to most that the 2008 elections also reaffirmed our nonbelonging. From racist and Islamophobic remarks and actions by the Obama campaigners and by the press to his unquestioned and undeniable support to Israel, my belonging, my safety and security, and my rights and those of my people in Palestine and Iraq were quickly and swiftly eradicated.[5] The campaign worked hard to distance Obama from Islam or any relation thereof, which his most sincere Muslim supporters saw as a way to ensure his being elected.[6] This position is itself an indication of the degree to which this nation may claim unity on bumper stickers and storefronts, but has no room for Muslims or Arabs. Obama's recent appointments in the offices of foreign secretary and chief of staff reaffirm the speeches Obama gave at the American Israel Public Affairs Committee and on the campaign trail.[7]

The discourse that takes place in the larger community is often also duplicated, though in different ways, within feminist and activist circles. Both cannot escape the history of images and representations that we have inherited from Orientalist and colonialist material relations. The paternalistic attitude of activists, mostly white, as well as some of those individuals on the margins seeking to "empower" Arab and Muslim women is another "veiled" racism that requires deeper internal reflection for the possibility of a more nuanced and true "sisterhood."[8] For many of us, violence is a daily reality that is experienced on multiple levels, in sympathy with and worry for our families, brothers and sisters living under military rule in Palestine and Iraq, and in being exposed to bumper stickers, news shows, and television screens that parade a convoluted sense of patriotism that can exist only by literally wiping out the other, Arab and Muslim, those people who "do not belong": us.

Beginnings and Carrying History in My Pocket

Stories have beginnings that inform, link, and set the stage for what is to follow. I trace my beginnings to 1982. It was that year my memory was born; 1982 was the year my consciousness emerged; 1982 was the year that defined my "belonging" and "nonbelonging"; 1982 was the year during which my city was invaded by Israel. Like many in my generation in Lebanon, I was born into conflict. My earliest memory that preceded 1982 is of myself, with my mother and my baby brother watching a city on fire from the balcony of our first-floor apartment to the east of Saida.[9] It was 1975, the year when the civil war in Lebanon started and my father was in the city that was aflame. A loud noise, I still hear sometimes, made me afraid. I recall that I ran and hid behind the couch. I was two years old at the time. Although we can assign a date to when the Lebanese civil war began, my region had been in turmoil since at least the turn of the century, with the famines, uprisings, and divisions culminating with 1948, the creation of the state of Israel, and the expulsion of Palestinians into neighboring Arab countries, including Lebanon.

What does it mean to be a product of war and conflict? It is an underprivileged position, I have been told, which strikes me as a curious positionality since I always thought of myself as privileged: I came from the South and had the ability to know and to understand my oppression and the oppressor's world very concretely. Marx and Gramsci argue that the exploited always knows more about the conditions of their exploitation and the life of the oppressors than those persons who oppress them. As Joanna (now Joe) Kadi puts it: "We lived it. We had our reality, the bosses had theirs, and we understood them both."[10] Theorists of color such as W. E. B. DuBois wrote about double consciousness, or the conditions that characterize the way in which African Americans understood their reality and the reality of white people at the turn of the twentieth century. This position of understanding is a tactic used by the oppressed to leverage some power over the oppressors. It is this tactic that I perceive of as privilege, as I would rather know than afford to be blind. This tactic can enable survival and empower a maneuvering of spaces and belonging during war and other conflicts.

Psychology defines war as a traumatic experience. Trauma, however, had been mostly assumed to be individual and personal. What happens, then, when a whole nation experiences the same trauma? My experiences during the war were by no means unique or extreme. Oftentimes I was luckier than others; after all, I made it out alive. Perhaps what may be specific is what I decide to do with these experiences, how I see them shaping my identity, my political consciousness, and how they inform my everyday life. All experiences are transformative. Certain watershed events, however, have the potential for being more transformative of our consciousness than most. It is dominant discourses, at particular historical moments, and how one experiences them that are then embodied in the way we think, feel, desire, and act—in other words, in the way one becomes a subject and enacts one's subjectivity. Social structure and the materiality of subjectivity are emphasized by Bourdieu's theory of practice and habitus.[11] Bourdieu's subject is shaped and made by a material world in which perceptions and ideas are experienced and enacted through practices performed at specific moments in time and space. In addition, feminists of color, including bell hooks, have emphasized multiple subjectivities through experience. "The multiple nature of subjectivity is experienced physically, through practices which can be simultaneously physical and discursive."[12] In fact, hooks has argued throughout her writings that this subjectivity translates itself onto the bodies of women as they are able to know oppression intimately in ways that makes the mental, or the symbolic, and physical inseparable. This personal experience then is transformed into political positionings and theorization about the world we live in.

The women activists of South Lebanon whose life histories I collected remembered the transformative moments of their lives very clearly. The events that marked their existence were often called by scholars "public political landmark events." However, these events were intertwined with the domestic and the personal on a deep level. It is in the best interest of persons in positions of power and privilege to maintain a particular version of history that rarely comes to terms (at least in the United States) with slavery, genocide, ethnic cleansing, and internment. This process of manufacturing consent of a monolithic history constitutes an attempt to erase history and a consistent and collective amnesia about the "forefathers" and the "discovery of America." Similarly in Lebanon, the dominant history taught at schools and written in books is of the center of Mount Lebanon and rarely the history of the marginalized South or of women. By contrast, the women I interviewed talked about their birthdays, love, marriages, and schools. And in the same breath, they talked about major political events such as the Balfour declaration of 1917, the fall of Palestine (1948), the "Million Martyr War" (1954–62) for the liberation of Algeria, the Sykes Picot Agreement, the Nakba, Nasser, the Baghdad Accords, and Eisenhower.[13] The women saw their lives as deeply intertwined with the history of their people in a style not much different from the text of Wilma Mankiller's autobiography.[14] Several African American feminist authors have written about their lives in the same vein.[15] This is not to say that people of color have a history and white folks in the United States do not; rather, I want to underline how a position of privilege and power makes that pretense possible and sometimes "necessary" for continued exploitation. Engaging with history on a personal level, having history that is alive in every bite and in every breath of air that you take, is a burden as well as a privilege. Carrying history in one's pocket makes one conscious of where one comes from and of what social structures attempt to define one's existence. It is about recognizing the roots that ancestors have laid for us. This process entails the assessment of one's role in that history, of seeing clearly my positionality today in relation to the random and purposeful events that preceded my existence in this world. The question that precedes it immediately concerns my exact place in this history and its future and what am I going to do about it. My work in the community as an Arab feminist, who is trying to help create a space for Arab Americans' safe belonging and to create institutions that cater to the needs of our youth and that are gender conscious at the same time, is partly a response to this question.

Obviously, not every person of color in the United States confronts her history and carries it around in her pocket. Hegemonic amnesia is also meant to make quiet, silence, assimilate, and appease the majority of people of color, to buy into the American dream of "try hard and you can make it," "try hard and you can re-create your individual self without any ties, attachments, or history," "try hard and be proud to be independent autonomous and an individual." These "American illusions of autonomy, American delusions of individuality," as June Jordan puts it, aim to erase history and pretend that every citizen or even individual (including "aliens" and immigrants) starts from point zero and thus by working hard can achieve it all. Some Arab Americans tried this path, renamed their children WASP names, spoke English to them, and tried hard to hide the smell of hummus, baba ghannouj, and kibbe. Such an approach, though, pushes people to be ashamed of their history as if they were the perpetrators of the injustices against them or their ancestors. As June Jordan puts it: "As though the horror and the dread of lynching and Jim Crow translated into something shameful about the victims, something the victims must keep secret, terrible years passed before these parents, mine among them, realized that they must publicly proclaim and publicly protest all of the injustice that their worn hands, slumped shoulders, and lowered eyes made clear. And even more time passed before these victims recognized the need to act, collectively, against that outside evil force of hatred."[16] Even those Arab Americans who tried to fit in and assimilate were eventually pushed back into facing that history with every new war between the United States and the Arab world (1967, 1982, the First Gulf War, and the Second Gulf War) and more recently with satellite television and the targeting of Muslims and Arabs under the pretext of waging a global and endless "war on terror" and protecting "homeland security." The 2003 invasion of Iraq and the public discourse that accompanied it made a Lebanese immigrant question his "belonging" to this U.S. nation. Assuming to have "assimilated" by using an American name, living and working in the United States for more than twenty-five years, achieving his version of the "American dream" by becoming the model minority (apolitical, uninvolved, and hardworking), he was shocked to suddenly realize that he still did not belong. He said, "We will never become an inextricable part of this society. They will never accept us."[17] The war on Iraq as the most recent example of wars involving the United States and the Arab world made him a suspect even to his long-term friends and neighbors. The discourse of "cells" and "terrorists within" transformed every Arab and Muslim into an automatic suspect and a potential enemy. Seven years later, these practices have become so normalized that even as television programs try to question them, they end up reinforcing the acceptability of racism against Arabs and Muslims.[18]

Second Beginnings

As an Arab woman living in the United States, I was at a loss as to which box I should fit into and whether I belonged. Not too long ago at a panel on Arab women, I was asked whether I identify as an American Arab, an Arab, or something of the sort. When does one become an immigrant? When does one become hyphenated, when does an immigrant move from being an Arab to being an Arab American? Is there a difference between being an Arab American and being an American Arab? Which aspect of one's identity do we "choose" to highlight and at what moment in time? What aspect of an identity can one wear or remove at will, and are there identities that cannot be revoked or denied? What does belonging to an ethnic group within a "nation" mean?

Historical and political circumstances influence one's ideology, behaviors, inclinations, and the choices we make. I arrived in the United States in 1995 in the middle of the winter to a midwestern college town in Iowa. For me and other Arabs, the nineties was the decade of the decline of student activism all over campuses in the United States. In contrast to the nineties, organizing in the eighties was fueled by the intifada of 1987 in Palestine as well as the struggle for South Africa and the divestment campaign. The First Gulf War and then the signing of the Oslo agreement had led to a sense of defeat as well as the fragmentation of the collective Arab organizing on Palestine. My experiences as an Arab student in the United States were thus framed by this backdrop of political activism. Nonetheless, I knew the moment I stepped off the plane that I was intent on making change; I was carrying my history in my back pocket, but I soon found out that it had no place in this country. I was bound to remain on the margins, even if I was to pursue an academic career. My representation of myself was to remain subordinated to the hegemonic Orientalist discourse.

The Racial Space

As an Arab student, I stepped not only into the ethnic space but also the racial space of the United States. My experience of racialization spans racism against people from Latin America, women of color in general, third world people, and Arab and Muslim women. When people saw me, their immediate reaction was to assume that I was a Latina. The de facto referent "other" that is not clearly black or Asian was Latino/a. Even though this misassumption may make more sense in California with its colonial history, the number of migrant Latino workers in the Midwest working on farms and in factories had been on the rise. I was visible as a member of a minority group, presumed Latina, but invisible as an Arab woman. Since women in the United States are categorized into white, African, Asian, or Latina, my invisibility as an Arab meant that to make sense of me and where I belong, the dominant culture had to fit me within the racial scheme that it understood.

Naber argues that Islam became a racial category in the late nineties.[19] This transformation became clearer as I moved to California in the fall of 1997. My middle name includes a "Mohamad," which makes it almost impossible to escape my identification as a Muslim. In the Midwest, I often was made to feel like a foreigner, but an interesting one, one who had made it out of the "jaws" of patriarchy back home. I often had to be the spokesperson for Arab women. I was eager to "represent" the "good side," the "nonstereotype," the "we are just like you" side. At the time, not fully understanding the complexity of race relations along with the social conditions associated with a long history of Orientalism and Orientalist representation, especially of women, I complied with telling my story to curious middle-class women in Iowa. A sense of shame toward those images and stereotypes so dominant in Western media of the "oppressed Arab and Muslim women" led to a feeling of responsibility to "change them" to "prove them wrong." I attempted to assert my Muslimness, even though it had not been an important aspect of my identity before. I naively thought, like many before me and after me, that seeing a Muslim woman who was not "veiled" and "oppressed" might be a transformative experience, leading Americans to change their attitudes toward Arabs. After moving to California, and being bombarded with imagined and convoluted notions of multiculturalism, I started to better understand this sort of "showcase" syndrome. I realized more so than ever that I was being treated as a "third world person," someone to be patronized and looked at approvingly: "You've tried hard and made it."

The Halls of the Academy: The "Enlightened"

I felt the most discrimination within the walls of academia and in the classrooms of graduate schools. I expected to find more enlightened people, yet most were acting in dangerous patronizing ignorance laden with power. They were supposedly the experts and the intellectuals. Silencing was probably the strongest form of racism I experienced. In classrooms, discussions of the Middle East or the Arab world were muted and silenced. When students dared to breach the domain of accepted social movements and dare to discuss or write about the struggles of Palestinians or Iraqis, their research topics and their political stands were often dismissed as being too "controversial and divisive" for open discussion. When fellow activists demanded a clear-cut position on the ongoing colonization of the Arab world, their concerns were dismissed under the pretext of the obscurity of our struggle and thus the impossibility to take a stand against or for it. Suddenly, social justice had multiple layers, and freedom became bound by historical junctures.

As a student, teaching assistant, and instructor, I felt the brunt of labeling, marginalizing, and silencing of issues of concern to me and members of my community. I recall classes where writings by scholars from the Arab world were rarely included on the syllabus. And when we criticized, we were sometimes asked to suggest extra readings. June Jordan said, "It never occurred to me that optional reading lists might actually imply that somebody powerful really believed there were optional people alive on the planet."[20] In anthropology, a discipline with a strong colonial past, the "other" was the object of study to be found on the pages of ethnographies but never in the theoretical reading assignments.[21] My nationality, ethnicity, language, and religious background were "the other" to be studied, observed, written about, and re-presented. It is the same "other" about whom that Napoleon's "army" of fifty or so scientists had documented volumes and volumes upon his conquest of Egypt in 1798. This knowledge helped define for "Europe/West" its "others" and a relationship of authority over those others.[22] As the "other," however, we do not speak and cannot represent our own selves or produce theory about the worlds we inhabit.

Therefore, strutting through the halls of the academy with the multiple identities that we hold (Arab, working class, African American, indigenous, Muslim, queer, Chicana, Japanese), we constitute a threat that requires silencing. Each of these identities was (and still is) silenced and deemed threatening to the "unity" of the patriarchal nation at one moment in the history of the United States or another. The slogan "United We Stand," so often displayed on bumper stickers and storefronts, focuses on the unity to the exclusion of the parts or, even more so, to the obfuscation and eradication of the parts into this unified red, white, and blue. Kadi argues that silencing is critical to the mechanism of oppression and more viciously internalized oppression: "All systems of oppression—from child abuse to racism to ableism—function most effectively when victims don't talk. Silence isolates, keeps us focusing inward rather than outward, makes perpetrators' work easier, confuses and overwhelms."[23]

Silencing can take several forms, including when a professor says to a graduate student embarking on a thesis research, "You cannot say this in a graduate seminar" or "This is not an appropriate topic for study" or "You cannot use these foreign sources as references." Indeed, intellectuals also act as gatekeepers to what is appropriate knowledge and who is an appropriate scholar. Policing thought and knowledge production is an important mechanism of maintaining oppression. Intellect becomes the exclusive realm of the "civilized" and "enlightened," those "experts" who write about the "other." The genealogy of Orientalist writings and images is too long to discuss in detail here.[24] However, it is a strong force that is still alive and well in the intellectual circles of the American academy of today. It is a force that attempts to silence and control the domain of representation, convoluting textual with political representation and assuming that the textual is apolitical.[25] Feminists of color such as bell hooks criticized the academy, along with white hegemonic feminism, for its inability to articulate and provide a space for knowledge produced by feminists of color.[26] As Arundhati Roy argues: "I think it's vital to de-professionalize the public debate on matters that vitally affect the lives of ordinary people. It's time to snatch our futures back from the 'experts.'"[27] When creating syllabi on gender in the Arab world, I made a conscious decision to include poetry, literature, ethnographies, and theoretical works by Arab women. It was part of my resistance on a college campus to bring in alternative forms of knowledge that are based on experience, other histories in the back pockets of women of the world. I am part of Arab and Arab American feminist Listservs where exchanging this information is crucial because looking over old syllabi or previous courses will not, we were convinced, produce the material we want.

The other form of racialization that many Arab and Arab American feminists face is in relation to our activism on behalf of our communities. Nadine Naber discusses the processes by which various state institutions target and oppress political activists working for Arab people's rights and more specifically those individuals or organizations working on Palestine and against Israeli and U.S. imperialism, such as the antiwar movement.[28] As a student and a teacher on campus, I worked closely with student and community organizations. Given the beginnings I have discussed above, it is not surprising that Palestine is central to our organizing. It is a fundamental and existential question that touches all aspects of our lives, including predominantly the support that Israel receives in this country from both the government and its various public institutions. Even though I can write chapters on the various issues that we had to deal with on my college campus, a few examples will suffice here.

- At an organized rally that was permitted and approved by the administration in 2002 on a California campus, a white male student held the American flag and wore a white T-shirt reading "Kill all Arabs." He circled the protesters, chanting at the top of his lungs, "Kill those Arab babies! Today's babies are tomorrow's terrorists!" for about an hour. Not only was he not removed from the premises, but we also had to restrain ourselves from engaging with him even as he stood two inches away from a close friend from Syria screaming those words into his face.

- A year later, an antiwar rally was organized. We met with the administration, obtained the permit, and made it clear that there would be counterprotesters and that there should be a way to deal with them. We were promised that counterdemonstrators would not be permitted on the lawn. However, we as students and faculty had to create our own barricade around the stage to prevent screaming counterprotesters from storming it. Counterprotesters, dispersed among the rest of the crowd, were screaming and arguing with people to distract them from listening to the speakers. One of them even faked an assault and a citizen's arrest against a Green Party student pacifist, which was actually caught on tape.

• Racist teaching assistants paraded racist cartoons and statements on the doors to their offices, and the administration's response to concerns raised by faculty and students was to claim that the door constitutes his freedom of speech.[29] On the other hand, a student was told not to wear a T-shirt reading "Free Palestine" in a center that serves marginalized communities on campus. This same center was won after a hunger strike and large student support in the early nineties. The center carries a large framed picture of the students on hunger strike all wearing *kufiyas*, the scarf most identify with Palestinian national identity. The irony notwithstanding, it was only after 9/11 that a Middle Eastern intern was finally established in a position at this center. However, whenever the intern dared to speak out or write, she was warned and chastised because she was making students of the colonial entity uncomfortable. In a meeting with the dean of students, where students and community were arguing against the imposition of an Israeli student as the Middle East intern, the administration went as far as indicating that it would have no problems with welcoming any group to the center, even if it was a member of the Ku Klux Klan.

San Francisco State University students struggled for more than a year with the university administration to approve an Edward Said mural to be placed in the Cesar Chavez Student Center. The administration tried so many different maneuvers, including sending a letter to the group indicating that it had decided to revise the process in total. The bottom line was that the administration wanted to remove an image of Handala and the key, both symbols of the right of the return that has been reaffirmed by the UN General Assembly more than 130 times through reaffirming the initial resolution UN 149.[30] The charge was that these images were violent symbols that aimed to eradicate another people, which could not be accepted. There was no consideration of history or the meaning of the symbols to Palestinians. Students, on the other hand, had to learn that struggles have a long history, as a beautiful mural of Malcolm X with his famous slogan, "By any means necessary," has become today an "acceptable" mural as black nationalism gets co-opted or folded into the fold of national unity.

The mechanisms of surveillance are becoming more and more apt as every aspect of our activities becomes monitored and reported on. Having lived through the Israeli occupation in South Lebanon, I was now living through the impact of Zionism here in the United States. The bottom line is that Arabs and Muslims are rarely seen as humans. We have no right to claim victimization or discrimination since only humans can be victims. By automatically making the "perpetrator" out to be anti-Semitic, the Zionist hegemonic discourse has been successful at stifling any criticism of Israel. Whereas Jews have the right to claim victimhood, which has become a privilege in Zionism's attempt to silence others, Arabs, who also have Semitic roots, cannot even claim such victimization status. We could not organize a lecture or show a movie without being harassed. By way of challenging the enforced silence and educating the public on issues of concern to women in the Arab region, I organized a film series while teaching at a university. Discussing women's oppression based on patriarchy or gender was acceptable, but discussing oppression based on wars and occupation was not. Showing movies about women in South Lebanon and Palestinian women earned me numerous tactics of intimidation and silencing. After attempts to silence us by knocking on the doors of all the various policing institutions available, such as the chancellor, deans, chairs of departments, local police station, and Daniel Pipes's Campus Watch failed, those individuals who aimed to quiet us resorted to intimidation tactics at the showings. We could not expect the administration to protect our rights and to make us feel safe, but we could expect it to question and ask us to explain ourselves.

As you read, racist organizations are being formed on many campuses, a matter aided by the "tolerant" atmosphere of the reelection of the Bush government. For the past several years, campus students across the country have been organizing an Islamo-Faciscm Week, prompted by David Horowitz and others.[31] The perpetuation of stereotypical images and the muffling of alternative voices in mainstream media and on campuses have led to a reinforcement of the status quo: Arabs and Muslims are not fully human. We have to endure questions like, "Aren't women oppressed where you come from? Can you belly dance for me?" even from friends whom we have known for a long time. We have to tolerate watching disgusting television programs that continue to depict women as oppressed chador-ridden or exotic belly dancers and men as violent, fanatical fundamentalists who enjoy reading Quranic verses just before they start shooting women and children (exemplified by such films as *The Siege* or *The Mummy*, to name a couple of examples). The portrayal of these demonic images and the silencing of alternative and informed images and discussions (such as my meager attempt of a film series on campus) are two mechanisms of reinforcing a violent exclusion from the "nation."

Is Sisterhood Truly Global?

In feminist circles, there has been some recent change in the ways in which feminists interact with their Arab sisters, a direct result of our insistence on engagement. However, this process is still greatly laden with problems. I used to feel, and still do sometimes, more like an outsider in feminist circles. It often seemed to me that we shared many of the concerns regarding the improvement of women's lives and the belief in the humanity of all people, and we shared similar struggles against oppressive patriarchal systems. Nonetheless, my white feminist colleagues often seemed to be more interested in pointing to how horrendous life for women in my part of the world is and in finding ways to "save" these women, than in actual meaningful dialogue with them or me. No matter what events we were organizing as Arab feminists, we can always count on an audience that would ask us questions about female genital mutilation and honor killings. Obviously, racism in U.S. culture has seeped through to these feminist circles. These practices continue today as I work outside of academia in a feminist organization where the all too common expression that I receive when at a fund-raising event or a conference of women's organizations, and when I explain that I work on the Middle East and North Africa, is "Poor thing, you must have a lot of work to do," or "That has to be tough given what is happening over there." The immediate almost knee-jerk reaction to place our people outside of history as an anomaly that has historical unchangeable oppressions is a legacy of Orientalist thought and a product of the current imperial project of the United States. It manages in one instant to make us exotic, objects of a complex desire to save and own.

At the same time, however, feminists of color have also often failed to see the connections and the humanity of their Arab and Muslim sisters of color. They launched legitimate critiques against the middle-class white feminist agenda, but failed to link up with those "others" on the margins. They may have identified race, and in some instances class, as the main element of oppression in addition to gender; however, they failed to accept and take notice that other ideologies have and do maintain the oppression of their sisters. A new breed of "home-grown" Arab and Muslim women and the internally colonized has also been contributing to this discourse.[32] They often contribute doubly to marginalizing their sisters by aligning with Islamophobic forces and as such delegitimating the important issues they claim they raise. Such narratives tend to make it much harder for women's rights activists in the Arab and Muslim world to struggle against patriarchal institutions and practices.

Arab and Muslim feminists have identified Zionism as an important determinant of the forms of oppression we struggle against in the United States and beyond. However, in feminist circles, this discussion was not acceptable, once again deemed too "controversial" or "obscure" at best. In *The Forgotten -Ism*, Nadine Naber, Eman Desouky, and Lina Baroudi discuss the various ways in which Zionism impacts our lives negatively as Arab and Arab American women in this country, including the silencing, the isolation, and the charges of anti-Semitism.[33] The pervasiveness of the Zionist ideology and support for it in the United States mean that sources of power are often aligned with it, including those sources with financial resources. Any questioning, for example, of the Israeli state and of its impact on women in Palestine, Lebanon, and the diasporas is not allowed and often actively silenced. In writing about the atrocities that women and men faced by the Israeli war machine in Lebanon in 2006, numerous challenges arose. Sister and feminist organizations found it necessary to silence my voice, thus doubly victimizing their sisters in Lebanon.[34]

As feminists, should our work toward dismantling patriarchy make us one-track, one agenda, and monovisionistic? Doesn't this narrow focus help segregate and weaken the movement? How and when do we notice that our discourses, even when sometimes fully legitimate, make us lie in bed with those individuals we should be struggling against, in one example Islamophobes? An example of such a struggle came from the U.S. World Social Forum around the position that a feminist organization, MADRE, took by issuing a press statement focusing on solidarity to Palestine in the age of Hamas, and by representing, meaning speaking in the name of, Palestinians on the panel at the forum. This action led activists attending the forum to first issue a quick letter to the organizers of the forum on their failure to include any Palestinian speakers in the panels but agreeing to those panelists who claim to speak on their behalf. Then, a press statement was released written by a wider set of Palestinian activists and organizations in the United States under the title "Defining Terms in the Age of Imperialism: Challenging Alleged 'Strategic Solidarity.'"[35] One of the main critiques by the activists is that "strategic" solidarity ends up reinforcing oppressive power dynamics. Whereas MADRE's critiques of Hamas's leadership and practices may be legitimate from a feminist standpoint, the fact that MADRE never issued a statement about Fateh's patriarchal and homophobic practices and perspectives calls into question the legitimacy of their claims and intentions and quickly places them in the same camp as Islamophobes. At the same time, as long as we ourselves do not openly lay claim to those necessary criticisms of our nationalist discourses, we lose a chance to articulate our vision for a more just and equal world, and we risk others defining them for us.[36]

Those issues came again to the surface during debates about whether U.S. organizations should attend the World Pride Event that was held in Jerusalem in 2006. I was invited to speak to the board of the International Gay and Lesbian Human Rights Commission about the negative implications of supporting World Pride and arguing for boycotting of the event. IGLHRC ended up sending delegates and participating at the event, explaining that they aim to do antioccupation work while there. On the other hand, QUIT (Queers Undermining Israel Terrorism) decided along with several other organizations to boycott the event.[37] The intersectionality of struggles becomes very clear in this example, and the differences in the understanding of these struggles and thus in the choices one makes. Stemming from QUIT's political consciousness and deep understanding of oppression along with their engagement with LGBTQI groups in Palestine and Lebanon, the decision to boycott was reached. Building movements that have the capacity to transform the world we live in has to be based in building coalitions to create countercollective narratives. To create a revolution and change, Gramsci argues, one needs a counternarrative, a counterhegemony, a movement that would produce its own organic intellectuals, whose interests are the interests of the community, a diverse community.[38]

Some feminists of color like June Jordan have made those connections and intersections between the various ideologies and mechanisms of oppression. Feminism of color, or third world feminism, though, is the only likely space where we could perhaps feel at home. The statements that feminists of color make about the centrality of their dual and multiple identities and the inextricability of race, class, gender, sexual orientation, and others are parallel to the demands and statements of Arab women. As an Arab feminist, I too am a product of all the histories I discussed. I am also aware of the conjunctures of my identity as an Arab, as a middle-class woman, as a member of a minority group, as an immigrant, as a feminist, and so forth. . . . This awareness of the multiplicity of my positionings makes it impossible for me to organize from a single one. I carry all of my histories in my pocket at all times.

Appropriation and Solidarity

On the eve of the invasion of Iraq in 2003, many demonstrations and lectures were organized. It was at once an invigorating experience and an eye-opener to the ever-deepening complexities of "third world"/"first world" relations. I found myself engaged with students and found a need to write about why it was important for students of color to oppose the war. To have to say that it was needed and necessary was a slap in the face. What I assumed to be natural alliances in the struggle against empire building were not fully clear here. Coalition building was thus another process of building bridges and relearning the basics of the commonality of struggles. The problematics of paternalistic discourses sneak into the antiwar movement. As Arab feminists, we need to question notions of solidarity and representation. It is one thing to stand in solidarity with an existential struggle and to see clearly its repercussions on you and a totally different matter to pretend that you own that struggle. In the first instance, respect should, I believe, be the underlying premise for any solidarity or coalition. Here is where we come full circle to carrying our histories in our pockets and understanding our privilege, be it as a white U.S. citizen or a privileged immigrant benefiting from education and a high-paying job. We face issues of cultural appropriation and the commodification and promotion of "ethnic" cultural artifacts as attempts at solidarity. We hear things like, "I married one of you," from the mouths of those traveling on Global Exchange's reality tours or the International Solidarity Movement to countries of "onflict." Solidarity has been essential in every struggle for self-determination around the world; nevertheless, every individual engaged in it must ask him- or herself: "With all the intersections of my history and my identity, what drives me to partake in this solidarity? Am I carrying my history in my pocket? And what have I learned from it? Is my solidarity conditional and, if so, on what?" These questions are not aimed at belittling the work in which solidarity movements are engaged, but to call into question motivations, processes, and notions of solidarity and ownership of struggles.

In addition, does standing in solidarity mean that one has the right to dictate to people the terms and conditions of their struggle? This conflict came into full view in the June 2006 war in Lebanon, where the perplexities particularly of feminist organizations around solidarity to their sisters in Lebanon came to be conditional on their rejection of Hezbollah, seen as violent and chauvinist and something that must be fought. The emphasis and almost obsession with telling Palestinians how to struggle nonviolently against the U.S. occupation abound among activist circles. Groups upon groups have been funded to go to Palestine and train people on nonviolent conflict resolution. This emphasis calls into question the notion of solidarity: is it conditional upon people's agreeing with one's pacifist ideology? It masks the history and present of multiple forms of resistance that the Palestinian people have engaged in, the everyday practices of survival that Palestinians are engaged in, and it masks power dynamics between the Palestinians and Israelis. It also avoids looking at the history of liberation movements across the globe, where an armed element was always present. In *The Wretched of the Earth*, Fanon discusses at length the nature of violent reactions to violent oppressions as an element of a liberation struggle: "Decolonization is always a violent phenomenon."[39] This is not to simply condone any kind of violence perpetrated in the name of liberation, but to call into question what realities some of the pacifist discourses imposed from afar mask.

Are Nonviolent Belongings Possible?

I still have perplexed feelings toward the terms "violence" and "belonging." I see them as connected on some level. However, I would like them to be more distinct. I grew up in a war-torn country, and thus violence has a very specific meaning to me. While in the United States, though, I see violence of a different kind perpetuated on a daily basis on different groups of people. Violence is on display, not only in television shows, supposedly fiction based, but also in the new disgusting fervor of reality television and on the news. It perpetuates a notion of being number one; it promotes as valued attributes conquering, mastering, and winning. A culture of violence and fear and violence justified by such fear is on display all the time. As Arundhati Roy argues, "Here, this whole regime of synthetically manufactured fear has bonded people to the government. And that bond is not because of public health care, or looking after the old, or education, or social services, but fear."[40]

The statistics on rape and crime are terrifying.[41] Walking down the street in the middle of the night in a city like Beirut is not even a question in my mind. Walking just after dark in "safe" cities in the United States is always accompanied by fearful thoughts and anxieties over rape and hate crimes. I see the American flag on cars and windows as a way to perpetuate violence and aggression on other people of the world. Belonging to the United States as a nation in the way that it is being portrayed on television, in political rhetoric of war and patriotism, in newspapers, and on people's bumper stickers is a violent act. At the same time, I am made to feel that my belonging to the Arab world, my belonging to a nation massacred by Israel and the United States, borders on terrorism. And again, this violence is committed against people to whom I belong and whom I love.

The escalation of both violence and the drums of war has in fact forced out into the public more defined spaces where I could start to feel a bit safe. Let me explain myself. I felt safe within a San Francisco demonstration of eighty thousand or more demanding an end to the war against Iraq and freedom for Palestine. I felt safe when people of all walks of life were marching beside me and condemning aggression against the children of the Arab world. I felt safe at a Women of Color meeting where a poet identified my aggressor and connected it/him/them to her aggressor. Nonetheless, the normalization of war on Iraq, Afghanistan, and Palestine among others as a daily occurrence that actually impacts the U.S. public and citizenry very minimally, despite the fact that these are U.S. wars, has raised added questions about these safe spaces and belonging. Some of us live a dual existence that sometimes feels schizophrenic, where we watch Arabic news channels in the mornings and make the frantic phone calls "back home" to see if everyone is okay, then go to our jobs like zombies on the streets of a nation that does not see, count, or mourn our dead.

Despite all the problematics I have discussed, those antiwar and feminist movements with progressive politics are the only locations in the United States where I could feel safe, where my belonging could start to take shape, where the history that I carry in my pocket can find room to breathe and dialogue. Perhaps the operative three words that are often thrown at me and others while walking in a demonstration, "Go back home," are true in the sense that I do not belong in the United States. Nevertheless, regardless of whether I make my home in the United States or elsewhere, I hope to see a world where belonging is not a violent act of nonbelonging to another. This change is essential in the Belly of the Empire.

6

Decolonizing Culture

Beyond Orientalist and Anti-Orientalist Feminisms

NADINE NABER

In this essay, Nadine Naber interrogates the ways that Arab diasporas remake "Arab culture" in the United States and the significance of this process to the issues of sexism and homophobia. Her analysis focuses on middle-class Arab immigrant discourses and the Arab American social movements to which she has belonged. Naber proposes a feminist approach that locates diasporic notions of "culture" within the historical lega- cies of European colonialism and Orientalism and the contemporary experiences of displacement, immigration, racism, and assimilation. Here, she argues that "culture" is "political." This approach considers how issues that are seemingly "internal" to our communities (such as sexism and homophobia) emerge with and through a range of "external" forces. From this standpoint, Naber calls for alternatives to social move- ment frameworks that subordinate gender or sexuality or both to a private-cultural- communal domain and mark gender and sexuality as secondary to the more pressing issues of our times—such as war and racism. Working beyond the notions of distinct and separate internal-private and external-public domains, she finds a sense of libera- tion from the fear of "washing our dirty laundry in public" that has haunted many Arab and Arab American feminist projects in the United States.

I was born in San Francisco, three years after my parents arrived from Al Salt, Jordan. Over the next twenty years, my parents moved a dozen times across the

This essay is an excerpt from my forthcoming book, *Articulating Arabness: Gender and Cultural Identity in the Diaspora.* I am grateful to Rabab Abdulhadi, Evelyn Alsultany, Lara Deeb, and Andrea Smith for their invaluable feedback on this essay. My deepest appreciation goes to all of the people who participated in my research. There are not enough words to thank them for their contribution.

Bay Area, creating for me a childhood and a sense of community that was both rigidly structured and ever changing. Throughout my childhood, "culture" was a tool, an abstract, ephemeral notion of what we do and what we believe, of who belongs and who does not. Culture was the way that my parents exercised their control over me and my siblings. The same fight, I knew from my aggrieved conversations with friends and relatives, was playing out in the homes of countless other Arab families. The typical generational wars—about whether we teenagers could stay out late at night, or whether we could spend the night at our friends' slumber parties—was amplified into a grand cultural struggle. The banalities of adolescent rebellion became a battle between two stereotypes, between rigid versions of "Arab" and "American" values. To discipline us, our parents' generation invoked the royal "we," as in: "No, you can't go to the school dance because we don't do that." Here, "we" meant "Arabs."

I hated these words. I hated these declarations of what "we" did and didn't do. Yet, they worked. Sort of. Sometimes, I actually listened. Or, more often as time went on, I simply tried to hide these parts of my life from my parents. Because even worse than disobeying my parents was the threat—always tangible in my house and in our community centers—that I might be disobeying *my people*— a term that signified anyone from the Naber family, to everyone in Jordan, to all Arab Christians, to *al Arab*. Transgressing my parents' rules was not merely adolescent rebellion, but was a form of cultural loss, of cultural betrayal. And even worse, each moment of transgression meant the loss of Arab culture to *al Amerikan*, that awesome and awful world that encompassed everything from the American people to the American government to the American way of life (at least as my parents seemed to imagine it).

Our Arab community, like so many immigrant networks, was wildly diverse, comprising Muslim and Christian, Jordanian, Lebanese, Palestinian, and Syrian families. Yet we all seemed to have a remarkably similar idea of what "American" and "Arab" meant. We seemed to share a tacit knowledge that *al Amerika* was the trash culture, degenerate, morally bankrupt, and sexually depraved. In contrast, *al Arab* (Arabs) were morally respectable—we valued marriage, family, and close relationships. It was not only our parents who put this pressure on us.[1] What we learned at school and from the U.S. media reinforced this dichotomy.

As with all products of human belief, there were caveats, and shades of gray, and matters of proportion. Our immigrant parents' generation disproportionately pressured girls to uphold idealized demands of Arab culture. Girls' behavior seemed to symbolize the respectability of our fathers and our families, as well as no less than the continuation of Arab culture in America. Particularly as my girlfriends, cousins, and I hit puberty, the pressure seemed to intensify. I couldn't wear my trendy jeans with the tear down the side for fear that my relatives and parents' friends would curse my sloppy clothes and my bare skin. By the time my friends and I graduated from college, young women's bodies and behaviors seemed to be the key signifiers in the stereotyped distinction between Arabs and Americans.

Compounding matters, our parents raised us in predominantly white suburbs and encouraged us—in certain ways—to assimilate. They encouraged us to befriend the "American kids" and dress up for colonial days at school. And many of us watched our fathers change their names from Yacoub, Mohammed, and Bishara to Jack, Mo, and Bob when they arrived at their grocery and convenience stores as the sun rose. It was only later that I came to understand that many men of my parents' generation changed their names after being called "dirty Arab" or "Palestinian terrorist," or after customers refused to shop at their stores.

Despite this, and despite the fact that our parents were encouraging us to adopt the values of middle-class America, the fundamental message in our family and community remained: *we* were Arab and *they* were American. It felt like we were living between two worlds, one within the confines of our modest suburban homes and the Arabic church, the other at the mall and in the unfettered streets of San Francisco. With each passing year, it seemed more and more impossible to live in such a bifurcated way. I fought with my parents all the time, and because I started to doubt which "side" of me was really me, the demands from both sides just made me want to rebel against everything.[2]

Even as I yelled at them, I knew that my parents wanted only the best for me. Because of my adolescent myopia, I had only the faintest sense of the difficulties of their lives and the concurrent struggle of their immigrant generation to simultaneously foster cultural continuity and be Arab in America. Just like I was with my ripped jeans, they too were trying to articulate who they were. It would be years before I grasped how each day they confronted not only the pressures of assimilation but also the realities of an expanding U.S. imperialist war in the Arab region and intensifying anti-Arab Orientalist and racist discourses in their new home.

More than thirty years ago, Edward Said argued that "Orientalism" is a European fabrication of "the East," that "the Orient" is shaped by European imperialist attitudes and assumes that Eastern or Oriental people can be defined in terms of cultural or religious essences that are invulnerable to historical change. Orientalism, he explained, configures the "East" in irreducible attributes such as religiosity or femininity. This political vision, he contended, has promoted the idea of insurmountable differences between the familiar (Europe, West, "us") and the strange (the Orient, the East, "them"). Like Said, critics of Orientalism have long argued that essentialist representations of Islam are crucial to Orientalist thought. In Orientalist thought, Muslims, Arabs, and other "Orientals" are hopelessly mired in a host of social ills, the cause of which is an unchanging tradition that exists outside of history and is incompatible with civilization.[3] Feminist scholars such as Rabab Abdulhadi have in turn argued that this strand of Orientalist thought has constructed our contemporary visions of Arab and Muslim societies as either completely decadent, immoral, and permissive or strict and oppressive to women.[4] This new Orientalism relies on representations of culture (Arab) and religion (Islam) as a justification for post–cold war imperial expansion in the Middle East and the targeting of people perceived to fit the racial profile of a potential terrorist living in the United States—Arabs, Middle Easterners, Muslims.[5] New Orientalist discourses have birthed a variety of widely accepted ideas: of Arab and Muslim queers oppressed by a homophobic culture and religion, of hyperoppressed shrouded Arab and Muslim women who need to be saved by American heroes, of a culture of Arab Muslim sexual savagery that needs to be disciplined—and in the process, modernized—through U.S. military violence.[6]

The impact of Orientalism, I began to see, was everywhere. Our Arab community had a plethora of cultural and political organizations to put on music concerts, festivals, and banquets and a range of political organizations that focused on civil rights issues and homeland politics. Yet there were no resources for dealing with the difficult issues within our families. As in many immigrant families, ours opted to avoid bringing attention to personal matters, particularly in public space and particularly among other Arabs. Throughout high school especially, many of my Arab American peers were devastated by the conflicting feelings of love, pain, and guilt toward our parents and the ideas about Arab culture that we learned from our parents and U.S. society. We joked about fleeing our community altogether. We swore to each other that we would never marry an Arab. It was clear that these problems were pushing Arabs away from each other. In addition, on my trips to Jordan to visit relatives, I learned that many of my neighbors in the Bay Area had more socially conservative understandings of religion, family, gender, and sexuality than their counterparts in Jordan. I was baffled: why were the stakes of family respectability so high in America?

Articulating Arabness

After I survived the dual gauntlet of high school and my parents' expectations, and after I moved out of their home, I began listening more carefully to the stories of our immigrant parents. I began asking why they came to the United States, what they experienced when they arrived, and what they dreamed of and worked for in America. Not surprisingly, our parents' commitments to cultural continuity were much more complicated than what I had understood them to be. As the twentieth century became the twenty-first, I spent several years researching these cultural ideas and exploring how they operated as a major site of struggle for middle-class second-generation Arab Americans then growing up in the San Francisco Bay Area. I worked with community-based organizations and did ethnographic research with eighty-six men and women, ages eighteen to twenty-eight, whose families had immigrated to the United States, primarily from Jordan, Lebanon, Palestine, and Syria. I interviewed fifteen immigrants from their parents' generation, immigrants who came to the Bay Area between the 1950s and 1970s, an era characterized by increased Arab migration to the United States, the expansion of American empire in the Arab region, and the intensification of racism and xenophobia in California.[7]

Despite a broad diversity in family origins and religious values, and despite access to socioeconomic class privileges, nearly all of these young adults told the same story: the psychological pressure to maintain the ideals of Arab and American culture felt overwhelming and irresolvable.

Bassam, a Palestinian Arab American who served on the board of the Arab Cultural Center in San Francisco during my research, placed the feeling of Nuha and so many others within the context of America at the turn of the twenty-first century: "We have real needs as a community. We are really under attack. We are being damaged severely in, and by, the U.S. There is a great necessity for pro-active behavior and community building. But it conflicts with the way our young people are brought up here. I'm so sympathetic to the need to perpetuate the community and yet, I'm horrified that the methods we think we must use to do so are going to kill us psychologically in this society."

For several years, as I conducted in-depth interviews with teens and twentysomethings, we shared stories about the norms and expectations of our immigrant communities. Orientalism was at the heart of this struggle. The dominant middle-class Arab immigrants' articulation of Arabness through rigid, binary categories (good Arab girls versus bad American girls, for example) was based on a similar framework that guided Orientalist discourses about Arabs. My parents and their peers simply reversed Orientalism and used its binary categories (liberated Americans versus oppressed Arab women, bad Arabs versus good Americans) differently and for different purposes. Articulating immigrant cultural identity through rigid binaries is not an unfamiliar resolution to immigrant and people of color's struggles in a society structured by a pressure for assimilation and racism.[8]

As Vijay Prashad argues, this dynamic, while a reaction to political and historical conditions, is an attempt to depoliticize the immigrant experience where culture is articulated not as living, changing social relations but a set of timeless traits.[9] In many ways, I found that in the San Francisco Bay Area, articulations of Arabness in America have been haunted by culture or, more precisely, by Orientalist definitions of culture.

The uninterrogated naturalization of a dichotomy between Arab and American culture among Arab Americans—usually associated as it is with essentialist understandings of religion, family, gender, and sexuality among Arab communities—allows Orientalist thought to be left intact and activated. Consigned to the "cultural," aspects of dynamic, lived experience come to be seen as frozen in time—essentialist Arab traditions that exist outside of history—which is the same conceptualization that operates as the basis for the demonization of Arab communities in the discourses of U.S. empire.

Within the dominant middle-class Arab immigrant discourse that circulated in my interlocutors' homes and community networks, gender and sexuality were among the most powerful symbols consolidating an imagined difference between "Arabs" and "Americans." Consider the ways some of my interlocutors described what they learned growing up about the difference between Arab and American culture:

JUMANA: My parents thought that being American was spending the night at a friend's house, wearing shorts, the guy-girl thing, wearing make-up, reading teen magazines, having pictures of guys in my room. My parents used to tell me, "If you go to an American's house, they're smoking, drinking . . . they offer you this and that. But if you go to an Arab house, you don't see as much of that. *Bi hafzu ala al banat* [They watch over their daughters]."

TONY: There was a pressure to marry an Arab woman because the idea was that "She will stand by her family, she will cook and clean, and have no career. She'll have kids, raise kids, and take care of her kids, night and day. She will do anything for her husband." My mom always says, "You're not going to find an American woman who stands by her family like that. . . . American women leave their families."

In the quotes above, concepts of "good Arab girls" operates as a marker of community boundaries and the notion of a morally superior "Arab culture" in comparison to concepts of "American girls" and "American culture." Idealized concepts of femininity are connected to idealized notions of family and an idealized concept of heterosexual marriage. These ideals underpin a generalized pressure for monogamy—and more specifically, for no sex before marriage—and for compulsory heterosexuality. Some interlocutors recalled their parents' reaction to what they perceived to be signs of homosexuality. Here is how Ramsy said his Palestinian mother reacted to photographs of him in drag: "My mom took one look at the pictures and said, 'My God! What are we doing in this country! Oh, look what this country did to us!' They definitely see it as an American thing. They don't know that there are a lot of gay people back home." Among the middle-class Arab immigrant communities I worked with, dominant articulations of Arabness were structured by a strict division between an inner Arab domain and an outer American domain, a division that is built upon the figure of the woman as the upholder of values and an ideal of family, heterosexuality, and, most important, heterosexual marriage.

This jumble of ideals about Arabness and Americanness was the buoy that guided and girded—but also threatened to drown—the middle-class Arab diasporas in the Bay Area. These ideals created a fundamental split between a gendered and sexualized notion of an inner-familial-communal (Arab) domain and an external-public (American) domain—a split that both provided a sense of empowerment and belonging and also constrained the lives of many of my interlocutors. This split was terribly familiar to me and, at the same time, largely undiscussed both in my own life and in the larger Arab American community. I have spent nearly a decade trying to decipher the divide within the Arab community between the internal and the external, the private and public, and figuring out how we find meaning and formulate a life within this imagined split.

As my research progressed, I began interpreting the predicament of growing up in new ways. Both my parents and the parents of my interlocutors constantly referred to Arab culture—as the thing that rooted us, and often, it seemed, ruled us. This amorphous entity shaped our calendar and our thoughts, what our goals were and who our friends were. But the more I searched, the harder it became to find this culture. All I could find, instead, was an amalgam of influences. The concepts of "Arab culture" my parents' generation relentlessly invoked are indeed historically grounded in long-standing Arab histories, yet they were just as much shaped by the immigrant journey of displacement and diaspora and the pressures of middle-class assimilation in the United States. Concepts of Arabness among my parents' generation, and through them my peers' and my interlocutors', have ultimately been shaped not by a ceaseless and unchanging Arab tradition but by a collision of historically contingent realities and varying modes of diasporic living in the American empire—of running a grocery store, of traveling to the

Arab world, of the travel of news and stories through the Internet and satellite television, by past and present Arab responses to European colonialism and U.S. empire, and by the words of the corporate media.

By interrogating the process by which middle-class Arab diasporas come to herald particular ideals as markers of an authentic, essential, true, or real Arab culture, I have learned that these ideals are best understood as cultural sensibilities that have permeated the Arab region for centuries and have become entangled in concepts of Arabness and Americanness that circulate in the United States. Even with regards to the Arab region, essentialist cultural frameworks cannot explain concepts and practices of family, marriage, gender, and sexuality, as these are very much entangled in European and U.S. discourses and are constantly changing in light of socioeconomic transformations.[10] Consider, for instance, that modernist nationalist concepts of gender and sexuality became dominant in the Arab region as European involvement in the region introduced certain new ideas about gender and sexuality.[11] These new European-influenced concepts replaced a much more varied structure of gender and ambiguous, fluid sexual attitudes that were common during centuries of Islamic rule.[12]

To a certain extent, I interpret dominant middle-class Arab American concepts of "Arab culture" as an immigrant survival strategy for replacing U.S. colonialist and Orientalist discourses about Arabs, Muslims, and the Middle East with seemingly positive or empowering concepts of cultural identity, a strategy that reverses the binary structure of bad, misogynist Arabs versus good, modern Americans and instead advances good Arab girls versus bad American(ized) girls. Specifically, the dominant middle-class Arab American discourse presented Arab cultural identity and community through the ideal of the good Arab family, good Arab girls, and compulsory heterosexuality, all of which was in opposition to an imagined America and its apparent sexual promiscuity, broken families, and bad women. Yet I also contend that this dominant middle-class Arab American discourse is shaped by the liberal logic of U.S. multiculturalism, a logic for imagining and performing cultural identity that becomes available to Arab diasporas upon their arrival in the United States. Liberal U.S. multiculturalism requires immigrants, people of color, and indigenous people to craft concepts of culture that are depoliticized and ahistorical.[13] Vijay Prashad contends, "Whereas assimilation demands that each inhabitant of the United States be transformed into the norm, U.S. multiculturalism asks that each immigrant group preserve its own heritage. . . . The heritage, or 'culture,' is not treated as a living set of social relations but as a timeless trait."[14] Conjoining masculinist nationalist binaries (good Arab girls versus bad American girls) with the logics of liberal U.S. multiculturalism, dominant middle-class Arab American discourses posit an essentialist, authentic Arab identity that exists outside of history. Furthermore, while the dominant middle-class Arab American discourse idealizes family and heterosexual marriage as *Arab,* and not American, in fact, patriarchy and idealized concepts of "family values" and compulsory heterosexuality are fundamental to the demands of white U.S. middle-class acceptability.[15] This small sampling from my research calls for a broader analysis of sensationalized issues such as "Arab" and "Muslim" patriarchy and homophobia. At the least, it points to an urgent need to transcend essentialist frameworks that explain structures of patriarchy among Arab families and communities as simply "cultural" matters. I believe that a diasporic Arab feminist theory, a theory that locates "Arab" patriarchy and homophobia at the interplay among long-standing cultural sensibilities, Orientalism and imperial formations, and the pressures of immigration and assimilation, opens up such possibilities.

Social Movements and "Arab Culture"

Working within various Arab and Arab American activist movements, I learned that it was not only conventional middle-class Arab American discourses that conceptualized family, gender, and sexuality as characteristics of an inner-communal-"cultural" domain. The concept of a distinct inner-communal-cultural domain has also constrained the Arab and Arab American activist movements to which I have belonged. In leftist Arab American political movements focused on Palestine and Iraq, for instance, many Arab and Arab American feminists have been working to liberate issues of gender and sexuality from a seemingly internal-cultural domain. In nearly every Arab and Arab American organization where I have worked, political actions were focused externally—on ending war and racism, on raising awareness about the links between sexual violence and U.S. and Israeli militarism, and on liberating Arab land from colonization. In 2002, I participated in a community-based organization that led a campaign to end U.S. sanctions on Iraq and launched a divest-from-Israel movement modeled after the South African anti-Apartheid movement. This leftist Arab movement operated according to a collective consciousness that Israel was killing and displacing Palestinians en masse, that the U.S. war in Iraq was looking more and more like genocide, and that U.S. tax dollars were paying for it. Mobilized by daily images circulating in alternative media sources of dead Palestinian and Iraqi children, activists operated as a community in crisis.

Crisis mode meant that certain issues were privileged over others. This point was most clearly evident in moments when people raised critiques of sexism or homophobia within our movement. These critiques were met with an official movement logic that contended that the issue of sexism was secondary to the fact that "our people are dying back home."[16] Alternately, it positioned discussions of homophobia as entirely irrelevant or outside the boundaries of acceptability. In this movement—as in many racial justice and national liberation solidarity movements—the official movement logic also subordinated critiques of sexism and homophobia in reaction to racism.

Not only were gender and sexuality barely discussed, but the official movement discourse insisted that discussing these internal issues in public could actually endanger the goals activists were fighting for. Many members of this movement shared the belief that U.S. Orientalist representations of Arabs and Muslims, specifically images of hyperoppressed Arab and Muslim women and Arab Muslim sexual savagery, were among the most common images Americans saw—especially from the news media and Hollywood. In their analysis, Orientalist representations were a key reason so many Americans supported U.S. military interventions in the Middle East and why many Americans, particularly liberals, expressed profound empathy for Arab and Muslim women—perceived to be victims of their culture and religion—but little concern over the impact of U.S. policies on Arab and Muslim communities.[17]

In response, many activists feared that discussing sexism and compulsory heterosexuality within Arab communities would reinforce Orientalism. Activists advocated an anti-Orientalist politics that reinforced the relegation of gender and sexuality to the margins. Activists feared that speaking out about sexism and homophobia could reinforce stereotypes of Arabs and strengthen the very violence they were fighting to eliminate. The tacit belief was that activists who publicly critiqued sexism or homophobia within Arab and Arab American communities were no better than traitors to their people. The result—of yet another binary structure—was that attempts to develop feminist or queer critiques were often confined between two extremes: untenable silence, on the one hand, and the reification of Orientalist representations, on the other.

◆　　◆　　◆

The fear of washing our dirty laundry in public has haunted my own experiences working on various Arab and Arab American feminist issues in the United States. Since 1993, I have been involved in a range of projects that presented various Arab and Arab American feminist perspectives at UN international conferences (the Durban conference on racism, the Cairo conference on population and development, and the Beijing conferences on women), various U.S. feminist conferences, and a range of U.S.-national political demonstrations and protests in support of Palestinian and Iraqi people.[18] All of these projects were anchored in a sort of anti-Orientalist feminism that disregarded issues internal to our communities because we were either cautious about the ways such issues could be used against us or because we felt that other matters such as war and occupation were the more pressing issues of our times. These efforts focused on deconstructing the proliferation of Orientalist U.S. discourses that represent Arab culture through images of oppressed Arab women, explaining the magnitude of these discourses to the legitimization of U.S. and Israeli militarism and war, and calling liberal U.S. feminists to task for reinforcing Orientalist feminisms and ignoring critiques of U.S. empire and its gendered and sexualized underpinnings.

In 2002, I joined the Arab Movement of Women Arising for Justice (AMWAJ), a new group of Arab and Arab American feminists, some of whom had been active in the previous projects but were tired of the privileging of "external" problems of racism and war among Arab feminist activists in the United States. Many of us were also tired of the silence surrounding forms of sexism and homophobia that take place among our families and communities. Yet we recognized that there were few spaces to talk about "internal" issues—particularly since we felt that most U.S. feminist spaces, as well as some Arab American feminist spaces—were dominated by Orientalist perspectives about Arab women. In fact, a few of us had recently left an Arab and Arab American feminist e-mail discussion group to which we belonged for several years because of the proliferation of Orientalist feminist perspectives within the group. We felt the list was no longer a safe space for discussing feminist issues internal to our communities. Yet many AMWAJ members felt that "internal" issues were crucial to the range of issues that shaped our lives as Arab feminists, queers, and transgender people living in the United States. We also came from a place that conceptualized gender and sexuality not within an isolated internal-cultural-familial domain but as interconnected to race and racism, class, empire, and so on. A shared desire for a space to discuss the range of issues that impact our lives—including the issues that we confront among our families and Arab communities—inspired us to organize a gathering for Arab women, queer, and transgender people living in the United States in Chicago in 2005. Yet we were cautious in moving forward since we shared one too many experiences where anti-Arab discourses co-opted our voices as fodder for anti-Arab racism and Orientalism and support for U.S. militarism. We were very clear that the project of addressing "internal" Arab community-based matters was fraught in the United States, but we were committed to going beyond Orientalism and anti-Orientalism. We strategically used the idea of "internal" and "external" domains for organizing our initial gathering. We began by fostering a space where people could speak openly about "internal" matters—since many of us rarely had this opportunity before-hand—beyond the intimate spaces of friendship and loved ones. We decided to close this first gathering to "outsiders," that is, people who do not share in an Arab self-identification. Here is what we wrote in what we called an "ally statement":

Who is invited to attend the gathering?

This gathering is open *only* to Arab and Arab American women, girls and transgender people.

Why a gathering for only Arab and Arab American women, girls and transgender people?

Currently, there are virtually no spaces in the U.S. for Arab women to speak to each other in candid, intentional ways. We have found that when we do speak about our issues, we end up spending a great deal of our time respond-ing to stereotypes or educating/explaining to other people about the Arab world; Arab history; gender and sexuality in Arab families and communities, etc. It is for this reason that we have created AMWAJ as a space expressly for women, girls and transgender people from the Arab region. We believe that in order to fully enrich and contribute to such a movement, every community needs spaces in which its members can focus on internalized issues and speak frankly about these issues that are difficult to give voice to.

AMWAJ activists modeled our gathering after the "I Am Your Sister" con-ference honoring Audre Lorde. Harnessing the wisdom of other "third-world" and women-of-color feminist collectives that have come before them, AMWAJ activists created new possibilities for transcending dominant masculinist and colonialist concepts of what can and what cannot be discussed or fought for. We were contributing to the emergence of a diasporic Arab feminist politics, a multi-issued, feminist politics that seeks to dismantle sexism, homophobia, imperialism, and racism and refuses to be silent on the ways these power structures operate within Arab families and communities. Yet while we maintained these commit-ments, we could not escape the predicament that has circumscribed antiracist, anti-imperialist Arab feminisms: how can we speak frankly about our experiences in ways that neither reinscribe Arab bashing nor engage in Orientalism?

Decolonizing Arabness

Collective projects such as AMWAJ have fostered new visions for social justice that are aiming to transcend bifurcated and simplistic options represented by the "cultural" self and the "political" self that force activists to choose between speaking about internal issues or working on externally focused causes such as war and racism. The overt ways that anti-Arab racism operates—with and through the themes of family, gender, and sexuality—elucidate that these categories of oppression are linked and cannot be dismantled separately. During the Israeli siege on Gaza in January 2009, I heard a guest on National Public Radio claim that Israel will continue to have the right to attack Palestinians as long as "Arabs love their guns more than they love their children." While this statement is loaded with assumptions about Palestinian culture and Palestinian mothers, it also reflects a dominant U.S. and Israeli discourse that justifies violence and occupation. A fuller analysis of empire takes seriously the gendered and sexualized logics through which empire works.[19] Yet we also need to take heed of critiques of U.S. empire that focus only on the center of power and turn a blind eye to the range of issues that matter in the everyday lives of the people who are targeted by the empire, thereby subsuming Arabs, Muslims, and South Asians, for instance, into scholarly and political discussions as but targets of the war, and contributing to their disappearance as human subjects and agents. I believe we need to broaden our analysis of the empire. How are Arab diasporas, for instance, articulating who they are, determining their community boundaries and who is included and excluded against the invasive and shifting relations of power central to U.S. imperial formations? I believe we need to struggle beyond crisis mode, create alternatives to the sense that the external attacks are so profound that "we can't take anything else on right now." What are the historical conditions and power structures through which anti-imperialist social movements determine what constitutes violence or what forms of violence are worth ending? How will we define the fragility of life and what forms of life are worth fighting for? Arab diasporas live life on multiple tracks—our days are built upon the divide between the internal and the external, "the communal" and "the political." Sometimes these tracks seem to exist side by side, and sometimes the gulf between the two seems impossible to bridge. Navigating the multiplicity can be maddening, yet, I believe, it can also be liberating. By unlocking the rigid back-and-forth between Orientalism and anti-Orientalism, we can respond to imperialism and Orientalism and we can also transcend the reliance upon the figure of the "woman" or compulsory heterosexuality to determine the survival of "Arabs" in "America."

7

Inanna

DUNYA MIKHAIL

Translated from the Arabic by Elizabeth Winslow[1]

Like many of my other poems, "Inanna" is a voice against the childish actions of war.
Inanna, in this poem, goes back to her country (Iraq) and meets with her people.
Although she loves them, she actually "yells" at them. Her voice is a mother's voice in
front of embarrassing actions.

I am Inanna.[2]
And this is my city.
And this is our meeting
round, red and full.
Here, sometime ago,
Someone was asking for help
shortly before his death.
Houses were still here
with their roofs,
people,
and noise.
Palm trees
were about to whisper something to me
before they were beheaded
like some foreigners in my country.
I see my old neighbors
on the TV
running
from bombs,
sirens
and Abo Al-Tubar.

I see my new neighbors
on the sidewalks
running
for their morning exercises.
I am here
thinking of the relationship
between the mouse and the computer.
I search you on the Internet.
I distinguish you
Grave by grave,
Skull by skull,
Bone by bone.
I see you
in my dreams.
I see the antiquities
scattered
and broken
in the museum.
My necklaces are among them.
I yell at you:
Behave, you sons of the dead!
Stop fighting
over my clothes and my gold!
How you disturb my sleep
and frighten a flock of kisses
out of my nation!
You planted pomegranates and prisons
round, red, and full.
These are your holes in my robe.
And this is our meeting . . .

2 DEFYING CATEGORIES

Thinking and Living Out of the Box

8

Between the Lines

YOUMNA CHLALA

These poems were written at the turn of the twenty-first century, during multiple global crises, and at a time when Arab identity was a contentious topic in the United States. They are about dislocation and reinvention, and the tension between the individual and the collective whole.

Heba always wears headphones when she paints. She takes a class every
    Tuesday
and Thursday. All because a critic in the local freebie newspaper said she had a
    great ability to create texture. She is like Tunis—turquoise and sunrises. In
    the next paragraph
he wrote: *unfortunately, Heba cannot draw.*

Still, she decided against Medicine, Geography, Architecture.
Every two hours she gets up to drink coffee. Her sketches are nude, hands at
    their side, throats throbbing between collarbones.

This makes all her boyfriends uncomfortable.

She imagines herself at the Whitney wearing all white, knitted cap and flat
    sandals,
like an old man. Her parents went to Hajj last week. Her father has been putting
    aside money since she was in high school and once, her brother stole it
    to buy music. She sent them money from her art scholarship. Her mother
    packed long robes, olive oil soap and
a box of fig cakes for the airplane. Heba was pretty sure her father was
    disappointed that
he could no longer smoke in the sky. She picked up that habit from him, early on,
when he came in her room to watch her paint at three a.m.

Mourning

syrupy marmalade spread on toast, burnt
the edges, a charred sandbox

irrepressible fires inside rivers, the Euphrates
screams and rises with the Tigris
emptied bells on ringing rooftops, the Church of the Nativity
stands and hollers parallel to Al Aqsa

in the tenderness of morning,

who would have imagined miles of mirrors, imploding?

Tangled

I circle my accent, seeking my tail. Clip a thousand articles about the weather
in Beyrouth, like stubborn hairs, stack them in a box without a lid, hope
that fire rescinds memory, moves back rain. Righteousness in simple acts of
solitude. Camus capitalized Suicide and we clerk and sort identity. You came
back with a diamond necklace, *Allah* spelled out like stars, the refugee camp
might miss it, don't believe in collective memory. Found a pen that belonged
to my childhood, a lake in the south, seven tones of blue, green, green, blue

9

Quandaries of Representation

MONA EL-GHOBASHY

Observant or not, Muslim women face a host of well-known stereotypes: that they are dependent, shackled by the strictures of their religion, and all-around unfree. Such stereotypes are compounded by the many "representational entrepreneurs" in today's media who are eager to speak for and about all Muslim women. The author discusses her experiences with the sometimes humorous, sometimes sobering expectation that she represent and embody the category of the Muslim woman. Rather than speak for all or even some Muslim women, she argues that she can speak only on her own behalf.

Ever since I was fifteen, I have been trailed by curiosity. Once in tenth grade, while waiting in my high school guidance counselor's office, an elderly secretary got up from her desk and came over to where I was sitting to ask me, in a too-good-to-be-true New York accent, "Excuse me, deah, are you in religion?" Perfect strangers have been no less inquisitive about my head scarf. "Excuse me, does your family come from the Caucasus?" asked an extremely solicitous and almost apologetic fellow passenger on a New York City subway car several years ago. She seemed to slink away in embarrassment as I shook my head and smiled, and I remember thinking that her demeanor suggested an academic elated at identifying a potential research subject.

Now that I reflect on it, the subway has been an especially rich space for strangers to graft onto me their passions, queries, and memories. Once, as I sat impatiently in a delayed subway car on the way to college one late morning in the early 1990s, a young African American man abruptly took off his massive headphones and turned to me, "Excuse me, can I read you a poem?" "Okay," I ventured hesitatingly, relieved that the train car was entirely empty save for him and me and a snoring man in the far corner. He unfolded a white piece of paper and began to passionately read its typed contents, an endearing ode to Malcolm X and Martin Luther King Jr. Then he folded the paper and carefully returned it to his pocket, explaining to me how it was wrongheaded to argue which leader was better, that both of their strategies were needed and had their place. He looked at me intently for affirmation, and I nodded smilingly. "Thank you, sister," he said, and then returned to complete absorption in the music piped through his headphones.

Once, in a subway car crammed with commuters returning home from work, an elderly Asian man got up from his seat and negotiated his way to where I sat. He leaned down to me and put his finger on the word "contrition" in the *New York Times* article he was reading. "Excuse me, can you explain to me the meaning of this word?" I was happy to oblige, as other passengers sneaked glances at us from behind their books and newspapers.

Once, on the N Train, an elderly olive-skinned man who had been eyeing me shyly gingerly volunteered that he was raised in Iran. I forced a polite smile; I was half-asleep and extremely fatigued from staying up all night to finish a paper. He said that he was Jewish, and that when he was a boy in Iran he memorized all of the Quran in school, and that his mother covered her head, "like you," making a hand gesture that framed his face to mimic a head covering. Perhaps he sensed some doubt in my eyes, perhaps he could not resist reminiscing about his childhood, but he then reached for his black wallet and carefully pulled out a remarkably well-preserved, sepia-toned photograph of a young, angelic-looking woman in a white head scarf. I leaned forward to look at the photograph, which he delicately placed in my hand. Its rippled edges were only slightly creased, and I was overcome by its beauty. He was positively beaming at me, and I beamed back at him.

Other encounters can only be described as bizarre, ranging from annoying but harmless quotidian intrusions to darker experiences that every woman faces in slightly different forms. On the extremely snowy Christmas Day of 2002, I made my way to Queens to meet my best friend who was in town for a short visit. Lost in a neighborhood suddenly made unrecognizable by mounds of snow and shuttered storefronts, I ducked into the only open store, a drugstore, to ask for directions to the café where I was to meet her. As I asked the security guard for its whereabouts, a customer standing in line a few feet away called out, "But do you know how to read? Will you be able to read the street signs?" The security guard stopped talking in midsentence, and we both turned to look at the man's smirking face in genuine puzzlement for several seconds, before it dawned on me that he was calling me illiterate. "You need to know how to read to figure out how to get there," he persisted. Cashiers, customers juggling their purchases and dripping umbrellas, and the security guard all turned to me, and time seemed to stand still. I sputtered, "I'm studying for a Ph.D., you bigot," and he retorted, "Yeah, well I have a law degree." I turned and sped out of the store, fighting back tears as I inhaled the bracing winter air.

My head scarf also attracts attention in Egypt, where I was born and now frequently return to conduct research and interviews. "You look like that over there, or do you wear that just when you come here?" I'm constantly asked. My interlocutors are puzzled and sometimes impressed when they learn that I look the same in Cairo and New York. Some seem to think of it as a badge of honor, though I point out that it entails absolutely no bravery to be *muhajjaba* at an elite institution like Columbia in a hypercosmopolitan, novelty-friendly metropolis like New York. After September 11, 2001, almost everyone in Egypt asked worriedly, "How do they treat you over there? Is it really bad?"

I have not experienced any harassment, but instead an outpouring of touching concern from colleagues, friends, and even solicitous strangers. But many hundreds of Muslims in less rarefied circumstances have indeed had their lives turned upside down by September 11. In the immediate aftermath, the most that I had to worry about was how my students would perceive me, and whether I could maintain my composure and walk into class on September 13 to steer a discussion about an event I literally could not comprehend. Other Muslims, Sikhs, and non-Muslim Arabs contended with physical harm, verbal abuse, social ostracism, loss of livelihood, and government harassment.

Over the years, as the American government's military and political intervention in the Middle East has intensified, the curiosity of others has honed in on my supposed exceptionalism. The vast majority of Muslim women are oppressed, goes the conventional wisdom, and I seem different. It must be because I live in "the West." "You look so elegant, but would you be allowed to dress this way in Egypt?" a woman I didn't know once asked. A perfect stranger sitting next to me on a flight from Cairo to New York tried to strike up a conversation by pointedly asking, "Do you always travel alone?" Instead of puncturing the widespread American conviction that all Muslim women are so downtrodden that they cannot dress freely (or elegantly) or travel alone, I am unwittingly deployed to confirm such certainties.

I have come to expect that, after delivering a public lecture on some aspect of politics in the Middle East, someone will invariably ask me a question about women and why they are so oppressed "in the Muslim world." At one and the same time, I am turned into a sanitized "liberal Muslim woman" who speaks unaccented English but also a credible insider able to "explain" my coreligionists' deplorable treatment of women. Equally revealing are the plaudits I receive for being "strong" and "articulate," well before my interlocutor has had a chance to learn anything about my politics or preferences. I cannot help but think that such projections have much more to do with what others graft onto me than what I am and how I see myself. And so I am alternately amused and sobered by how others wish to package me.

Lest I appear to be whiny or caviling, let me concede that there is a necessary amount of reduction in every quotidian transaction. Superficial cultural small talk is often serviceable in everyday conversation, particularly between strangers. Since I am identifiably Muslim because of my head scarf, it is inevitable that my appearance will become the subject of attention. As I wait to pick up clothes from the cleaner, it is entirely ordinary for the owner to make friendly conversation by referring to my head scarf and asking whether it means I come "from the Arab," which segues into a comparison of the weather in South Korea and Egypt and how New York's weather is really quite ideal because there are four distinct seasons, a discourse that ends with me claiming my cleaned clothes and the dry cleaner pleasantly wishing me a nice day.

Yet there remains a fine line between harmless everyday cultural interactions and the quandary of unwittingly being made to represent and somehow stand in for all Muslim women, everywhere, at all times. The task of representation entails negating the manifold stereotypes that stubbornly cling to Muslim women, a task I am reluctant to take on. As it was and continues to be for African American and Asian American women, the burden of deflecting stereotypes is especially acute for Muslim women at this historical juncture, buffeted as they are by unceasing attempts to "reform," "liberate," "uplift," and "empower" them by a motley crew of individuals, institutions, and national governments. As an identifiably Muslim woman, I often feel torn between countering pernicious stereotypes and resisting the mantle of representation that battling stereotypes entails.

When I am called upon to speak from a Muslim, Arab, or Muslim female "perspective," I always wonder: is there one Muslim/Arab/Muslim-female point of view? Do all Muslim women have the same positions on all issues, or even one single issue? I doubt that anyone would claim that Episcopalian or Reform Jewish or Catholic women have a single perspective, so why are millions or even thousands of Muslim women assumed to hold a uniform point of view? Muslim women are divided by national origin, generation, class status, level of religious observance, level of education, and political orientation. What is meant by statements such as "Muslim women are oppressed" or even "In general, Muslim women are unfree"? Conversely, it makes no sense to me to think that one person can be emblematic or representative of "Muslim women," even if it is done positively, as when attempting to identify a spokeswoman or "positive role model" for Muslim women, such as former Turkish prime minister Tansu Çiller or former Pakistani prime minister Benazir Bhutto or Iranian human rights lawyer and Nobel Prize laureate Shirin Ebadi.

There is a reason to be suspicious of the zeal to represent Muslim women. I have in mind the cottage industry of instant celebrities and "public speakers" eager to speak about and for "Muslim women." This sort of representational entrepreneurship is especially prevalent in the United States and countries in Europe with substantial Muslim minorities, where every few years a Muslim woman is trotted out as an exemplary role model to her "sisters." Inevitably, she is carefully packaged as a freethinker and courageous gadfly eager to "speak the truth" to her coreligionists.[1] Such entrepreneurs almost always adopt a lecturing, hectoring tone, speaking down to real Muslim women. They excoriate "Islam" for its oppression of women (sometimes its "Muslim men") and demand that Muslims "speak out against the fundamentalism in our midst," or some similar trope that is strategically deployed to launch lucrative careers as professional identity peddlers.

As is so common with disingenuous attempts to address "the community," the audience for such self-appointed spokeswomen is not their community but the publishers, talk-show hosts, and think tanks eager for more sordid tales of the backwardness of Muslims and the oppression of Muslim women. Far from valiantly subverting stereotypes, such manufactured missionaries are deeply invested in upholding stereotypes, confirming the comforting belief that Muslims are a benighted lot, incapable of any positive action and clinging to not a single redeeming value. So they must wait for the brave missionary to come and save them from themselves. Without the stereotype, the entrepreneurs have no traction.

Self-anointed representatives are a far cry from people with more modest and truer aspirations, those individuals who work away from the limelight, who live and work among the communities they seek to empower, who understand the sociological structures and intricate layers of inequality that ensnare Muslim and non-Muslim women alike. I cannot help but recall Virginia Woolf's cutting words, no less true today than when she published them in 1938:

Money is not the only baser ingredient. Advertisement and publicity are also adulterers. Thus, culture mixed with personal charm, or culture mixed with advertisement and publicity, are also adulterated forms of culture. We must ask you to abjure them; not to appear on public platforms; not to lecture; not to allow your private face to be published, or details of your private life; not to avail yourself, in short, of any of the forms of brain prostitution which are so insidiously suggested by the pimps and panders of the brain-selling trade; or to accept any of those baubles and labels by which brain merit is advertised and certified—medals, honours, degrees—we must ask you to refuse them absolutely, since they are all tokens that culture has been prostituted and intellectual liberty sold into captivity.[2]

I do not share Woolf's suspicion of all institutions, but I wholeheartedly identify with her aversion to loud publicity seeking and self-promotion, the sort of entrepreneurship and scramble for representation now routine when it comes to "Muslim women."

Any organized attempts to reduce Muslim women, whether ones that seek to "represent" them or ones that seek to "liberate" them or both, ignore the variation in their life circumstances. Some Muslim women are indeed downtrodden; others are not. Those Muslim women who are oppressed are oppressed in different ways and for different reasons. The same goes for those Muslim women who are emancipated. A genuine concern with diagnosing and alleviating oppression must grapple with unsexy sociological facts and political dynamics that do not make for good copy or riveting confessional narratives. Serious students of gender oppression tackle the variation head-on; hawkers of Muslim women's oppression smother inconvenient facts to serve their agendas.

On a more rarefied plane, attempts to represent or speak for Muslim women by definition must mute their unique selves. Real Muslim and Arab women are extraordinarily diverse, as the contributions to this volume make so amply clear. Like other human beings, they are fraught with ambiguity, contradiction, and inconsistency. I understand the need to suppress idiosyncrasy for purposes of sociological classification and policy intervention for poverty alleviation or literacy promotion, but I do not trust the zeal to flatten Muslim women's diversity by self-appointed spokeswomen and overnight do-gooders.

Each Muslim woman is an irreducible self, capable of speaking on her own behalf. When conceptualizing the self, I find myself returning again and again to Edward Said's final words in his beautiful memoir, *Out of Place*, where he ruminates on the multiple sources of the self:

I occasionally experience myself as a cluster of flowing currents. I prefer this to the idea of a solid self, the identity to which so many attach so much significance. These currents, like the themes of one's life, flow along during the waking hours, and at their best, they require no reconciling, no harmonizing. They are "off" and may be out of place, but at least they are always in motion, in time, in place, in the form of all kinds of strange combinations moving about, not necessarily forward, sometimes against each other, contrapuntally yet without one central theme. A form of freedom, I'd like to think, even if I am far from being totally convinced that it is.[3]

10

Dyke March, San Francisco, 2004

Many Are Intrigued by the Fact That I Am Also a Belly Dancer

Happy/L. A. Hyder

Happy/L. A. Hyder spoke at the 2004 Dyke March in San Francisco. Held the night before the Pride Parade in June, it is attended by thousands of lesbians from around the world. The 2004 theme was "Uprooting Racism," and authors-activists Jewel Gomez and Elana Dykewoman also addressed the gathering. As it turned out, they used similar words to talk about our local lesbian community and the world at large, focusing on strength, diversity, respect, and freedom when speaking to the necessity of "uprooting racism."

Thoughts of strength also pepper her writing about being a belly dancer—along with feminism and sensuality. It is really not an oxymoron to put these side by side, since the art of belly dance, leaving off the negative connotations given to it, celebrates the strength of women.

Dyke March, 2004

Let me look
drink in the energy of these hills
the revelry in our corner of eden . . .

Welcome to those here from around the globe joining us as we do the Dyke March San Francisco style . . . showing off our strength and growing numbers as young to old make choices to live in a way that is still new and being sorted out.

It's been only thirty years since dykes started coming out in record numbers. Much had to happen from there to here, where the word "lesbian" is spoken openly and seen in daily newspapers without always being in a denigrating context.

And here we are—together . . . from the very old-school style to the new-style gender benders—for it is true that even the most high femme among us is bending gender to her own desires.

The dyke community has always been, at our best, available to the processes that make this day's inclusive, open, and fired-up energy possible. This same energy is what we must use to change the face of racism—and to manage the great efforts it is taking to heal a society mired in racism—just as we are changing the face of who one can be in this world. We were all raised to be racists. It is endemic to our society and kept vital by a corporate-controlled media whose job is to keep us from questioning the profit motives that perpetuate wars and a poverty-based society.

We were all raised to be racists, and for many people of color this has taken a heavy internal toll. For everyone, the external toll is devastating.

The blatant racism against Arabs in this country is nothing new . . . nor is it isolated. It's cousins with the racism against all people of color.

It's just that we Arabs are the people to hate at the moment—we are the most visible "other," a position foisted upon any population being decimated . . . and let's be real—the Palestinians are being decimated, the Iraqi civilization has been bombed to dust, there is a push in the government to make a preemptive strike against Iran, and the list goes on—and it goes around the globe and its face is also Latin, African, Asian, those native to all lands, and most especially those who are Native to the U.S.

As dykes, we are hardly fooled by the stated desire of the U.S. government to help the women in Arab countries. This government has, for years, been installing right-wing fanatics in positions of power around the globe as they undermine women's rights here as well.

Women in Middle Eastern countries were not veiled under punishment of death until quite recently (and are not all Muslim). Women in Middle Eastern countries enjoy many freedoms and are highly educated. These women have always participated, and continue to, in their countries' struggles at all levels of the spectrum—by educating girls in secret as well as openly demanding and participating in the reforming of their governments. Women of Middle Eastern descent—meaning from North Africa and from Southwest and Central Asia— have always been politically active within the U.S. as well.

So what can we offer in the midst of our celebration and keep right on celebrating? Looking at our rainbow of colors within all our ethnicities gathered on this hill in the name of "Uprooting Racism," I see strength.

I believe that as dykes, knowing what it is to be spit upon and made *other* puts us somewhat ahead of the game. The trick is to bring this afternoon's energy and spirit with us for use on a daily basis.

That means we give each other the respect we deserve, we strive to understand each other in a compassionate way, and we keep the lines of communication open in dialogue. Remember—"difference" is not a dirty word.

Neither is "forgiveness." We've all made mistakes we've regretted deeply and all hold on tight to at least one grudge. When we come together in respect, with compassion, and in dialogue, we can forgive ourselves and others . . . and we can gather our strength into a power we can wield in the world.

We are more powerful than we can imagine—otherwise, why has so much energy been expended to keep us invisible? Now take a look around at how visible and vibrant we are!

And, imagining a world where peace and justice are respected and lived concepts, let's use this energy from today to do whatever it is we do best, and let's, collectively, vote for people who work with peace and justice as their goal.

Many Are Intrigued by the Fact That I Am Also a Belly Dancer

Many are intrigued by the fact that I am a belly dancer. I have lived and worked in San Francisco since 1969. Within two months of landing here from Worcester, Massachusetts, I purchased my first real camera. Within the first year, I began jazz and then belly-dance classes. Each of these endeavors came from long-held desires to be an artist (I was so tired of trying to take artsy photos with an Instamatic camera) and to dance.

Raised, as we all are, to be heterosexual, I held that role as my own until the early 1980s, when I came out, claiming a lesbian identity. At that same time, I became involved at the San Francisco Women's Building as a member of the Vida Gallery collective. It was here that I learned to bring my visceral knowledge of racism, classism, and sexism into the theoretical and into a practical proinclusion stance.

I have at times been questioned, because of my very feminist sensibility, about my belly dancing . . . especially how I justify performing, considering the less than feminist way this dance is viewed. For me, it all stems from my first real belly dancer, whom I saw at the age of five or six at a huge *maharajan* at an outdoor pavilion in Connecticut. The day was gloriously sunny and an adventure. My family sat at a round table covered with food and drink. The orchestra played classical Arabic music. At some point, a dancer was introduced, and I ran up to the stage to watch.

Although I had seen dancers before at smaller venues, mainly church picnics, this time it was different. I was mesmerized. I remember the dancer as tall, with very long black hair, wearing a red, black, and gold costume with a shiny gold-coin belt. She was so majestic, and she could spin and spin and spin. Then and there, I knew, I would belly dance someday, and although I always held the kernel of this desire, I never really considered it until I was in San Francisco where belly dance was already very popular in the early 1970s.

I worked for a year with Jamilla Salimpour, well known as *la mama* of early belly dance, getting down the basics. I feel it takes about a year to be comfortable with moves unfamiliar to our bodies. The next year I worked with Nakish, an African American dancer with years of jazz behind her. Here I got a sense of performing large. I have been shaping my solo performance on my own since then, and I occasionally collaborate on a piece. I should mention I was the only Arab and one of the few women of color in these classes and in my social circles at that time.

I understand belly dance to be many things and watch as tribal dance is embraced, where dancers are more covered up, have tribal markings on their faces, and wear heavy tribal jewelry. Their beautiful dancing is very choreographed and tight. My training is cabaret—it is more playful and, yes, seductive. I prefer a good-size space to dance in, allowing me to move across the floor with large movements.

There are well-defined theories of the dance coming from imitating and celebrating birthing, and although I can see that as true for some steps, I like to think it came, also, from women simply entertaining each other in the harem. Music and dance are in all cultures.

Truth is, cabaret belly dance is a sexy and sensual dance. What dance isn't? Even ballet can be overtly sexual. My guess is it is the amount of skin shown in a belly-dance costume that is the problem—plus the overt nature of seduction— and the image of belly dancers that has been shown in film as dancing for (nasty-seeming) Arab men. It seems to me that in mainstream media this depiction is part of the overt racism toward Arabs, and so the dance is made sleazy.

Another example of the misconception of belly dance comes from a number of years ago, when I attended a huge belly-dance event. Performers from around the globe danced for the discerning eyes of their peers and for admirers of the dance. One local dancer was around six years old. While performers were given the space to perform (that is, it was not a tip-the-dancer event), this youngest of performers was interrupted by a man in his (my guess) late forties who sexualized her by walking from the back of the auditorium and placing his (most likely) single dollar bill in her dance belt. I was the only one, at least in my immediate vicinity, to be outraged. This man not only sexualized the little girl but also turned her dance, and by extension the art of belly dance, into something needing male approval and specifically performed for male pleasure.

Wherever it began, most of the Arabs I know love this dance for many reasons, including showing our exuberance and celebration of life as a people. Most other connotations given it have come from outside of our societies and cultures.

A few years ago, I danced at a Hyder family reunion. My brother, Ed, an excellent drummer, had two other fabulous musicians playing, and Marie, a cousin I had not seen since my preteen years, sang beautifully. My favorite comment came from an older female cousin who called my dancing "elegant."

In the Bay Area lesbian community, I am known as a visual artist and a dancer. In the early 1980s, I met dancers Sharon Page Ritchie, African American, and Sylvia Castellanos, Mexican American. We perform in various configurations to this day. We were the first out lesbian belly dancers, and I do not recall being confronted with questions about our choice of dance in what was then a jeans and flannel-shirt culture. I believe this is because we always dance from a place of strength and power. Our lesbian and feminist audiences loved us—and still do.

My mother and the church ladies love the dancers too and occasionally get out on the floor themselves, handkerchief in hand or using hand gestures. I remember a woman in a shimmy dress coming to a small church picnic and dancing in the middle of a circle of about twenty smiling and clapping women. My mother always encouraged my dancing and came with me the few times I performed when visiting her on the East Coast.

My favorite story concerning my mother and my dancing happened when she was visiting me in 1989. Although I had come out in 1981, I was not out to my family. Many of us refrain from coming out to families who do not live nearby. I wanted so deeply to tell my mother, who was seventy-four at the time, so I could be fully honest about my life. We went to Golden Gate Park, and I told her as we sat and watched swans on a beautiful pond. We cried together, and we held each other, and we confirmed our love.

A few days later, I was scheduled to perform with Sharon and Sylvia at a dance celebrating a lesbian-of-color conference, which I also attended. My mother came to see me perform. She had met a number of my friends and so was taken care of as I donned my costume. I could see she was enjoying the performance as we three danced together to open the set. When it was time for my solo, I made sure to spend some time dancing near her front-row table in the large hall. As I was dancing and women were yelling, my mother sat with a big smile on her face, throwing me kisses.

This is the essence of belly dance to me. It is a joyous dance, really. It is performance as ritual with the dancer as an emissary of the erotic, bringing the sacred with the profane, holding the sensual and celebrating the sexual.

Belly dance is one of the few dance forms where the audience is actively engaged by the dancer. Is it any wonder that this dance of power and strength performed by flagrantly seductive women sure of their own abilities is denigrated?

Postscript 1, 2006

Lebanon is being bombed and attention has been successfully drawn away from the apartheid wall and the plight of the Palestinian people.

In reading the above writing, I was surprised by my mention of voting in my Dyke March speech until I realized I still had some hope that Al Gore, a reasonable man, could become president in 2004. I am generally unavailable to hope and was not surprised by the chicanery and the outcome. I am, by the way, a Green Party member.

I am from the first generation to grow up with television as part of our daily lives. We saw firsthand the growth of the black civil rights movement out of a harsh reality largely hidden from most of us in the 1950s post–World War II haze of seeming abundance. As we came into our teen years, a favored president was assassinated, and we left those teen years protesting, or going off to fight, and many to die in, the Vietnam War. We came into our twenties with determination to change the world. And, indeed, much has grown out of the many movements to follow the civil rights model.

On a good day I still hold the belief that peace is possible—or do I see it this way in order to hold on to the semblance that sanity will outlast the destruction? I have great shame and great anger toward the United States, my country of origin, for the cruelty and oppression and inhumanity perpetrated daily in my name . . . within this country and around the globe . . . and at those politicians who refuse to listen to the people they work for.

Only knowing of the many good people and projects happening to counter the destruction keeps me from becoming a puddle of grief. I look at my writing from 2004 and understand the need for a hope based in reality and wonder at the resilience that keeps people dancing all over the world.

Postscript 2, 2008

Recently, I attended a panel on traditional arts. Enjoying the speakers, I was brought upright in my seat when the male Romany presenter declared, "My people see belly dancers as being no better than strippers."

Rather than speak out in the moment, which I now regret, I waited to speak to him after the panel. He was not available to hear my comments and was dismissive from the start when I told him my ethnicity and that I have been performing what is called belly dance for forty years. He later argued with me while I attempted to explain where I believe the denigration of dancers comes from, which I will pass on here.

Photo Discovery, a book of rarely or never-before printed images, contains three pictures with women performing in the streets with male musicians— "Berber Entertainers, Tangiers" (Albumin Print by Fred Hardie, presumed American, 1870s), "Egyptian Dancers and Musicians" (Photochrome, Anonymous/France, ca. 1890), and "Gypsy Girl with Lion" (Gelatin Silver Print, Lala Deen Dayal, India, 1901).

These women, covered from head to toe, were often the sole moneymakers for their families. Just as often, the women may have been rejected by their families for performing in public—although their financial support was not rejected, and the family may have sent them into the streets to make the money in the first place as the only alternative to starvation.

Whatever the reason, many of these women were seen as bringing shame on the family, and, whether they ended up as prostitutes or not, a very real possibility, they were treated as outcasts.

(A bit of an aside here: The reality of prostitution lies with the male species and with women being denied access to most ways to make a living without being dependent upon a male. Prostitution, obviously still existing in our modern day, has "sister" professionals dancing in strip clubs. Although I believe both professions are legitimate, I also believe these women are still caught in that double bind of being needed and being denigrated for their services.)

I was thrilled when I saw Jack Shaheen's portrayal of the portrayal of belly dance in his film *Reel Bad Arabs*, as he respected the dance and dancers at the same time as lambasting the way the dance was used to denigrate Arabs. I was in an almost all-Arab audience at the DIWAN Arab Artists' conference at the Arab American National Museum, and I had held my breath when that segment began, wondering where it would take us. Jack was there, and I thanked him later for his comments, telling him I had been dancing for many years. He, in turn, thanked me, saying he thought long and hard about how best to include that segment.

It is an interesting thing, being a feminist and a belly dancer. Performing the dance is exhilarating, and I am always a little dazed when I am through. Since I do not dance all of the time, I immerse myself in the music and movement whenever I am to perform. Having an appreciative audience is a wonderful thing. To still be dancing and performing in my sixties is, too.

11

The Pity Committee and the Careful Reader

How Not to Buy Stereotypes about Muslim Women

Mohja Kahf

A surge of publication about Muslim women recasts old Orientalist fodder, the Western stereotype of the Muslim woman as Victim, and its companion stereotype, the Muslim woman as rebellious Escapee from Islam. The author calls the widespread discourse of this stereotype "the Pity Committee" and calls the equally biased, apologist reaction against it "the Defensive Brigade." A close reading of a New York Times column titled "Sentenced to Be Raped," about a crime against a Pakistani Muslim woman, illustrates almost all the seven key elements of the composite Victim-Escapee stereotype. The author cautions that real sexism exists among Muslims and should not be brushed aside; it is just not that different from sexism among other peoples. Demonizing Islamic difference and assuming Islam and Muslims to be inherently or exceptionally sexist do not help the work toward gender justice. Five strategies, the author suggests, can deconstruct the stereotype about Muslim women and keep the focus on the work toward gender justice. They are thinking critically, engaging in dual-fronted critique, finding cross-cutting parallels, remembering history, and refusing to erase economics.

Publication about Muslim women is a hot commodity today. We have had the *Princess* trilogy by Jean Sasson, *Infidel* (2007) and *The Caged Virgin* (2006) by Ayaan Hirsi Ali, *Honor Lost* by Norma Khouri (the 2000 book about honor killing in Jordan that was proven a hoax), and hosts of others. "Muslim" is not the same category as "Arab," and such writings cover Muslim women from varying ethnicities. All this new discourse on Muslim women, on closer glance, is not so new; much of it rehashes an old story: the Muslim woman as Victim, and its flip side, the Escaped Muslim woman.

In the Victim stereotype, the Muslim woman is chained to a harem lattice being beaten, raped, murdered for honor, or fill in your choice of oppression here by the Muslim father, husband, imam, or fill in your choice of harem master, while Islam, the tribe, her society, and so on look on approvingly; "the West" rides up on a white horse and rescues her; fade to The End. This story dates back to romantic literature, and the Byronic plot of a white man saving a harem girl continued to thrive throughout the heyday of colonialism, part of the White Man's Burden narrative. The Escapee story follows the same plot but is narrated by the Victim herself, who casts off the shackles of Muslim patriarchy all by her Nancy Drew self. Then she runs into the arms of the waiting West, or at least embraces a Victoria's Secret shopping spree.

This Victim-Escapee narrative is promoted by what I call the neo-Orientalist Pity Committee. It is not a real committee, but the Orientalism is real, no matter how many people think Edward Said outdated. The Victim-Escapee stereotype appears at every level of culture, pop to high. It is hegemonic, which means it is not seen as a stereotype but as The Truth: that Islam is exceptionally, uniquely, inherently evil to women seems to be one of the received truths of our era, axiomatic. It knows no bounds: left- and right-wingers, feminists and nonfeminists, religious and secular folk in the global Western conversation subscribe to it. Self-Orientalizing Muslims assume that the things this discourse says must be true, given the overwhelming "evidence." The Pity Committee thrives in imperialist contexts, so it is riding high today with the U.S. occupying Iraq and waging war in Afghanistan, its story becoming dearer to its subscribers by the hour.

Join the Pity Committee, and you too can consume a fresh Muslim Woman Victim Flavor every season. The job of mascot for the Pity Committee, Escapee of the Month, is a tempting career opportunity, if you are a Muslim woman. If you sign up, the Pity Committee will give you a book deal much plumper than the one I got from my small publisher. All you have to do is have a victimization story—clitoridectomy or arranged marriage will do as well as honor killing. If you do not have one, you can make one up, like Norma Khouri, and still be believed by a readership primed by centuries of bigoted images of Islam.

Real Muslim sexism, like Christian, Jewish, Hindu, Buddhist, secular, and other sexisms, exists. Real Muslim women have victimizing experiences. But to be the feted mascot of the neo-Orientalist Pity Committee, you have to use your Escapee Story to demonize the whole Muslim world, or at least one whole Muslim country (Afghanistan, Saudi Arabia, and Iran make good choices today). And you will locate the salve for women's oppression only in the West, which earns sainthood for gender equality in your narrative. Your story, for best effect, ought to align with U.S. foreign policy and consumerism, or at least with the war on terror.

However, let's not leave out what I call the Defensive Brigades, or Muslim Apologists, the underdog camp in global discourse dominated by Western terms of reference, but no less wrong because it is the underdog. Books speaking this discourse are not typically sold at Barnes and Noble. To find it, you must read mosque newsletters, Muslim chat rooms, and conservative-press offerings in Muslim locales. This camp's knee-jerk defensive discourse on Muslim women demonizes anyone attempting to change the status quo and, more important, utterly fails to address the real issues of sexism in Muslim societies.

What gets lost in this ideological tug of war (besides Truth and Beauty, which are always, you know, sacrificed)? The jihad for gender justice pays the price. Yet the work goes on, often in quiet little underrecorded ways. Meanwhile, readers committed to gender justice without demonizing can resist the pull of both sides, the Pity Committee and the Defensive Brigades, through critical thinking, dual critique, and other strategies.

Case Study: The Pity Committee and the Careful Reader

In June 2002, a woman named Mukhtar Mai, in the remote village of Meerwala, Punjab Province, Pakistan, was gang-raped by members of a powerful feudal clan. A provincial tribunal without the authority to render such a verdict decided that she would be raped as revenge for the alleged sexual assault the overlords claimed that her fifteen-year-old brother had committed against a woman in their clan, a charge apparently concocted to cover one of their cronies' own rape of the boy. Mukhtar Bibi's father pounded on the door of the house where he learned she was being raped, and later put his shirt over her and walked her home, where he and her mother comforted her. The village imam, Moulvi Abdul Razzaq, expressed outrage about the crime at his pulpit, defying the rich clan, as did a Pakistani journalist who wrote of the crime in a local paper. The story did not gain the attention of the international presses for some time. Shariah justice came swiftly: within weeks, Mukhtar Mai was awarded a half-million rupees in damages, and the rapists were given death sentences. However, the defendants appealed to the higher Multan court, where (Western) evidentiary law helped them get their death sentences revoked. Ms. Mai took the case on to the country's supreme court. Pakistani women's groups rallied to her support.[1] Meanwhile, Ms. Mai took the monetary award and built a girls' school in her village. This place is where she chooses to remain: in her provincial hometown, doing the tasks she has taken on for her community.

Mukhtar verified the facts in an interview appearing in *Islamica* (2005), an English-language magazine published by an ethnic mix of Muslims based in Amman and Chicago and oriented toward traditional Islam.[2]

I first heard about the Mai incident from my colleague at the University of Arkansas, Susan Marren, an American feminist literary scholar. She sent a link to a *New York Times* article by a Nicholas Kristof, titled "Sentenced to Be Raped," which broke the story to the U.S. public on September 29, 2004, more than two years after the incident.[3]

Kristof opens with jocular reference to his being in Pakistan to "help Bush track down Osama." (Are we framing the Muslim woman's victimization within the war on terror yet?) Kristof says, "I can't say I've earned the $25 million reward. But I did come across someone even more extraordinary than Osama." Mukhtaran is not the sort of "rogue" he usually writes about, he says. (We do not hear about Muslim women who are rogues in mainstream Western discourse, by the way, because a rogue is not a victim figure.)

Kristof issues this missionary statement of ideological purpose: "I firmly believe that the central moral challenge of this century, equivalent to the struggles against slavery in the 19th century or against totalitarianism in the 20th, will be to address sex inequality in the third world." If only he had put a period after "inequality." The *New York Times* columnist goes on in terms that suggest he has never set foot in a women's studies department in his native country: "The plight of women in developing countries isn't addressed much in the West, and it certainly isn't a hot topic in the presidential campaign. But it's a life-and-death matter in villages like Meerwala, a 12-hour drive southeast from Islamabad." Gender injustice is never a life-and-death matter in the West, it seems. Kristof then narrates the rape itself: "As members of the high-status tribe danced in joy, four men stripped her naked and took turns raping her. Then they forced her to walk home naked in front of 300 villagers."

"In a society that values modesty, how would three hundred villagers watch her walk home naked?" my friend Susan Marren asked me. Even though she has no background in Middle East studies or South Asian culture, Susan at once spotted this plot hole in the *New York Times* journalist's story.

"In Pakistan's conservative Muslim society," Kristof goes on, "Mai's duty was now clear: She was supposed to commit suicide." Apparently, Pakistanis think alike on this issue across all urban and rural classes. A quote from Ms. Mai's brother that, if read outside Kristof's loaded context, simply explains why being raped drives many to consider suicide is cited by Kristof as if to suggest that her brother wanted Mukhtaran to commit suicide. It is Kristof's sole quote from any of Mai's family, so it almost implies that this stance is her family's position, which is scandalously misleading, compared to what Ms. Mai herself says in the *Islamica* interview about her parents' staunch support. Kristof cites another village gang-rape victim who did commit suicide.

His "fieldwork" for establishing the suicide mandate thus finished, Kristof constructs the next sentence to suggests that Pakistanis do not find rapist behavior shocking or criminal: "But instead of killing herself, Ms. Mai testified against her attackers and propounded the shocking idea that the shame lies in raping, rather than in being raped." The reader is excused for assuming, based on Kristof's passage, that Ms. Mai is the first rape victim to press charges in Pakistan and that shame is never an issue for rape victims in America.

Absent from this conclusion is another (alleged) rape victim in the story, the upper-class woman whom Mai's younger brother was accused of assaulting. And where is any discussion of Mai's young brother, himself a rape victim? These other rapes complicate the claims Kristof makes about gender and Muslim or Pakistani attitudes.

Following the lead of Susan's careful reading, we find more spotty logic here: If the overlords did not think rape a shocking crime, why would they have arranged brutal vengeance for the alleged first rape? Even if the first charge was fabricated, they had to fabricate something that would make a plausible motive for revenge.

Next, Kristof mentions the sentencing of Mai's rapists: "The rapists are now on death row, and President Pervez Musharraf presented Ms. Mai with the equivalent of $8,300 and ordered round-the-clock police protection for her." We are not told how a society that unanimously views rape victims as worthy only of suicide sentences the rapists to death and awards punitive damages to their victim. Kristof seems to minimize the money by putting it into dollars, a unit where it looks like a pittance, out of its context in a poor region of Pakistan, where it is a small fortune. He glides into a portrait of what Mukhtaran Bibi did with the money—open a girls' school in her underserved village.

Here Kristof injects a plot-thickening moment—he stalks around, with Bryonic drama, one imagines, in "the area where the high-status tribesmen live," and senses danger! It is almost as if he is the hero in this story, as if the government had not already, uh, recognized this threat and given Mukhtar an armed guard. Kristof here says he talked to a "matriarch in a high status family," who belittles Mai—surprise—with malevolence worthy of Joan Collins's *Dynasty* character. This partisan woman's insult is made, without sense of irony by Kristof, to represent the view of all Pakistan toward Mai.

Kristof concludes with this wild-eyed sentence, which should live in infamy, so broad a spray of hatred does it emit: "So although I did not find Osama, I did encounter a much more ubiquitous form of evil and terror: a culture, stretching across about half the globe, that chews up women and spits them out." He concludes, in classic Pity Committee fashion, "We in the West can help." In a postscript a few weeks later, he promises that if you send a check for Mai, he will be sure she gets it, bringing the reader into the role of Western rescuer of the Muslim woman Victim.

My friend Susan, the careful reader, said, "How does a woman as shunned and isolated as he paints her up and open a school? Wouldn't there be *people* helping her do that?" Indeed. Prodded to investigate by Susan's queries, I found online Pakistani forums where vastly different versions of the story were floating amid lively debate. "Not that they're the whole truth either," Susan said, but the possibility of these variations makes the narrative more understandable. Kristof's story by itself did not make sense to an intelligent reader.

Key Elements of the Victim-Escapee Stereotype

Kristof's column illustrates many elements of the Pity Committee story of the Muslim woman as Victim-Escapee.

Mute Marionette or Exceptional Escapee. The Pity Committee's Muslim woman is not a speaking subject in her own right but framed within the narrative of the Westerner giving her a voice, who alone is able to construct and analyze her plight. The modern-classic example is Jean Sasson's original 1992 *Princess*, which the American author wrote ostensibly because her fabulously wealthy, well-traveled subject could not speak for herself.

In the late 1980s, there was a clamor for "authentic voices" to represent minorities; it was thought that only someone from that same identity could "get it." This idea turned out to be misguided; in the end, it is about discourse, not identity. But discourse from "authentic voices" of Muslim women dutifully came out, playing largely the same game at one less narrative remove. When the story is told by the woman herself and not a Western proxy, she is constructed as exceptional, a solo act, who against all odds escaped from this brutal culture and found her voice—never because there were factors within the culture that enabled her to develop a voice.

Meek Mother. Muslim mother figures are made meek, minimized, or invisible in the Victim-Escapee stereotype. For example, the English version of first-wave Egyptian feminist Huda Sharawi's memoirs (misnamed *Harem Years* in the English abridgement and translation by Margot Badran of 1986) leaves out the strong personality of her Circassian mother.[4] In constructing the Victim's victimhood or the Escapee's exceptionality, the Pity narrative tends to eliminate empowering relationships with sisters, grandmothers, and girlfriends and to ignore homegrown feminisms. Kristof's mise-en-scène admits no indigenous Pakistani feminisms and portrays other local women as either helpless doubles of the victim or evil pawns of patriarchy such as the "high-status matriarch."

Forbidding Father. Lurking about the Victim or Escapee story is a cruel male authority figure. The Muslim father figure is no kindly Austenian Mr. Bennet, who is equally patriarchal, but endowed with ambivalent feelings and an understandable wish to see his daughter protected through conformity to accepted social norms. The Muslim father's motivations are inscrutable, or thoroughly evil. Mai's father, who played a heartbreaking role of trying and being unable to protect his daughter and then holding her hand through the aftermath, is completely absented from the *New York Times* story. The reader is given the vague impression that the father gave his daughter up to be raped.

Rotten Religion. The idea that Islamic values could play positive roles for women is inadmissible in Kristof's Pity Committee perspective. Mukhtaran Bibi's strong Islamic faith, which she says in the *Islamica* interview was an integral part of how she coped with the horrific experience, is left out. Ubiquitously, Western media, and many secular Muslim feminists, take the word "shariah" (Islamic law) as code for "oppression of women." In Mai's case, shariah championed the woman, punishing the perpetrators in the initial ruling far more severely than any Western law code would. The term "shariah" is erased in Kristof's telling (remember, it is only a Western value to punish rapists). Islamic terms are mentioned only when they can stand as icons for misogyny. The concerned local imam, whom Mukhtar Bibi in the interview describes as having been "a continuous source of support," is absent from Kristof's version. In the 1993 film *Not Without My Daughter*, a classic of anti-Islam hysteria, the Islamic call to prayer is used as a voice-over during a wife beating. This metonymy, suggesting that the very rites of Islam are implicated in sexism, has a concrete effect on Muslims living in the West, training a hostility on the symbols and practices of their religion that can make them the target of court actions, harassment, or Islamophobic violence.

Cruel Country. The Pity Committee's Victim-Escapee story casts the Muslim country (any of them, take your pick) as unmitigatedly woman hating. Kristof's title, "Sentenced to Be Raped," implies that Pakistan itself approved Mai's gang rape. The country's police and court systems count for nothing in the syntax of Kristof's writing, but these authorities arrested, booked, charged, tried, sentenced, and jailed the rapists. They appealed, as defendants do, even in the United States. Even their appeal is based on due-process law, a requirement for a democracy, but Pakistan gets no credit for having this legal protection for all defendants.

The *New York Times* columnist does not even acknowledge his fellow journalist, the local writer who was the first to publish anything about the incident, despite the risk to him (but not to Kristof) of vengeance by the rich local clan. Here is another Pakistani man in the story who is not behaving like a villain, wiped from the *New York Times* version.

Kristof's Mukhtar, unlike the Mukhtar who speaks in the *Islamica* interview, is unconnected to her own society by bonds of love, relationship, and self-identification; she is without succor, except for that which he urges from the West. Audience members who hear me present this material sometimes come up to me saying they did walk away from reading the *New York Times* piece believing that Pakistan, and Islamic shariah, condoned the gang rape. Careless reading, or a result of the rhetorical strategies of the column itself?

Erased Economics. Absent from Kristof's column is any analysis of class. If you include class, the cruelty in the story starts to look awfully familiar to American readers, not exotically "Izlahmic." Mai's words in her *Islamica* interview, in sharp contrast, indicate that she sees herself suffering from her class positioning, not from her religious identity and only faintly from her gendered subjectivity. While she expresses bewilderment that anyone would think her rape condoned by Islam, she repeatedly brings up her status as a poor person. Asked why most villagers did not support her, she says, "The others were afraid. They would think 'we're poor, and maybe if we stand up, the tribal lords will abuse us in the same way.' In their hearts these people were with us, but they were scared to show this." She adds a class-based critique of the police and the government: "They never pay attention when such things happen to poor people anyhow." The *Islamica* interviewer, bent on scoring Defensive Brigade points about religion, glides over Mai's class analysis, too. But the interview form lets her articulation of the problem come through, whereas Kristof obliterates her voice under the weight of his condescending, Islamophobic, culture-war triumphalism in pseudofeminist drag.

Vile Veil. One element lacking in Kristof's column that is usually found in Pity Committee narratives is the veil, starring as the most oppressive device since the rack. The veil—inexplicably to most of those women who wear it—has become a visual icon of Islamic sexism. You can almost always spot a Pity Committee book by its cover: the image of a woman with face half hidden by a veil is nearly de rigueur. Although covering the face, a mode of dress preferred by many women on this earth, is not in itself oppressive, this image is used on these book jackets within a discursive community where such a sign signifies "Islamic sexism."[5]

Ms. Mai never asked to be enrolled as the West's Victim of the Month. Her story spills over the edges the stereotype. If Pakistan were such a dungeon for women, for example, why does Mukhtar Bibi choose to go on living there, now that she has the means to leave? Nevertheless, the editorial and publishing discourses in which Kristof operates shape the story to their Pity Committee horizon of expectations. Muslim women get recruited to Victim or Escapee roles whether they go willingly or not.

The Charge of the Defensive Brigade

There's more to the Mai story, illustrating the second half of the dynamic, where the Defensive Brigade enters. This damage-control squadron (not a real armed troop, mind) is generally reactive, whereas the Pity Committee is powerful and proactive and sets the agenda. It is a discursive community that sees its role as "defending Islam" against ideological onslaught. It reifies or freezes Islam into one mold, much as does the Pity Committee, but from the opposing direction. Where the Pity Committee vilifies, the Defensive Brigade sugarcoats, rather than seeking genuine complex analysis of gender relations in the world of Islam.

After the U.S. press gets hold of the Mai story, there is a defensive backlash in the Muslim presses, in Pakistan and globally. The president of Pakistan, who is in a category of Autocratic Rulers, not the same as the Defensive Camp but here overlapping with it, rightly perceives the American espousal of Mukhtar as mired in neo-Orientalist Pity Committee agendas. Wrongly, he bans her from traveling abroad. When this textbook Defensive Brigade move backfires, making more negative press for Pakistan than her trip abroad might have done, he lifts the ban, grumbling, with inexcusable insensitivity, about women making money off being raped.

Due to the efforts of pro-Islam Muslim feminists such as Asifa Quraishi of the Muslim women lawyers group KARAMA, several important U.S. Muslim organizations were not deterred by the Defensive Brigade, and supported her visit, arranged by the Asian American Network Against Abuse of Human Rights. Mukhtaran Bibi comes to the United States, speaks at women's rights venues, and collects money for Pakistani earthquake victims and her expanded school project. However, Aslam Abdullah, editor of the *Minaret*, a publication of the Islamic Center of Los Angeles, questions the veracity of Ms. Mai's version of the rape in a posting on Pakistan Link, and some other Muslims decry her U.S. appearances as opportunistic "publicity stunts." Turning from substantive criticism to ad hominem attack is a typical Defensive Brigade move. At the extreme, and most reprehensible, end of this mode of response, she becomes the target of threats from hyperdefensive Muslims.

Muslim women are recruited to be mascots for the Defensive Brigades as well. This mascot is Good Daughter, in contrast to Rebellious Escaping Daughter on the other side. The Token Muslim Woman on boards and committees often finds herself in Muslim Apologist roles, whether she is comfortable in them or not.

The Apologist Camp also typically accuses any initiative to change the gender status quo as being tainted with Western imperialist influence or funding. The life-altering, country-altering, brutal violence done to many countries by colonialism cannot be forgotten. Nor is imperialism in the past; its new invasions continue. But there is a time to acknowledge that whatever injustice imperialism has done and is doing, there are indigenous injustices needing redress.

In Jordan, for example, there is a campaign to strengthen laws against honor killing, a crime not condoned by shariah but originating in pagan tribal values and violating Islamic principles. (Honor killing *is* treated as a crime in every Muslim country; the problem is the lack of severity with which it is treated.) The Jordanian law pertinent to honor killing, Article 98, comes from Napoleonic Code, in fact, not from Islamic law. Yet the local Jordanian initiative against Article 98 and its sister, Article 340, has been smeared by Jordanian Islamists as a Western-inspired, Zionist-aided attack on traditional Jordanian family values.[6]

Dealing with fallout from the tug of war between bigoted Pity Committee discourse and bigoted Defensive Brigade reactions is a terribly secondary thing to have to worry about when your time should be spent fighting honor killing itself. And this example is just one illustration of how the Pity Committee and its nemesis, the Defensive Brigade, create a bad dynamic that throws a wrench in the gears of actual struggles for gender justice. Thus, we see how stereotypes distort us as human beings; they take our energy away from real ethical development. When we say that Muslim women do not fit the Victim stereotype, we must not step away from our moral obligation to change the realities of Muslim sexism, just as we must work against endemic sexism in America.

Is it possible to participate in gender justice initiatives, to produce discourse on Muslim women, to include Islam and gender issues on one's syllabus, or even simply to read a book about women and Islam and not reinforce the battle lines? Yes, with some strategizing.

Slipping Past the Pity Committee and Dodging the Defensive Brigade

Native American activist Winona LaDuke says use multiple strategies.[7] Five strategies might help to counter Pity Committee and Defensive Brigade discourses: critical thinking, dual critique, cross-cutting parallels, refusing historical amnesia, and awareness of economic inequities.

Critical Thinking. Good old-fashioned "If p, then q" logic works. Thank you, Aristotle, no matter how sexist you were, and thank you al-Farabi and Ibn Rushd, the medieval Muslim Aristotles. My colleague questioned the story for logical inconsistencies, and this examination led her to seek other versions for comparison.

Dual Critique. Critiquing oppression in the global Muslim community while simultaneously critiquing oppression committed by and in Western societies, waging a double-fronted battle, pries gender work out of both camps. Here we might recall 4:135 from the Quran's chapter on, appropriately, "women." It is a passage that construes the criticism of one's own society as a strength: "Stand out firmly for justice, as witnesses to God, even against your selves, or your parents, or your kin, and whether it be against rich or poor: for God can best protect either; and follow not your desires that conflict with justice, and if ye distort or decline to do justice, then truly God knows what it is that ye do."

Cross-cutting Parallels. Kristof demonizes a far-off culture, one he sees as stretching across the *other* side of the globe, but how far away from New York is the misogyny that produced the rape of Ms. Mai? Ask Kitty Genovese, whose screams were heard by thirty-eight of her Manhattan neighbors when she was raped and murdered in 1964. Or ask the victim of the 1989 Glen Ridge, New Jersey, rape, in which four football players raped a mentally retarded young woman. Is it so hard to imagine, in an American setting, that star athletes from prominent families might find some local support for their abuse of a woman without many resources? "Supporters Surround Coach Accused of Sex Crimes," reads an August 11, 2008, headline about six girls at a Warrensburg, Missouri, high school who reported sexual molestation by their popular coach, only to have their school and town turn hostile on them.[8] Muslim sexism exists; it is just not that different from sexism among other people, despite having its specific local forms. Bizarrely, some reified notion of religious and cultural difference is made the culprit of sexism in Kristof's column. Sexism in a "conservative Muslim society" is not seen as akin to sexism in "the West." Seeing the world of Islam as utterly alien in this way, as an "It" rather than a "You," involves one amnesia and two blindness, against which the careful reader can strategize.

Remembering One's Own History. Historical amnesia strikes those persons who posit inherent Islamic misogyny, amnesia about the fact that the same debates about women's rights, which have been swirling in the Islamic world in the past 110 years, have been raging in the United States and Europe for the past 150 years. The variation amounts to a few decades more or less of social change, depending on the Muslim country, even despite the added difference that religious law is still in play in many Muslim nations and not in the West. I know it is not politically correct to say Muslim countries are two decades behind, or three or four, on some issues. Nor is it accurate in every case, but it is a useful start for comparison: The United States was a traditional agrarian patriarchal society around the time of the Industrial Revolution and went through lengthy stages of development with concomitant social change. Many Muslim countries started as traditional preindustrial agrarian societies a number of decades ago. The specific decade differs by country, but all have crammed into a shorter time span many developmental stages similar to the ones that served as catalysts for social change in Western countries. In many Muslim-majority countries these processes were complicated, also, by the debilitating effects of foreign colonial subjugation.

First-wave feminism happened in the United States from the 1860s to the 1910s, in Egypt from the 1880s to the 1930s, and although some specific issues differed, the processes were similar. The 1930s to 1950s were actually more progressive in the Arab world, the Indian subcontinent, Iran, and Turkey than in the United States. In the United States, in the 1950s a woman could not get a bank loan without a husband, and the cult of feminine domesticity held sway. Feminism woke up again in the United States and flowered into a mass movement in the 1970s. The feminist campaign to change American attitudes about domestic violence, for example, got a toehold on public policy only in the late 1970s (later in Texas, I am told). Why, then, should it be a surprise that in the 2000s, Saudi anchorwoman Ebtihaj Mubarak is spearheading the first major public campaign against domestic violence in Saudi Arabia, a country preindustrial until 1936, and that she is encountering Neanderthal attitudes? Do Americans simply not remember how recent was their own society's Neanderthal resistance to feminist reforms and that gender equality is still a jihad in progress, unevenly realized across states?

Economics Not Erased. Martin Buber once wrote, "When a culture is no longer centered in a living and continually renewed relational process, it freezes into an It-World."[9] An It-World sees people as commodities, treating Muslim women's stories as chips in a global game of domination and consumption. Those people who reify "Islam" as the ultimate cause of the abuse of women in the "third world" seem blind to the fact that the global devastation of organic communities by transnational corporations with terrifyingly little accountability and the frightening gap between the world's poor and those countries whose consumption levels have strip-mined everyone else's economies are the biggest factors in the well-being or lack thereof of the vast majority of Muslim women. These economic injustices have likewise undermined the well-being of poor American women and have impoverished working-class people in the United States. Here is the biggest cross-cutting parallel, and the biggest abuser of women, and we are all kin in the struggle against it. It is why the wars are being fought. Not over culture.

In this equation, an individual Muslim woman can be just as much the oppressor and the rogue as can a Muslim man, and a Western man and woman. Go on, ask me how: because we who are privileged consumers and happen to be Muslim women have just as much power as any other privileged person to consume and destroy, particularly when we ally with institutions of power. And if you think that what we wear or do not wear on our heads has anything to do with that power or its misuse, I will need to bop you on the nose.

12

History's Traces
Personal Narrative, Diaspora, and the Arab Jewish Experience

KYLA WAZANA TOMPKINS

In this essay Kyla Wazana Tompkins looks at the politics of feminist autobiography in terms of the specific intersections of race, gender, and diaspora that construct the Arab Jewish experience. She theorizes the possibility of an Arab Jewish experience that is oriented not toward or through Zionism but rather in the politically and culturally productive possibilities of diaspora.

I was asked to write this piece, theorizing my experience as a non-European or Arab Jew, in the fall of 2005, but it took me quite a while to make myself sit down and write. In one of my initial e-mail exchanges with my dear friend Evelyn Alsultany, she wrote: "I know that theorizing personal experience induces nausea for you, but I think you have an important contribution to make around your experience on how few people (both Jews and non-Jews) get that one can be an Arab Jew." To which I replied: "Well, as you know, nausea for me usually masks raging ambivalence. So this should be an interesting place to explore."[1] I am marking this ambivalence because I want to be clear that I have mixed feelings about self-narration as a genre of feminist writing, such that, as you can see, I am hesitating before beginning.

Life writing has a hallowed place in feminist theory, both as a liberatory practice and as a teaching tool. Chandra Talpade Mohanty has discussed the importance of "testimonials, life stories, and oral histories [as] a significant mode of remembering and recording experiences and struggles." Writing, she argues, "often becomes the context through which new political identities are formed."[2] These genres have been both politicizing for those women who have read these texts and recognized themselves and educational for those women for whom these texts functioned as doorways into subjectivities of which they had not previously conceived.

Life writing and autobiography assert the political importance of memory and agency as rhetorically and methodologically opposed to the otherwise hegemonic practices of History (with a big *H*, in which the canonized written record serves as the only record through which the past becomes visible) and Anthropology (in which the third world subject becomes visible as the subject of a first world gaze, a gaze that has typically identified the third world subject as bound to tradition). As such, autoethnography, the writing of one's life story into public visibility, is a hallowed and important genre of feminist writing, one that emerged directly out of the tradition of consciousness raising, and, as Mary Louise Pratt has written, postcolonial resistance.[3]

The other narrative genre that this mode of feminist writing comes out of is the nineteenth-century sentimental novel. In the United States the tradition of politicization through feminist writing goes back to the women's novels of the nineteenth century and the political movements to which they were tied. In particular, I am thinking of the early white women's feminist and abolitionist movement in which, to quote Christine Stansell, "women emerged into the public through novels long before they emerged politically." The reading politics of these novels encouraged women to *feel*, to identify and sympathize with the other in spite of difference, a politic that has been criticized by feminist critics in recent years for flattening out and obscuring the differences between subject and object of sympathy and thus upholding asymmetrical relationships.[4]

Despite Gloria Anzaldúa's radical intervention into the politics of identity, with her groundbreaking essay "La Concienza de la Mestiza," in which she asserts the fluid and strategic self-making of intersectional identities, many women's studies classrooms continue to use first-person narratives by women of color as positivist testimony and, worse, as an instrumentalization of suffering that facilitates the dream of diversity while reducing the work of understanding difference to the sentimental pleasures of witnessing someone else's injury.[5] Using writing by women of color solely in terms of the "realm of the experiential" implicitly makes the claim, as bell hooks has written, that writing by women of color has "no connection to abstract thinking and the production of critical theory."[6]

Thus, an unfair burden of realism is placed upon writers of color in both literature and women's studies classes. In classrooms where faculty are under pressure to provide coverage, that is, to provide visibility to as many subject positions as possible, first-person narratives are still seen as sufficient evidence of the critical presence of women of color in the syllabus. I do not want to deny the historical importance of theorizing experience, or the radical potential of the women's studies classroom, but before performing this role, I want to mark the importance of engaging these texts through strategic reading—and writing—practices.

To theorize from one's own experience calls upon the subject of the text to open herself and her story up to the world, to in some way make herself vulnerable at the same time as she makes a claim for political visibility. Effective life writing resists too easy spectatorial pleasure and guards the self against injury, but it also strives to work from something more than the classic—and incidentally, Christian—story of injury and redemption around which so much life writing has organized itself. Effective life writing seeks visibility for histories that are otherwise invisible, and in turn identifies and acknowledges the shared histories within and against which we, as readers and authors, are *mutually* made and obscured. Life writing is thus useful in the ways that it links the production of diverse subjects to history and strategizes about the possibilities for agency within a contemporary political landscape.

To know the other, Judith Butler has written, one must ask the question, "Who are you?" But, she argues, the ethical imperative is to leave the question always open: the question "Who are you?" must be asked again and again, and the answer must always be seen as incomplete. This point is crucial to understanding what it means to theorize experience, to narrate it, to read about the experience of the other, because it means beginning from the understanding that this narrative is always ongoing. "Who are you?" is a question that is never entirely answered; listening, like standing witness, can be a radically humble practice, one that functions without the expectation of completion.

Thus, I wish to be clear from the outset that in operating from a place of ambivalence about confessional writing, my own self-narration here is limited and strategic. I unveil myself, as it were, to answer the question that this book's authors have asked me: who are you? But I can offer only a contingent answer.

A Short Story about Crossing Borders

About a decade ago, my mother and I went to Morocco, she for the first time since she had left Morocco for Canada in 1963, and I for the first time in my life. Though I now shudder to think about how obnoxious it is, I had recently seen *The English Patient* and was pretty much taken up with khaki-and-linen romance. After a long flight from Toronto, I arrived at customs in Casablanca, wearing khakis and linens, and presented the officer with my passport, where my name is marked by my father's very English name, Tompkins. The agent looked at my passport and then back at my face two or three times, bewildered. "But," he said to me in French, "aren't you of Moroccan origin?" "Yes," I said. "Well," he said, stamping my passport casually, and with one more skeptical look at my outfit, "Welcome home."

I note this moment because it was the first time in my life that I was ever recognized as Moroccan, despite my ridiculously Orientalist outfit. I am not sure why it is, but my trip to Morocco was also the first time that I realized that I had facial and physical features that were indigenous to somewhere, someplace. A few weeks later, after traveling around the country, we flew back to Paris for a few days before going home to Toronto. The first night we went out to a bistro for dinner, where we had the bad luck to sit next to two really extremely rude Parisian couples. Assuming that we did not speak French, because my mother and I speak English with each other, they spent their dinner talking about us as though we could not understand what they were saying: "Filthy Algerians. Why can't they get their dinner somewhere else?" Once again, recognized as Arab, this time in an entirely different way.

I mention these incidents because they seem, even fifteen years later, burned into my consciousness as pivotal moments in my identifying as a Moroccan; they are much clearer in my mind than my time in Israel. Perhaps it is because the experiences were so entirely different from each other, yet, at the same time, they complemented each other so entirely: welcome in a country I had spent my life hearing stories about, recognized as exactly the same ethnicity three weeks later, with entirely different consequences. In both situations, I felt like I came into view, within the framework of a history I had always thought of as secret or private; there, in Paris and in Casablanca, I was visible in terms of a public history.

Interpellation: it is funny how you can be happily starring in the movie in your own mind (in my case and at that time, *The English Patient*) when the hailing gaze of another slaps you into history.[7] I have never been particularly committed to identifying with my paternal lineage (half-English, half-Irish), but growing up in Canada as a voracious reader of Victorian literature, I suppose I cannot deny that I grew up as a bit of an Anglophile. My cousin Claire and I refer to those moments in which we forget our roots as "cottage moments": those moments when you are trying on some item of clothing or contemplating buying some object and you think, "That would look great at the cottage," and then you remember that not only do you not own a cottage, but you have never owned a cottage and neither has anyone in your family.

Traveling from Canada through France to Morocco and back again, my mother and I traversed multiple colonial and postcolonial histories, and thus had to negotiate the different ways that we were read. In Morocco I put on a caftan and walked around invisible in an entirely new way: covered from neck to toes, no one looked at me twice, until I violated some corporeal norm, as I did frequently. One time, sitting in the front seat of a taxi on the way to Tangiers, I placed my bottle of orange Fanta (oh, the flavors of colonialism!) between my legs as I turned around to talk to someone in the backseat, only to be greeted by the shocked and disgusted eyes of the cab driver at my immodest body language. In Casablanca, I walked into the hotel bar by myself and had a drink with a group of men from the conference I was attending. Walking back to my hotel room, one of the men tried to kiss me: only later was it explained that my presence in the bar had somehow signaled my availability. Much of the time my crossing of gender norms seemed all the more serious because I look Moroccan; had I been blonde or more obviously Euro-American, well, that kind of behavior was to be expected. But to be Moroccan and behave this way: what a slut!

Since my trip to Morocco, I have thought and rethought these interpellatory moments. I have come to realize that they signify a kind of recognition that is not or has rarely been available to me in North America. In all of these situations, I faced different expectations because I am Moroccan, because I look Moroccan.

Growing up in Canada and now living in the United States, there has been less visibility. This invisibility is both a pleasure and a burden. On the one hand, like many others, I have borne the burden of self-explanation in a culture dominated by paradigms of assimilation into whiteness, in which, as Caren Kaplan has so lucidly written, "Jews and not others become 'white' in the specific context of U.S. white supremacy as it interacts with Euro-American anti-Semitism."[8]

But on the other hand, there are pleasures and privileges to being misrecognized, limited though they may be. I think of these pleasures as somehow linked to the geography of Morocco, which is located at the Gibraltar gateway between Europe, Africa, the Mediterranean, the Middle East, and the Atlantic. I feel identified with other Jews, with other Arabs, with Africans, with Mediterranean peoples. My physical presence is such that I am inevitably misread in North America, but that misreading opens up other pleasures, most particularly in the slippery freedom of misrecognition.

But this experience is true only some of the time, and it is a small pleasure compared to the lack of institutional power: for non-Ashkenazic Jews, to live as the product of a history that is largely invisible to History, as subjects whose contours are either not recognized or misrecognized, means balancing the politics of visibility and assimilation—the basic human need to *be seen* against the tiresome necessity of narrating yourself to the many who have no idea who you are. The last consideration, perhaps, involves trying to figure out how to do all of these things without figuratively blowing your own, or someone else's, top off. Yes, rage. Invisibility can be as enraging as it is strategically useful.

Many Arab Jews have experienced this invisibility in relation to common understandings of Jewishness: the expectation that we know or relate to Yiddish as the Jewish language, or that our religious practice takes the same shape as Ashkenazic or European practice (and thus that Ashkenazic religious institutions are sufficient to meet the needs of Sephardic communities). This invisibility functions through the equation that Ashkenazi = Jewish, through the unspoken but often articulated sense that we are less than other Jews, that we are backward, primitive, dirty, or uneducated—*barbarit*, as I was once called in Israel. But it also happens through the occlusion of Arab Jewish history from mainstream Jewish history itself, echoed through such benevolently ignorant responses as, "Really? You're a Moroccan Jew? I didn't know such a thing existed."

To be "such a thing" has meant living as the object of Euro-American Jewish disgust and ignorance; living against that sentiment has, at least for me, meant refusing to have my Arab identifications split from my Jewish identifications. For me, there simply is not one without the other; there is no hyphen, no halving of the self, no balancing act. The one simply means the other; they are synonymous.

Why do people not already know this history (about "such a thing" as us)? As they say, a question can be answered only when it ceases to be rhetorical and becomes material. I propose, as a starting point, five problems that both define and obscure the history of Arab Jews. The first is that we are a minority within a minority: out of an estimated 14.5 million Jews on the planet, only 20 percent define themselves as Mizrahi or Sephardic, and within that number, there are many smaller ethnic and national groups.[9] This diffraction of the Jewish experience undermines the political function of much mainstream Jewish history, which operates through putting forward a unitary Jewish experience generally organized around European history. Directly related to the politics of Jewish historiography, the second reason for our historic invisibility is that Sephardic-Mizrahi history has been overshadowed by the Holocaust, which has dominated Jewish historiography for the past half century. The third reason is that there are almost no Jews left in Arab countries, and thus the term "Arab Jew" has come to seem obsolete. The fourth is that the anti-Arab racism inherent to Israeli-Zionist state policy has worked, since 1948, to render the idea of Arab Jews oxymoronic, even impossible. The fifth is that it is almost impossible to conceive of non-Muslim Arab subjects within the public sphere today, inflected as it is by anti-Arab hysteria.

These five historical and historiographic problems form the framework within which Mizrahi identity and history has to struggle for space. For those

Mizrahim of my own generation, that is, we who were born into the diaspora, these issues are achingly immediate, because we face the possibility that those cultural ties that we grew up with, embodied in our parents and grandparents, are now becoming more tenuous, as those generations die off.

This issue is particularly powerful for those of us who live outside of Israel, who might choose our parents' homelands as primary sites of identification. I certainly grew up hearing more stories about Morocco than I did about Israel; my trip to visit Morocco with my mother was far more meaningful to me than was my trip to Israel.

Given these possibilities, what might it mean to articulate a critical Mizrahi politic? As a feminist committed to progressive social change, and to preserving an Arab-identified Jewish identity, this question is critical, particularly given the lack of cultural and social structures, Jewish and non-Jewish, that might exist to support such a project.

Gramsci has written, "The starting-point of critical elaboration is the consciousness of what one really is, and is 'knowing thyself' as a product of the historical process to date, which has deposited in you an infinity of traces without leaving an inventory."[10] In this formulation, history works as a process through which identities and subjects are created; to elaborate on or propose the possibility of new selves thus means first situating and taking account of oneself as a product of history. This taking account of oneself also involves placing the self in a critical relationship to what Chandra Mohanty and Jacqui Alexander have called the "archaeology of state practices," that is, the "dialectical relationship between the old and the new [that] provides theoretical and political cues in understanding contemporary relations and hierarchies."[11] I do not mean to imply that one can propose the formation of a new self as a radical departure from the present, or even as an idealized excavation and reencounter with the past. Rather, it is clear that in order to ask what might come, we must investigate the horizon of possibilities formulated by history, the contemporary workings of power, and the spatial dislocations of multiple diasporas. We must ask: what is the historical situation of the Arab Jew in diaspora?

(Some of) the Story So Far

Although I have used the term "Arab Jew" from the beginning of this essay, I am speaking about the populations that have been known as Sephardim and Mizrahim within the Jewish global community. These communities of Jews for the most part lived in Arab countries. The term *Sepharad* means "Spanish" in Hebrew and refers to those Jews who escaped the Spanish Inquisition in the fifteenth century, scattering to different parts of Europe, North Africa, and the Americas. *Mizrahi,* by contrast, comes from the Hebrew word for "East" and has been used to describe those Jews who lived in what might be referred to as the Orient: Iraq, Iran, Egypt, Lebanon, Libya, Syria, and Yemen, among other places. My own family comes from the country with the largest concentration of non-European Jews, Morocco, a country that contains several different ethnic Jewish groups, including indigenous North African populations, families whose ancestors fled the Spanish Inquisition in the fifteenth century, and families who have been in Morocco for millennia. These communities have not always existed in peace with their Muslim rulers: in many countries Jews were subject to repeated and cyclical violence, as well as sartorial and other restrictive and identifying laws.

In 1948, the year in which the state of Israel was created, there were 856,000 Jews living in Arab countries. Some historians believe that Israel established Zionist organizations in Arab countries to, as Sami Chetrit has written, "mobilize local Jews for emigration to Israel." By 1958, the population of Jews living in Arab countries had already been cut in half: by 1976, there were 32,190 left in Arab countries. Today, there are fewer than 8,000.[12]

The actions that Israel took to encourage emigration to Israel—however they are understood—and the congruent rise in anti-Zionist and anti-Semitic violence in Arab countries disrupted and nearly destroyed these cultures, scattering families and destroying communities.[13] Even after Arab countries outlawed emigration to Israel, there was massive immigration to the new state. However, communities also scattered to France, Canada, and the United States, leaving families like mine struggling to maintain relationships across several continents, languages, and cultures.[14]

To say that the Zionist state has been indifferent to the destruction of thousands of years of Mizrahi culture is an understatement. As Israeli Mizrahi intellectuals and activists have documented, from the arrival of Mizrahim in Israel until today, Israel has worked to construct an ideal Israeli subjectivity and culture organized around Ashkenazic norms and through the rejection of the Arab or Oriental.[15] From its inception, Israeli culture identified itself with European values and against what was termed the "primitive" characteristics of Mizrahim.

Following waves of immigration from Iraq, Yemen, Morocco, Algeria, and other Arab countries in the sixties and seventies, Ashkenazi-Israeli scholars puzzled over how to elevate the backward cultural mentalities of immigrant Mizrahim and Sephardim. Variously seen as "traditional," antimodern, and tainted by their Arabness, Mizrahi families arrived in Israel to be treated as second-class citizens. In turn, their children were subjected to aggressive discrimination in schools and taught to hate their own parents' ethnicity. To this day, the history of Jews in Arab countries is not a part of the public school history curriculum, denying Mizrahi children access to their own histories and their parents' and grandparents' languages. Zionist educational policies have ignored the histories of Mizrahim, focusing instead on Europe, the Holocaust, and a narrative of Israeli exceptionalism emerging out of a history of Jewish European (or Ashkenazic) thought.[16]

Constituting more than half of the Israeli population, Mizrahim and Sephardim long occupied, as Sami Chetrit has written, "the lowest rungs of Israeli Jewish society." And although, as Chetrit documents, Mizrahim have organized resistance movements to Israeli-Ashkenazi cultural hegemony and supremacy, notably with the "Black Panther" movements of the 1970s, only recently, with the rise of the ultra-Orthodox Shas Party, has Sephardic and Mizrahi cultural consciousness reemerged as a political force to be reckoned with in Israeli politics.[17] At times radically anti-Palestinian, at other times more moderate, Shas has attracted some of the Sephardic and Mizrahi vote by capitalizing on the lack of a Mizrahi presence, and lack of attention to Mizrahi issues, in either of the two leading political parties, Labor and Likud. Interestingly, liberal Ashkenazi Jews have responded by characterizing Sephardim as more likely to vote for a right-wing party; in fact, Ashkenazim and Sephardim in Israel vote for the "Left" and the "Right," such as they are in Israel, in equal numbers.

Mizrahim are often represented as "traditional" or "religious," in opposition to what is seen as the secular, more progressive first world Ashkenazic (sometimes, but not always, Zionist) culture. This opposition, which phrases Sephardic religiosity in Ashkenazic terms, disguises the progressive contours of historical Sephardic religious practice in countries like Morocco. Although much has been made of *dhimmitude*, the historical legal status of Jews in Arab countries required to pay extra taxes to maintain residence, and the *mellah*, the contained and segregated Jewish neighborhoods, much less documented are the intimate everyday connections between Jews, Muslims, and, importantly, indigenous peoples such as Imazighen and Bedouin in predominantly Arab countries.[18] The history of Jews in Arab countries includes civic and cultural partnerships between these populations, intermarriage, and conversion. As one might expect, Arab Jews and Muslims shared cultures, cuisines, traditions, and languages. Arab Jewish liturgy has a distinctively Arab sound.

Not to put too fine a point on it, a significant number of Jews *are* Arabs: we are Jewish Arabs; we are Arab Jews. The oxymoronic status of these otherwise simple and historically accurate statements seems remarkable but makes sense when we understand the ways in which the founding of the state of Israel, as a culmination of several generations of European Zionist activity, had to render the Palestinian Arabs abject and other, in order to justify what was an unconscionable theft of land and denial of legal status.

Judith Butler has argued that establishing the subject of a movement, or of any claim to rights, necessarily entails exclusion and abjection of the other.[19] The subject of the European Zionist movement was a "New Jew" whose Oriental traces had been resolutely rejected. European, secular, masculine, and, above all, militarized, the New Jew, as Todd Presner has shown, laid the racial foundations for the Zionist body politic that was formed against the *Ostjude*, or Eastern Jew.[20] This Eastern Jew was, within this early cultural Zionism, generally an Orientalized version of the German Jew, usually from Russia or any country east of Germany. As a foundational figure for the modern Jewish state, this important early Zionist figure of the "New Jew" was always already constituted against the Orient.

Mizrahi feminist scholar Ella Shohat has written about the strategies by which hegemonic Zionist ideas of Jewish history disrupted Mizrahi lives, histories, and cultures:

> In order to be transformed into "New Jews" (later Israelis), the "Diasporic Jews" had to abandon their diasporic culture, which, in the case of Arab Jews, meant abandoning Arabness and acquiescing in assimilationist modernization, for "their own good." . . . This rescue narrative also elided Zionism's own role in provoking ruptures, dislocations, and fragmentation for Palestinian lives, and—in a different way—for Middle Eastern and north African Jews. These ruptures were not only physical (the movement across borders) but also cultural (a rift in relation to previous cultural affiliations) as well as conceptual (in the very ways time and space, history, and geography were conceived).[21]

Shohat has written extensively about the links between Israeli anti-Arab racism and the terrible discrimination and psychic damage done to Mizrahim in Israel. The primary justification for the establishment of the state of Israel is now and has always been the Shoah, the Holocaust, making Israel and Zionism, as Chetrit has said, "European solution[s] to a European problem."[22]

The North American Context

In 1992, after the five hundredth anniversary of the European incursion into the Americas, radical Mizrahi and Sephardic activists began to rethink their own identities in relation to what has come to be called the "golden age" of Muslim Spanish rule, specifically the period between the tenth and the fourteenth centuries.[23] Because the first phase of the project of Spanish colonialism over-lapped with the final expulsion and forced conversions of Spanish Moorish Jews—in fact the same year—the five hundredth anniversary of 1492 provided an opportunity to rethink Mizrahi and Sephardi history and identity in conversation with the modern emergence of colonialism and empire and to turn back to the golden age of Spain as a model for interreligious, interethnic coexistence. Since then many new Marrano and Converso communities have been rediscovered in such places as Brazil, Colorado, and New Mexico.[24]

After that promising start, however, there has been very little scholarly work on the lives of Sephardim and Mizrahim in relation to the Americas; most writing is about the Mizrahi experience in Israel. But Mizrahim have suffered cultur-ally and economically in their North American experiences as well. In North America, the relative poverty of Mizrahi immigrants, and the entrenched racism of mainstream Ashkenazic institutions, meant that there was a lag time in creat-ing new institutions such as schools, synagogues, and cultural centers. Although Sephardim first emigrated to the Americas in the sixteenth century, the over-whelming number of North American Jews are Ashkenazic, particularly since the large waves of European Jewish immigration in the 1840s and 1880s. Those few Sephardic congregations that have remained intact since the North Ameri-can colonial period do not reflect the cultural and religious practices of the more recent immigrant groups. For instance, in Toronto, it took more than twenty-five years from the first arrival of Moroccan immigrants to create a Moroccan syna-gogue. As a child, I remember celebrating the high holidays in people's basements for years before there was an official Sephardi synagogue.

As I have written elsewhere, part of the decline of Mizrahi culture has involved the Ashkenazification of the Sephardic religious practices.[25] Dependent on Ashkenazic religious institutions, Sephardic liturgical and daily religious prac-tices have been colonized by Ashkenazic yeshivas, while even newly discovered Marrano communities have quickly been taken up by what might delicately be called the Lubavitcher outreach program.[26] The desire to preserve Sephardi reli-gious practices is in part the reason for the rise of the ultraconservative Shas Party; it has also led to a widespread new religious conservatism at least among the first wave of Sephardi immigrants, my grandmother's generation. This conser-vatism is profoundly alienating to those of us who would like to formulate egali-tarian religious practices while retaining a connection to our Sephardic history.

This situation is a critical problem for Jews like myself who long to find places where our ethnic and political identifications can be recognized, articulated, and developed. As recent immigrants facing, on the one hand, largely Ashkenazic

North American Jewish mainstream culture (for instance, B'nai Brith, Hillel, Canadian Jewish Congress, Hadassah, and the American Jewish Committee) and, on the other hand, largely Zionist Sephardic institutions (the American Sephardi Federation and Sephardic Education Center, among others), we need to find ways both to maintain a relationship to the cultures that our families came from and to recognize that living in diaspora offers the opportunity to create new alliances, borrow from other cultures, and reinvent ourselves.

There are groups, like the World Organization of Jews from Arab Countries, and the recently founded Jews Indigenous to the Middle East and North Africa (JIMENA), who are doing the critical work of preserving and articulating a Mizrahi culture. However, both of these groups seem to define Arab Jewish identity entirely within the terms of the Israeli state, thus failing to make progressive connections between their own Arabness and the cultural and political situation of non-Jewish Arabs, including Palestinians. In particular, JIMENA seeks to claim reparations for Jews who left or were expelled from Arab countries, leaving assets behind. The latter's mission statement problematically demands that "whenever the rights and concerns of the Palestinians are addressed in law or action, that the Jewish Refugees from the Arab Countries also be mentioned." Whatever the historical specificities of this claim from country to country, the goal of tying Arab Jewish rights to the Palestinian cause seems opportunistic and politically dubious, in the extreme.

Toward a Radical Mizrahi Subjectivity

In the recent past, the project of formulating a progressive Arab Jewish identity has come to seem more necessary but more difficult than ever. On the one hand, the Israeli-Zionist project has rendered the idea of Arab Jewishness oxymoronic, in the North American context; on the other hand, to put forward this subject, the Arab Jew, both flies in the face and puts oneself in the path of heightened U.S. racism toward Arab Muslims. As U.S. aggression in the Middle East has escalated following 9/11 and during the "war on terror," the two terms "Arab" and "Muslim" have become even more conflated than they were previously. More specifically, as Nadine Naber has written, Islam has become a racialized category, as American Muslims increasingly respond to dominant post-9/11 racism by constructing new racial formations organized around religious practices.[27] At the same time, the category of "terrorist" has become increasingly associated with Muslim Arab men and women. Thus, within public U.S. culture, the idea of a non-Muslim Arab is becoming obscured, while the choice to identify publicly as an Arab—when one has that choice—has become increasingly dangerous. To make oneself politically visible as Arab today is to risk being dangerously misread in the way that Arab Muslims are every day.

Perhaps this explanation is why many Arab Jews can and do choose to identify more as Jews than as Arabs (or, as a friend once said, more J than A), either suppressing any possible cultural identifications with the Arab communities and countries that they came from or giving in to the Israeli vision of Jewish history as inevitably leading to one Jewish people organized under the Israeli flag. One effect of these identifications is an intensified racism toward other Arabs on the part of Arab Jews, in an effort to disavow their own ethnic location.[28]

Yet racism against Mizrahim does not go away. Even when it takes the form of a benevolent ignorance on the part of Ashkenazi-dominated organizations or the Israeli government, racism against Arab Jews takes many forms, and in my experience, whatever a Mizrahi group's political affiliations, few are not aware of that fact. Thus, despite the absence of visible, politicized progressive Arab Jewish organizations, my own experience tells me that in diasporic Mizrahi communities a healthy dose of ressentiment still simmers, even as we have reorganized and reformulated communities in new countries. Whatever their reasons for identifying as Jew before Arab, Mizrahi assimilation is not seamless.

In reviewing some of the Mizrahi-Sephardi literature for this article, I was amazed to see how little of it, in particular those articles that address racism within Israel, also take up the problem of Zionism. Many of the articles that I read, including, surprisingly, most of the Israeli feminist articles on Mizrahi women in Israel,[29] took the existence of Israel as a given, leaving Palestinian losses at the hands of the Israeli state unquestioned while addressing the systematic exclusion of Mizrahim from positions of power in the Israeli public sphere.

Against the rise of the Shas Party and the ongoing desire on the part of Ashkenazi intellectuals to conflate Mizrahi political agency with the extreme Right, I believe it is crucial that Arab Jews begin to excavate the history and possibility of a radical Mizrahi identity, one that both rescues and protects the cultural legacies of those individuals whose ancestors and families lived in Arab countries while simultaneously opposing the ongoing oppression of the Palestinian peoples.

I am not arguing for a naive or ahistorical identification with Palestinians; too many progressive Mizrahim, and certain progressive Ashkenazim as well, seem to wish to use the Arabness of Arab Jews, and their undeniable victimization at the hands of Israel, to rescue an innocent or politically unimplicated Jewish subjectivity. This desire, it seems to me, was one reason for much of the 1992 celebration of the "golden age" of Moorish Spain, that fabled period of Jewish, Christian, and Muslim coexistence.

However much we can learn from that history, and there is a lot to learn, we cannot ignore the past six decades in which Mizrahim have not only paid an enormous cost, culturally and spiritually, but also participated in the survival of the Israeli state. Without indulging in nostalgia or denial, it seems necessary to find spaces (critical, geographic, cultural, and spiritual) where new Mizrahi identities (Israeli, European, in the Americas, and elsewhere) may be allowed to flourish, both locally and transnationally, that is, in conversation with each other across national borders.

I am thinking here about a sophisticated, transnational politics of location, one that includes the perspectives of Mizrahim in Israel, Europe, and the Americas. I am also thinking literally about space: the need for institutions, for religious, spiritual, and cultural spaces where progressive Mizrahim can convene to formulate new religious practice, compare histories, articulate strategies, and excavate diverse cultural practices in the service of formulating Jewish identities that will not be put to the service of an anti-Arab or anti-Semitic agenda.

Imagine a Jewishness that claims its Arabness without using that Arabness to naturalize claims to lands that are not or should not be ours, a Jewishness that rests comfortably in its transnational dimensions instead of seeking to force their resolution, a Jewishness that takes its displacement as a starting point for affiliation and alliance with other displaced peoples, and, perhaps most radically, a Jewishness that takes account of religiosity as a starting point for a logic of radical democratization that refutes both the secularization of liberal-democratic rhetoric and the lie that liberal democracies are secular. I do not mean to propose that the dream of such possibilities lies in one community alone, but I do hold that dream for myself and for future generations of diasporic Arab Jews.

Riffing off of Gramsci, I proposed earlier that the radical possibility of theorizing experience lies in rediscovering oneself as "a product of the historical process to date, which has deposited in you an infinity of traces without leaving an inventory." Consider what might happen if we, as Mizrahi Jews, cataloged our own inventory: what might we find, and what might our communities become?

3 ACTIVIST COMMUNITIES

Representation, Resistance, and Power

13

The Burden of Representation

When Palestinians Speak Out

NADA ELIA

> We must be specific, and we must be the people whose voice, whose proposals, whose values are considered by the international community to provide an end to war, to unceasing violence and to endless devastation.
> —Edward Said, memo to Palestine National Council, 1983

> Please do not bring up Palestine in your speech. This is a women's conference, not a political conference.
> —Betty Friedan to Nawal el Saadawi, at the UN International Conference on Women, Nairobi, 1985

Nada Elia explores how Arab American feminists are frequently invited to speak at various "progressive" events and conferences. The expectation, however, is that they will deliver some variation of one single narrative: the oppression of Arab women by Islamic fundamentalism. A discussion of the broader political context, namely, ongoing settler colonialism and the criminally racist nature of Zionism, is met with extreme hostility and the much abused charge of anti-Semitism. Nevertheless, after decades of being pushed to the margins, Arab Americans are forcefully moving center-stage and speaking truth to power. It is an extremely difficult position to be in, but the alternative, silence, is not a viable option for activists.

In late January 2009, in the wake of Israel's massive slaughter of innocent civilians in the Gaza Strip, which left more than thirteen hundred dead, more than five thousand injured, entire neighborhoods wiped out, and more than twenty thousand homeless, the British Broadcasting Corporation (BBC) refused to broadcast a video appeal by the Disaster Emergency Committee (a coalition of leading British charities including the British Red Cross, Oxfam, Save the Children, and ten other charities) to help the people in Gaza.[1] The reason given by the BBC was a desire to maintain "impartiality" in its coverage of the massacre, a twenty-two-day offensive launched by Israel from the air, sea, and land, against a weakened, quasi-starved, imprisoned people, the majority of whom are refugees and children. To maintain this supposed "impartiality," the BBC had not once referred to this carnage as anything but a war of self-defense on Israel's part, thus omitting all reference to the more than twelve hundred Palestinians killed by the Israeli military between 2005 and 2008. Also in its supposedly impartial coverage of this supposed "self-defense," the BBC had somehow failed to mention that, regardless of its own claims to the opposite, Israel is still considered the occupying power by the United Nations.[2] Occupying powers have no right of self-defense, only an obligation to withdraw comprehensively.

However, even as the voices that would have spoken for Gaza's dead and injured, for the refugees made homeless yet again, were not given airtime on the BBC, a parade of Israeli government officials and military officers used that channel to brush off the charge of war crimes, explain away, and justify the bombing of schools and residential homes.

The BBC's censorship of a Palestinian perspective may have been especially egregious, but it is does not constitute a departure from "Western media as usual." A few years earlier, on November 12, 2004, one day after Palestinian president Yāsir 'Arafāt passed away, the *New York Times* published five articles of analysis about him. Not a single one was by a Palestinian. As Hugh Sansom correctly pointed out in a letter to the *Times* editor, no other culture is so often spoken for by others, denied a public forum to express itself.[3] But this silencing too had occurred in the hegemonic media, and I, for one, know better than to expect the *New York Times* to allow for Palestinian self-representation. My essay here addresses the silencing of Palestinians that occurs in places where we are supposedly welcome, given a chance to speak for ourselves, rather than be (mis)represented. Although diaspora Palestinians are finally breaking through the wall of absolute censorship that once gagged us in mainstream Eurocentric discourse, many of us still regularly find ourselves in very hostile circumstances, where we are indeed invited to speak, but what we say, as we denounce our oppression, proves too jarring to our audience. In public lectures, in our workplaces and classrooms, in open-floor discussions with "progressive activists," in e-mail discussions with "transformative spiritual activists," in "grassroots antioccupation coalitions," or at conferences on "collective historical wrongs," Palestinians and their supporters are, at long last, making themselves heard, eloquently demystifying "the Middle East question," and speaking truth to power about oppressor and oppressed in Palestine, and many in the audience are objecting very loudly. Betty Friedan's patronizing comment to Nawal el Saadawi, made twenty-five years ago, still echoes today in various forums around the world where privileged and disenfranchised meet, supposedly to engage in productive dialogue. The arrogance of an American academic presuming to tell one of the foremost internationally recognized Arab feminist activists what she should and should not talk about is exemplary of the power dynamics in such settings. How would Friedan have reacted if an Arab woman had suggested she "control herself" and refrain from discussing anti-Semitism? What authority does Friedan have over Saadawi that entitles her to say, "Please do not bring up Palestine in your speech. This is a women's conference, not a political conference"?[4] Or did Friedan possibly think there is no such creature as a Palestinian woman, hence there could be no need to discuss Palestinian women's circumstances at an international women's conference, just as Israeli prime minister Golda Meir had declared in 1969 that Palestinians "didn't exist"?[5] Yet, even in 2010, Palestinians continue to encounter instances of this censorship and arrogance, as they seek to educate allies about the wrongs they have suffered, and continue to endure, while also trying to organize to end and redress these wrongs.

A more recent example of such silencing, or, rather, attempt at silencing, on a global scale, occurred at the 2001 World Conference Against Racism, Racial Discrimination, Xenophobia, and Related Intolerance in Durban, South Africa. There, the United States accused the pro-Palestinian contingent of "hijacking" the conference, because it insisted on having Zionism viewed as an unacknowledged form of racism. Yet surely, had a discussion of Israel's brand of racism and racial discrimination been welcomed at this conference, the Palestinians would not have been accused of "hijacking" it rather than merely contributing to it.

Zionism, the establishment of a settler-colonialist Jewish state in historic Palestine, achieved through the dispossession and displacement of that land's indigenous people, is indeed a form of nationalism that cannot be dissociated from racism, and as such fully belonged at the Durban world conference. Four hundred and fifty Arab Palestinian villages, out of a total of 550 in Palestine in 1948, were deliberately destroyed to allow for the creation of the Jewish state, and 82 percent of the Arab Palestinian population was displaced in that historic tragedy Palestinians call *Al Nakba* (the catastrophe). Today, 70 percent of the Palestinian population is denied the right to return to their homes, so that Israel can secure its exclusionary status as a "Jewish state." Indeed, as one reads the

UN definition of "genocide," it is evident that Israel was founded on the genocide of the non-Jewish natives.[6] Yet when Palestinians denounce this political
system, which privileges one religion and perceived ethnicity over another, they
are called racist themselves.

Nor did the Palestinians "hijack" the 2001 Durban conference, as was obvious
to all but Israel and its longtime champion, the United States. "This conference
presents a unique opportunity for the nations of the world to define, condemn,
and remedy racism and racial discrimination," said Reed Brody, advocacy director
of Human Rights Watch, emphasizing that the question of Israel's treatment of
Palestinians is only one of many before the conference. "This meeting is about
the millions of refugees who are fleeing racism but who find intolerance, about the
so-called untouchables of South Asia, about how HIV/AIDS disproportionately
affects people of color, about the unique ways racism and sexism interact, and
about racism in the application of the death penalty." But the United States, self-
proclaimed defender of freedom and democracy for all, staged a joint withdrawal
with Israel from the international conference, when it became clear that a significant number of delegations were also critical of Israel's treatment of the Palestinians. Then secretary of state Colin Powell explained that the U.S. delegation was
leaving because the conference was bound to fail because of its denunciation of
Israel. "I know we do not combat racism by conferences that produce declarations
of hateful language," Powell claimed.[7]

As was obvious to most participants worldwide, however, there was an addi-
tional layer to the cynical exploitation of the Palestinian tragedy going on at this
conference, for the "Palestinian hijack" accusation provided the United States
with an excuse to opt out of the conference, thus avoiding any discussion of reparations for slavery. As international human rights activist Ibrahim Ramey put it,
"Most of the NGOs in Durban suspected that the real reason for the [U.S.] withdrawal was the reluctance of the government to confront the issue of systemic
racism within the U.S. itself, and the African-American case for reparations."[8]
Thus, the United States avoided any discussions of the issues Brody mentioned
(racism in the death penalty, world responsibility for the AIDS epidemic, and so
on), as well as reparations for the descendants of enslaved Africans, by claiming
Palestinian "hijacking" of the conference. This move could have hindered coalition building among international projustice activists, were it not for the already
tarnished image of the U.S. government in the world, an image sadly further
tarnished since that conference, by the Bush administration's warmongering and
unconditional support for Israel, as the latter engaged in ever more serious violations of international law.

When the world's bullies continue to blame the victim, using any available pretext to avoid addressing the crimes they are committing, we need to keep in mind Audre Lorde's ever-pertinent observation, that we were never meant to survive, that our silence cannot protect us, because "the machine will try and grind you into dust anyway, whether or not we speak."[9] Lorde explains that only death can come from silence, whereas death, pain, fear, but also, hopefully, change can result from speaking out, and it is that last possibility that makes speaking out imperative.

How could the silence of the Palestinians protect them? Would the United States have addressed Israeli racism against the Palestinians, had the Palestinians not brought it up at the conference? History shows us otherwise. For decades, the United States has paralyzed international criticism of Zionism's violations of the Palestinian people's inalienable human rights by vetoing every UN resolution condemning Israeli policy or actions. Would the United States have stopped its financial, military, and political support of the Israeli juggernaut, bent on the utter destruction of Palestinian society, had social justice activists not clamored that this oppression be named for what it is? As American politicians from the neoconservative Right to the neoconservative Left vie for the "Jewish vote" by proclaiming endless support to Israel, it is obvious to Palestinians that they have few allies in this country and that we must persevere in educating the Left as well as the wrong. Senator Barack Obama's volte-face, during his successful presidential campaign, provides a very sobering reminder, for anyone who needed it, that few American politicians dare to venture into real change, as far as support for Israel goes. From his early years as a Chicago politician, Obama was well informed about the Middle East, expressed a sympathetic understanding of the plight of the Palestinians, and demonstrated critical and nuanced views of the need to secure justice in order to achieve peace. Yet, as he campaigned for president, Obama successfully distanced himself from his recent past, seeking to reassure American voters that he is as unequivocally Zionist as the rest of the candidates, and proclaiming, as all presidential hopefuls are bound to, that he is a "stalwart friend of Israel." As far as Palestinian rights are concerned, the only "change" Obama has delivered so far is the change of heart he apparently experienced on the campaign trail, which, sadly, seems to be more than a short-lived strategy. More than ever today, as Israel is further emboldened to engage brazenly in war crimes, we must speak out. Only death can come from our silence, whereas our denunciation of our oppression will ultimately bring about an improvement of our current moribund circumstances.

Our silence cannot protect us. Indeed, when U.S. politicians speak of courting the "Jewish vote" by flaunting their support of Israel, they are demonstrating the Manichaean reductionism that is characteristic of the simplistic American worldview, a reductionism we must speak against. In the United States, there is an unfortunate and erroneous conflation of "Jews," Judaism, and Zionism. This strategic conflation leaves no room for a nuanced appreciation of anti-Zionist Jews, or of Israelis critical of their government's actions, who nonetheless do not qualify as "self-hating." Moreover, the equation of Zionism with Judaism leads to the equally flawed conflation of "criticism of Israel" with a "dislike of Jews"—anti-Semitism. Palestinians, then, face a double challenge: they must resist their occupation, as well as the unfounded but crippling charge of racism. The Algerians fighting for independence from French colonialism were not called "antiwhite," nor were the blacks in South Africa accused of "reverse discrimination." In fact, no other colonized people rising against their occupier have been accused of racism. But because the hegemonic discourse in North America equates "Jews" with Israel, Palestinians who seek an end to their oppression are vilified here as anti-Semitic. Below, I discuss three incidents I have personally experienced that illustrate the ongoing silencing of pro-Palestinian activism. I have chosen three different types of "progressive spaces" where such incidents occur—international academia, cyberspace, and a suburb of Seattle—to show how widespread the censorship is. Additionally, from my discussions with numerous social justice activists who support the Palestinian struggle for freedom and self-determination, as well as my own history of activism in various parts of the United States, I know that this censorship occurs consistently, all across the country. The examples I give must therefore be seen as no more than a minimalist sampling of the intolerance we still face among progressives. And while many on the U.S. Left are finally waking from their treacherous slumber, which enabled their government's atrocities in the Middle East, Islamophobia remains sadly pervasive among American liberals today. Consequently, despite the U.S. Left's commitment to denouncing (and, hopefully, resisting) racism, colonialism, militarism, and occupation, this camp remains home to many who fail to appreciate that our struggles are one and the same.

◆   ◆   ◆

In October 2004, I was an invited panelist at an international conference in Montreal, Canada, discussing historical wrongs, collective traumas, and communal healing and recovery.[10] The conference, modeled on the Durban UN World Conference Against Racism (as indicated in the registration packet), opened on a Wednesday evening with two keynote speakers. The first, a scholar from an eastern African country, spoke of the universal duty to remember slavery, which has been affecting hundreds of millions worldwide, for centuries, the legacy of which is lived by hundreds of millions all over the world today. With regards to the slave trade, this speaker correctly pointed out that it is still premature to speak of forgiveness, as the full implications of this historical wrong remain unacknowledged to this day. The second keynote speaker, an indigenous chief, spoke of the ongoing legacy of the colonization of the Americas, again indicating that the wrong is not over and done with, as its repercussions are lived on a daily basis by indigenous peoples today. The chief was adamant in his opposition to "sanitizing language," arguing that we must name the wrongs for what they were: ethnocide and cultural genocide. Both speakers spoke of the poverty, unemployment, diseases, depression, violence, and incarceration rates that still plague people of African or indigenous descent in various African and American countries, North and South. Clearly, both keynote speakers were addressing wrongs of a global scope, with ongoing consequences, detrimental to the victims, preferential to the victimizers, and the need to acknowledge those consequences. Amnesia is too convenient, said the African scholar, as the indigenous chief again urged the conference participants not to mince words, not to sugarcoat reality, for only when one acknowledges the magnitude of evil, rather than attempt to minimize it, will one seek to adequately redress the consequences.

I was elated. At the opening ceremony, both keynote speakers had reminded the audience that we all need to speak the truth about the ongoing misery inflicted by racism, colonialism, slavery, and imperialism. Tomorrow, I thought to myself, we will grapple with these issues that have for so long been swept under the rug. We will finally discuss, as victims and victimizers together, some of the world's historical wrongs as we are experiencing them in the twenty-first century.

The euphoria was short-lived. The next day, during the opening panel, which was supposed to engage with the key issues of memory, recovery, and healing, we had three white scholars who spoke at great length of "Europe's diseased memory"—diseased in that it still has not gotten over the Holocaust. And as the conference was winding down, by Friday afternoon, it was painfully clear to me that something was seriously amiss. The keynote speakers had urged us to grapple with the ongoing consequences of slavery and colonialism. But the "experts" had presented us with an academic discourse so Eurocentric it placed Germany at the center of the contemporary world's memory of any and all wrongs. Germany must be taken as the "starting point of any discussion of the contemporary world's memory," one of these European experts asserted, in a sweeping dismissal of such momentous developments as the emancipation of enslaved Africans throughout the Americas, the advent of communism in Asia and Eastern Europe, decolonization (sixty-two countries gained their independence from Britain alone), and an end to apartheid in South Africa and to legal segregation in the United States. All of these events, and many more of equal import, inform the memory of the majority world, if not necessarily Europe's. Surely, equating Europe with the "contemporary world" is a form of racism?

Imbued with an unflinching sense of entitlement and authority, the aca-demic "experts" had spoken beyond their allotted time, giving the other partici-pants absolutely no opportunity to dispute their claims. So, when I finally had the floor, on Friday afternoon, as the conference was winding down, I neglected my own prepared essay to denounce the pervasive Eurocentrism of this inter-national gathering, arguing that Europe does indeed have a diseased memory, if the only wrong it can acknowledge is the Nazi Holocaust, without so much as a passing reference to colonialism and slavery, despite the urgent reminder, two nights earlier, to finally address these crimes. (Clearly, they had not deemed it important to rework their prepared talks so as to respond to the plea made by the keynote speakers.) Then I went on to critique the fact that the panel of "experts" on historical wrongs and traumas was all white, and apparently inca-pable of comprehending the crimes so many millions of victims have experienced. I added that since these experts had addressed only the Nazi Holocaust, and how that episode has affected Germany and divided the French, and how Europe as a continent had still not overcome the trauma, they were clearly not talking to us, but at us. For two days we had discussed our pains and traumas, as colonized peoples who had lost our languages, our countries, indeed, in the case of the indigenous peoples, our entire continents; we had talked about the immediacy of our circumstances—the fact that we remain dispossessed today, with alarming unemployment, poverty, and incarceration rates. We had talked to the descen-dants of colonizers and slaveholders, to white Europeans, Canadians, and Ameri-cans, about the differential of power and privilege resulting from these historical wrongs. But the Euro-experts did not engage in a dialogue with us. The Nazi Holocaust is a stain on Europe's memory, involving as it did the genocide, by Europeans, of fellow Europeans; hence, it remains, in Eurocentric discourse, "the greatest wrong," and Germany becomes "the launching pad" of any discussion of global memory in the contemporary world. Colonialism, imperialism, and geno-cide *outside of Europe* apparently need not be addressed, for they are not traumatic to Europe and its descendants.

As I finished talking, having intentionally spoken less than my allotted time, to allow for discussion, it became immediately clear to me that the organizers were extremely upset with me. One of them actually shouted his anger at me, only inches away from my face, as soon as we stepped out into the hallway. The other organizer simply walked away from me as I approached her to say good-bye. As she stood there, smiling and shaking hands with everybody else, she looked away whenever I managed to make eye contact with her, until I figured she clearly was unwilling to talk to me. Additionally, one of the "experts" I had criticized called me stupid, to my face, but without addressing me. "A chaque conference, il y a un moment de bêtise" (At every conference, there is a moment of stupidity), he said to his fellow European panelists, while looking at me, as I stood a mere foot away from their group. Just as I had pointed out in my own critique of the conference, that critique that so infuriated the "experts," this particular expert was talking at me, about me, but not to me, despite his full awareness of my presence. I must presume he felt that I was no worthy partner for dialogue, no reliable partner for any peace attempt. I have not valued his Eurocentric worldview over my experience as a dispossessed diasporan Palestinian. I had claimed agency, and I had denounced his bias.

The gender dynamics of this academic confrontation were truly interesting. When I criticized the format of the conference, the male organizer, an Arab, spontaneously expressed his anger, while the white woman "ignored" me. Similarly, the only man among the Euro-experts I had criticized actually insulted me to my face (which I take as a validation of my critique), while the rest of the panelists, all female, would not acknowledge my presence among them. Privileged men feel that they can confront a woman they perceive as a threat to their authority, while women, even when in a position of relative power or equality, often adopt the "feminine" strategy of evasion. I wonder, in retrospect, how the response to my talk would have differed had I been an Arab man, saying exactly what I had said. Would the men who raised their voices against me have refrained from doing so, viewing me as an equal? And if not, would we have gotten into a shouting match, for I, too, would have considered it my prerogative to raise my voice in response? Would the women I had offended have nevertheless smiled at me, instead of completely avoiding eye contact? Interestingly, both conference co-organizers told me, while I was still in Montreal, that they had read my paper (which we were required to submit ahead of time in order to facilitate the process of simultaneous translation) and thought it provocative, powerful, and incisive in its analysis of global racism. They assured me that they would publish it, and the Arab man who had been vocally angry at me even told me I could address the conflict that had happened, in a brief preface, before submitting the edited version. But the woman organizer, who had the final say in the publication of the conference proceedings, eventually rejected my submission.

In the final analysis, the silencing, the betrayal had come from a white woman, not an Arab man . . .

Since I had been invited as an Arab American feminist, a women's studies professor, and a member of a number of feminist organizations, were there any unspoken expectations that maybe I would denounce "Islamic fundamentalism," when in fact I spoke out against my other oppressor, racism, in both its Zionist and Eurocentric manifestations? It cannot be overemphasized that a Palestinian woman's dignity, her individual rights, and her freedom are denied her by Israel, not her Muslim next of kin. Thus, Arab women speaking out against their oppression must of necessity speak out against racism, both Israeli and American, colonialism and imperialism (once mostly British and French, but today also Israeli and American), and overall Western intervention in our countries' politics. Why had my brief talk provoked so much anger?

It was Friday night in Montreal, a city I love. I had the evening to myself, and I absolutely cherish evenings to myself. Yet I felt miserable, deeply troubled by this experience. I tried to walk it off. I walked for close to three hours that evening, trying to shake off the gloom that had descended on me as I absorbed the reaction to my critique of the conference's Eurocentrism. Why was I giving so much weight to the anger I had caused, even as I remain convinced that my own criticism was absolutely justified? Why could I not focus instead on the women who came up to me and thanked me for speaking out? Was it not the master's tool at work again? Much later, back at home, I looked up my copy of Lorde's *Sister Outsider* and read: "Those of us who stand outside the circle of society's definition of acceptable women . . . know that *survival is not an academic skill*. It is learning how to stand alone, unpopular and sometimes reviled, and how to make common cause with those others identified as outside the structures in order to define and seek a world in which all can flourish."[11]

Despite the superficial veneer that makes me an acceptable woman, I had clearly not been successfully tamed; I had not assumed that my duty consists of patiently, laboriously educating my audience, over and over again, about the most basic fact, namely, that the colonized have been wronged by the colonizers. As the choke hold around the livelihood of my people gets tighter by the day, I can no longer devote my energy to pointing out, on a map, where Palestine *should* be. . . . I expect allies with a sense of justice to do the necessary work of unlearning racism enough to reach out a helping hand where it is most needed, rather than have the colonized, the oppressed, the wretched of the earth, explain to them why our circumstances are unacceptable. To quote Lorde again: "Women of today are still being called upon to stretch across the gap of male ignorance and to educate men as to our existence and our needs. This is an old and primary tool of all oppressors to keep the oppressed occupied with the master's concerns. . . . This is a diversion of energies and a tragic repetition of racist patriarchal thought."[12]

I went back to my hotel room, determined not to let this setback paralyze me any longer. Yet the disappointment was an all too familiar feeling. One memory haunted me, as I lay down, exhausted yet sleepless: the experience of the Arab American contributors to *This Bridge We Call Home: Radical Visions for Transformation*.[13]

My own piece in *This Bridge We Call Home* addressed how the first anthology, *This Bridge Called My Back: Writings by Radical Women of Color*, had completely erased the existence of radical Arab American feminists, since it was supposed to be by "all women of color" and for all women of color, but did not include a single Arab voice.[14] *This Bridge Called My Back* was a groundbreaking book, and remains extremely important to this day, as it illuminated the voices and experiences of women of color at a historical moment in which feminism was defined largely by the experiences of middle-class white women. To their credit, it must be said that the coeditors of the second edition, AnaLouise Keating and Gloria Anzaldúa, had actually accepted not one or two but all of six Arab and Arab American contributors. However, I also know, from conversations with a number of contributors, that many of us were unaware this edition would not be a "women of color" anthology but would include white women and men, some of whom would not acknowledge any privilege, while others actually celebrated their privileged status. In her preface, Keating claims, "We had made it clear in our call for papers that we were interested in receiving work from men." Actually, the call for submissions said, simply, "We welcome work by people of all colors and genders," while repeating, five times in a 260-word announcement, that this anthology, initially titled *This Bridge Called My Back, Twenty Years Later*, was to pick up where the groundbreaking volume had left off.[15] How could we have assumed that the follow-up collection would stray so far from the spirit of its parent, that it would now include white men who acknowledge their privilege only to dismiss it in the most cavalier manner? Thus, one contributor, Max Valerio, for example, acknowledges the privilege that comes from the fact that he passes for white, despite his mixed-race background, but dismisses it with two simple words: "Privilege aside," he writes, "and contrary to what some people may assume, I have never liked being so light, and only accepted it with great effort over time." How were we to know how *essentially* different this new anthology would be?[16]

But the betrayal did not come from the white male contributor(s). The new anthology had essays by some seventy contributors, and the editors formed a

Listserv to communicate with us all about formatting, deadlines, and other such technicalities, but also to get input about the title of the projected collection. Because Anzaldúa was already very weakened by the disease that would soon claim her life, Keating was the Listserv owner and did most of the communication with the contributors, although she explained that all decisions were made jointly by Anzaldúa and herself. Ideally, we all wanted a title that closely echoed the first edition's while indicating that it was not a reprint. Naturally, the Listserv quickly developed into a political forum, as many contributors suggested titles, presenting the rationale behind their choices, while others responded. Occasionally, someone would forward a message from a progressive activist organization they were affiliated with, calling for action about specific causes. The overall tone of our communications was extremely jovial, we were all excited to be part of this wonderful project and fed off of each other's enthusiasm, and all was going very smoothly, until one of the contributors posted a message inquiring whether the contributors to *Bridge* wanted to issue a collective statement condemning the latest Israeli violence against Palestinians. This inquiry was during the Second Intifada, and Israel was once again engaging with impunity in the massacre of civilians. Suddenly, the tone on the Listserv changed dramatically, as that contributor was called racist, anti-Semitic, a hatemonger who should not even be included in the anthology.

The hostility quickly escalated, as the other Arab contributors (many of whom did not know each other at the time) participated in the discussion, explaining that a critique of Zionism is a critique of a political project and could not be conflated with anti-Semitism or racism of any sort. At no point was our criticism directed at some homogeneous "Jewish community," but very specifically at Zionism, a political movement that some Jews, as well as a growing number of Christians, embrace. Every pro-Palestinian e-mail on that Listserv was met with a barrage of accusations from Jewish contributors who charged that we were blind to the continuing oppression of Jews and that we had zero tolerance for "the Jewish perspective." We tried to explain Jewish women's privilege vis-à-vis other women of color in general, and Palestinian women in particular, but the Jewish contributors participating in this discussion saw their Jewishness exclusively as a site of oppression, never privilege. At no point was there so much as a dismissive gesture, a statement such as "Jewish privilege aside, we have to confront numerous stereotypes . . ." Clearly, those supposedly radical women were incapable of comprehending multiplicity, even as they lived it in the flesh, for many of them said they were Latina Jewish, Jewish lesbian, Jewish Native American. But they could not conceive of "Jewish oppressor," "white/Jewish privilege," or "non-Zionist Jew." Hence, they were accusing us on the basis of their own blindness, their own failure to go beyond George W. Bush's Manichaean "Either you're with us, or you're with the enemy."

Despite our most articulate arguments, we were unable to bring these contributors to an understanding that the Palestinian denunciation of the Zionist policy of illegal occupation, dispossession, and racial discrimination stemmed not from anti-Semitism but from women of color's desire to be free of multiple sites of oppression. The anti-Arab rhetoric kept coming, unprovoked, until we finally contacted the editors, urging them to intervene and put an end to what had become a hate list, with zero-degree tolerance for Arab voices. They did not.

As with the Canada conference, here, too, the dynamics of censorship and silencing were fascinating. As the discussion evolved, every time a pro-Palestinian message was posted, Keating (and Anzaldúa, presumably) immediately reminded us that the list had been created to communicate about the book and must not be turned into a political forum. (So much for that basic tenet of feminism, "The personal is political"!) But when an anti-Arab message was posted, it was generally followed by numerous others supporting whatever ugly accusations had just been made, without the immediate reminder that this Listserv was not meant as a political forum. Such consistent oversight on an editor's part can only come from complete socialization into the privileging of one party over another and closely resembles the dynamics that made it possible for the "experts" at the conference on historical wrongs to devote their whole panel to Europe's anti-Semitism, even as speakers from Peru, Argentina, Algeria, Palestine, Djibouti, and numerous First Nations had discussed how they had been impacted by racism, colonialism, slavery, and sexism.

Toward the end of this debacle, one contributor accused the Arab contributors who had expressed criticism of Israel of being so racist that we were in league with the Ku Klux Klan. Once again, we were categorized based on the hegemonic discourse's failure to see the world beyond the binary of "good guys and bad guys." The KKK is anti-Semitic, we are critical of Zionism, so therefore we must be in league with the KKK. But this wrong inference fails to take into account many important variables. Not all Jews are Zionists, but that notion apparently is a very challenging concept for Americans to comprehend. Not all non-Zionist Jews are self-hating Jews. Not all anti-Zionists are racist. I would even contend that since a critique of Zionism is a critique of racism, in all likelihood an anti-Zionist is anti-racist. As a matter of fact, Klan members are anti-Semitic but not anti-Zionist. Shouldn't progressives understand that concept?

The hatred continued, until the entire book project was threatened, as a few contributors indicated that they were considering withdrawing their pieces.

Then, and only then, Keating finally shut down the Listserv. The centrality of the Palestinian issue to women of color generally—namely, the fact that we are a colonized people seeking to break through the distorted hegemonic narrative that either completely erases or totally misrepresents us—was once again pushed to the margins, as Keating suggested creating another Listserv, where whoever was engaged in the political discussion would have the opportunity to continue that debate, without hindering the *Bridge* project. By doing so, she was contributing to our further marginalization, our erasure, as she took away our opportunity to engage in a meaningful discussion with our potential allies, simply because one group of contributors had accused us of being racist. In retrospect, I can only guess that Anzaldúa and Keating's decision to include Arab American voices did not stem from a sincere and deep appreciation of our circumstances, but was—sadly-part of the overall "dilution" of this anthology, as compared to its predecessor, *This Bridge Called My Back*.

We asked that the editors address the "behind-the-scenes" hostility in the introduction to the collection and were seriously disappointed when the book finally came out, sanitizing the hatred beyond recognition. Here is what Anzaldúa wrote about the e-mail discussion in her preface:

> I recalled the internal strife that flared up months earlier in the postings on the listserv we set up for our contributors. I think the listserv conflict also masked feelings of fear—this supposedly safe space was no longer safe. The contentious debates among Palestinian women and Jews of Latina, Native, and European ancestry churned a liquid fire in our guts.
>
> Conflict, with its fiery nature, can trigger transformation depending on how we respond to it. Often, delving deeply into conflict instead of fleeing from it can bring an understanding (conocimiento) that will turn things around. In some of the responses to the heated discussions, I saw genuine attempts to listen and respond to all sides. With generous conciliatory responses a few contributors tried to heal las rajaduras split open by mistrust, suspicions, and dualisms.[17]

I would venture that the contributor who accused us of being in league with the Klan was not making a "genuine attempt to listen." On the other hand, those few contributors who were trying to heal the rift saw their efforts curtailed by the decision to move the discussion elsewhere. And I must assume that the editors did not feel that this conflict was worth their delving into, for the understanding and healing that could come of such an effort were clearly not part of the transformative work their anthology would facilitate. Betty Friedan's arrogant request,

"Please do not bring up Palestine here. This is a woman's conference, not a political conference," echoed on, more than twenty years later . . .

However, it was also obvious to us, the Arab American contributors, that we had transformed ourselves, despite the attempt to silence and marginalize us. We did not accept the offer to join an alternative list. We have given ourselves permission to narrate "center-stage," and we are not going to fade away, even though we are experiencing immense backlash. We are shouldering the burden of representation, and once again, we are reminded not to assume that those individuals claiming to follow in the footsteps of "radical women of color" will necessarily bear some of the weight with us. Decades ago, Friedan, beacon of second-wave feminism, had tried to silence Nawal el Saadawi at an international conference on women, and contributors to *This Bridge We Call Home*, as well as its editors, had shown little progress in terms of understanding the dispossession of Palestinians. Yet, we must continue, "for to survive in the mouth of this dragon we call america, we have had to learn this first and most vital lesson—that we were never meant to survive."[18]

As I reflected on this episode, as well as the conference in Montreal, I was reminded of another incident where I experienced intolerance and open hostility in a supposedly friendly space. In October 2004, in a suburb of Seattle, I was moderating a sophisticated political discussion, with most participants eager to learn about specific actions they could engage in, ahead of the U.S. presidential elections. The last question raised during the discussion was: "So how does John Kerry compare to George W. Bush on the Palestine question?" I responded that there was absolutely no doubt in my mind that Kerry was significantly better on U.S. women's issues, civil rights issues, and environmental issues, but if I were to think in terms of Palestine, then he fared no better than Bush on Palestinian women's issues, civil rights issues, and environmental issues. I explained that anybody who believes an Apartheid Wall can bring about peace, anybody who approves of Ariel Sharon's policies, cannot possibly be supportive of the Palestinians' most basic human rights.

I could not claim ignorance. Kerry had made one Zionist statement too many. A smart man—for we must sadly acknowledge that "smartness" is not to be taken for granted as an attribute of a U.S. presidential candidate—Kerry had proactively responded to the argument that criticism of Israel is not necessarily racist, explaining, on his Web site, that anti-Semitism is "often masked in anti-Israel rhetoric," thus also implying that he would not tolerate anti-Israel rhetoric. "John Kerry and John Edwards believe that anti-Semitism—often masked in anti-Israel rhetoric—is a dangerous trend threatening both Israel and Jewish communities around the world," proclaimed Kerry's presidential campaign Web site, which reproduces the usual American politician's statement of unending, unquestioning, unfaltering support for Israel.[19]

I explained that, as a Palestinian, I could not look my own mother in the eye and tell her I voted for Kerry. My mother, just like my father, is a native of Jerusalem; both were displaced in 1948 and have never been allowed to return to Palestine. My father had since died, in the Diaspora. I explained that I could not tell my mother: "Mom, I looked up Kerry's election Web site, read about his support for Ariel Sharon, and for the 'security fence,' as he chooses to call the Apartheid Wall, and about his pride in having consistently voted for continued financial, political, and military support for Israel, throughout his nineteen years as senator. But Mom, forgive me, I voted for Kerry, because he believes American women should have the right to terminate an unwanted pregnancy, and that Pacific salmon should be placed on the endangered species list." The Palestinians are an endangered species themselves, I added, and for us, a vote for Kerry would not necessarily be better than a vote for Bush. This question was the final one, and as we prepared to leave, one woman came up to me, warmly congratulating me on my eloquence, my composure, my knowledge, and so on—because Arabs, I suppose, rarely display such qualities . . ."But you just blew it, at the end," she added hastily. "For me, everything you said lost all validity after you claimed that Kerry and Bush are two sides of a coin. As a Jew, I really resent what you said."

Following the 2004 election fiasco, progressives did come out and say that Kerry was perhaps even more pro-Israel than Bush and would have continued to "crush" the Palestinians.[20] But when I had suggested that, for me as a Palestinian, a vote for Kerry based on his electoral statements would be almost equivalent to a Jew voting for Hitler, I was told I "lost all credibility" with my audience, for how dare anyone, whatever their circumstances, compare anyone with Hitler.

I do not want to conclude this essay on a negative note. have made gigantic strides toward demystifying the plight of the Palestinians. I am convinced that the truth will ultimately prevail, and that Israel will eventually be recognized by most for what it is: an apartheid state. I also believe most Americans will not support apartheid. But it has not been easy, and we still have a long way to go.

◆　　◆　　◆

The *New York Times*, the editors claiming to be midwives of social transformation and activism, and this participant in the discussion in Seattle are unfortunately representative of a problem still plaguing the American "Left." Incapable of fully comprehending multiplicity, they fail to address a historical wrong that is obvious to the rest of the world, a wrong perpetrated by a victim-turned-victimizer. Yes, one can acknowledge the continued presence of anti-Semitism, while denouncing the fact that Israel itself is a racist apartheid state. Progressive Palestinians and their allies are ever cautious never to be associated with neo-Nazi organizations because they know that such organizations are racist and that our critique of Zionism is political. It is really not so complicated, yet, as we are accused of "being in league with the KKK," it is painfully obvious that the United States needs much education. Isn't it sad that no "progressive" Eurocentric expert finds it outrageous that, today, it is the Palestinians who hold on to the dream of "next year, in Jerusalem"? Instead, when I explain that both of my parents are from Jerusalem but that my mother is denied the right of return, I am told that it would be "inconvenient" to grant Palestinians the right of return.

Inconvenient for whom? Has anyone asked the Palestinians if they find it inconvenient to return to their homes? "But it would present a huge problem," I am told, and again, I need to respond with some basic questions: A huge problem for whom? Would it be a huge problem for the Palestinians to be allowed to return to their homes? And what if it were a huge problem? Do we not have a huge problem now, and wouldn't the solution, difficult as its implementation might be, actually solve the problem? The Gaza Strip is one of the world's most densely populated areas, and a full 80 percent of the population of Gaza are refugees. Would it be a "problem" to put an end to the ongoing violation of their human rights? Would it be "inconvenient" to demand that Israel respect international law? And what if Israel were "inconvenienced," for the sake of justice?

Protesting voices are not soothing. It is not in their nature to lull the listener to sleep, comfort them, reassure them that all is fine. Protesting voices must shake the listener out of their slumber. And yes, that is discomforting for the listener. I do wish I had a fairy tale to share, a story with a happy ending. I would like to be able to tell such a story. I would like to tell my own son, a fourth-generation Diaspora Palestinian, such a story: And then the Palestinians got their land back, and were able to go back to their homes, and everyone lived happily ever after in peace, freedom, and dignity. And yes, I do firmly believe that when Palestinians have their freedom and dignity back, *everyone* in Palestine-Israel will live happily ever after, as the Israelis (who will not be pushed into the sea, whatever the fear-mongers say) also finally break free from the need to engage in ever-greater crimes in order to maintain an illegal occupation.

So until I can tell such a soothing story without lying, I am bound to raise my protesting voice. So long as there are worldwide denunciations of every known or potential genocide except the genocide of the Palestinians, I will continue to speak out. So long as there are efforts to prevent the forced displacement of any community from its historical home, except for the Palestinians, I owe it to the world and my people to speak out. I will seize every opportunity to call attention to the ongoing massacre of Palestinians, in such hostile places as international conferences against racism and racial intolerance, (supposedly) radical women-of-color Listservs, and the suburbs of "progressive" cities like Seattle. So long as antiwar activists denounce the U.S. occupation of Iraq but not Israel's occupation of Palestine, I will keep drawing the parallels. So long as Western feminists denounce the oppression of Arab women as a result of Islamic fundamentalism, but not as a result of Israeli occupation, I will raise my voice. I will explain that Palestinian women are without any doubt more oppressed by Israel and Zionism than they are by their fellow Palestinian men, that a Palestinian woman's freedom of movement, her right to an education, her right to vote, her right to work, her right to live where she wants, her right to sufficient food, clean water, and medical treatment in her own homeland are denied her not by her fellow Palestinians but by the illegal occupying power, Israel.

I do not like having to always explain. I wish I did not have to. I wish I did not have to face hostile audiences at the various "progressive" events I go to. Yet I feel that I must go on; I must continue to speak out. That is what is euphemistically referred to as the burden of representation.

14

Taking Power and Making Power

Resistance, Global Politics, and Institution Building

An Interview with Anan Ameri

NADINE NABER

Anan Ameri discusses her experiences as the founder and director of the Arab American National Museum (AANM) in Dearborn, Michigan. She reflects upon the vision behind the museum and its significance to diverse audiences. Ameri shows how her history of grassroots activism in the areas of social justice for Palestinians, Arabs, and Arab women has shaped her approach to leadership within the museum. She illustrates that she is committed to a feminist politics that does not separate the issues of racism and sexism but takes them on simultaneously. She considers it a feminist politics that motivates her vision for social change and is based on a commitment to coalition building with other people of color, women of color, and third world women.

Nadine Naber: What was the goal or vision behind the Arab American National Museum?

Anan Ameri: The vision behind the AANM is to create an institution that documents, preserves, and presents the Arab American presence in this country. We want to tell our own story, which has been told for too long by others and often with malice.

It is important to note that in the last two decades we have witnessed the creation of a number of ethnic museums in this country. The motivation behind creating these museums is the fact that minorities are rarely represented in mainstream museums. For example, there are fifteen thousand museums in the USA, and not one of them represents Arab American presence, experiences, or contributions.

NN: How has the museum been received by different audiences?

159

AA: The AANM opened to the public in May 2005. By our third anniversary our audiences reached fifty thousand annually; almost half of them are students and educators. At least one-third of our audience comes from neighboring states or from other countries like Canada, European countries, and the Arab world. In spite of their diversity, the overwhelming majority give us positive feedback. The most common comments have been: "I never knew that Arabs have been part of this country for so long" and "I never knew that he or she is an Arab," like Danny Thomas and Ralph Nader. Many identify with Arab American history in the U.S. and would say: "This is just like us Italians, or Greeks, or Latinos." Many people also comment on the physical beauty of the place.

NN: What is the significance of the Arab American National Museum as an institution?

AA: What is most significant is that the museum is part of a larger institution, the Arab Community Center for Economic and Social Services (ACCESS), which is committed to empowering the Arab American community in all aspects of life—economic, social, cultural, health, education, et cetera. We believe that art and cultural life are just as important as food and jobs, and that is why we created the Arab American National Museum. It is a museum that genuinely reflects the diversity of Arab Americans and was conceptualized with the help of the Arab American community nationwide. Finally, it is the only museum in the USA that is dedicated to telling the story of Arab Americans.

NN: What do you think is the significance of the museum's being directed by a woman?

AA: I am an activist who has been working with the Arab American community for over thirty years. So I come not from a "professional museum" background, but from a grassroots perspective. This, coupled with ACCESS's history, made it possible for this museum to be truly rooted in our community and reflective of our people's vision(s).

At the same time, I do not see my role as a director different from that of a male role, in terms of the functional operation of the museum. However, I am probably more aware of the importance of the role women play in our society, and thus more sensitive to ensuring that women are represented in our exhibits and public programming. When other women, Arab and non-Arab alike, see the stories of the women we present, or when they attend a book reading or performance by an Arab American woman, they realize the potential in themselves as women.

NN: In addition to your recent work with the museum and your history as a scholar, you also played a key role within the Palestinian women's movement in the U.S. What was the vision behind this movement, and what were your contributions to these efforts?

AA: My vision was, and continues to be, that Palestinians in the Diaspora have a moral responsibility to support the national struggle of the Palestinian people for liberation and independence. As a woman myself, who lived in both Jordan and Lebanon at the time of the 1967 war and 1973 war, I witnessed firsthand the determination and strength of Palestinian women to organize, to contribute to the steadfastness of Palestinian people, and to deliver in a tangible way. Palestinian women in the occupied territories and Lebanon played a leading role in organizing and in leadership. They were especially instrumental in sustaining nongovernmental organizations.

In the late 1970s, I, along with other Palestinian activists, men and women, established the Palestine Aid Society (PAS), a nonprofit, tax-exempt organization with the objective of supporting women's organizations in the Palestinian occupied territories and in Lebanon. Our approach was to support vocational and educational organizations that promote women's education, training, and economic independence. We believed that women's economic independence is critical to equality. One cannot talk about women's equality when women lack education, job opportunities, and economic independence. In the USA we also promoted women's leadership and participation in the organization. Although PAS is not a women's organization, from the first year of its establishment, women played an important and leading role. Unfortunately, with the current political situation, including the continued Israeli repression, the unconditional support by the U.S. government of Israeli occupation, and hence the lack of hope for a peaceful and just solution, the organization lost most of its momentum.

NN: You have also played a central role in the process of increasing the visibility of Arab American people, ideas, and institutions, locally and nationally. What are the ways that gender struggles have played out within your work among Arab American community organizations? What I mean is, what have been the gender issues that have emerged within your work among Arab American communities? And how do gender struggles play out among community organizers and leaders?

AA: When I came to the USA in 1974, I was struck by the level of hostility toward Arabs. I was especially struck by the stereotyping and negative images of Arab women that unfortunately continue in this country. That of course made me angry, and I felt that I had a responsibility to prove them wrong. I would say that two major events shaped my identity and, consequently, my work: first, the 1967 war brought my Palestinian identity to the forefront; second, coming to the USA and realizing the extent to which Arabs are portrayed negatively and how little people in this country know about us, as Arabs, as Palestinians, and as women. While the 1967 war pushed me to activism on the Palestinian issue, coming to the USA pushed me to activism on Arab issues and especially Arab women's issues. That is how I became an activist and feminist.

I remember very clearly the 1967 war. Although I am a Palestinian, and my family became refugees after 1948, I grew up as an "ordinary" person from a middle-class background. My hopes and dreams were purely individualistic, like getting a higher education, a job, travel, and possibly get married. In the summer of 1967, I had planned with a friend of mine to go to Bethlehem for a summer job. Also at the time, I had many friends from Jerusalem, Ramallah, and Nablus. We used to go there for weekends. Suddenly, the 1967 Israeli occupation of East Jerusalem and the West Bank made it impossible for us to even visit. The humiliation I felt, and the agonizing feeling of powerlessness, made me very angry and pushed me into political activism. I can say without exaggeration that since that moment, the issue of the Palestinian rights, and their struggle for independence and statehood, dominated my life.

When I was young, I thought that I, along with a few who believe in the same causes as I did, could change the world. As I grew older, I came to understand that goodwill and good work are not enough. I came to realize that what we need here in the U.S., in Palestine, and in the Arab world are institutions. Although I understood this early enough, it has not always been easy.

Now, if we were to examine nonprofit organizations in the USA, or any place in the world, we would realize the significance of women's roles in these institutions. They not only work in nonprofit organizations in large numbers but are often the founders, executive directors, and board members. Nonprofit organizations are very important institutions in all societies and often address critical needs of the underdogs—the poor, the immigrants, and all those who are marginalized because of their race, gender, physical and mental challenges, age, or any other factors. In other words, they fill a vacuum or need that governments and corporations choose not to address. Unfortunately, we have to recognize that part of the reason women dominate the nonprofit world is because it pays much less than other professions—otherwise, we might find more men working in the nonprofit world.

Gender is always an issue in the Arab world and in the non-Arab world. Yes, I did reach leadership positions, and at one point in the 1980s, I was the only woman who was the executive director or president of an Arab American national organization. I was the only woman from the USA who was a member of the Palestinian National Council. I have to admit that, for the most part, I was treated with a lot of respect and appreciation. That does not mean that once in a while a male would not challenge my leadership.

NN: Can you give an example of how your leadership was challenged?

AA: That challenge demonstrated itself by some males being patronizing, or totally ignoring what I said, or men talking about me in my presence as if I were not even there. But to be fair, I have gained the support of most of the Arab men that I have worked with.

NN: Your contributions have also extended to the broader realm of U.S. multiculturalism as you have worked with various communities of color and in the context of white middle-class cultural contexts. Have you dealt with struggles over gender and race in the process of working with non-Arab communities?

AA: I believe that sexism and racism are alive and well among Arab communities, as in other ethnic communities and among mainstream America. You only have to look at the U.S. Congress and the corporate world, where power and money are located, to find out that we still have a long way to go. In general, European Americans continue to be the privileged class, and today we hear a lot of people in power complaining that Affirmative Action is reverse discrimination. What they fail to mention is that this country had five hundred years of Affirmative Action that favored European Americans, which put them in control of government, corporations, educational institutions, and media.

If white America has higher levels of education, income, and health, it is because of all these years of racism and anti-immigrant laws that institutionalized these practices. For that reason, European American women have made more progress on gender issues; they are, simply put, better equipped to fight for their rights as women. They are also better equipped to fight for more resources for their children's schools and for their "right" to go to Ivy League universities. This not-so-vicious circle had been, and continues to be, in their favor and in the favor of their male and female children.

As a woman of color, and as a person who fights for Affirmative Action and who believes in the power of collectivity, I think that Arab Americans need to work with African Americans, Latinos, and other minorities. We at ACCESS and the museum have used the arts as a way to bridge different communities. Of course, there is a lot more that needs to be done.

NN: What kinds of coalitions have you seen or do you envision between Arab Americans and other people of color? What would this entail or look like?

AA: I think that we can create a number of coalitions, or one coalition that addresses the many issues that are, and must be, of concern to Arab Americans as well as many other minorities. There is of course the issue of immigration and immigrant rights. Also, many of us deal with Affirmative Action as if it were an issue that concerns only African Americans. This is an issue that we should create a national coalition around, not only from a principled position but also from a pragmatic point of view. All minorities in this country, including Arab Americans, were the indirect benefactors of Affirmative Action. There are also the issues of the PATRIOT Act and profiling. While many of these issues should be of concern to *all* Americans, we all know that the burden lies on minorities, and unless we stick and work together, we cannot and will not win all of these battles.

NN: What is your view of feminism? Do you identify as a feminist? What does the term "feminist" mean to you?

AA: I simply believe in equality regardless of gender, race, religious beliefs, or nationality. As a result, I believe in equality of women, and their right to equal education, equal access to jobs and promotions, and equal access to resources, being it power or money. In the meanwhile, I know that we do not live in a perfect world—far from it. In all societies everywhere, women are not equal to men. For me, feminism means to work toward ending all forms of discrimination toward women. However, my priorities might be different from the priorities of other feminists. I believe, also, that women of color and women from third world countries have different agendas than women in the West. Women in war-devastated areas also have different agendas and concerns. For example, they are more concerned about basic rights such as food for their children and want to be protected from violence, including rape. Low-income women in this country, most of whom are minorities, are concerned with health care for themselves and for their children; they want an increase in the minimum wage and need affordable housing. There are basics that many Western feminists do not even address. So, I do get frustrated sometimes by some feminists who try to impose their agendas on others or try to dictate to other women what they should be concerned with.

NN: As you work toward putting an end to various forms of oppression, what does your vision of social change look like? What do you think are the key elements necessary for ending global oppression?

AA: In the world that we live in today, there are those who have and those who don't. The gap globally, as well as within each country, between the poor and the rich is rapidly increasing. After the collapse of the Soviet Union and the end of the cold war, some were optimistic and were talking about the peace dividend. Now that the enemy is gone, we should spend our money on food and development of the poor in third world countries. The U.S. corporations, and those with political power, saw the vacuum created by the end of the cold war as a new opportunity to expand their hegemony and to increase their control over the resources of the world—hence all the trade treaties that were primarily responsible for allowing U.S. expansion without any control and creating the most unfair system of economic exchange. The economic boom of the 1990s was the immediate result of this expansion. In my view, global oppression is economic oppression. My view of social change entails more equitable distribution of resources between the rich and the poor, among nations, and within nations.

15

Inside Out

Youth of Color Organizing from Multiple Sites

An Interview with Janaan Attia

NADINE NABER

Janaan Attia makes links between her engagements with U.S. identity politics and her experiences as a community-based organizer. Attia addresses the positions of Arab youth within people of color-based movements and the place of Arab women and queer Arabs within movements based on women of color and queer people of color. She calls upon the many communities to which she belongs to take issues of sexism, homophobia, and racism seriously. She approaches these issues carefully, within the broader context of the tokenism and exclusion of Arab communities within progressive U.S. politics after September 11, 2001. Although Attia approaches the Obama era with caution, she remains optimistic about organizing strategies that work from the "bottom up" and incorporate more and more creative methods into their strategies for resistance.

Nadine Naber: You are an organizer and have played a significant role in raising awareness about the ways that Arabs in general and Arab women in particular are racially marked in the U.S. You have especially contributed to spaces where youth of color are grappling with social justice issues. How did you become involved in youth organizing and activism?

Janaan Attia: Whenever I am asked this question, I always start that I started as a youth! In high school I became involved in organizing other youth to support the South African people during Apartheid. With other high schoolers, I also started an organizing collective that was focused on educating our peers about systems of oppression; we held small teach-ins and reading groups focused on texts written by revolutionaries. It was very important to me because high school counselors were not encouraging me, the curriculum in school was absolutely irrelevant to my life and interests, and nothing came close to understanding what my new politicized identities meant to me.

Almost half my life later, after organizing with mostly adults, I started working at a high school here in the Bay Area through an amazing nonprofit, Youth Together. My job was to organize youth and teach them to organize each other to fight for educational justice in their school, teach them about social justice issues and ethnic studies. It absolutely changed my life. I was reminded of my own struggles in high school, and it made me reflect back on how I had been excluding youth in my organizing.

NN: Can you tell us about your work with young people of color?

JA: First, I think it's important to clarify that not only are the youth of color I have worked with grappling with social justice issues, but, more particularly, they are just learning about their own racial-ethnic identities in empowered ways. They know how society sees them, and my role is to share my experiences and help them place theirs in social justice contexts, equip them with language necessary to name the injustices, and, often most important, work with them to create new languages around identity and social justice. I think this is very different for some Arab American youth, because there isn't a historic Arab American power movement like those of Chicano/Latino and black communities to draw from, so they often identify with other communities of color. And Arab American student movements have often been made invisible, so they just do not have access to that information. Besides, their struggle often starts with the fact that many people don't know the difference between Pakistan and Palestine!

NN: What have been some of the challenges you have faced in terms of building an understanding among youth of color about the ways that Arabs in general and Arab women in particular are racially marked in the U.S.?

JA: Some of the challenges are just that some youth of color have limited contact with Arab communities and do not have the basic understanding of Arab cultures, religions, et cetera. Of course, given the way gender and Arabs are played out in the media, oppression of Arab women by Arab men is something I always hear when I do the stereotype piece of the Arab 101 workshops. The information they have says all Arab (and Muslim) women are controlled by Arab men, that Arab women don't know how to read, that they can't leave the house. They often mention that the Arab girls in their school always stick together and don't talk to anyone else, which clearly plays into stereotypes of Arab women being timid and even evokes images of the "harem." So the information they do have is marred with racism and stereotypes, through different mediums that often target youth such as music, video games, and so forth. It isn't much different than with adults, really. The other day I did a workshop for a group of youth of color (no Arab youth present) about the peoples, cultures, and histories of the Southwest Asian and North African region. They had so many questions I hardly had time to get through the workshop, which to me meant it was a success; the group was letting me know what they needed information about, and it was an encouraging first step toward unraveling so much of the silence and misinformation about our communities. What really excited me is that they were seeing commonalities with their own experiences and were enraged that they never hear about what Arab youth and their families have to endure at school and on the streets. In general, I think once the information is in their hands, they really get it.

The problem is that we are not doing much to empower Arab youth to speak for themselves, and so they often remain invisible to other youth. I know there are some programs at cultural centers that work with youth, but they are often quite conservative in their approach. We know that many of the girls don't want to talk about the issues they face in front of their brothers and male cousins, so one approach I took with a group of high school students who wanted to start an Arab Student Union was to meet with the girls separately and really get to the core of their concerns (I did the same with the boys, but they really needed a male to do this work with them). It's simple, but it opened them up considerably and empowered them to take positions in the Arab Student Union, which they had refused when the group was all together. We are afraid to talk much about patriarchy in the Arab communities because of the way it gets special negative attention, but we can't ignore it because of this. We have to spell out the racism in that view so that we can also work on issues of sexism and patriarchy in our communities. Otherwise, we continue to perpetuate what we do have going on, and the youth aren't empowered to change anything.

I have seen a growing Arab youth movement in recent years in the Bay Area, one that includes social justice education and youth empowerment, and it is encouraging that it is the youth that are taking it on and building it with adult ally support.

NN: How have some of these issues played out in your interactions and in your work with people of color- or women of color-based organizations in the Bay Area of California?

JA: As I mentioned, I think adults are severely misinformed as well. My experiences organizing as a culturally and politically identified Arab but ethnically identified African woman often become a point of contention in organizing in people of color spaces. Identity politics is of great importance in people of color spaces, but too often I have found that I am expected to fit into neat categories (not Arab and African together). So, sometimes it can be difficult to talk about serious issues Arab communities are facing because there is tension around my own identity politics. I don't find that this completely rules my experiences by any means, but it does color it in significant ways. At the same time, it's the Bay Area and California, so many organizations are somewhat keen to Arab issues, at least since 9/11, when people decided they'd better get caught up on what's happening in Palestine or make an Arab friend! I am joking, of course—well, maybe somewhat.

One thing that is especially a sticking point is the hypervisibility and yet invisibility of Arabs in this country, which complicates things a great deal in organizing spaces. In one women of color group I worked with post-9/11, group members expressed that they felt the Arab sisters are so angry that we have been marginalized in women of color spaces, but now, suddenly, we want to work with other women of color. Even more complicated was the tension between the queer women of color in the group. There was a sentiment among some of the women that the queer Arab women were acting as if they were "more oppressed" by homophobia than the other queer women. This came up when the queer Arab women tried to have a conversation about how homophobia plays out in our communities, not that it is more or less than anyone else's community, but that it has some different ways of existing. So even radical women of color spaces are riddled with stereotypes and false notions leading to a certain amount of silencing of Arab women. After 9/11, all kinds of women's events wanted an Arab speaker, so there was that tokenism without dialogue going on quite a bit. I think we are really working harder at changing that now.

NN: In your view, what are the commonalities around which coalitions can be built among Arab American youth and other youth of color? What are the differences or sites of tension between Arab American youth and other youth of color, and how does gender or sexuality come into play in the process of coalition building?

JA: I can't necessarily think of Arab American youth as being one group with common experiences. Certainly, class differences and immigrant experiences or growing up as a first- versus third-generation Arab American changes things. I have mainly worked with immigrant youth from working-class backgrounds, and with them there is such a variety of experiences and perspectives. Here in the East

Bay, Oakland and Berkeley, Arab youth do not have any center or group really working with them in the schools, like youth have in San Francisco through the Arab Cultural Center.

A group of boys asked me to help them start an Arab Student Union at their high school. They felt that the girls weren't going to come unless I invited them because they wouldn't take invitations from boys. So I literally begged the girls to come to the first meeting; they came and would not engage at all. We were trying to assign positions, and none of the girls would step up. Finally, one of them yelled at a cousin and said to him, "Why should I be treasurer? So you can tell my dad?" I say all this to illustrate that we need to be doing some serious work around systems of oppression in our communities and in society in general with Arab youth independent of other youth before we can really think of coalition building. Other communities of color are active with their youth around issues of social justice, and we need to do the same in sustainable ways with Arab youth so we can move into coalitions. At the same time, the growing awareness about Palestine in youth communities has been a successful tool in building the connectedness of oppressions—as in the similarities between the police in Oakland and the IDF [Israel Defense Forces] in Palestine.

NN: What are some of the tensions around issues of homophobia, sexism, and racism that you have experienced in the different communities to which you belong?

JA: This is a big question! The biggest tension is how to enter any space as your whole being, for me as a woman, as a Copt, an African, an Arab, a queer woman, as woman centered, et cetera. I used to just float by in women of color spaces as "the Egyptian" or in queer spaces as just a queer woman of color. When I was finally able to merge the queer and the Arab, after running away from the queer Arab community here in the Bay Area for so long, things may have become more whole for me personally, but they became way more complicated as an organizer. Like so many other queer folks of color, it sometimes feels I have to pick between my identities, which just isolates me from so many of my communities. The queer "community," which is often dictated by white supremacist, classist, and sexist ideas, has many issues with me being Arab, and the Arab community (like so many other communities) isn't quite working on its homophobia. So for now, it's about pushing my own boundaries and those of my communities, not only to accept the queer or the Arab but to be active and have an analysis of what is creating that isolation for so many.

NN: What have been your experiences with feminisms in the U.S.? What does women of color feminism mean to you? Or, are there other feminist spaces that have meaning to you?

JA: My first memories of a feminist identity came in high school when I read Alice Walker and other women writers of African descent. Walker of course coined "womanism," and though that spoke to me to a certain extent, I was not really comfortable with feminism, womanism, or any other label. I find myself continually grappling with what feminism means to me because so many of my first experiences are been tainted by white feminists exotifying me, especially my queerness coupled with my Arabness. And then add Zionism and Orientalism to the mix, and this Egyptian girl growing up on the West Side of Los Angeles went running from feminism if that's what it meant.

But I have definitely been part of many amazing women of color spaces that identified themselves as feminist. However, until I really came to identify myself as Arab, I never felt there was space for me. It is complex; race politics hardly allows Egyptians to be African in the U.S., so I floated around for a long time, confused about where I could organize and not be the only one with my cultural background. I finally realized that I was experiencing a major disconnect. There was the reality of how my family was being perceived and racialized as Arabs, and then there was the reality that my family does not identify as Arab (as many Copts do not). So I had to understand all of this to finally become comfortable with identifying as Arab politically. After that point, I demanded a place for myself and now am finally able to work with other Arab women to think about what Arab American feminisms look like.

We have such a rich history of feminist thinkers and organizers in the Arab world and in the U.S., so we definitely don't have to completely reinvent the wheel; work has been done, but only to a certain point. We need to push Arab American feminisms into more action. What's important to me is a collective, progressive identity for Arab women in the U.S., however we decide to name it. A movement that understands we cannot wait for other communities of women to acknowledge our experiences as important but for us to really do the work. We need to challenge women of color spaces to think more about who is invisible, how certain groups are made out to be hypervisible without having them at the table, et cetera.

NN: When you hear the words "violence" and "belonging," what do these terms evoke for you?

JA: My initial reaction is thinking about my family. I grew up in a family that was struggling with the belonging part, just as many immigrant families. My parents had no idea what they were coming to in 1969. When they saw that their papers labeled them as "Caucasian," they had no idea what it meant, but I think they understood they were being erased. They were given a television shortly after arriving, and when they turned it on, they were shocked at the way people of African descent were being treated in the U.S. They gave up dreams of belonging long before my father came home from work one day almost in tears because somebody at work called him "Ayatollah Khomeini" and told him to go home. So, given all of that confusion and pain, the violence they experienced externally often found its way into family dynamics. We don't often talk about pressures and experiences of racism and classism on families of color as one of the sources of the violence within the home.

NN: What strategies have you used in the process of creating social change? What do you think could be different within the progressive circles where you do your work? What kinds of changes do you think could make an important impact?

JA: We can sit in meetings and process group dynamics all we want, but when it comes down to it, we as politically active Arab communities need something to push our boundaries, something that speaks languages that are not academic- or organizing-speak, something we can create and be visible through. I am speaking here of languages that are accessible. One example is Theater of the Oppressed and Augosto Boal's work; it really is about creating ways of communicating complex ideas about oppression, social justice, power in ways that embody the every-dayness of our lives.

Art, particularly theater, is how I became active in social justice organizing as a youth, and though I haven't used art in the way I am speaking of here in recent years, I see it as essential for making change. I need to return to it, and the youth I have worked with always remind me. They would never dream of doing an action or event without art, and not art for art's sake. I think all organizing needs to use art as the work and in the work, so this is one way that the progressive circles I am in could be different, one thing we must return to in organizing. Not to say that it is not happening; certainly in the Bay Area and other cities there are vibrant and politicized art communities. I would just like to bring art in to cultivate more creative ways of organizing and sustaining ourselves while organizing.

NN: How have any of your views on these issues changed in this new Obama era?

JA: Certainly, youth seemed to become more politically engaged during Obama's campaign, but I think it actually says a great deal about youth movements and not necessarily just about his campaign. By this I mean that youth have been increasingly using their voices, art, and experiences in empowering and visible ways in the past few years, and that momentum picked up during this Obama campaign. Just like so many, youth saw their communities ravaged by oppressive economic and race systems and were excited at the prospect of change and a president who inspires them, not to mention reflects them. I actually voted for Cynthia McKinney myself because I felt she truly reflected my politics and my communities' real needs; at the same time I understand why Obama is exciting to communities of color—and don't get me wrong, I am glad he won over McCain. During the campaign, when I have spoken with youth, women of color, and even my parents about Obama, I tried to engage in conversation that looks at what he says and what he voted for in the Senate during the Bush administration. Palestine is a central issue for me; during this recent massacre in Gaza, I saw little evidence of Obama's commitment to justice. I don't think this is the only example, and I still have concerns for our communities here and abroad. I do hope that his administration makes some positive changes for our communities, but my politics have always been that change occurs from the bottom up, so we still have work to do and leaders to hold accountable.

16

Arabiya Made Invisible

Between Marginalization of Agency and Silencing of Dissent

NOURA ERAKAT

This piece describes the process of exercising one's agency as a Palestinian law student–activist while confronting narrow stereotypes concerning Arab and Muslim women's identity, on the one hand, and being dismissed as a radical anti-Zionist, on the other.

"I thought you were Latina."

"Why?"

"Because you're loud and outspoken. Girl, you've got attitude."

"Lucy, you just described most Arab women."

"I always thought Arab women were demure and submissive. Besides, your hair is wild."

"No one's as loud as my mama, and she wears *hijab*. Wait, and besides, not all Arabs are Muslims, Lucy."

◆　　◆　　◆

Lucy is an African American woman. She was a fellow student at Berkeley Law School at the University of California. Her remarks characterizing Arab women as a subjugated community within the Arab world are certainly not exceptional. Were they exceptional, perhaps the Bush administration could not have used the liberation of western Asian women as a justification for war against Afghanistan and Iraq so flippantly. Perhaps large U.S.-based feminist organizations would have challenged the simplistic notion that veiling oneself is a form of oppression rather than endorsing such notions in their support for war.[1] Instead, the sweeping characterization of Arab women as an oppressed population is as widely accepted as it is commonly made.

While major feminist groups and U.S. political pundits justify war against sovereign nations in the name of women's liberation, the women whom they purportedly seek to liberate are made invisible to mainstream North American audiences. Such invisibility contributes to the consistent assumption that I am Latina. And whereas I do not take issue with "looking Latina," as an Arab woman, or *Arabiya*, I do take issue with "being Latina." My characterization as non-Arab because of my "wild hair" and outspoken nature reinforces stereotypical images of Arab women as Muslim and the image that all Muslim women are veiled and oppressed. The marginalization of Arab women as passive agents incapable of their own liberation is exacerbated by the counternotion that those Arab women who support Palestinian self-determination are anti-Semitic and therefore incredulous.

The equation of anti-Semitism to anti-Zionism is systematically used as a silencing tactic. Anti-Semitism refers to the historic oppression and vilification of Jews that led to such tragedies as the Nazi-engineered Holocaust. Zionism is the theoretical notion that global Jewry should have a homeland, and in its practical application, Zionism has meant the establishment of a Jewish state in Palestine. Israel's establishment necessitated an ethnic-cleansing project that destroyed 450 Palestinian villages and displaced 750,000 indigenous Palestinians. Moreover, Zionism demands that a Jewish majority be maintained in historic Palestine. However, naturally in the region, the Palestinian population within Israel will outnumber the Jewish population.[2] Therefore, in order to maintain its demographic balance, Israel's Jewish majority must be engineered. Within Israel today, there are 4.6 million Jewish citizens, 1.3 million Palestinian Christian and Muslim citizens of Israel, and 0.5 million citizens who are neither Jewish nor Palestinian. Israel explicitly privileges its Jewish citizens over its non-Jewish citizens by implementing de jure and de facto policies. Consider that within the Israeli legal system, there are twenty discriminatory laws, seventeen of which are discriminatory on their face in that they relate only to the rights of Jews in Israel or alternatively abridge the rights of Palestinian Israelis. Moreover, it maintains that Palestinians should be transferred to neighboring Arab nations.[3]

To drive out Palestinians in the West Bank and the Gaza Strip and to control the water and land resources in the territories, Israel also maintains a belligerent military occupation of the West Bank and the Gaza Strip. Anti-Zionism therefore refers to the opposition of the establishment of a Jewish state that seeks to maintain a Jewish majority, even if contrived, and privileges its Jewish citizens, at the expense of pluralist and egalitarian principles, in historic Palestine. By equating anti-Semitism with anti-Zionism, pro-Israeli advocates silence dissent in places of public discourse, including on university campuses.

In the first instance, my identity as a strong Arab woman is marginalized as an agent of my own liberation, and in the second, I am silenced as a pro-Palestinian political activist. This dual process, the marginalization of agency and the silencing of dissent, is incredibly dangerous when liberating the subjugated western Asian woman serves as a justification for war. On the one hand, I cannot refute the manufactured (mis)conception of Arab women as hopelessly subjugated using my lived experience as an example, and, on the other, I cannot work to unravel the colonization of Palestine that has exacerbated patriarchy among Palestinian society and denied Palestinians their national self-determination.

On Becoming *Arabiya*

My affirmation of self as a strong Arab woman is not surprising in light of my upbringing. As the daughter of displaced Palestinians, I grew up in a community that struggled to resist its assimilation into American society. For my large extended family, assimilation meant evisceration of its Palestinian identity. To resist our cultural and ethnic erasure, my parents spoke only Arabic at home, traveled to the Arab world regularly, limited their social life to the extended family, and distanced themselves rhetorically and emotionally from their new home: the United States. My parents also feared that outside of their own control and purview, if left to roam free in the United States, their children would shed their Arab Muslim identities and become "Americanized." For that reason, they limited our social mobility as well. For example, I was allowed to go to school dances—if one of my male cousins accompanied me. I was allowed to participate in school activities like journalism and theater—but only during school hours. I was allowed to go to friends' slumber parties—but I could NEVER spend the night out of the house. My parents consistently tried to limit my immersion into American society. They did their utmost to shelter me in an Arab Muslim community. When I stepped out of line, they threatened to send me "back home" where I could be raised without the threat of becoming Americanized. I rebelled against my parents' efforts but within limits: I violated my curfew to participate in student government activities; I slept outside of the home to participate in leadership camps; I missed family events to volunteer in senior centers and homeless shelters.

My upbringing is simultaneously unique and common: unique because it has been created within the context of Arab diasporas among Arab immigrants in the United States, common because most Arab American women whom I have encountered can recount similar stories. This upbringing has shaped me into the woman I am today: proud, rebellious, culturally rooted, politically active, and family oriented. I never hesitate to assert my Palestinian identity. I also embrace my identity as a woman of color, which is a function of several things, including my frustration at the U.S. colonization of Iraq, its support of Israeli colonization of

Palestinian land, and its economic and military domination of the Arab world in general. I am even more frustrated by media coverage of the Middle East. I believe that imperialist ambitions of conquest and the accumulation of wealth drive U.S. foreign policies. I believe that people of color within the United States and the Global South, generally, incur similar repression and marginalization due to such U.S. imperial exercises. I therefore identify as a woman of color from the Global South. In doing so, I may overtly share similar struggles with Latina women, but I am not Latina; I am an *Arabiya*.

On Being an *Arabiya* at Berkeley Law School

Taking the specificities of my history and experiences seriously, I wondered where I fit in the consciousness of progressive law students of color who, despite their best intentions, may have failed to understand the nuances of being an Arab woman. Whereas I indeed endure repressive patriarchal practices, I simultaneously exercise my agency and struggle against those norms, thereby negating my image as victim.

Still, during my time in law school I felt that in the eyes of my "allies," I am a fiery and passionate activist *in spite* of my Arab identity, not at all as a function of it. Additionally, for my allies my ethnic background paled in relation to the work in which I engaged.

Although my identity is seemingly irrelevant to my allies, to me it is of primary importance. As a part of a movement that aims to counter Orientalist conceptions of western Asia and as a woman who had grown up constantly battling stereotypes and enduring biased media coverage, it matters a great deal that I am *Arabiya*. However, due to the hyperdiplomatic, read as politically correct, environment on the law school campus, I was rarely given the opportunity to engage my student counterparts about my Arab identity.

Aside from Lucy, who honestly confessed her conception of Arab women, no one ever mentioned it. For the sake of diplomacy, it seemed as if my history, my upbringing, my family, and my language were nonexistent, especially on a campus where Arabs constituted 0.004 percent of the student body. The invisibility slowly crushed my enthusiasm for achieving radical solidarity work among people of color. My characterization as an Arab woman who exercises her agency for change as an anomaly rather than a common characteristic of Arab women served to marginalize me as an Arab woman. This portrayal coupled with the tactics used to systematically silence me as a pro-Palestinian activist constituted a dual process that threatened to completely dismiss me as a sociopolitical agent for change.

On Being a "Terrorist Anti-Semite"

[Jewish law student]: "Boalt is the only place at UC Berkeley, where I feel that it's safe to be Jewish."

[Transgender Asian law student]: "Privilege! As an Asian American transgender male, I can't feel safe anywhere. You're complaining because Students for Justice in Palestine is protesting Israel's apartheid policies—what does that have to do with your Jewish identity?"

"They're calling Jews murderers!"

[African American woman]: "Look—I don't know what's going on over there in the Middle East. It's too confusing, too emotional, whatever. Right now I am concerned with the fact that the Berkeley Law Foundation's scholarships for students of color are under attack. It is offensive to me that anyone or any group would attack the presence of students of color on campus for any reason."

◆   ◆   ◆

Upon beginning law school at Berkeley, I helped form the Law Students for Justice in Palestine (LSJP) along with a couple of other students. The idea was to create a sister organization for Students for Justice in Palestine–UC Berkeley at the law school. The mission of both organizations was to urge the UC Regents to divest their holdings from corporations with subsidiaries worth five million dollars or more in Israel. Presently, those holdings total more than seven billion dollars. The divestment movement was inspired by the divestment movement from South Africa during the 1980s. One of the first events we organized was a speaking event for Na'eem Jeenah, a South African activist who was then on a speaking tour throughout the States. The topic of his talk was a comparison of South African and Israeli apartheids. The LSJP used Jeenah's transnational analysis to obtain the sponsorship of nearly all the progressive organizations at Boalt, including the Berkeley Law Foundation. The BLF is a public-interest law foundation with 501(c)(3) status dedicated to increasing the number of students of color at Berkeley Law School by providing scholarships to two incoming students every year, among other things. The BLF is able to generate funds for the scholarship by organizing an annual auction as well as directly soliciting funds from students and faculty.

Jeenah's talk stirred a huge controversy before he even came to campus. Accusations of anti-Semitism began flying around, and a new group called Friends of the Middle East mysteriously appeared on campus. Only two members of this new organization attended Jeenah's talk. One of them painted Jeenah as an anti-Semite by drafting a memo that took four of his comments out of context and distributed it to all of the law school's faculty and student body. Thereafter, the Friends of the Middle East threatened the BLF that if it would not retract its cosponsorship of the event and publicly apologize to Berkeley Law's Jewish community, then it would divest from the BLF. In effect, the Friends of the Middle East, predominantly composed of Ashkenazi Jews, threatened to divest from the funds meant to enable students of color to attend the law school. As the controversy escalated, the LSJP became increasingly marginalized from the debate. At a BLF student board meeting, one African American woman said that she had no idea what was going on in Palestine or in Israel but that this was offensive to her as a woman of color working to increase the number of people of color on campus. Another Jewish woman explained that she felt that the BLF should retract its cosponsorship because, since the LSJP launched its divestment campaign in February 2001, Berkeley Law was the only safe space for her on the UC Berkeley campus. And although issues of anti-Semitism and issues of students of color in higher education actually represent a common struggle against the dominance of wealthy, heterosexual white males in legal institutions, in this context not only were they framed in an antagonistic relationship, but they also trumped the core issue of the conflict: the struggle for Palestinian self-determination.

The Friends of the Middle East tactic, of equating anti-Semitism with anti-Zionism, is one only too familiar. By equating anti-Semitism and anti-Zionism, the Friends of the Middle East threatened to label all students critical of Israel or its policies as anti-Semitic. The group thereby silenced all dissent on campus.

Behind the scenes, the BLF board decided not to apologize, but it discussed the possibility of adopting a new policy whereby the BLF would not sponsor any talks related to the Israel-Palestinian conflict. I nearly suffocated on my own silence. As the only Palestinian woman of the approximately one thousand law students on campus, as the cofounder of the LSJP, a member of the BLF, and an organizer of the Jeenah event, I did not just feel invisible; I felt erased. I thought that surely if I appealed to the students of color on campus, they would support our efforts as pro-Palestinian solidarity activists. So I drafted a counter memo to the one written by the Friends of the Middle East. Titled "Silence Is Not the Alternative," the memo encouraged the Boalt community to promote debate about sensitive topics pursuant to the mission statement of the BLF, which seeks to "promote dialogue on difficult, and often controversial issues." I wrote a separate memo strictly for the student of color community, and I insisted that Arabs and Arab Americans are part of a people of color movement and that the community should not abandon us now in a moment of controversy. Rather than build on my political gesture, an Iranian Jewish student quickly silenced me by insisting that Jews are and have always been the marginalized community among the people of color movement. And although his assertion was too true, in this case, he prioritized maintaining the status quo of Israel's abominable practices over principles of antisubjugation. Consider that rather than reconcile the BLF's sponsorship of Jeenah's talk with his pro-Israeli views, he chose to demonize the BLF for supporting an antioppression speaker. He led the divestment campaign from the BLF and consequently from the funds available to people of color at Boalt. He did not pause at his own demonstration of hypocrisy, and no one publicly responded to him about his contradictory stance as a person of color who sought to divest from the BLF. No one responded to me, either. The fear of being labeled anti-Semitic was too great.

More than five years have passed since then, and student organizations are still afraid of being associated with the LSJP for fear of being labeled anti-Semitic. Zionist students subjected the LSJP to a smear campaign, and thereafter the Berkeley Law community contained it as one of its shameful secrets. The year after the Jeenah controversy, I assumed leadership of the BLF in an effort to heal the blow endured by the public-interest organization and also to create stronger, more explicit linkages between people of color in the United States and Palestinian Arabs in the United States, Israel, and the Occupied Territories. My efforts to rehabilitate the BLF were successful, but those meant to build stronger ties were not.

During my tenure as the BLF's cochair, I also chaired the LSJP and organized educational events to illuminate the violations of human rights and humanitarian law involved in the Israel-Palestinian conflict. The events drew mostly non–law students from the UC Berkeley campus. Progressive law students maintained their distance and never engaged me on the most salient topics, including the differences between anti-Semitism and anti-Zionism or on Palestine's ongoing occupation as a function of U.S. imperialist interests in the Middle East. In my last year of law school, the Boalt Hall Women's Association sought to sponsor a student talk for a blind female student who had done research on the disabled population in the West Bank. The BHWA solicited the cosponsorship of other law student organizations but explicitly rejected the idea of approaching the LSJP because of its "reputation." Instead of resolving the issue regarding the LSJP's political stance, progressive students masked their ambiguity about the LSJP with silence. If they did not say anything, they could be considered neutral, neither anti-Semitic nor unprogressive.

Moving Beyond the Impasse of Immobility

Shortly after the BHWA's event, an announcement was forwarded to its Listserv inviting the group's members to attend a Women in Black rally. Women in Black planned a silent vigil in protest of the occupation of Palestine, Iraq, and Haiti. In response, an Israeli member of the group, whom I shall call "Oly," responded with the following:

> It is absolutely unfathomable to me how feminists and gay activists can denounce Israel—a democracy, and the only country where women and homosexuals enjoy basic rights, and not hold three times as many protestations against the Palestinians. . . . Just a few examples: Palestinians conduct honor killings. Palestinians execute homosexuals. . . . I simply don't understand. Israel can be criticized for many things . . . but THE LAST THING Israel deserves is to be attacked by women and gays in the name of *Palestine.* Moreover, the Israeli occupation has NOTHING to do with Arab oppression of women and gays.[4]

This student asserts that misogyny and gender inequality are inherent to Arabs in general and Palestinians in particular. According to her, "the Israeli occupation has NOTHING to do with Arab oppression of women and gays." She fails to consider that structural violence waged on women in the context of war and occupation is the most extreme of its form. Moreover, she swiftly disregards the nexus of colonial occupation and patriarchy. Cynthia Enloe, a scholar on gender and militarism, writes, "When a nationalist movement becomes militarized . . . male privilege in the community usually becomes more entrenched."[5] For Oly, this point may be true in other situations, but among the Palestinians, gender inequality has nothing to do with military occupation—it is just their culture. This statement is not to excuse patriarchy in Palestinian culture on my part. To the contrary, I recognize that absent military occupation, Palestinian society would be challenged by structural gender inequities and misogyny. However, a few points are relevant here: first, military occupation has exacerbated such inequities within Palestinian society in several ways that I will not discuss here, and, second, failing to recognize the relationship between occupation and patriarchy works to justify the intransigence of the former injustice in the name of mitigating the latter.

The denial of Palestinian self-determination is justified by racist notions of Arabs as subhumans, including, but not limited to, the beliefs that Palestinian mothers send their children out to kill themselves and that Palestinian women and men are inherently patriarchal. Moreover, the continuing denial of Palestinian self-determination limits the potential of gender equality among Palestinian society, and the lack of gender equality among Palestinian society is offered as a justification for the denial of Palestinian self-determination. Consider the following critique of a Students for Justice in Palestine talk titled "Occupation 101" and published in *Campus Watch:*[6] "And then as I looked at the Palestinian coeds dressed in the current Berkeley coed uniform of tight jeans and tighter pullovers, I wondered if they would feel comfortable living in the Sharia-dominated state advocated by Hamas. Would they be able to walk down the streets of Ramallah the way they do the streets of Berkeley? Would they be free to buy *Lolita* in Jericho and read it without first closing the blinds and locking the doors?"[7]

Whereas the author wonders whether I would be able to comfortably walk around in tight jeans in Palestine, I wonder, if this man is truly concerned with my personal freedom, then why isn't he protesting the twenty-five-foot Apartheid Wall built between my village of Abu-Dis and Jerusalem? If he really cares whether I can read *Lolita* comfortably, then shouldn't he be more concerned that Palestinian children are denied a roof over their heads because of consistent home demolitions? His concern with my personal liberation seems disingenuous in light of the fact that he fails to mention Israeli military occupation as a significant, if not the most significant, factor contributing to the subjugation of Palestinian women's rights. Instead, he uses the lack of gender equality in Palestine as a justification for its continued colonization.

The erasure of context in the discussion of gender equality and Palestine is an irresponsible act. It is nothing short of racist to attribute a society's behavior to its character rather than its environment. Countering this discourse is made increasingly difficult when one's identity as a strong Arab woman is taken for granted and her political activism is conceived as extreme and irrational. Like Lucy, other students on campus did not conceive of me as an Arab woman because of my outspoken character and "wild hair." Perhaps the reading of Oly's e-mail may have been different were her sweeping generalizations of women in Arab society not so strongly affirmed by popularly held beliefs among an American mainstream. Were it not the case, my exercise of agency on the Berkeley Law campus may have worked to counter her assertion that "empowered" and "Arab woman" do not belong in the same sentence. Moreover, if my activism is indeed considered as extreme, then whatever rational rebuttal I present can be disregarded with ease, thereby diminishing my efficacy as a political activist.

In fact, students critical of my work falsely signed my name on a petition and in the "Comment" column wrote that I support terrorism, and if nothing else I am a nuisance to my professors. I was made to feel as though I was tolerated as an activist because of my progressive beliefs but that my political beliefs, vis-à-vis U.S. foreign policy, were not.

In a similar vein, my identity as an Arab American woman was not understood and therefore not embraced. Whereas my identity was not denied, I felt that students considered me an anomaly rather than an accurate representation of an Arab woman. On campus my identity as a strong Arab woman was marginalized, and I was silenced as a pro-Palestinian political activist.

The dialectical tension between national liberation and gender inequality works to maintain the status quo of foreign colonization and gender inequality. Shattering this cyclical paradox requires the end of Israel's gendered violence against Palestinian women and men, as well as the gendered ways that the United States and Israel use negative images of Arab women to justify colonialism and war. Simultaneously, we must work to end gender oppression within the Palestinian movement for liberation and Palestinian society. Failing to recognize the interplay between gender inequality and the struggle for self-determination will only exacerbate existing misconceptions, including Lucy's understanding of Arab women as passive, progressive students' fear of being labeled anti-Semitic for their criticism of Israel, and Oly's assertions that "the Israeli occupation has NOTHING to do with Arab oppression of women and gays." Not only does Israeli occupation have much to do with the oppression of Palestinian women, but the Israeli occupation of Palestine would not be so successful were it not for its insistence that it is a more civilized alternative to Palestinian society. The only civil, just, and humane alternative to a military occupation is its absolute destruction. Anything less will fail to afford Palestinian society its right to self-determination and subsequently its ability to realize gender, economic, and racial equality.

As an Arab woman and a Palestinian activist, I certainly want to participate in both my gender and national liberation. Doing so necessitates dismantling the dual process of marginalization of agency and the silencing of dissent. In practice, it means mounting a serious challenge to the conception of Arab and Muslim societies as homogenous structures that collectively oppress their women as a function of a reactionary culture—which is why I can be only an anomaly rather than an example. It also requires broadening the acceptable discourse on Israel's policies without using reprehensible silencing tactics that collapse political critique with unacceptable bigotry. Shattering taboos and unpacking politicized stereotypes will effectively help me participate in my own gender and national self-determination.

17

On Rachel Corrie, Palestine, and Feminist Solidarity

THERESE SALIBA

Rachel Corrie, a twenty-three-year-old white activist from the United States, was killed in the Gaza Strip in 2003 by an Israeli military bulldozer driver as she defended a Palestinian home from demolition. This essay, written by a member of her community, examines Rachel's witness to the extremes of violence inflicted on the Palestinians as a model of feminist solidarity that embraces our global connectedness and transcends borders of identity.

The varied responses to Rachel's death, locally to internationally, expose the advances and obstacles that Arab American feminists face working within academia and in the community in solidarity with Palestinians, Arabs, Muslims, and other oppressed groups. This essay, rooted in a gendered analysis of violence, power, and privilege, traces the racialized meanings of the Palestinian-Israeli conflict, emphasizing Israel's investment in deracializing the Arabs to deny the immense inequities between Israel and the Palestinians. It also documents the growing humanitarian crisis in Gaza; the unrelenting U.S. economic, military, and political support for Israeli human rights violations; and the gendered implications of occupation and siege for Palestinian women. Nevertheless, Rachel's story, lauded by such prominent intellectuals as Edward Said and Susan Sontag, has broken through the climate of intimidation surrounding critique of Israel and its censorship of the Palestinian story and spurred increasing activism and expressions of solidarity. We recommend reading this essay alongside the play My Name Is Rachel Corrie *or* Let Me Stand Alone: The Journals of Rachel Corrie.

Special thanks to Anne Fischel, Joe Kadi, and Tom Wright, and to the editors, Nadine Naber, Rabab Abdulhadi, and Evelyn Alsultany, for their insightful comments on this essay, their encouragement, and their solidarity. Sections of this work were first presented at "The Search for Peace: The Palestinian-Israeli Conflict; Women's Movements," sponsored by Evergreen State College, Olympia, Washington, March 2, 2004.

. . . And how do I
scream when I have no voice left? And who
will answer these questions for me?

Not Rachel Corrie. She is dead. And no matter
what any army says, I have seen the photos
and that woman was wearing orange,—
bright and alive one minute and dying
under rubble the next. Even I, it seems,
have developed a callous to the deaths of
Palestinians, because the murder of this white
girl from Olympia Washington has
my heart breaking and my blood faint.
Something like ten Palestinians have been killed since
yesterday, when a Caterpillar bulldozer driven
by a man demolished the home that was her body.
—Suheir Hammad, "On the Brink of . . ."

I also think it's important for people in the United States in relative privilege to
realize that people without privilege will be doing this work no matter what, because
they are working for their lives. We can work with them . . . or we can leave them
to do this work themselves and curse us for our complicity in killing them. I really
don't get the sense that anyone here curses us.
—Rachel Corrie, e-mail correspondence

Above this desk where I write, I keep a newspaper photo—two Palestinian
women, one in a black head scarf, the other in white, walking with their eyes
downcast. On their shoulders they bear a coffin wrapped in a Palestinian flag.
The coffin could be any of the thousands of Palestinians killed since the *Al-Aqsa
Intifada*, any woman or child. The women's faces, strong and solemn, marked with
a quiet dignity, remind me of the beautiful faces of the young women I taught at
Bethlehem University back in 1995–96. They remind me of the first time I went
to Gaza in 1991 to interview Palestinian women involved in the intifada, despite
my adviser's warning that I would risk getting an academic job by including a
chapter on Palestinian women activists in my dissertation. The coffin, though
empty, is carried in memory of Rachel Corrie. The photo reminds me of Rachel.
It reminds me of a similar procession where I lent a hand with a similar coffin
(heavy even in its emptiness), carried up to the steps of our capitol building in
Olympia, Washington, where Rachel grew up, attended college, and became a

young community activist. Two days after that AP photo was taken, hundreds of us gathered in the pouring rain to protest the renewed war on Iraq, the continuing assault on the Palestinians, and Rachel's brutal death. As the skies opened up in downpour, I took the bullhorn and read Suheir Hammad's poem, "On the Brink of . . ." each word like a salve to my soul and this broken world. Hammad's words, the community before me, the image of Palestinian women bearing Rachel's coffin through the dusty, devastated streets of Gaza—all resonate in resistance and feminist solidarity.

On March 16, 2003, Rachel Corrie was crushed by an Israeli bulldozer as she tried to prevent the demolition of a Palestinian home in Gaza. Rachel was a student at Evergreen State College, a public liberal arts college where I teach. Through her letters and involvement with the International Solidarity Movement (ISM), Rachel bore witness to the extremes of violence that Palestinians have been subjected to in the name of "combating terrorism," especially in the Gaza Strip, and was vilified or ignored by the U.S. mainstream media and government for her expression of solidarity. She became a national and international figure of "sacrifice, killed by the forces of violence and oppression to which [she was] offering nonviolent, principled, dangerous opposition."[1]

I start with Rachel, killed beneath the blade of a D-9 Caterpillar bulldozer, to honor her life and commitment and to examine the reactions to her death, which came from across the seas and close to home. These varied responses reinforced for me the advances we have made, as well as the many obstacles we face as Arab American feminists working both within academia and in the community in solidarity with Arabs, Muslims, Palestinians, and other oppressed peoples as we stand against the multiple violences of this purported "war on terrorism." Moreover, Rachel, through her dignified actions and writings, exemplified the meaning of feminist solidarity in that she consciously used her privilege to stand with the Palestinians and to support their most basic human rights—to their homes, their water and fields, and to a homeland—against a massive U.S.-made machine of destruction.

I start with Rachel because, as Suheir Hammad wrote, I felt her death tore at my heart, even though, as many of us who knew Rachel know, she would have hated to have her life mean more than the lives of those she sought to defend. Rather, she recognized her white U.S. privilege and used it to stand with the Palestinians. As the graffiti on the walls of a demolished building reads in Rafah, "Rachel was a girl from Olympia who came to stop the tanks," and on the wall across from the ISM office, "Rachel has Palestinian blood." And I start with Rachel because the concerted response to her death in our community was often

a shockingly vicious attempt at silencing. In her poem in response to the massacres of Sabra and Shatila, African American feminist poet June Jordan wrote:

> I was born a Black woman
> and now
> I am become a Palestinian.[2]

When my friend and colleague Anne, who is Jewish and was very close to
Rachel, told me she did not understand the vehemence with which Rachel was
attacked in the wake of her killing, I told her simply, "She has become Palestinian, and she will be attacked in the same way the Palestinians have always been
attacked and their struggle discredited. She will be called a terrorist or a terrorist sympathizer." I write this now with a certain distance, but for Anne and me,
in those first days and weeks after Rachel's death, we could not speak or come
together without tears and a deep emptiness that tore at our hearts.

On Feminist Solidarity and Rachel

I first met Rachel Corrie in the fall of 2001, when she contacted me to be on a
panel called "Women, War, and Militarization." A group of young women activists was coordinating this discussion to counter the growing male-dominated
antiwar movement in our community. Like many feminist activists in the wake of
9/11, the student organizers and speakers, faculty, and community members were
trying to formulate feminist and grassroots interventions to the Bush administration's policies in the "war on terrorism." As Arundhati Roy has said, few of us
(activists) "can afford the luxury of retreating from the streets for a while in order
to return with an exquisite, fully formed political thesis replete with footnotes and
references."[3] With this sense of urgency, we spoke out against the militarization
of women's lives; the racist and colonialist invocation of women's rights used to
justify war; the rising assault on women in the military and in their homes; the
erasure of social programs supporting welfare, health, and education to enhance
an already monstrous military budget; and the marginalization of women's voices,
both in the "war on terror" and in the global justice movement. But a feminist, or
gender, analysis is not only about the lives of women; it also offers a critique of the
workings of power and privilege—the power of men (or patriarchy) over women,
but also the power of occupier over occupied, the power of the economically
advantaged over the poor, the power of a country with the fourth-largest army
in the world against a stateless, dispossessed population without rights. Feminist
analysis also looks at, for example, the relative privileges enjoyed by Palestinian
urban women as compared to women in the villages and refugee camps, who are

often characterized as "the most oppressed of the oppressed." In addition, feminist analysis examines the intersecting forms of oppression faced by certain groups. For Palestinian women, these intersecting oppressions include the occupation and ongoing Israeli military dispossession (since 1948), the patriarchy of Palestinian society, the corruption of the Palestinian Authority, and the deliberate and systematic impoverishment of an entire people (more than three million within the territories alone) by the Israeli government—in other words, gender, class, racial-ethnic, national, and militarized oppression. It is this multilayered feminist critique that leads June Jordan to identify as "a Palestinian" and not exclusively as "a Palestinian woman."

"The greatest struggles of resistance," argues Zillah Eisenstein, "are located with anti-racist feminisms against Empire." Many of us sought to place those struggles at the center of our activism and academic work, even as we strove to build broad-based coalitions, both locally and nationally. With the rise of transnational feminism in the 1990s, we challenged global power structures in the form of economic and cultural globalization, as well as the globalization of militarized violence. Lisa Suhair Majaj, addressing the imperatives of Arab American activism, has written, "At this time of global interconnection, individual causes can no longer be viewed in separation from the global structures of power that situate them, nor can the effects of these structures of power be isolated to a single group."[4] Through "hate-free zones," international solidarity, and coalitions, these global interconnections were forged quickly after 9/11—in defiance of the limiting borders of identity, both discursive and spatial, set for us.

People often ask how Rachel became interested in the Palestinian issue. I cannot say for sure, but she seemed to see that global interconnection that Majaj describes—she worked at the Evergreen Labor Center and had done environmental work and education for youth and mentally disabled adults. After 9/11, it seems, I saw her at every community event and antiwar demonstration, often working diligently behind the scenes to pull things together. In February 2002, she stopped by my office because she heard that I needed help putting up flyers to advertise a talk and reading by Joe Kadi and Trevor Baumgartner (who had just returned from ISM work in Palestine). I remember Rachel in the audience that evening, dressed in jeans and a sweatshirt, her sandy-blonde hair in rain-damp strings, listening attentively to the speakers. I never had Rachel in class, though she sat in at times on our lectures in International Feminism, but I came to know her through her committed antiwar organizing with the Olympia Movement for Justice and Peace, then with our local chapter of United for Peace and Justice. On the first anniversary of 9/11, she took leadership in organizing a citywide conference called "Choosing Peace" and stood out on the Olympia pier all day while young schoolchildren wrote messages of their hopes for peace and local religious leaders and activists spoke of their visions for a more unified world. In her writings and talks, I never saw Rachel explicitly use the term "feminist," but through her organizing and solidarity work, she consistently involved children, women, Arabs, Muslims, and other underrepresented groups to forge a broader movement for social justice in our community.

I spoke with Rachel a few times before she left for Palestine. Rachel was not naive—she had studied the conflict as well as Arabic language, had friends who had worked with ISM in Gaza and the West Bank, and had built connections with both Israeli and Palestinian nonviolent activists prior to and during her six-week stay in the Palestinian territories. Before she left, when she told me of her intentions to go to Gaza, I said, "Gaza's a rough place. Have you seen the film *Gaza Strip*? You really should." Later, with intense insight, she wrote in a letter from Gaza, "No amount of reading, attendance at conferences, documentary viewing and word of mouth could have prepared me for the reality of the situation here. You just can't imagine it unless you see it—and even then you are always well aware that your experience of it is not at all the reality."[5]

Yet, like a parent, I had wanted to affirm her commitment but provide her ample warning for her safety. Rachel went to Gaza because she feared the ethnic cleansing that might take place under the cover of the renewed U.S. war on Iraq. When she told me she wanted to set up a sister-city project with Rafah, I told her it would be easier to have such a relationship with a West Bank town, like Bethlehem. I do not remember her exact words, but she looked at me like, "That's why it's so important to go to Rafah." I had been to Rafah in 1991, when I visited a family of fifteen living in the ruins of their demolished home. At that time, the father told me, "Lots of people come and take pictures, but nothing ever changes." Rachel was determined to change things. On a small scale, she initiated pen-pal exchanges between the children of Rafah and Olympia, but on a larger scale, she saw the need for more political intervention. As she wrote to her mother a few days before her death: "This has to stop. I think it is a good idea for us all to drop everything and devote our lives to making this stop. I don't think it's an extremist thing to do anymore."[6] What Rachel conveyed was an extreme urgency, the sense that many of us have felt, especially after the violent Israeli repression of the second intifada and the post-9/11 assault that have so imperiled our communities and made activism imperative to our survival.

Edward Said, in his essay "The Meaning of Rachel Corrie: Of Dignity and Solidarity" (first presented at the American Arab Anti-Discrimination

Committee Annual Conference, 2003), offers a sharp critique to the Arab and Palestinian community in the United States that has failed to embrace with self-respect and dignity the struggles that so many, like Rachel Corrie, have come to embrace. He concludes:

> Isn't it astonishing that all the signs of popular solidarity that Palestine and the Arabs receive occur with no comparable sign of solidarity and dignity for ourselves, that others admire and respect us more than we do ourselves? Isn't it time we caught up with our own status and made certain that our representatives here and elsewhere realize, as a first step, that they are fighting for a just and noble cause, and that they have nothing to apologize for or anything to be embarrassed about? On the contrary, they should be proud of what their people have done and proud also to represent them.[7]

According to Said, the problem for Arab and Palestinian Americans may be in our shame for our own people and struggles, our failure to recognize the importance of our cause, as others, like Rachel so eloquently through her letters and her dignified actions, have done. Feminists might call this internalized oppression or even assimilation to the mainstream American construction of citizenship. Indeed, although a few in our communities have taken leadership roles, speaking out to the media in demonstrations and protests, many of the major Arab and Muslim organizations have taken a more apologetic approach to the current crisis and sought to minimize our visibility in a charged political arena. For example, the national chapter of the American Arab Anti-Discrimination Committee publicly supported the war in Afghanistan and encouraged Arab American cooperation with FBI officials in the wake of 9/11.[8]

Said draws on Rachel's example to inspire Arab Americans to action, much in the same way that Rachel draws on Palestinians' daily resistance to inspire U.S. citizens to take responsibility for U.S. economic, military, and political support for Israeli human rights violations. Rachel expresses a human solidarity with the Palestinians, but I also see her actions in Gaza as expressing feminist concerns and consciousness, as she did in her local Olympia organizing. Rachel's e-mail messages (published in the *Guardian*, *Ha'aretz*, the *Monthly Review*, and *Harper's*) became a powerful testament to the world of her impressions of Gaza, her intentions in her solidarity work, and her fears for the people with whom she came to share meals, tea, blankets, and cartoon videos. Many wrote of Rachel's heroism: Susan Sontag compared her to Archbishop Romero, as well as Israeli Refuseniks, in her ability to move beyond her "tribe" and to stand in solidarity with others;

the Palestinian ambassador to Cuba called her "the beautiful face of America" in contrast to Bush's ugly face; and Egyptian Ahmad El Khameesy said she represented "the conscience of America" at a time when it seemed the United States had none, especially in its policies toward the Arab world. Rebecca Gould wrote of her hope that Rachel's death would "mark the end of the alliance between Israel and the United States." As Gould points out, the word in Arabic for martyr, *shahid*, has the same root as the word "witness," and she takes Rachel's life as "a feminist manifesto for the 21st century" because "her political consciousness did not end with a desire to overcome her own oppression." In a similar vein, June Jordan draws on the words of Lebanese writer Etel Adnan to capture the foundation of this feminist solidarity: "It is when we women, the New women of the world, 'stand up to our brothers to defend the Stranger,' it is only then that we can hope to become innocent of the evil that now imperils the planet." In this way, Rachel's depth of compassion for the Palestinians, her attention to their daily indignities, her witness to their ability "to remain human" and maintain their dignity "in the direst of circumstances," and her deep connection with the women and children capture this sense of feminist solidarity.[9]

E-Racing Palestinians and Arabs and the Politics of Anti-Semitism

Rachel Corrie recognized the racist nature of the Israeli military occupation with its U.S. backing. She wrote, "If the Israeli military should break with their racist tendency not to injure white people, please pin the reason squarely on the fact that I am in the midst of a genocide which I [as a U.S. citizen] am indirectly supporting, and for which my government is largely responsible." Yet the invocation of a racialized framework for understanding the Israel-Palestine conflict has a long and contentious history. By "racialized," I mean the ways in which a particular racial character is imposed on Palestinians, and Arabs more generally—a character that is assumed to be inferior, less civilized than the Israeli or Euro-American, and therefore less deserving of basic human rights. Rabab Abdulhadi argues for "a more nuanced understanding of [how] Zionism, anti-Semitism, discrimination, racism, and prejudice work; where we apply certain terms; and how we produce a complex analysis of these labels' particular flavor and context." In the U.S. context, Said has asserted a particularly American brand of Orientalism that is tied to our country's special relationship to Israel. In discussion of Palestine, I see the denial of racist treatment of the Palestinians as a variation on what Edward Said termed denying the Palestinians victim status because they are the victims of victims. Although references to the racist occupation seem to invoke the controversial "Zionism Is Racism" resolution passed by the UN General Assembly in 1975, then revoked, under considerable pressure, in December 1991, it is perhaps instructive to recall the complexity with which Said dismantled Zionist ideology in *The Question of Palestine*, its expansionist designs, assumptions of cultural superiority, and denial of Palestinian rights or even existence. He concludes that "Zionism is Zionism," an inherently colonialist project to its victims, justified by an ideology that "today we would call racist," yet one more complex than the concept of "racism" can contain.[10]

In my previous work I have argued that "Arabs and Arab Americans remain victims of racist policies, even as they are rendered invisible by the standards of current racialized discourse."[11] In other words, although race is a social construction, Arabs, including Palestinians, are denied a racial category, at the same time as they are racialized—that is, marked as racially or culturally inferior—within a racist system. Furthermore, unlike other European countries with a marked history of colonization in the Arab world, the United States, with its special relationship with Israel, consistently denies the racialization of, and therefore the racism projected against, Arabs in general, and Palestinians in particular. Moreover, there is a consistent denial of a racialized motivation for Israeli policies and a clear investment in deracializing the Arabs to promote this illusion.

One of the most contentious issues in our community after Rachel's death was around the racist nature of the occupation and charges of anti-Semitism affecting the campus climate. Shortly after Rachel's murder, a few members from the Jewish community and a couple of Jewish faculty met with college administrators to voice their concern about rising anti-Semitism on campus. Middle East studies faculty (including myself and Israeli feminist Simona Sharoni) were accused of promoting "covert anti-Semitism," and a lively debate ensued, most of it carried out on campus e-mail, about a student-initiated plan to wear *kufiya* at graduation to commemorate Rachel and to carry on her vision of solidarity with the Palestinians. A few faculty attempted to pass a resolution banning the wearing of *kufiya*; at least one suggested that wearing *kufiya* could be considered "hate speech," whereas others invoked free speech in support of wearing *kufiya*. Yet many campus members quickly learned that once they supported the *kufiya* campaign or building a campus memorial in honor of Rachel, they would be charged with anti-Semitism or not understanding the complexity of the issue.[12] In an absurd twist of logic, those individuals mourning Rachel's death and condemning the U.S. government's political, economic, and military backing of Israel's occupation suddenly became the purportedly guilty party. These charges effectively intimidated and silenced many; however, there were also many students, staff, and faculty (including many Jews) who felt they knew enough about the issues to talk back and challenge the discourse. As it turned out, several hundred people wore *kufiya* at the Evergreen 2003 graduation, and Cindy Corrie delivered a moving speech in acceptance of her daughter's posthumous degree.

In response to the conflict at Evergreen, the college administration agreed to hold a lecture series titled "The Search for Peace: The Palestinian-Israeli Conflict," dealing with issues of dialogue, historical narratives, religious dimensions, human rights, and women and peace movements. In the opening presentation, "Difficult Dialogues," the local rabbi stated that "too often, the apartheid metaphor obscures dialogue because it adds a rhetorical dimension of race to a conflict that is not race-based." He went on to argue that "racism" is ill-applied to the conflict, because "Zionism is a multiethnic national movement and Israel is a multiracial society."[13] Of course, such an argument can be made that the United States is also a multiracial and multiethnic society, but this does not mean that it is innocent of a long history of white supremacy and racist policies. Although charges of anti-Semitism made up a substantive part of his speech, with arguments such as "anti-Zionism is insensitive at best, and anti-Semitic at worst," the rabbi rejected paradigms of colonialism, racism, apartheid, and globalization as applicable to the Israel-Palestine conflict. His argument crystallizes the investment in deracializing the Arabs: while Jews have the charged claim to anti-Semitism, Palestinians and Arabs are denied a similarly charged claim to "racism" and left bereft of a charge on which to base their oppression, apart from what the rabbi described as their "struggle with stereotypes and stigma," certainly not a systematic form of oppression. Moreover, the discourse of "balance" in approaching the conflict assumes both peoples are on equal footing (although anti-Semitism, as usual, was not applied to Arabs), that a "balanced approach" is necessary with no critique of power relations. In effect, deracializing distracts attention from the exercise of power and privilege and denies the immense inequities between Israel and the Palestinians, and, closer to home, between American Jewish communities and Arab and Muslim American communities.

Although real anti-Semitism does exist and should be combated, the use of the charge to silence political critique of Israeli policy is well documented in Alexander Cockburn and Jeffery St. Clair's *Politics of Anti-Semitism*. Indeed, when St. Clair visited Olympia, he explained how the book was inspired by Rachel Corrie's death and the virulent charges their Web site, Counterpunch.org, received in response to their reporting on her death. Just as the antiwar movement was increasingly addressing the occupation of Palestinian lands and incipient divestment campaigns bloomed on campuses across the country, charges of anti-Semitism both in the mainstream and on the Left reached an increasing pitch. The most famous case involved Harvard University president Lawrence Summers, who argued that "a petition signed by 600 Harvard and MIT faculty, staff, and students to divest university funds from companies that do business in Israel to protest the occupation . . . [was], along with other criticisms of Israel 'anti-Semitic in their effect if not their intent.'" In her incisive rebuttal, "The Charge of Anti-Semitism: Jews, Israel, and the Risks of Public Critique," Judith Butler characterized Summers's comments as a "blow against academic freedom" and argued for preserving the public sphere as a space where Jews do not "monopolize the position of victim," but rather where both the violences of "suicide bombers" and of "the Palestinian child atrociously killed by Israeli gunfire" are "challenged insistently and in the name of justice." Furthermore, Butler insists that the conflation of "Jews" with "Israel" and "Zionism" denies not only Palestinian struggles for self-determination but also "the reality of a small but dynamic peace movement in Israel itself," as well as the work of American Jewish organizations that oppose the Israeli military occupation.[14] Butler situates her critique of Summers within the framework of certain discourses: academic freedom, critical engagement with Israeli policies, the separation of Jewishness and Zionism, as well as Palestinian human rights; however, she avoids racialized discourse concerning the Palestinian struggle.

Yet as we confronted similar charges of anti-Semitism on our campus, I was also reminded of June Jordan's critique of the feminist community and the political Left in 1984, in the wake of the Israeli invasion of Lebanon: "There were those for whom Israel remained a sacrosanct subject exempt from rational discussion and dispute, and there were those to whom Israel looked a whole lot like yet another country run by whitemen whose militarism tended to produce racist consequences; i.e. the disenfranchisement and subjugation of non-white people, peoples not nearly as strong as they. . . . Now it is one thing to disagree and quite another to prohibit disagreement."[15] Jordan brings up two simultaneous critiques here: a racialized understanding of the conflict as the subjugation of nonwhite peoples and Israel as exempt from critique and, thereby, the suppression of discussion or disagreement regarding Israeli policy.

Clearly, the charges of "covert anti-Semitism" leveled against Middle East studies faculty at Evergreen were not isolated events, but rather part of the larger national discourse and assault on academic freedom and the long-standing attempt to silence any critical discussion of U.S. and Israeli policies. For example, House Resolution 3077, which passed in the fall of 2003, includes a provision to establish an advisory board to monitor campus international studies centers in order to ensure that they advance the national interest; it mainly targets the seventeen federally funded Middle East studies centers.[16] This bill, along with the attack on the Middle East Studies Association by Martin Kramer and Daniel Pipes on their "neo-McCarthyite Campus-Watch website" show that Middle East studies is merely first in the neoconservative line of assault against academics.[17] Indeed, the discourse of "academic freedom" and "diversity" is being used by conservatives to argue for more hires that support conservative perspectives, all in the name of "political diversity" at universities.

Moreover, these debates on racial-ethnic inclusion and strategies have larger implications in the ongoing "war on terrorism," which masks its political-economic intentions of "remapping the Middle East" in the guise of fighting terror. In fact, while U.S. and Israeli policies deny the racialization of Arabs to promote an illusion of "just [nonracist or imperialist] wars," Arabs are continually racialized both domestically and internationally through U.S. foreign policy in the Middle East, which equates "Arab-looking" persons with terrorism. In effect, the tragic events of 9/11 and the readily available discourse of terrorism accorded victim status to both the United States and Israel and further reified the terrorist trope of Arab as other. More than twenty years ago, in response to events in Lebanon, June Jordan wrote, "The problem was that the Lebanese people, in general, and that the Palestinian people, in particular, are not whitemen: They never have been whitemen. Hence they were and *they are only Arabs, or terrorists, or animals.* Certainly they were not men and women and children; certainly they were not human beings with rights remotely comparable to the rights of whitemen, the rights of a nation of whitemen."[18] Today, as scenes of the destruction of Falluja, of Mosul, and of Baghdad call to mind the bombardment of Beirut, we can replace depictions of Lebanon's fate with Iraq, while Palestine remains Palestine, even as it is reduced to rubble and its people fragmented into Bantustans or reservations, surrounded by the "Separation Wall."

Palestinian Women and Our Sister City, Rafah

When Rachel was in Rafah, she stood watch by night over the last remaining water well in the area that Israel was trying to demolish, and she described what she saw there as a kind of "genocide," the systematic destruction of people's ability to survive.[19] Her predictions for Rafah were prophetic, and the violence of Israeli invasion that initially shocked the world—such as the destruction of Jenin in 2002—has since become normalized. Indeed, Israel's siege and war on Gaza from 2007 to 2009 has escalated economic warfare and military violence to their highest levels since the 1967 war.

More than a year after Rachel's death, in May 2004, Israel mounted a massive assault against Rafah, which has been documented by Human Rights Watch in its 135-page report "Razing Rafah: Mass Home Demolitions in the Gaza Strip." The report also calls for the Illinois-based multinational company Caterpillar, Inc., to suspend sales of D-9 bulldozers, the vehicle used by the Israel Defense Forces (IDF) to carry out illegal home demolitions (and to kill Rachel). The report documents the destruction of 298 homes in Rafah, many far inside the border, and describes the indiscriminate destruction of roads, shops, agricultural fields, and water and sewage systems. It documents how IDF operations to "widen the buffer zone" have left "16,000 people or ten percent of [Rafah's] population homeless over the past four years, regardless of whether their homes posed any genuine military threat, as the IDF has always claimed." In short, it describes the process of clearing Palestinians from the border areas that Rachel described a year earlier in her letters home, or that Gazans, such as Dr. Mona El Farra, with the Union of Health Work Committees in Gaza, have been reporting since November 2000.[20] Indeed, one of the ironies of solidarity is that the Palestinians still need international solidarity workers and human rights organizations to lend legitimacy to their firsthand reports of suffering.

This ethnic-cleansing operation that Rachel witnessed in Rafah is part of a larger assault on Palestinians in general and Palestinian women in particular.[21] In February 2004, the United Nations issued a report on the situation of Palestinian women. It states that "Israel's repressive policies in the West Bank and Gaza have had a devastating impact on Palestinian women and children" and that "only an end to Israel's occupation will reverse that trend." The capacity of women to cope with the situation is declining, and more women have become dependent on emergency assistance, especially food assistance. In addition, women are subject to increasing Israeli military violence, and responsibilities within the household have expanded owing to death, imprisonment, or unemployment of male members. In the five months following September 2003, the number of poor in Palestine had tripled to nearly two million, and a 2002 report by Johns Hopkins University showed that 30 percent of Palestinian children are suffering from chronic malnutrition. Much of this malnutrition is caused by water shortages, for Israel controls aquifers in West Bank and Gaza and channels water for use by Israeli citizens and settlers. According to a 2008 World Bank report on Gaza, 29 percent of Gazans are unemployed, and two-thirds of the population live below the poverty level of two dollars per day, excluding remittances and food aid. In addition, Israeli restrictions on movement have increased the number of births at home or in ambulances. In the last six months of 2003, forty-six women delivered babies while waiting for permission to pass through checkpoints. As a result, twenty-four women and twenty-seven newborns died in a six-month period.[22] These structural violences of deliberate starvation and denial of medical care and livelihood are other methods used to make life untenable for the Palestinians.

Over the past five years, Israel's assault, particularly on Gaza and its 1.5 million inhabitants, has continued unabated. In September 2005, Israel withdrew its Jewish settlers from the area, yet maintained control of airspace, borders, and territorial waters, effectively enclosing Gazans under heavy surveillance behind the wall in what has become known as "the largest open-air prison in the world." After Hamas's victory in a democratic election in 2006, Israel, with the backing of the United States, the European Union, and others, implemented an economic siege on Gaza in which Israel controlled the passage of goods and resources, including food, fuel, and medical supplies, in an attempt to weaken the Hamas government. In a celebrated act of resistance, in January 2008, Gazans broke through the border wall at Rafah, flooding into Egypt to purchase essential goods and food supplies denied them under siege.

In late December 2008 through January 2009, Israel's militarized violence reached unprecedented levels during a three-week air war and ground invasion of Gaza. During this period, approximately fourteen hundred Palestinians were killed, including more than three hundred children and one hundred women.[23] International aid organizations and human rights groups, including the United Nations, International Red Cross, and Amnesty International, have documented Gaza's humanitarian catastrophe, resulting from Israeli shelling of hospitals, mosques, schools, UN refugee centers, ambulances, and civilian areas; some document the use of white phosphorous and cluster bombs banned under international law.[24] Both Israeli and Palestinian human rights organizations have accused Israel of "war crimes" in its indiscriminate destruction of Gaza.[25]

◆　　◆　　◆

In the United States, in the wake of Rachel's killing, some activists made hopeful predictions that her death would "mark the end of the alliance between Israel and the United States." Yet even during Israel's brutal war on Gaza, the United States continued its unrelenting military and political support of Israel's actions, against world opinion. For example, the United States was the lone abstention vote for UN Resolution 1860 calling for an "immediate, durable, and fully respected ceasefire," thereby signaling to the world that our government would allow Israel to continue its vicious assault on the Palestinians in Gaza. Moreover, both houses of Congress passed near-unanimous resolutions "recognizing Israel's right to defend itself," and in effect condoning Israel's military assault and its breaches of international law and massacre of Palestinians.[26] This unrelenting U.S. complicity was also evident in Rachel's case, when House Resolution 111 calling for a U.S. investigation into Rachel's death received minimal congressional support. Indeed, the U.S. government response to Rachel's death was pathetic—the usual endorsement of Israeli policy with impunity, giving the IDF a green light to kill other internationals.[27]

Furthermore, in 2005, when the Corries joined five Palestinian families in a major lawsuit against Caterpillar, charging the corporation with aiding and abetting war crimes, the U.S. government stood with Caterpillar, arguing that U.S. foreign policy cannot be implicated in criminal violations, and the case was dismissed.[28] For many in the Olympia community, especially Rachel's family, the unrelenting obstacles to justice reinforced by the U.S. government's backing of Israel's brutal occupation have been a painful, yet awakening, lesson in what it means, at least in small part, to "become Palestinian."

Nevertheless, Rachel's courage and sacrifice have given the community a point of identification with the Palestinians in their struggle for justice and dignity and have spurred increased activism against the occupation. Since Rachel's death, nearly twenty people from our community, including Rachel's parents, Cindy and Craig Corrie, have gone over to Palestine as witnesses in solidarity with the Palestinians. Some have engaged in direct nonviolent action with the ISM; others have worked with children and women cooperatives in Rafah to build support and promote exchanges of women's craft work at a fair-trade store in Olympia. The Olympia-Rafah Sister City Project has raised thousands of dollars in medical relief for Palestinians in Rafah.[29] Many young women and men are spreading Rachel's work. Many have been unable to enter Rafah because of the extreme closures on the Gaza Strip, but those individuals and groups that make it in remind people in Rafah that they are not forgotten by the world.

In the summer of 2005, seven members from our community worked in Rafah, and several months later Rafah activist Fida Qishta, founder of the Rachel Way Group, visited Olympia. Before the Olympia City Council, Fida explained how when she heard the news of Rachel's death, she asked, "How can an American be killed for the Palestinian people?" She stopped her normal life of teaching and school and founded the Lifemakers Center for children, and began to work for the International Solidarity Movement. The next year, Fida's family home was also destroyed by the Israeli military; nevertheless, inspired by Rachel, she continues her committed work, and her center now serves more than three hundred children.[30] During Israel's recent war on Gaza, Fida worked with ISM volunteers and reported on the impact in Rafah. In an interview with *Democracy Now!* she stated:

The war that Israelis started with Palestinians in Gaza, it's really unbelievable and not acceptable. It's genocide. And all the world should stop and say to Israel, "Stop it. That's enough . . ." And for us, as Gazans, we try to continue our lives, no matter what happens. We keep the hope, and we keep the struggle for the future and for our families. We don't think, for example, if the Israelis destroy a house or kill a son or a daughter, that means our life is ended. We try to survive and continue our life. We try to do our best with it, but Israel is trying every single day, every single minute, to destroy the Palestinians' hope.[31]

Feminist Solidarity and Arab American Feminism

The model of feminist solidarity that Rachel embodied—a feminism beyond the borders of "tribe" or identity—comes often from privilege, the privilege to act or not. As Rachel wrote, Palestinians will be doing the work anyway, because their survival depends on it. Yet Said, in pointing to Rachel as an example of the international solidarity expressed toward Arabs and Palestinians, challenges especially relatively privileged Arab Americans in our complacency and inaction. In the Olympia community, given Rachel's sacrifice and her parents' unrelenting commitment to pursuing Rachel's vision in ending the injustices of the occupation, many of us have been compelled into action. Yet many in our community have seen their privilege quickly erased when they stood in solidarity with the Palestinians. As a graduate student, I was forewarned that Palestine was a dangerous subject, despite the work done by Edward Said, June Jordan, and others to lend it legitimacy. And despite our gains over the years in many spheres, "Palestine" and "Palestinian" remain unspeakable subjects, or if you speak them, your words will be censored, edited, and distorted, often in violent ways. For example, when Rachel's mother, Cindy Corrie, submitted an op-ed piece to the *New York Times* on the anniversary of Rachel's death, she was told she had to insert a false sentence that said the home that Rachel was protecting had underground tunnels used by terrorists to bring in weapons. When she refused to be (in her words) "a mouthpiece for the Israeli government," the *New York Times* pulled her piece; it was, however, published in the *Washington Post*.[32]

Yet in March 2006, three years after Rachel's death, attempts by the New York Theatre Workshop to censor Rachel's story backfired. The theater's decision to indefinitely postpone *My Name Is Rachel Corrie*, the Royal Court play that had two successful runs in London, unleashed national and international campaigns to publicize Rachel's story (see rachelswords.org).[33] These campaigns brought unprecedented attention to Rachel's witness to "the horrors of Israeli occupation." The theater justified the indefinite postponement of the U.S. premiere with "concern for the sensitivities of (unnamed) Jewish groups" unsettled by both Prime Minister Sharon's ill health and Hamas's victory in recent Palestinian elections.[34] Yet, as Philip Weiss asserts in the *Nation*, Rachel's story and literary gifts have granted us (in the United States) the freedom to break through the climate of fear and intimidation surrounding critique of the Israeli occupation. In this sense, Rachel's witness and solidarity with Palestinians in their struggle for human rights demonstrate a significant break in the silencing and censorship of the Palestinian story as a human story.

Since 2006, *My Name Is Rachel Corrie* has been reaching audiences worldwide, on stages in Lima, Montreal, Athens, New York, Des Moines, Seattle, and scores of other cities. On the fifth anniversary of Rachel's death, the play opened in Haifa, in Arabic; other performances are scheduled throughout Europe, and in South Africa, Australia, even Iceland. In several U.S. cities, theaters have backed out due to political pressure, yet artists and activists offended by the censorship and silencing usually find creative ways to stage the play, bringing even more attention to Rachel's story, and to the Palestinian struggle.

Moreover, March 2008 saw the release of *Let Me Stand Alone: The Journals of Rachel Corrie*, a major publication by W. W. Norton. Here, as in the play, Rachel becomes more than a political symbol. As Cindy Corrie explains, "Sometimes she is demonized; sometimes she is lionized, but it makes it more possible for her to have more impact if people see her as human." The sustained beauty of Rachel's writings and sketches and her incisive observations into personal and global relationships, from ten years old into young adulthood, expose a young woman who is deeply caring, creative, quirky, wise beyond her years, anything but naive. In a press release from March 2003, Rachel writes, "We can only imagine what it is like for Palestinians living here, most of them already once-or-twice refugees, for whom this is not a nightmare, but a continuous reality from which international privilege cannot protect them, and from which they have no economic means to escape."[35]

Although Rachel's international privilege did not ultimately protect her from the U.S.-made bulldozer that crushed her to death, Rachel recognized that she moved through this world with privileges denied the Palestinians. I, too, live in a community marked by privilege, where most of the activism is carried out by allies struggling against occupation, war, and U.S. imperialism. Since 9/11 I have often felt that Arab and Muslim communities are so under siege that we are struggling for our survival—for the Palestinians, the Iraqis, for Arabs and Muslims in America—on a daily basis, that it is difficult to extend ourselves beyond the borders of our community in the way Rachel did. How do we extend ourselves beyond this "virtual portal of luxury" to people on the front lines of the war zones? As Said argues, we need to gain "respect for ourselves as Arabs and understand the true dignity and justice of our struggle" in order to appreciate the solidarity extended to us. I would add that without a critical mass of participation from within the Arab and Muslim communities, we will remain defined by the discourse of others. Moreover, as Nada Elia has written, "Coalition building is vital to our visibility, to our very survival." In other words, we need to continue to make the necessary links with other folks that will pull us out of our isolation, not just strategically but also out of real concern for their struggles. As Arab Americans working in a climate of urgency and crisis—of occupied peoples, profiled, and under surveillance—we need to maintain this globally connected view. And as Arab-American feminists, we must constantly ask how we can assert a "radical, anti-racist, and non-heterosexist" feminism as we stand on the front lines in this "war on terrorism."[36]

I have often asked myself this question when I hear young people of color here say there is too much focus on the Middle East at Evergreen and not enough on the racism on our campus and in our communities. Or when I read a book about Arab women and globalization and wonder about the lack of reference to other third world women (Filipinas, Sri Lankans, and others) who are brought to Arab countries to serve as maids, or even sex workers, for the Arab elite or U.S. military.[37] And how do we speak of the occupation of Palestine and Iraq without attention to Native Americans, for as Suheir Hammad reminds us,

> In America
> right now you are standing
> on stolen land no matter
> where you are reading this poem.[38]

And what do I tell my queer student who just returned from the Palestinian territories with ISM and is disillusioned by the silencing of issues of sexuality in Palestinian society? How do we build hope when nonviolent resistance is met with militarized force? As Hammad writes:

> What can we theorize from all this?

> What do we tell young
> people? How do we say, "Your
> voice means nothing to those
> who think life is about power
> over others and greed?" And where

is it safe to think for yourself and try
real hard to not want to hurt nobody?[39]

The need for solidarity with ourselves and coalition building with others is still imperative for "subverting the mechanisms of occupation," and subverting all the destructive mechanisms of militarized violence—war, imprisonment, occupation, torture, the Apartheid Wall—that destroy life, homes, and the security of our planet. As a feminist, I take my inspiration from the Palestinian people who remain and resist against great odds. I take my inspiration from the many Palestinian women I worked with, learned from, taught, and interviewed over the years—women who are engaged in creative collective actions in the face of their people's systematic destruction and dehumanization. I take my inspiration from Rachel Corrie, who worked with Israeli human rights groups to document the water crisis in Gaza and stood with Palestinians to defend their most basic right to their homes. Rachel perceptively described the Palestinian struggle "to defend such a large degree of their humanity against the incredible horror occurring in their lives and against the constant presence of death."[40] I take my inspiration from Rachel's family, who has been tireless in their commitment to meet with people on all sides of this struggle and to carry out Rachel's vision to stop these injustices. I am inspired by the growing divestment movement, led by students on college campuses and the Presbyterian Church (USA), calling for divestment from corporations, like Caterpillar, that are directly benefiting from Israel's repression of the Palestinians in the Occupied Territories. I take my inspiration from many feminists of color who argue for a feminism without borders to counter the globalizing inequalities of capitalism, racism, and militarization, and from tireless Israeli human rights and peace activists like Tikva Honig-Parnass, who told me quite simply, "I believe in human beings, I believe in their need for freedom, so nothing that we see now is going to last forever."[41]

Indeed, Palestinians should not have to prove that they are worthy of the basic rights and dignity that we take for granted. As many feminists have argued, and as Rachel Corrie stood for, the future worth living for is one that affirms life, justice, dignity, and security for all peoples.

18

Just Peace Seder

Toronto Just Peace Seder Community

The Toronto Just Peace Seder is a joint Jewish-Palestinian community-building initiative launched in the spring of 2002 and organized annually since by a group calling itself Cooks for Peace. The collaborative text is a testament to the successful partnership developed over a period of ten years between an informal, unaffiliated group of Jewish, Palestinian, and Arab Canadian women (as well as, at times, men).

Reinventing the Seder

Kathy Wazana: In the spring of 2002, with the deteriorating situation in the Occupied Palestinian Territories, the reinvasion of Ramallah, and the siege of Bethlehem, my sons and I found it increasingly difficult to contemplate the upcoming traditional Jewish Passover holiday, which celebrates the freedom of the Jewish people.

Ameena Sultan: When, in March 2002, Kathy asked me to be part of a Jewish holiday celebration dedicated to the Palestinian victims of the Israeli occupation, I was intrigued.

Kathy and I had met at an Arab Jewish dialogue group and soon discovered that, more than our common political values, we shared a cultural heritage: she is an Arab Jew from Morocco, and I am an Arab Muslim from Egypt.

Kathy and Ameena: The concept of a peace seder is neither new nor unique. Over the years, many Jewish communities throughout North America have adopted the tradition of a "third seder" dedicated to universal issues of liberation or peace. These initiatives have usually involved the reading of a text (liberation seder, freedom seder, peace seder, and so forth) and a dinner hosted by progressive Jews, with non-Jews invited to attend as guests.

Rejecting the host-guest model, we chose instead to create a space where Jews and Arabs could participate jointly in a reinterpretation of the biblical story of the Exodus and its ritual retelling during the Passover holiday, as part of a process of reclaiming and affirming our common heritage. It has meant rejecting the premise that this ancient history belongs only to the Jews and that it is theirs to merely "share" with others.

From this starting point, we began to deconstruct the traditional seder (meaning "order") and the biblical references that have contributed to the perpetuation of the Jewish ethos of fear of persecution and exile. In the context of today's reality, the fear of persecution and exile belongs to the Palestinian people. And the Jewish freedom that is celebrated on this holiday has cost the Palestinian people their freedom.

The "Just Peace Seder" is an evolving document, as each year the reality changes and our understanding of the historical and political context grows. First drafted in 2002 and revised, updated, contextualized each year since, this text was read at the last Toronto Just Peace Seder, attended by more than one hundred people from the Jewish, Arab, Palestinian, and other communities gathered in a restaurant owned by a Palestinian member of the group.

Just Peace Seder, 2006
Programme
Monday, April 17
6:00 p.m.
Toronto, Canada

MENU
Baba Ganoush
Moroccan Olives & Oranges Salad
Fennel & Preserved Lemon Salad

———

Matzo Ball Soup
Moroccan Fishballs in Saffron Lemon Sauce

———

Braised Lamb Shanks
with
Herbed Roasted Potatoes
Cumin-Spiked Beets
Spicy Carrots

———

Dessert
Moroccan Mint Tea

Welcome and Introduction

Shalom, *Salaam Aleykum*, Peace be with you.

Welcome one and all to the fifth Toronto Just Peace Seder.

It's just about peace, and it's about a just peace. People have different ideas about the relationship between peace and justice, and the words of Jewish philosopher Baruch (Benedict) Spinoza offer one important way of thinking about it: "Peace is not an absence of war; it is a virtue, a state of mind, a disposition for benevolence, confidence, justice."

What Is the Significance of the Seder?

"Seder" means order. Traditionally, the celebration of Passover follows a specific order. Each item on the seder plate before you is placed in a particular order and is symbolic of an aspect of liberation. The purpose of these symbols is to make the story of freedom from bondage more tangible for us.

The seder is part of the commemorative practice of Jews to keep alive the vision of freedom in the Passover story. The literal story of Passover, the one recounted in the biblical book of Exodus, involves the journey of the Jews from slavery in ancient Egypt to emancipation.

But Passover is not only about telling a biblical story as a prelude to a great meal. It is about retelling, reliving, and reinterpreting the themes of oppression, enslavement, exile, and liberation into a more inclusive and relevant context right here, right now.

As we recount the Passover story, we are compelled to acknowledge the timely, sometimes uncomfortable correlations between that ancient narrative and the realities of those persons who live in various conditions of oppression.

This Just Peace Seder acknowledges the gulf in power between oppressor and oppressed, occupier and occupied, and recognizes that they inhabit a shared world of violence, fear and hopelessness.

Today we gather for a Just Peace Seder, during a time when both justice and peace are in woefully short supply, in Israel and Palestine, in Iraq, in Haiti, in Afghanistan, in too many places around the world. Coming together on this night—Jews and Muslims and Christians, Israelis and Palestinians, believers and atheists—is a gesture of hope and defiance against cynicism, a moment of resistance to the overwhelming wave of despair that threatens to engulf us. It is not a solution to the conflict, it is not a recipe for peace, but it matters nonetheless.

Although the Haggadah instructs us to tell the story as if only Jews were the enslaved, we cannot evade the fact that the Israeli occupation places every Jew in the role of the one who enslaves, and that our own history of victimization is used to rationalize and justify the oppression of the Palestinian people.

The core meaning of Passover demands that we connect our observance to this reality in the Middle East today. For this reason, we can no longer recline and retell the story of freedom; we must instead contextualize the seder meal and look forward to a day when Jews and Palestinians are both free from oppression, fear, and mistrust.

◆   ◆   ◆

Candle Lighting

Reader 1

We open the seder by lighting candles: they mark the transition from an ordinary day to a special one; they illuminate the darkness; they are a symbol of enlightenment. This year, we observe with great sadness the building of a wall that is enclosing millions of Palestinians living in the West Bank, as people living in Gaza have been for years. This wall of shame and oppression is the physical manifestation of a process whose ultimate goal has been to separate and to erect social, psychological, economic, and political barriers between Palestinians and Jews. It is a devastating example of the darkness within which political leaders operate, guided by hatred, greed, mistrust, and fear.

Seventeen years after the world celebrated the dismantling of the Berlin Wall, the world is now standing by as Israel builds a wall thirty feet high, with razor wire, electric fences, and armed guard towers and promotes it as a viable option for peace. By being here tonight, we say a collective no to this wall of shame and oppression.

We now ask someone at each table to light their candles in the hope that all leaders involved turn on the light of hope and peace.

◆   ◆   ◆

The First Cup of Wine

Reader 2

Spring is the season of rebirth. From a ground that seemed still and cold springs new life. There are moments in our interior life when we feel stunted and sterile, unable to nourish hope. There are times when the exterior world seems hostile and deadly—no place for hope to take root, much less flourish. And yet the world can be repaired.

Spring also reminds us of the time for planting fruits and vegetables. This year we remember the tens of thousands of olive trees that have been uprooted by the Israeli army in deliberate violation of international law and in a flagrant, concerted attempt to economically suffocate the Palestinian people by depriving them of a livelihood that is so rooted in their historical, tangible relationship to the land.

Let us raise our first cup of wine to olive trees and for what they stand for: rootedness, sustenance, hope, and rebirth.

Let us all now drink the first cup of wine.

◆　　◆　　◆

The Four Questions

Reader 3

Tonight, instead of asking four questions, we ask one important question: "How can we celebrate Passover this year, as the occupation of the West Bank and Gaza enters its fortieth year?"

The ability to ask questions, to challenge and to seek answers, to disagree, to be open to changing one's mind are all signs of freedom. It also connotes a responsibility to be open to listening to answers, to weighing and considering them, and even to begin thinking about whether we are asking the right questions. Having that kind of discussion is why we are gathering here tonight.

◆　　◆　　◆

The Story of Passover

Reader 4

The Haggadah tells a story about physical enslavement, which even today is real and powerful. But it is not the only form of bondage. We may be politically subjugated, denied the ability to exercise self-determination and to govern ourselves in accordance with our priorities and values. We may be socially oppressed, constrained by demands and expectations of the roles assigned to us as man and woman, as young and old, as gay and straight, that we did not freely choose or consent to. We may feel psychically imprisoned, unable to break free of the demons and the fears that haunt us and make it so hard for us to move forward, to live and love freely. A form of enslavement most often overlooked, especially by the people who live it, is of the one who enslaves others. The one who believes his or her own freedom can be secured only by the subjugation, the erasure, the negation of others. As that great sage and rock and roller Steve Earle wrote, borrowing the voice of a prisoner:

There's a guard on the second shift comes on at three
And he's always about a half inch off of me
Like he needs to keep remindin' me that I'm not free
God forgive him 'cause he doesn't see
He's no less a prisoner 'cause he holds a key.

Tonight, we celebrate not only freedom from harm. We also embrace the freedom to live in peace, with dignity and with hope for a bright future. This evening, let us address our thoughts to those individuals who are trapped physically, politically, and psychically in the vicious circle of victim and victimizer, enslaver and enslaved. Rather than enter that circle, let us think of ways to undo it.

◆   ◆   ◆

Second Cup of Wine: The Struggle for Human Freedom

Reader 5

This second cup of wine is dedicated to the struggles of all people seeking a secure life free of fear and persecution.

Let us all now drink the second cup of wine. May we all stand by those people who are struggling for freedom and peace and self-determination.

The Dayenu, which means "It would have been enough," is said after each stanza. Let us bring the Dayenu into the present tonight by striving for a vision and say together:

◆   ◆   ◆

When the wall of shame and oppression is bulldozed and the bricks are used to rebuild demolished Palestinian homes, THAT WILL BE ENOUGH.

When all Palestinian children and Israeli children can play safely on the streets of their cities, THAT WILL BE ENOUGH.

When Palestinian and Israeli mothers and fathers no longer live in fear of losing their sons and daughters, THAT WILL BE ENOUGH.

When Palestinian families are reunited, and return home, THAT WILL BE ENOUGH.

When all political prisoners are free, THAT WILL BE ENOUGH.

When Israeli citizens no longer live in poverty because of the diversion of government resources into the war machinery, THAT WILL BE ENOUGH.

When Palestinian farmers can once again live off their land, THAT WILL BE ENOUGH.

When Israelis and Palestinians are living in justice and peace, THAT WILL BE ENOUGH.

When Palestinians can celebrate their freedom and self-determination, THAT WILL BE ENOUGH.

◆　　◆　　◆

The Ten Plagues

Reader 6

Our sages say that we must never rejoice in the pain of others, even if they are those people we deem our enemies. There is a beautiful tradition that during the recitation of the ten plagues visited upon the Pharaoh and his people, we remove a drop of wine from our glasses for each plague. Wine symbolizes joy, and our joy is diminished each time humanity suffers.

As the pain of others diminishes our joys, let us diminish the wine in our glasses as we repeat the names of these modern plagues:

1. the killing and maiming of Palestinian and Israeli children and innocent civilians

2. home demolitions and the seizure of Palestinian lands for settlements

3. the uprooting of olive trees

4. the isolation of an entire people

5. checkpoints and roadblocks, curfews and closures

6. walls and fences

7. the silencing of dissent

8. physical and psychological abuse and torture

9. the erasure of history

10. the militarization of Israeli and Palestinian societies

◆　　◆　　◆

The Seder Plate

Reader 7

The seder plate, the perfect vehicle for contextualizing this ageless story of oppression, holds the principal symbols of the Passover story.

Matzo: Unleavened Bread

When Moses and his followers fled, they had to leave so quickly that the bread they baked did not have time to rise.

Symbolically, matzo reminds us that when the opportunity for liberation comes, we must seize it even if we do not feel fully prepared; indeed, if we wait until we feel prepared, we may never act at all.

It is said that matzo tasted just like the manna that fell from heaven in the desert, food they could not save or accumulate because it went sour each night. The manna taught the Israelites to overcome their belief that they had to compete for scarce resources, and to trust that there would be enough for everyone. Only once they had let go of their terror of scarcity could they learn to open their hearts to one another in empathy. Here is a central spiritual message: there is enough, if we want there to be.

Break off a piece of matzo and eat.

◆   ◆   ◆

The Bitter Herb

Reader 8

Martin Luther King Jr. said, "Let us not seek to satisfy our thirst for freedom by drinking from the cup of bitterness and hatred." At the Passover seder, we eat the bitter herb to remind us of, and repel us from, the bitterness of oppression and slavery anywhere, anytime.

One of the most radical messages of the Torah is that cruelty is not destiny. Though we are treating others the way we were once treated, the message of the Torah is that the chain of oppression can be broken, that we do not have to pass on to others what was done to us. One of the most frequently repeated injunctions in Torah comes from Exodus: "And you shall not wrong or oppress the Other, for you know the feelings of the Other, as you were strangers in Egypt."

Dip a piece of matzo into the bitter herb and eat.

◆   ◆   ◆

Dipping Greens in Saltwater

Reader 9

The saltwater represents the tears of anguish shed by slaves and by all people who are not free. On this night, we remember the tears shed by Palestinian and Israeli mothers and fathers for their daughters and sons who have perished in the conflict.

The green vegetable we dip in the water suggests the possibility of growth and renewal, even in the midst of grief.

Dip and eat.

◆   ◆   ◆

Haroset

Reader 10

This mixture of apples, wine, dates, and nuts is meant to resemble mortar. We can give it at least two meanings: it can remind us of the bricks that the slaves used in their toil; its sweetness can also signify the bricks and mortar that we use to build our homes as free people and to build bridges between free peoples.

On this evening, the mortar symbolizes the thousands of Palestinian homes that have been destroyed by the Israeli army and the even greater number of houses that continue to be built for Israeli settlers on Palestinian land, and of course, and again, the "Separation Wall."

Dip matzo in haroset and eat.

◆   ◆   ◆

Egg

Reader 11

Nurturing life requires warmth, love, security, guidance, hope, and vision. To reach their full potential, human beings need the support and encouragement of family and community. The egg symbolizes the fragility and interdependence of life; it is the potential for new life, spring, eternity, and renewed hope. Tonight, we observe the loss of lives of thousands of Palestinians and Israelis over the course of this conflict.

◆   ◆   ◆

Shank Bone

Reader 12

The shank bone represents the "strong hand and the outstretched arm." Tonight we condemn the strong arm of violence and celebrate the hand extended in friendship, solidarity, and peace.

The shank bone also represents sacrifice. Tonight we reflect on the growing number of Palestinians and Jews whose lives have been sacrificed for political gain.

◆   ◆   ◆

The Third Cup of Wine: Remembrance

Reader 13

We drink the third cup of wine to those persons who were taken from us and those who fought for freedom and life.

This year, again, we observe Passover with great sadness. We mourn the Palestinian civilians—children, women, and men—who have lost their lives in acts of terror by the Israeli state. We also mourn for those Israeli civilians—Jewish and Palestinian children, women, and men—who have lost their lives to acts of terror.

Let us remember, let us learn, and let us act for a just peace, so that we can gather to celebrate life, instead of mourning death.

◆　　◆　　◆

Final Cup of Wine: Elijah's Cup

Reader 14

According to Jewish tradition, the prophet Elijah was a brave man who denounced slavery in his day. It was customary during the Passover seder to open the door of the house for Elijah, in the hope that the age of universal peace may soon be at hand.

We, too, open the door to peace, knowing that Elijah's task is really our own. As the prophet Isaiah said, "They shall beat their swords into ploughshares, and their spears into pruning hooks, nations shall not take up sword against nation, they shall never again know war. But they shall sit every one under their vines and fig trees, and none shall make them afraid."

That day has not yet come; we do not drink the wine.

Supper

The Haggadah says, "Let all who are in need come and eat." This statement is understood to mean not only those persons who are literally hungry but also those who are spiritually famished. Tonight, we should all be grateful that we are not among the hungry, the homeless, the destitute. But we all hunger for peace. Amen.

19

Dissidents, Displacements, and Diasporas

An Interview with Dena Al-Adeeb

NADINE NABER

Through an interview-style narrative, Dena Al-Adeeb explores the multiple and multilayered displacements and dislocations that color her Iraqi diasporic experiences. This article maps out her dissident trajectories through her political and social-cultural activism and artwork. Dena outlines almost thirteen years of work against the war and sanctions in Iraq, against anti-Arab (including other West Asians and North Africans) racism and xenophobia, and on Palestinian solidarity efforts. The interview traces her commitment to coalition building and transnational solidarity campaigns through her efforts in people of color, third world, immigrant, and indigenous peoples and transnational-radical women of color feminist formations. Al-Adeeb situates her artistic productions within movement work and as a catalyst for social change and transformation.

Can you tell me a bit about your history? When and why did you end up moving to the United States?

My immediate family avoided the Baath regime's forced deportations waged in the 1980s against Iraqi Shiites of presumed Iranian descent.[1] We escaped to Kuwait after members of my father's family were deported from Iraq to the Iranian borders. Two of my cousins were also arrested at that time, and we recently found out that they were executed in 1982 and 1983. My early lived experience taught me from a young age to question the very construction of borders, nation-states, and citizenship. In retrospect, I realized that they were created in order to organize and control us based on the political interests of governing elites. That was my first encounter with displacement, and it also served as an early catalyst to introduce me to the fluid, shifting, and destabilized nature of identity, home, and belonging. In Kuwait, the presence of the Iraqi Mukhabarat threatened the safety and security of politically displaced Iraqis.[2] We never spoke about the deportation and especially kept

213

quiet about it in public. These ten years were filled with fear and censorship; the active presence of the Mukhabarat was so threatening that people refrained from calling their families out of concern that the phone lines might be tapped. The trepidations my family negotiated were owing to both the formal and shadowing surveillance of the Iraqi secret police in Kuwait and their collaboration with the Kuwaiti authorities as well as the informal or public consent to this surveillance. My mother, sister, and I returned only briefly to Iraq in the late 1980s, toward the end of the Iraq-Iran war; it was a remarkable risk since my father's name could have been on the Mukhabarat's "red list." It was only after the 2003 U.S. invasion of Iraq that my father was able to return to Iraq after twenty-three years of exile.

I experienced a second displacement during the Iraqi invasion of Kuwait in 1990. My family and I came to the United States a few days before the invasion. We planned to return to Kuwait after a few weeks, as we needed to briefly stay in the United States to uphold the requirements of our green cards. A few days after we arrived, on August 2, 1990, we learned about the Iraqi invasion of Kuwait and realized that we would not be able to return. The ruptures I experienced as a result of the multiple displacements became a position for me to explore my multiple and complex identities. The ruptures caused not discontinuity, but rather a continuity flavored by layered and multifaceted experiences that inspire me to find different modes of expression.

Hoping I could finally escape living in the "belly of the beast," I returned to Iraq several times throughout the 1980s, 1990s, and after the U.S. invasion and occupation in 2003. In 2004, I was ready to go "home," to return to Iraq, especially after the escalation of violence and hatred toward Arabs, Muslims, West Asians, and North Africans in the region and in the diasporas. Shortly after arriving in Iraq, I came to realize that this time there might not be a place to go back to in my lifetime since the "beast" had unleashed decades of carnage. The place I once called home was no longer.

After experiencing displacement from Iraq to the United States, what have the terms "violence" and "belonging" come to mean to you?

Violence, displacement, belonging, and not belonging paved the path to the formation of my identity, sense of self and community, and eventually political, academic, cultural, and artistic work. The struggle, determination, and resilience of my family and our experiences gave birth to a spirit of resistance and struggle for survival.

Displacement defined my experiences in the United States from the first moment I realized there is no place to return. The invasion, the sanctions, the

Gulf War in 1991 that lasted for thirteen years, the second "intifada," and the events of September 11th and its aftermath in Afghanistan, Iraq, Iran, Palestine, and Lebanon were all experiences of violence that splintered my ability to belong in the United States and magnified my sense of alienation. My identity was defined to a large extent by these events that took place not only "back home" but via racist, imperialist, and violent U.S. propaganda media campaigns that were aimed at glorifying the obliteration of my peoples and country. For the first seven months of our arrival in the United States, we lived the war virtually in our living room, glued to the television. We were practically transported to the "war zone" in Iraq via satellite television; we were privy to the bloodbath and mass destruction on the ground. We had intimate sensory access to the scene of carnage as well as the familiar demolished landscape. As the ongoing war escalated, the family gathered in the "war zone," a liminal space between the war in Iraq and its impact on our lives while we were forced to remain in the United States. We stared miserably into the toxic rays of the tube as we witnessed so-called smart bombs obliterate "collateral damage." The living room continued to be the gathering place where the war unfolded through the tube. We especially came together during the height of the bombing campaigns in solidarity and as support for each other, though the way we internalized the events and related to each other seemed to reflect another form of war, an inner war that we struggled to survive and at times transferred onto each other, reflecting our rage and sense of powerlessness. In the midst of this, my sister, father, and I attempted to create a new life for ourselves while dealing with the separation of my mother and brother, who returned to Iraq and Kuwait in 1990. They returned to the Bay Area just before the bombing campaign in 1991. The war for us and many other Iraqis did not cease after the First Gulf War and resumed during the Second Gulf War, but rather it was an ongoing escalation of violence and devastation through sanctions and unrelenting bombing campaigns throughout the 1990s that led to the 2003 invasion and occupation.

Our initial encounters in the Bay Area were shaped by the launching of the Gulf War. As marginalized immigrants, we experienced a microscopic gaze that interrogated our identities and our belongingness, casting us as the threatening "Other." Since my sister and I had access to "American" culture more than my parents did, we became the cultural and at times linguistic translators, which meant buffering all the racist and anti-immigrant comments. I recall an incident where several neighbors came to my parents' house during the war (none of them had any contact with my parents before then, and they purposefully avoided my parents' greetings on the streets of the neighborhood). They asked to inspect our house. I remember the rage I felt as one of them audaciously made his way through my parents' house, inspecting room by room as if we were hiding "weapons of mass destruction" in our bedrooms. My father graciously led him into our rooms in order to divert any suspicion of us in the neighborhood. I held back my rage in respect for my father as I painfully watched the tall white man who supposedly was sent as a representative of the local church and neighborhood; he scavenged through our most sacred inner worlds. I remember telling my mother and father in Arabic not to let him trespass and attempted to explain to them that they do not need to be hospitable to his racist, xenophobic, and violent behavior.

Such and other racially prejudiced behaviors were a common theme in our daily reality while living in the Bay Area. Hence, every moment of my existence in the United States affirmed that I do not belong; that my brother and father (as constructed in the United States) could be terrorists, violent and criminal; that my sister, my mother, and I are seen as backward, oppressed, and silent; that my peoples are savages, uncivilized and dispensable; that I do not belong and will never belong. Such masculine and feminine constructions are not only common in mainstream U.S. propaganda campaigns but also embraced by many, including other oppressed and marginalized peoples, as well as some in our own communities, not to forget how we in our own communities might have internalized some of these constructions.

The streets in the Bay Area became the new "war zone" where other activists and myself utilized public spaces to demonstrate, educate, and organize; the occasional spitting, cursing, and assaults seemed calmer than the family living room since I was now actively engaging instead of passively internalizing the news and images on the screen. As my activism evolved, I began working with other displaced and marginalized communities in the United States, forging solidarity based on some of our shared experiences.

My existence and identity continue to be negotiated, torn, and redefined through forced displacement and nonbelonging; it inspires in me an immense sense of self, home, identity, community, and culture that is based on resistance, resilience, and a refusal to accept injustice. It is from such a place that I create and build home and community and seek justice.

How did your trips back to Iraq in 1999 and 2004 affect your life, your sense of self and identity, and your political work? Can you talk about one of the trips?

In 1999, I returned to Iraq with my mother and two fellow Iraqis living in the United States, Nadia and Shami. It had been nine years since I had returned to Iraq, and it was my first trip back since I arrived in the United States. I wanted to return to see family and Iraq, and I also felt that this trip could be an extension of the brewing antisanction- and antiwar-movement work and could potentially be a collective effort to express solidarity with people in Iraq. In collaboration with the Arab American Anti-Discrimination Committee, the San Francisco chapter, we organized an antisanction community event and gathering, reached out to community members, and were able to fund-raise and elicit donations of toys, medical journals, and medicine. We received donations up until the departure date. It was inspiring to witness the collective energy and efforts of our communities and their commitment and support. These moments speak to the significance of activism, community organizing, and political work; these efforts were not simply about the material contributions and their effects. Obviously, these gestures are symbolic. The trip and the community work building up to the trip were an attempt to build community, to create solidarity, to engender consciousness about the political situation through education and media campaigns, and to mobilize the resistance needed to fuel our dreams and the potential for a more just reality.

In Iraq, Nadia, Shami, my cousin Zena, and I spent a day at the children's leukemia ward in a hospital in Baghdad where we distributed toys, medicine, and money. There was medical consensus in Iraq that the impact of the Gulf War increased leukemia incidents as a direct result of the depleted uranium used by U.S. and British forces. The sanctions escalated this dire reality. As I walked along the run-down, dimly lit hospital corridors, I looked through the cracked glass window at the frail and failing bodies of children and witnessed the color of life fading from them. It was a horrifying vision. Six children lined up in rows on sheetless old mattresses; they looked up at their parents' sad eyes, in utter hope for the slightest respite and consolation. Parents nursed their children as the short-staffed hospital devoured one by one, the angel of death hovering over them. These symbolic offerings paled against the threat of death that loomed around them.

We retreated to the doctor's office and humbly performed the offerings. He accepted but informed us that the best way to support is by offering the families funds so they may be able to visit their dying children since some of them could not afford the trip all the way from northern or southern Iraq. He stressed that at this point nothing could be done to save the children's lives, but to have their families around in their last few days would be an important offering. He introduced us to a family that could not afford to come all the way from Kurdistan to see their child. The mother's weary and perplexed eyes still haunt me, and I recall Secretary of State Madeleine Albright's comments on the U.S. sanctions against Iraq. On May 12, 1996, Lesley Stahl asked her on *60 Minutes*, "We have heard that a half million children have died. I mean, that's more children than died in

Hiroshima. And, you know, is the price worth it?" Secretary of State Albright responded, "I think this is a very hard choice, but the price—we think the price is worth it."

In retrospect, I learned that moments like this one have immense impact. My cousin and others living in Iraq were surrounded by the direness of the situation and the hopelessness it caused. Since she is a doctor, she engaged her vast network of physicians and pharmacists to distribute the supplies. Through these efforts, her hope emerged anew; she made a tangible contribution, in addition to herself. In the midst of surviving such monumental circumstances, a sense of powerlessness can prevail; the capability of helping, of witnessing the impact on people's lives, empowers one and intervenes in the psychological battle waged by an invasion intent on breaking a people's spirit. My cousin smiled again; in those moments she had hope. She is one example of many who were able through such activities to reclaim their faith in their abilities to effect change and begin to hope and dream.

As I witnessed the impact of our collective efforts, my commitment was invigorated; I had a renewed sense of faith that organizing could and was having a potent impact. The social landscape actually shifts as the work builds momentum. These types of projects affect long-term organizing, movement building, and vision. Our work nurtured solidarity with our families and communities "back home" and helped to build a transnationalist community based in the United States with political, cultural, and socioeconomic ties "back home."

Can you reflect on your experience as an Iraqi woman activist in the United States and on the place of Iraq and Palestine in U.S. progressive movements? What is your perspective on coalition building in the U.S. context? When and why were you attracted to working with particular organizations at particular times in your life? What kinds of perspectives did you bring? What do you think you gained from working in this context? What kinds of challenges did you face?

In the mid- to late 1990s, I worked on antisanction and antiwar campaigns with the International Action Center (IAC) against the war in Iraq. I was drawn to the IAC because it was the only organization in the Bay Area that continued to engage assertively and publicly in antiwar and antisanction campaigns long after the First Gulf War began. Iraq continued to be sanctioned and bombed throughout the 1990s under the Clinton administration, though this fact did not receive the attention and outrage it deserved by most in the United States. The IAC, on the other hand, continued to be steadfast in its activism, tactics, and public activities, such as mass demonstrations. I was also attracted to working with the

IAC because of its progressive and leftist internationalist political orientation and its mobilizing strategies. Growing up outside of the United States in a politicized household, as well as the circumstance we went through as a family, provided me with a conceptual understanding of imperialism and colonialism. My active involvement and politicization with the IAC and other organizations in the Bay Area, as well as my own lived experiences, gave me access to exploring the links among class, race, indigenous people's struggles, and immigrant and third world struggles with U.S. imperialism and hegemony. It was a critical time since I was exposed to political and ideological analysis that resonated with my own lived experiences. My work with the IAC mainly focused on educational and demonstration campaigns, which proved to be informative, analytical, and inspirational. The demonstrations were an outlet to rally people as well as to demonstrate our criticism and outrage at U.S. foreign and domestic policies.

At times within the antiwar and progressive movements, I felt that I was the token representative of a diverse Iraqi community. Therefore, I attempted to engage with members of the Iraqi community and invited some to attend several events, since I felt that we needed to speak for ourselves and assert our voices. As I initiated creating a space for us within progressive movements, I realized that differences began to emerge, such as the community's need to voice its critiques of the Iraqi regime and U.S. foreign policy. As an Iraqi who endured both Iraqi and U.S. systematic oppressive regimes in multiple ways, I continued to critique both governments and held both responsible, though I understood the need to focus on U.S. foreign policy since we are living in the United States. Other members of the Iraqi community felt the urgent need to vent their voices mainly at the Iraqi regime. The issue of being an Iraqi who was against all oppressive regimes including Saddam Hussein's as well as the U.S. government's continued to raise questions for some in the movement and outside of it. I was continuously asked to choose between those oppressive regimes, especially after the 2003 U.S. invasion. Some would argue that Saddam Hussein's regime was more horrific than the invasion and neocolonial occupation of Iraq under the U.S. administration, while others would argue that the disastrous situation today in Iraq is much worse than Saddam Hussein's regime. I felt and continue to assert that I should not have to pick between resisting only one of two interrelated oppressive situations, the dictatorial tyrannical rule of Saddam Hussein or the neoimperial-neocolonial invasion and occupation by the United States.

Since I was the only Iraqi organizing in predominantly white leftist progressive spaces, I found the need to organize among other Iraqis, Arabs, and other West Asians and North Africans.

Therefore, I began to engage with other Iraqi activists in order for us to begin brainstorming ideas about our needs and visions. A small group of us came together for several months, attempting to sort out what we wanted to do collectively; we spent most of our time exploring different frameworks that we should engage in: legal and social services, educational and activity-based events, as well as humanitarian relief work. We occasionally came together during rallies, educational events, and social gatherings. I look back at that time and cherish our unspoken understanding and intimate bond, especially since we did not have such spaces to come together as politicized active Iraqis concerned with what was happening.

In 1997, a small group of Arab and Arab Americans gathered at the Arab Cultural Center and decided to revive the Arab-American Anti-Discrimination Chapter in San Francisco (ADCSF). After many years of experiencing institutional marginalization, we came to realize that we needed a place to organize as an Arab community. It was a turning point for me and for Arab organizing in the Bay Area, as our efforts culminated in the creation of a grassroots organization that addressed and dealt with our systematic institutional marginalization as well as united and empowered our community to work toward justice and self-determination.

Continuing to work with the ADCSF on the antisanction, war in Iraq, and Palestine solidarity work, our work intensified with the second intifada and the continuous bombing campaigns in Iraq. We began attracting individuals from the community and carving a space for ourselves within progressive movements, branching out to other immigrant, indigenous, and people of color organizations, movements, and communities. Our vision of justice and liberation of Iraq and Palestine was tied to other progressive struggles both domestically and internationally. Building solidarity among progressive movements became a core component of our work by linking Palestine to other indigenous struggles, including apartheid South Africa. For example, we showed that police brutality that targets people of color in the United States was an extension of the same military-industrial complex that occupied the streets in Iraq and Palestine. In addition, parallels were drawn that explored the violence of the Israeli Apartheid Wall in Palestine and that on the U.S.-Mexico border. We were able to show the links among imperialism, colonialism, neocolonialism, Zionism, racism, classism, and other oppressions against all of our communities and how we must tackle them collectively. Our attempts at solidarity building were both strategically as well as ideologically oriented, since we believed that justice and self-determination could be reached only through our collective liberation.

Have gender and sexuality been important themes to your political activism and commitments? In what ways?

As Arab feminists, we understood the struggle for gender justice and liberation as central to our activism and commitment toward movement building and achieving social and political change. Some of us continuously felt silenced and undermined as women organizing in ADCSF and other spaces in the community. We took a step forward and embarked on creating a space for ourselves as feminists by reviving the Arab Women Solidarity Association, San Francisco Chapter (AWSASF). We understood that committing to a practice of challenging patriarchy and centering gender justice within our struggles against other forms of oppression paved the path for a united and stronger community front. Only when women can participate equally, acquire leadership roles, and center our liberation struggles as women within the community are we in fact working toward our liberation. All systemic forms of oppression are interrelated, and only an intersectional analytic lens and practice understands as well as resists the ways imperialism and racism, for example, deploy the gendered projects of military campaigns and invasions. Through our critiques, activism, and political efforts, we reclaimed our voices in our own communities as well as claimed a space for ourselves within transnational, radical, and women of color feminist circles.

As we continued to affirm our feminist visions and solidarity, we began to work through heterosexism and homophobia in our organizing efforts. Sexism, heterosexism, and homophobia are prevalent in most communities, and as Arab women we were concerned with a framework that constructed our communities as hypersexist and hyperhomophobic and heterosexist and the impact that it had on our work and lives.

Organizing with AWSASF was a transformative experience, and sisterhood began to take on a new meaning and depth for me personally, politically, strategically, and collectively. I began to explore my own identities in a more complex manner as well as to understand the depths and meaning of building sisterhood personally, politically, and strategically. My search for sisterhood led me to pursue organizing within other radical transnational, immigrant, and women of color feminist spaces. Building movement and solidarity with these spaces proved to be liberating, though at times silencing and marginalizing when it came to consistency in resisting Zionism and its links to imperialism, neocolonialism, racism, and sexism. We saw these contradictions manifest, for example, when AWSASF disseminated a paper we wrote and published in 2001 titled, "The Forgotten '-Ism': An Arab American Women's Perspective on Zionism, Racism, and Sexism."

Zionism is so deeply entrenched within progressive spaces, which makes it extremely difficult to talk about Palestine. Palestine and Zionism continue to be the divisive point within progressive U.S. politics. Asking potential allies to be consistent in their politics and practices has proved to be dangerous terrain. Organizations like San Francisco Women Against Rape (SFWAR) attempted to bridge the gap between their politics and practices. In response, they were met with severe threats, attacks, and budget cuts; they were systematically marginalized and silenced. SFWAR became an example to any other organization that dared speak up against Zionism. Coalition building in the United States will continue to face challenges until we systematically address and deal with Zionism's role within U.S. hegemonic and imperial interests as well as how it plays domestically within progressive movements.

My attempt to bridge the gap between movement work against the war and anti-Zionism activism and women of color spaces led to my hiring as the first Iraqi immigrant woman to work at the Women of Color Resource Center (WCRC). The politics of the moment also signaled a ripe time for groups like the WCRC, AWSASF, and INCITE! Women of Color Against Violence to bridge the gap between more domestically oriented women of color politics and transnational feminisms. At the WCRC, for example, we organized a gender-analysis working group that consisted of scholars, activists, and cultural workers who examined the gendered transnational dimensions of the war and militarism in order to deepen the intersectional analysis of the war's impact specifically on women as well the misogyny at the core of militarism and imperial projects.

I came to realize that my main contribution in the movement was the need to stress a radical shift in our collective efforts, which centers all of our marginalized voices, and the varied needs of our multiple communities. This realization was based on a vision of social change that called for justice and liberation of all oppressed peoples as well as an understanding for the need to create the necessary spaces and efforts to radically shift the existing framework in order to center all marginalized narratives and peoples; otherwise, our fragmentation will make us susceptible for attack.

Can you tell me how you have used art as a medium for social change? What is your perspective on the significance of art to social justice movements?

Art is a critical component of culture and the preservation of a community. Artists are producers of culture. As marginalized immigrant and diasporic peoples, we are faced with the challenge of upholding and safeguarding our culture, as well as producing art and other knowledge and aesthetic productions in the pursuit of challenging problematic cultural norms, isms, and oppressions within our own communities and in society as a whole. As artists we are responsible for finding ways to reflect on our experiences as well as to collaborate with others to build community, institutions, and movements.

Art builds social movement by documenting and creating an interpretation of historical moments and memory. It is an important branch of political movement work that aims to educate and to invigorate and inspire critical thought, inquiry, and ideology. It can potentially serve to heal the wounds of injustice by accessing an emotional and psychological realm that can also channel people's creative energies toward envisioning and manifesting a political vision.

I have used my artwork as a catalyst for social change and transformation. In 2004, I documented my trip to Iraq through film and photography. This documentation was stolen, and I was determined to find alternative methods to relay the information and document my experiences and encounters. In 2006, I reconstructed the experience through an art installation.

The art installation interprets Iraqi Shia women's experiences by reconstructing sacred space and ritual through creative practices. The art installation serves as a lens into multiple historically informed and conditioned narratives and experiences that shed light on silenced histories of Iraq, Iraqi Shia, and diasporas. I evoke my own and other women's experiences to tackle marginalized histories and to shed light on the tumultuous present realities in Iraq and its diasporas. I bring into play the tragic events of the battle of Karbala in the exhibit in order to explore its expression in rituals.[3] I chose these creative practices in order to elucidate their methods of dealing with oppression and trauma, which in turn provide mechanisms for healing and transforming individual turmoil into collective memories while instigating collective resistance. I utilize a similar approach to the concept of the Karbala tragedy and 'Ashura rituals to map out through memories a narrative based on my own and the memory of the women's stories and creative practices.[4]

As the participants walk through the four rooms of the art installation, they are invited to enter into a journey that encapsulates my interpretation of Karbala, 'Ashura, the sacred, and women's reconstruction of identities. The installation was an attempt to explore the meaning of narratives, creative practices, sacred spaces, and rituals. The material objects in the rooms symbolize and signify my intent to represent the past in light of the present. I ask the audience to explore my reconstruction of the pilgrimage place, an interpretive gendered meaning of 'Ashura, the cityscape of Karbala, and Shia narratives.

This work highlights the centrality of understanding the relationship between creative expressions and social change. Through such creative practices, the Karbala narratives of oppression, resistance, and justice are resurrected, as they keep a history and a memory alive. And as the reader engages with the Karbala narratives, I aim to demonstrate to her or him how powerful the link is between rituals, art, and social movement, and how they are fused into imaginative expressions that tap into the participants' senses and powerfully move them into catharsis and collective resistance.

4 ON OUR OWN TERMS

Discourses, Politics, and Feminisms

20

Arab American Feminisms

Mobilizing the Politics of Invisibility

AMIRA JARMAKANI

> If you want to hear me, you'll listen to my silences as well as my words.
> —Joanna Kadi, "Speaking (about) Silence"

This chapter explores Arab American feminisms as mediated by the paradoxical framework of being simultaneously invisible and hypervisible. Calling this idea the "politics of invisibility" (since hypervisibility also functions to obscure the creative work of Arab American feminists), Amira Jarmakani looks at the ways Arab American feminists have worked in coalition with U.S.-based feminists of color, deploying what Chela Sandoval has called "oppositional consciousness." Ultimately, she argues that one way of responding to the complexities of the U.S. context is to strategically mobilize the politics of invisibility, transforming it from a weakness into a useful and powerful tactic.

A few years ago, I walked into a coffeehouse in Atlanta, ordered a drink, and placed the book I was reading, *Opening the Gates: A Century of Arab Feminist Writing*, on the counter while I paid for my drink.[1] "Arab feminism," the barista exclaimed. "That's just an oxymoron to me!" Her comment, cloaked as it was in certainty and self-assurance, demonstrates a particularly precarious positioning into which Arab and Arab American feminisms are often thrust. Given the prevalence of popular misinformation about Arab and Muslim womanhood in the United States, Arab American feminists face a complicated context that simultaneously seeks to define our realities as well as obscure the issues we consider to be pressing. The barista's comment, disarming in its nonchalance, glosses over the nefarious meaning in both the content and the tone of her statement, which quietly insinuates a rich field of feminist thought out of existence. Furthermore, far from unique, the idea that Arab (or Arab American)

227

feminism is oxymoronic gains credibility against the backdrop of U.S. official discourse about the "war on terror," which appropriates feminist logic in order to justify militarism and neoliberal imperialism. The barista's comment, uttered in September 2002, is indicative of the intensification of Orientalism and Islamophobia following the events of September 11, 2001; her presumed knowledge that Arab feminism could not exist was framed and bolstered by the U.S.-led invasion of Afghanistan, cast by the Bush administration as a project of liberation meant to save Afghan women from the oppression of the Taliban.[2] Indeed, this one anecdotal interaction exemplifies multiple layers through which Arab American feminism tends to be perceived. At the most obvious surface level is the narrative of the imperialist-colonialist civilizing mission, which capitalizes on the image of exotic, oppressed women who must be saved from their indigenous (hyper)patriarchy. Adopting the "women's rights" civilizing mission stance, in turn, depends on an appropriation of feminist logic, yet it must be a logic that is amenable to the imperialist position. In the case of the U.S.-led invasion of Afghanistan, for example, the U.S.-based Feminist Majority Foundation had been advocating on behalf of (but not with) Afghan women since at least the early 1990s. In what could be called a form of "global feminism," the Feminist Majority worked from the position of savior rather than one of solidarity with feminists in Afghanistan, and therefore developed a position easily appropriated in the service of militarism. Importantly, the military-imperialist and feminist-imperialist stances collude to reify stereotypical notions of Arab and Muslim womanhood as monolithically oppressed. They depend on a set of U.S. cultural mythologies about the Arab and Muslim worlds, which are often promulgated through overdetermined signifiers, like the "veil" (the English term collapsing a range of cultural and religious dress expressing modesty, piety, or identity, or all three). These powerful symbols, in turn, threaten to eclipse the creative work of Arab American feminists. Because the mythologies are so pervasive, operating subtly and insidiously on the register of "common sense," Arab American feminists are often kept oriented toward correcting these common misconceptions rather than focusing on our own agendas and concerns.

Perhaps owing to its actual dynamism and flexibility across multiple historical and cultural contexts (and known by various names and practices), the cultural mythology of the veil serves as a salient example of the paradoxical framework Arab American feminists must negotiate. The image of the veil has been appropriated and deployed, as I have been arguing, by colonialist and imperialist powers to justify domination (for example, Britain in Egypt,[3] France in Algeria,[4] and the United States in Afghanistan and Iraq). It has also been utilized as a symbol of cultural authenticity in anticolonial nationalist movements and as a loaded marker in debates about "civilization," modernity, and liberal-democratic citizenship,[5] all of which tend to obscure discussion of the ways Muslim women negotiate faith and piety.[6] With the exception of the last, most deployments of the veil eclipse the complex sociohistorical realities of the women they purport to represent. Functioning according to what Minoo Moallem has called a "semiotic war," the cultural mythology of the veil easily becomes a signifying tool among competing patriarchies or imperialisms or both, a framing that constructs Arab and Muslim women as either hidden or revealed objects rather than thinking subjects.[7] The paradox is that, as a marker (supposedly) of invisibility and cultural authenticity, it renders Arab and Muslim womanhood as simultaneously invisible and hypervisible. As I have been noting, Arab and Muslim female subjectivity is obscured by the mythology of the veil, while the notions of oppression, tradition, and civilization become animated in the service of imperialist or nationalist agendas that render the mythology, if not the women, hypervisible. As feminists of color analyzing the impact of the faulty levees after Hurricane Katrina have pointed out, both invisibility and hypervisibility can operate as tools of oppression.[8] As demonstrated by my opening anecdote, the cultural mythology of the veil has largely signified invisibility in the U.S. context in order to corroborate dominant assumptions about the oppression of Arab and Muslim women. The powerful presence of these women is therefore subsumed under the louder message of their supposedly helpless silence. As hypervisible, the mythology of the veil is so powerful and prolific in the United States that it is virtually impossible to talk about the realities of Arab and Arab American women's lives without invoking, and necessarily responding to, the looming image and story that the mythology of the veil tells.

Although I have been focusing on the U.S. cultural construction of the "veil" so far, it is by no means the only signifier, or sensationalist issue, that impacts the work of Arab American feminists. Indeed, the point is not that Arab American feminists are unconcerned with the questions raised by the cultural and religious customs women negotiate in various contexts and the way these customs—and women's subjectivity—are circumscribed within patriarchal, nationalist, imperialist, and local realities. Rather, the problem is that a range of complex, nuanced concerns are flattened into convenient symbols, which then become fodder for mainstream debates about the "death" of (U.S.) feminism.[9] Take, for example, the opening sentence of a 2007 article by Christina Hoff Sommers:

The subjection of women in Muslim societies—especially in Arab nations and in Iran—is today very much in the public eye. Accounts of lashings, stonings, and honor killings are regularly in the news, and searing memoirs by Ayaan Hirsi Ali and Azar Nafisi have become major best-sellers. One might expect that by now American feminist groups would be organizing protests against such glaring injustices, joining forces with the valiant Muslim women who are working to change their societies. This is not happening.[10]

Sommers's opening statement demonstrates a number of things. First, it reiterates the laundry list of issues—"honor killings" and "stonings," for example—that have become the primary lenses through which Arab, Iranian, and Muslim women's realities are filtered in popular U.S. discourse. Second, it invokes native informants—figures like Ayaan Hirsi Ali and Azar Nafisi—who are indeed widely popular in the United States, no doubt because they corroborate the images their audiences already hold about the status of women in Arab and Muslim societies.[11] Finally, and perhaps most revealingly, its true focus is a critique of "American feminist groups," who are (according to Sommers's logic) supporting (Islamic) "terrorism" by failing to denounce the absolute subjugation of women in the Arab and Muslim worlds. The problem, again, is in the framing of the issue. It capitalizes on the idea of Arab and Muslim women's oppression, signified through overdetermined symbols (like the "veil") and sensationalized, decontextualized news stories (about "stonings" and "lashings"), in the service of another project altogether: building a case for the "war on terror" by characterizing the Arab and Muslim worlds as widely supporting terrorism and oppression. Notably (and significantly), any critical space for Arab American feminists is either obviated or filled by native informants who speak to the monolithic logic of absolute oppression through ready-made symbols and news stories.

Building on this idea of the way Arab American feminisms have been circumscribed within a paradoxical framework, I would also like to suggest that such a position might be put to strategic use. In her essay "Speaking (about) Silence," Joanna (now Joe) Kadi argues that stories of silence (or being silenced) are political, a point that has much salience for the case of Arab American feminisms. While she largely frames silence as a form of oppression that can be alleviated through coming into one's voice, I want to build on her argument here to suggest that silence can also be a potential strategy (among many others) in crafting an oppositional consciousness through which to both define Arab American feminisms and build alliances and solidarities with other women of color feminists in the United States.

A Historical Context for Arab American Feminisms

The anecdote with which I began also demonstrates a general context of misunderstanding about and misrepresentation of Arab womanhood and Arab feminisms, which help to determine the framework for the articulation and reception of Arab American feminisms. Because Arab American feminism often finds itself necessarily engaged with an incomplete and monolithic understanding of Arab womanhood, it equally often speaks from a corrective, and therefore defensive, stance.

This type of oppositional stance is nothing new. In fact, it closely resembles Leila Ahmed's experience at the 1980 National Women's Studies Association (NWSA) conference as she recounts it in her article "Western Ethnocentrism and Perceptions of the Harem." Ahmed's article, though certainly not the only or the oldest example of Arab American feminism, provides a point of reference for tracing the trajectory of Arab American feminism in the United States. Since the attacks on the World Trade Center and the Pentagon in 2001, Arab American feminism has been portrayed and perceived, from a mainstream perspective, as suddenly relevant or newly forming. Yet, using the 1980 and 2001 NWSA conferences as a loose framework, I am interested in exploring the way in which Arab American feminists have been participating in critical feminist dialogue for the past few decades. Charting its intersections with women of color feminisms in the United States, I will be particularly exploring the development of oppositional consciousness as a defining, integral feature of Arab American feminisms. A preliminary example comes from Leila Ahmed's experience at the 1980 NWSA conference. While attending a panel entitled "Women in Islam," Ahmed was surprised to hear what she found to be an overly optimistic view of women's status in Islam. Although Ahmed agreed that "Islam had, as that panel maintained, brought about a number of positive gains for women in Arabia at the time, and had granted women certain rights," she felt that fact "still did not warrant playing down Islam's blatant endorsement of male superiority and male control of women, or glossing over the harshness of, in particular, its marriage, divorce, and child custody laws." Having attended a conference devoted to critical interrogation of the status of women across multiple contexts, Ahmed was no doubt confused to find the panelists' analysis of gender oppression within Islam strikingly underdeveloped. Nevertheless, as she explains in her later reflection, she had not yet lived in the United States and, therefore, did not yet understand the defensive position from which the panelists had begun. Before discussing the rich complexity and dynamics of female oppression within the Islamic tradition, the "Women in Islam" panelists first had to address those certainties and assumptions that existed in the audience about the hyperpatriarchal and overly oppressive nature of Islam. There was no space for the panelists to offer an honest and productive critique of the status of women in Islam without first confronting U.S. misperceptions about Islam. As Ahmed discovered, these misperceptions were (and are) deeply entrenched in the mainstream psyche: "Just as Americans 'know' that Arabs are backward, they know also with the same flawless certainty that Muslim women are terribly oppressed and degraded. And they know this not because they know that women everywhere in the world are oppressed, but because they believe that, specifically, Islam monstrously oppresses women."[12]

This type of "knowledge" about Islam, which is often conflated with an understanding of the Middle East as the two have become virtually interchangeable in U.S. discourse, is the same sort of certainty that has reified the cultural mythology of the veil as an all-encompassing signifier of Arab and Muslim womanhood in the United States. As Ahmed points out, there is not simply a dearth of information about Arab and Muslim women; rather, there is a plethora of misinformation about the nature of female oppression in Islam. Consequently, Arab American feminists often find themselves absorbed in the task of addressing and correcting this misinformation, which ultimately subverts and redirects Arab American feminist energy and analysis.

A contemporary example of such a double bind can be found in the public discourse surrounding "Islamo-Fascism Awareness Week," which was staged by the "Terrorism Awareness Project" (an affiliate of the David Horowitz Freedom Center). As described by Horowitz in the magazine *Front Page*, the goal of the October 2007 event was to "confront two big lies of the political left: that George Bush created the 'war on terror' and that global warming is a greater danger to Americans than global Jihad and Islamic supremacism."[13] Although "Islamo-Fascism Awareness Week" mostly drew criticism for its sloppy conflation of "terrorism" and "fascism" with Islam, in part through its rhetorical use of dubious terms such as "global jihad" and "Islamic supremacism," it is perhaps most notable for its tactical deployment of gender oppression and its strategic targeting of women's studies departments across the United States. Despite purporting to care about women's oppression, the argument goes, women's studies departments in the United States have been inexcusably silent about "Islamic misogyny," the brutal oppression of women in the Muslim world, and "Islamic gynophobia."[14] If equating "the Left" with so-called Islamo-fascists (or, in another formulation, "feminists and Islamists") has been a clever, yet disingenuous, strategy of the David Horowitz Freedom Center to discredit widespread critique of the "war on terror" and to demonize Islam by attributing all intimate violence against

Muslim women to the religion itself, its appropriation of Muslim womanhood in the service of its own argument is a well-worn Orientalist and imperialist trope.[15] Most important, though, it sets up a familiar dichotomy of actors (the freedom-loving U.S. liberators on one side, with "feminists and Islamists" on the other, for example) warring over the presumptive task of saving Muslim women. Though I am loathe to give the Freedom Center more credit than it is due, the fact is that it is part of a larger discourse (including voices as diverse as the Freedom Center, the Bush administration, the National Organization for Women, and mainstream newspapers) that speaks about Muslim women, invoking them symbolically as part of a rhetorical strategy. Indeed, this rhetorical strategy is often so effective as to reify the false binaries of liberation and oppression forever hovering around Arab and Muslim women.

Despite her seeming attempt to undercut the types of claims made by David Horowitz and Christina Hoff Sommers, for example, Katha Pollitt (in her "Open Letter from American Feminists") reinforces the same binary that situates Arab and Muslim women as objects of sensationalist (cultural-religious) violence, such as "female genital mutilation (FGM), 'honor' murder, forced marriage, child marriage, compulsory Islamic dress codes, the criminalization of sex outside marriage, [and] brutal punishments like lashing and stoning."[16] In her rush to defend U.S. feminist organizations against the accusation that they do not support gender-justice struggles for Muslim women, she uses the same sensationalist examples that have inscribed Muslim women as victims of their culture or religion, thereby perpetuating a rhetorical framework that ultimately appropriates Arab and Muslim womanhood for the sake of argumentative strategy. For Arab American feminists concerned with gender and social justice for Arab and Muslim women worldwide, this common discursive framework does violence to the very women it purports to represent. It attempts to provide an analysis isolated from the very conditions (for example, military occupation and global economic restructuring) that help give rise to the violences they face, while simultaneously objectifying them as convenient talking points.

The Politics of Invisibility

Given the way Arab women become objectified in popular discourse, it is no wonder that Arab and Arab American feminists often find themselves cast into a liminal space, compelled to engage in a debate constructed by a set of false binaries about whether veiling is oppressive or liberating, for example, or whether feminism is a "Western" concept. These kinds of debates consistently privilege the notion that gender oppression can be understood in isolation from other actors of oppression, and they routinely center an analysis of the individual as abstracted from larger structural axes of oppression. In short, they enact what I am describing as a politics of invisibility, where the politics of invisibility describes the systematic elision of a nuanced analysis regarding gender justice for Arab women and an overemphasis on sensationalist issues and stereotypical categories associated with Arab womanhood. The politics of invisibility, then, is the complicated process by which Arab and Arab American women are doubly silenced by the very categories that claim to give them voice. Invisibility here is meant to signify both the ways that Arab and Muslim women are silenced and the ways they are made hypervisible, paradoxically, as markers of invisibility, exoticism, or oppression. Far from being absent from the public domain, Arab and Muslim women are represented prolifically as veiled women, as harem slaves (particularly in the 1970s in the context of the 1973 oil embargo), and as exotic belly dancers (in contexts as varied as the popular sitcom *I Dream of Jeannie* to a 2002 Camel cigarette advertising scheme titled "Exotic Pleasures").[17] However, these popular representations of Arab and Muslim womanhood serve to circumscribe them within a totalizing shroud of silence and oppression (recent images of the veil are only the most obvious examples). They speak for Arab women's realities in the shorthand of stereotypical categories. Furthermore, these categories of representation are insidious in that they present themselves as accurate and authentic reflections of Arab women's realities, and they are deployed by the dominant discourse in the same way—as proof of the condition of Arab womanhood.

Because these images are so pervasive, Arab American feminist thought is often overlooked or not heard unless it engages the dominant myths and categories through which Arab womanhood has been filtered in the United States. The continuous need to identify and deconstruct stereotypical images of Arab womanhood functions as a double silencing of Arab American feminists whose energy could be better spent theorizing new spaces of possibility for Arab American women rather than responding to the misinformation promulgated by the dominant discourse. To the extent that Arab and Arab American women, and particularly Arab and Arab American feminists, have been able to carve a space in which to give voice to their own issues and concerns, they have found much of that space reluctantly, yet inevitably, filled with corrective responses to mainstream misunderstandings.

Even those Arab and Arab American narratives that refuse to engage stereotypical categories are often reinterpreted or translated through them. Amal Amireh gives a salient example of this phenomenon in the case of Nawal el Saadawi, a famous Egyptian feminist, whose book *Al-wajh al-'ari lil mara'a al-arabiyyah*

(The naked face of the Arab woman) was translated into English with the title *The Hidden Face of Eve: Women in the Arab World,* literally covering the Arab woman's face in the process of translation.[18] Though hardly the only example of the way Arab womanhood gets translated through stereotypical categories,[19] this one demonstrates both the power of the metaphorical cover that everywhere threatens to obscure the textured realities of Arab and Muslim women's lives and the politics of reception that privilege the "cover" to the extent of eliding women's subjectivity.

The complicated ways in which the politics of invisibility impact the articulation of Arab American feminism was brought home to me during my own experience at the 2001 NWSA conference. Though I was giving a paper about Arab American literature, I was scheduled on a panel titled "Construction of Gender and Sexuality in International Literature," thereby highlighting popular U.S. perceptions of the Arab as perpetually foreign, even (especially?) in the case of Arab Americans. The conference organizers did not seem to have a framework for understanding Arabs as Americans. Yet it was the audience response to my paper that gave the clearest indication of how Arab American feminism is affected by the politics of invisibility. Remember that I was scheduled on a panel that was meant to discuss international literature, so the U.S. nationality of the writers was subsumed under the organizers' understanding of a dichotomy between domestic-U.S. and foreign-Arab, eliding the possibility of a transnational framework, reinscribing Arabs as foreign within a U.S. context, and pointing to another way in which Arab American women writers did not fit dominant conceptual categories. Moreover, the women in the audience seemed to have no frame of reference for understanding Arab or Arab American women as writers, since the activity of writing requires a subjectivity that is incompatible with the stereotypical frames of reference that are widely available for understanding Arab and Muslim womanhood. Indeed, these dominant interpretive categories were clearly in play for the woman who posed one of the main questions I received, though it must be said that the overwhelming audience response to my paper was characterized by silence, despite the fact that there was ample time left in the session for discussion. It struck me as telling, then, that one of the main questions I did receive was from a white woman who wanted me to explain why Arab and Arab American women react negatively when she tells them she is a belly dancer. Her indignant tone suggested that she was asking for validation and reassurance about her performance of the belly dance as a white woman. Her question can be contextualized within a larger phenomenon of the rising popularity of American interpretations of belly dance and the increasing popularity of belly-dance exercise classes. These are further embedded in a larger history of the

American belly-dance community, which has seen itself as reclaiming and honoring the belly dance as a celebration of female power since at least the 1970s and has, in some instances, presented itself as saving the dance from its excessively patriarchal cultural heritage.[20] I can only assume that my questioner was coming from the righteous perspective of such good intentions when she inappropriately, and rather shockingly, expected me to speak for other Arab and Arab American women's reactions to her. More to my point, however, her question exemplified the fact that the only way in which Arab womanhood can be understood is in terms of the already entrenched stereotypical markers of Arab female sexuality, particularly because I made no mention of belly dancing in my talk.

Regardless of which stereotypical category was invoked during my presentation, the fact remains that the audience had either no frame of reference for understanding Arab womanhood (in the case of Arab American women writers, for example) or could understand Arab women only through the filter of preexisting stereotypical categories (like the harem, the veil, and the belly dancer). The implications of this sort of politics of invisibility are explored by Japanese American writer Mitsuye Yamada in *This Bridge Called My Back: Writings by Radical Women of Color:* "No matter what we say or do, the stereotype still hangs on. I am weary of starting from scratch each time I speak or write, as if there were no history behind us, of hearing that among the women of color, Asian women are the least political, or the least oppressed, or the most polite." I reference Yamada here because of the way in which she writes about the "double invisibility" of Asian American women.[21] As I elaborate on what I mean by the politics of invisibility in relation to Arab American women, Yamada provides a useful model for analyzing the insidiousness of a stereotype that reinforces the image of Asian American, or for my purposes Arab American, women as already inscribed in a space of silence or oppression. Like Yamada, I felt as if I were "starting from scratch" in that I had to name the stereotypes of Arab women as stereotypes before I could begin the work of dispelling them. In this regard, then, the politics of invisibility has impacted Arab American women's lives and, by extension, the articulation of Arab American feminism in insidious and complicated ways.

It is not simply that Arab American women are not seen because they are, as contemporary U.S. popular culture would have us believe, "hidden" behind the veil. Rather, as the barista's comment indicates, it is a matter of not being credited with the possibility of existence. Arab feminism appears as an oxymoron not only because Arab women are perceived to be silent and submissive according to the mythology of the veil. It is an oxymoron because Arab women are not afforded the subjectivity of thinking, theorizing individuals. We are not merely silenced; we are wholly displaced and, therefore, ontologically elided, by sensationalized news stories and images of oppressed and exoticized Arab women. Arab and Arab American women as actively engaged in the process of creating and producing knowledge is incomprehensible to those individuals who understand Arab and Arab American women through the filmy lens of stereotypical categories. My own experience at the 2001 NWSA conference speaks to the ways in which Arab American feminism has gone unrecognized and unacknowledged within the mainstream movement. With no frame of reference by which to understand it, it has all too often either been ignored or been displaced by the very stereotypes it seeks to critique.

The Cutting Edge of Invisibility

Three months after the 2001 NWSA conference, following the events of September 11, the politics of invisibility would take on another dimension in relation to Arab American feminisms in the academy. The explosion of stories and images of Afghan women's brutal oppression at the hands of the Taliban (an issue that had utterly failed to garner public and widespread U.S. interest for years) in many ways highlighted the hypervisibility of Muslim (often conflated with Arab) womanhood. Again, it was not a matter of not being seen. Indeed, the U.S. public seemed to believe that it was finally seeing Muslim and Arab women in a way that it had not seen them previously. However, the seemingly sudden hypervisibility of Muslim and Arab women's lives had, predictably, shrouded their realities even further. The sheer proliferation of the image of the veil, coupled with the way in which it was reproduced as a monolithic signifier of the oppression of Muslim and Arab women, effectively displaced any potential for understanding the complicated network of power relations, patriarchal and imperial, that impact women's lives in Middle Eastern and Muslim countries.

In September 2001, I was teaching a course at Emory University titled "American Identities," and as I struggled to acknowledge and voice the disturbing reality of violence and racism enacted against the Arab American community as a corrective to my students' assured assertions that hostility and hate crimes did not exist, I realized something about the mechanics of invisibility. Despite evidence and news stories to the contrary, my students could not see the violent and dangerous reality of Arab Americans' lives after 9/11, in part, because their understanding of the Arab American community was already determined by the dominant narrative of terrorism. As with the mythology of the veil, the narrative of terrorism had prefigured my students' understanding of Arab Americans. Their knowledge about Arab Americans was informed by the prolific image of the terrorist, which was incompatible with the realities of hate crimes and victimization that I wanted them to acknowledge. The conditions of Arab Americans' lives were already displaced by the interpretive categories through which they had come to be understood.

Regrettably, my colleagues' responses to me and to my work after September 11 also highlighted the problematic ways in which Arab American women's realities continued to be elided. The immediate connection that my peers made to my work on representations of Arab womanhood in U.S. popular culture after the horrific events of September 11 was to suggest, with a tinge of jealousy, that my work was at least now "cutting edge." I did not, and still do not, know how to respond to heartbreaking destruction and grief with the consideration of how I might capitalize on or benefit from that destruction and grief. Yet the "cutting edge" comment once again exemplifies the way in which the hypervisibility of Arab womanhood actually worked to further eclipse Arab and Arab American women's realities. The assumption that my work was now suddenly interesting or useful in a way that it had not previously been participates in the construction of 9/11 as the origin story for perceptions and representations of Arab women, and, in so doing, ignores the history of representations of Arab womanhood in the United States. It also suggests that an understanding of Arab womanhood is important only in relation to larger political and international conflict and achieves a moment of recognition in the shadow of such events.

Perhaps most problematic, however, is the suggestion that I can capitalize, through my research, on the increased attention given to representations of Arab women since it condones and reinforces an uncritical commodification of such representations. Even if unwittingly, it advocates for the appropriation of representations of Arab womanhood at the expense of examining the complex realities that characterize Arab women's lives. In fact, my colleagues' comments failed to acknowledge a much more problematic and insidious academic climate for scholars writing about issues related to the Middle East, particularly since 2001. As Beshara Doumani argues, "The academy is in the midst of a transformation driven by the increasing commercialization of knowledge . . . buffeted between conflicting but intimately related forces of anti-liberal coercion and neoliberal privatization." In other words, to the extent that scholarship about Arab and Muslim womanhood can be commodified and marketed (and the celebrity status of Orientalist native informants like Azar Nafisi and Ayaan Hirsi Ali are good examples of this process), such commercialization goes hand in hand with both overt and covert forms of censorship. In a climate in which the David Horowitz Freedom Center deploys the language of "academic freedom" to chastise women's studies departments for their lack of attention to "the plight of Muslim women" and to coerce those departments into promulgating Islamophobic and simplistic lessons about women and Islam, the conversation about Arab and Muslim womanhood once again gets reduced to an obfuscating binary.[22] In such a context, in which surveillance and privatization work in tandem, Arab American feminisms seem to be presented with two options: be appropriated or be censored and censured.

NWSA Revisited

One of the most troubling features of the politics of invisibility is precisely this ability to simultaneously silence Arab American feminist analysis and produce discourse that further obscures that analysis. As I see it, the primary task for Arab American feminisms is to find a way to reject both disingenuous appropriation as well as more insidious forms of censure. My suggestion for responding to the politics of invisibility actually brings me back to my discussion of the "Women in Islam" panel at the 1980 NWSA conference and to a recognition of the ways that Arab American feminist discourse has long been engaged in mobilizing, or deploying, the politics of invisibility as a strategy. In the context of a hegemonic white women's movement, the panelists addressing Arab women's issues at the 1980 NWSA conference spent much of their time working to dispel mainstream U.S. feminist narratives that cast Middle Eastern women as unwilling victims of a seemingly hyperpatriarchal society. In so doing, they were employing a critical perspective that participated in a mode of analysis that paralleled the experience of women of color at the 1981 NWSA conference, as documented by Chela Sandoval in her article "Feminism and Racism: A Report on the 1981 National Women's Studies Association Conference."[23] Sandoval's account of the way in which women of color organized in response to the title of the 1981 NWSA conference, "Women Respond to Racism," offers a useful framework for understanding the work that has already been done by Arab American feminists. Although Arab American feminists were not clearly identified with what Sandoval calls "U.S. Third World feminists" in the context of the early 1980s feminist movement, both groups of women were clearly utilizing some of the same strategies.

In many ways, the fact that Arab American feminism has had to construct itself negatively has facilitated the development of its greatest strength: an oppositional consciousness. Sandoval's comments regarding the experiences of feminists of color at the 1981 conference can apply to Arab American feminists as well: "U.S. Third World feminists must recognize that our learned sensitivity to the mobile webs of power is a skill that, once developed, can become a sophisticated form of oppositional consciousness . . . which creates the opportunity for flexible, dynamic and tactical responses." This sort of flexible, dynamic, and tactical response to power is what Ahmed witnessed at the "Women in Islam" panel in 1980, and it is the type of critical consciousness and resistance that Arab American feminists have continued to cultivate in response to multiple forms of oppression propagated by racism in the white feminist movement, sexism in Arab and Arab American communities, and the racist, sexist, and patronizing effects of imperialistic projects of so-called liberation. What Arab American feminists need most urgently is to continue to use the skills and tools we have gained from an oppositional consciousness in order to forge more spaces of possibility for the lives of Arab and Arab American women. The work of Arab American feminists contributes to the work of those feminists, both in the United States and transnationally, who "are calling for new subjectivity, a political revision that denies any one perspective as the only answer, but instead posits a shifting tactical and strategic subjectivity that has the capacity to re-center depending upon the forms of oppression to be confronted."[24] Indeed, Arab American feminists demonstrate a "shifting . . . strategic subjectivity" by creatively mobilizing a politics of invisibility. Mobilizing the politics of invis-ibility can mean using silence as a strategy; it is a response that understands contextual clues to determine when speech will simply reinforce the false binary that frames so much of the public discourse about Arab and Muslim woman-hood. It employs oppositional consciousness in flexible ways, and therefore does not solely operate as a counterdiscourse, since counternarratives run the risk of legitimating the problematic assumptions of the very discourses they resist. Most important, mobilizing the politics of invisibility helps to disarm the notion that silence and invisibility are necessarily oppressive and opens up a wider field of intervention for Arab American feminists.

The powerful and potent shorthand of cultural mythologies (like the images of the belly dancer and the terrorist, for example) and of sensationalist stories about the "plight" of Arab and Muslim women is not going to disappear—these tropes are unfortunately too useful as interpretive categories. Simply advocating for a rejection of current stereotypical categories and narratives would inevitably lead to the establishment of equally limiting categories of representation, and spending energy to create a counterdiscourse will perhaps unwittingly reify the false binary that already frames much of public understanding. The work of Arab American feminists, then, must continue to encourage a fruitful fluidity that con-stantly forges new possibilities for understanding and contextualizing the com-plex realities of Arab and Arab American women's lives. In solidarity with social justice and liberation projects worldwide, we must mindfully utilize the tools of an oppositional consciousness in order to support the urgent work of carving and crafting new spaces for the expression of Arab American feminisms. Rather than simply resisting the politics of invisibility that have denied us a full presence, we must mobilize it, thereby reinventing and transforming that invisibility into a tool with which we will continue to illustrate the brilliant complexities of Arab and Arab American women's lives.

21

Class Equality, Gender Justice, and Living in Harmony with Mother Earth

An Interview with Joe Kadi

NADINE NABER

Joe Kadi reflects upon the vision behind the groundbreaking anthology edited in 1994, Food for Our Grandmothers: Writings by Arab American and Arab Canadian Feminists. *Joe addresses how personal history coupled with writings by U.S. women of color inspired development of this book. Kadi addresses similarities and differences between the issues the book addressed and the issues facing Arab American communities in a post-9/11 historical moment. Joe talks about an identification as both a feminist and a transgender/genderqueer person. Joe also affirms a commitment to a vision for struggles against imperialism, racism, and sexism that do not ignore issues of class, homophobia, and environmental justice, within and beyond Arab American communities.*

Nadine Naber: Your edited anthology, *Food for Our Grandmothers: Writings by Arab American and Arab Canadian Feminists,* was groundbreaking. It challenged the invisibility of Arab Americans and Arab Canadians and produced a key shift in feminist studies by providing a reference point for understanding some of the issues that impact Arab American and Arab Canadian women's lives. Can you tell us about the vision behind the book?

Joe Kadi: I love reading. Ever since I was a kid I'd lose myself in books. It's one of the ways I survived my childhood. Later, trying to make sense of the world, I again found myself lost in books, this time written by feminists, working-class people, queers, Arabs, other people of color. It was so healing and liberatory. These writings helped me make sense of the world, and they helped me figure out how to understand my life in relation to social, cultural, political structures. Feminist literature in particular just blew my mind. In the early '80s I was married to a man who was abusing me, although abuse was so normal for me that I didn't really notice. During that time, I connected with other feminists who shared with me the writings of bell hooks, Gloria Anzaldúa, Cherríe Moraga, Dorothy Allison, Chrystos. Wow—talk about opening up my world. I especially loved the anthologies written by women of color, such as *This Bridge Called My Back*. I found that the anthologies offered this amazing diversity of voices, this wild array of history and culture where pieces both connected with each other and stood on their own. I would always think, "Gee, I wish we (that is, Arab feminists) had an anthology like that!" We just didn't have books like this. At a point in the late '80s several women, who had the same desire, encouraged me to take on the task. And I, naive as I was about the world of writing, publishing, and editing, said "Okay!" I really had no idea how much work was involved, and how hard it would be to find a publisher. It was a whole new world for me, and I had a difficult time navigating it.

NN: The book impacted me tremendously by validating my experiences and providing a tool for teaching about Arab American femininities in a context in which literature on Arab American women is limited. Can you tell us more about the impact of the book? How do you think it has impacted feminist thought or feminist studies in the U.S.? How has it impacted Arab American women's lives?

JK: It's hard for me to answer this question in any kind of accurate way. I only know when people seek me out and tell me what the book means to them. Occasionally, someone will take the time to write me a letter and tell me she read about her own life in a way that made sense for the first time ever in *Food for Our Grandmothers*. Sometimes South End Press tells me that a professor in such-and-such a place is using it as a course textbook. Other times people will come up to me at readings and let me know how positively the book has impacted their life. But there is no way for me to track the book's impact except through these sporadic exchanges. I will say, though, that when people write to me or come up to me after a reading and tell me the book has given them a sense of culture, history, or identity they didn't have before, that is a precious gift.

NN: It has been twelve years since the publication of *Food for Our Grandmothers*. In your view, how have some of the issues the authors who contributed to *Food for Our Grandmothers* spoke to changed since then? How would you frame an anthology on Arab American and Arab Canadian feminists if you were going to publish it today?

JK: Have the issues changed? Basically, I do not believe so. We are still battling very tough issues, some from the broader society, some from without our own community. In terms of the broader society, we're still dealing with sexism, ableism, classism, heterosexism, and virulent anti-Arab racism pushing the myths about passive, downtrodden Arab women and brutally oppressive, demonized Arab men. Issues of sexism, classism, heterosexism, and ableism in our own community are still prevalent and need to be challenged. However, within these basic frameworks, I believe the oppression we experience has intensified and deepened since the attacks on the World Trade Center in 2001 and since the U.S. invaded Iraq (perhaps I should say: since the U.S. attacked Iraq in a more forceful and violent way than it had during the years of the embargo).

If I was going to take on the task of editing another anthology, I would need to address that. I would also want to make the book more diverse than *Food for Our Grandmothers*, by ensuring there were more immigrant women, queer or trans women or both, working-class women, and Muslim women.

NN: Despite the fact that many Arab American feminists use the framework of "intersectionality" (which tends to refer to the links among race, class, and gender), there has been little written on socioeconomic class. You have written an entire book entitled *Thinking Class*. What would you say the significance of socioeconomic class is to the study or practice of feminism in general?

JK: As a working-class person who thinks a lot about class and perceives the way it impacts us in our daily lives, I simply cannot stress the importance of this issue enough and the need for all caring, thinking people to take this issue seriously. Of course, I include feminists in the phrase "caring, thinking people." To me feminism is at its root concerned with justice for all living beings, and a cornerstone of justice is that basic needs of food, shelter, and dignified, safe work are met. These are critical class issues. They aren't the only critical class issues (culture springs to mind as another), but they are cornerstone ones, and working-poor and working-class people are routinely deprived of these basic needs.

Right now we are seeing a terrifying assault on working-poor and working-class people in the United States. The rates of homelessness have skyrocketed—the average age of a homeless person in the U.S., the richest country in the world, is nine years old. The middle class is disappearing. The gap between rich and poor is heightening. Up until five years ago I was living in rural Wisconsin, which is, as all of rural America, economically depressed. Most people work shit jobs for shit wages. They juggle two or three jobs and have no health insurance. Friends of mine currently had their heat turned off or lived without phones because they simply cannot pay their bills—and these are people working more than forty hours a week. It is a national disgrace. We need campaigns for living wages; we need national health care; we need decent jobs that do not harm the environment. I am fearful about the upcoming national election. While I don't believe the Democrats are the be-all and end-all, I do want them to come to power so there is not another four years of Republican rule. I can only shudder when I consider that possibility.

NN: You have also critiqued homophobia during a historical moment in which few Arab American writers have raised LGBT (lesbian, gay, bisexual, transgender) issues.

JK: There's a lot of homophobia within the Arab American community. Absolutely. Yet, I have to add, there's a lot of homophobia everywhere; our community is no different from the larger society. I usually say these two statements together because there's so much anti-Arab racism right now that if I were to simply say the first statement and not add the second, I would be adding fuel to the fire of racism. One of the ways anti-Arab racism works is that our community is tagged as more homophobic than the white mainstream culture held up as the norm.

It's hard to always have to qualify these things. If I were simply having a conversation with you, the editors of this journal, a group of Arab American women, I would be able to say, "There's a lot of homophobia in our community." You would understand what I mean and nod in agreement, and we'd have a discussion about our community with all of its flaws and grace and infuriating qualities and goodness. But if I'm talking to non-Arabs (and I don't just mean white people here!), and I say, "There's a lot of homophobia in Arab American society," the nodding would be of a very different quality. The nod of "Oh, yeah, those Arabs. They're totally homophobic, and they're so misogynist. You poor thing! How do you put up with it?"

I hope you're following me here. What I'm trying to say is that many of us inside the community are operating from a holistic understanding of the community, but pretty much nobody else is. So we always have to explain, to contextualize, our words and ideas. Which isn't a totally bad thing. I mean, clarity is good; explaining things fully in their proper context is good. On the other hand, it does get a bit tiring!

NN: What have been your experiences with feminisms in the U.S.? What does women of color feminism mean to you? (Or are there other feminist spaces that have meaning to you?)

JK: My experiences with different feminists have pretty much run the gamut, as I expect all of ours have. I have experienced great support and inclusion from different white women and different women of color, and I have experienced disrespectful and painful dismissal by different white women and different women of color. Sometimes feminists have argued that "Arabs aren't people of color"; others exhibit absolutely abysmal ignorance about Arabs generally; others actually believe the crap about "Arab men are the most sexist men of all!" and "Arab women are the most oppressed women of all, and gee, it's lucky your husband let you come to this event, and why aren't you wearing a veil?" Rather mind-blowing.

I always state that there is a wide array of responses to Arab women within feminist circles, and that I have, over my twenty-five years as part of this movement, encountered many feminists who are supportive and concerned about my community. I am very disturbed by the current mainstream media discussion of feminism, in which the women's movement is continually painted as a very white movement that is very racist. In my own experience that is an inaccurate portrayal—I have always participated in a multiracial women's movement that actively fights racism. This inaccurate portrayal has filtered down to progressive young women, both white and of color. I have, several times in the past few years, found myself talking with a group of young women and had to dispel their notion of a completely racist women's movement made up solely of white women. This has become especially obvious to me in recent years, as I have been teaching in the women's studies program at the University of Calgary.

I do want to make it clear that, as a transgender/genderqueer person, I am still a feminist, still concerned with feminist issues. I know there can be questions, even anxieties, about what it means when someone who has clearly identified as a feminist woman suddenly emerges as a transgender person. My feminist values, my concern about what is happening to women globally and locally, my love for the common woman have not changed. I imagine it will be an interesting experience for me to experience these key pieces of my feminist self from a different vantage point.

NN: What are your visions for transformation? What I mean is that if you could create a different world, a world without oppression, what would it look like? What do you think needs to change? And what do you suggest that we do differently in order to get there?

JK: I want to help transform our society, our world, into one where social justice, active participation, and sustainability are foundational building blocks. My absolute priority vision is that my species—humankind—live in harmony with Mother Earth and take care of her. What will this mean? For starters, stop clearcutting forests; stop building subdivisions on open, healthy land; stop dumping toxins into our rivers and into our soil. Stop acting as though we can continue to run our society on a limited, finite natural resource—oil—when it is a cold, hard fact that we will be running out of oil at some point in the future, possibly sooner than we think. Stop acting as though we can live disconnected from the planet that is our home.

And of course environmental issues are so connected to all other issues—you can't fully make sense of what imperialism did in the Arab world without understanding the environmental degradation that went along with that. You can't make sense of pollution patterns—such as the locations of toxic-waste dumps—in this country if you don't take a hard look at race and class demographics.

It's difficult, but I hold on to my vision of all of us living in harmony with Mother Earth and caring for her.

I am now back in Canada, which is my home country. I am living in the Rocky Mountains of western Canada, where there are still huge tracts of unspoiled wilderness. But even here, the assault on the earth is continuing. The oil and gas industries are wreaking tremendous havoc here, and are pushing to do more. The Alberta provincial government, which is a right-wing government and has been in power for three decades, tends to allow business to do what it wants. It's quite painful seeing the destruction of pieces of beautiful wilderness.

I wonder if I might close with the last stanza of my poem "Relatively Small Pieces of Land" that expresses some of these ideas:

Each day I make the choice to stay
on, with, by the land.
Is it the ruffed grouse, or my heart? The
coyote's howl of anguished desire, or mine?
Who shed her skin last night,
transformed by the light of the
moon? Who called to the night sky? Who
embraced with her whole heart? Who risked
it all, for love, simplicity, a precious
small piece of bluffland in a driftless region?

22

Personal and Political

The Dynamics of Arab American Feminism

Susan Muaddi Darraj

In this personal essay, the author shares several experiences that reveal how Arab American feminists battle sexism in their personal lives as well as on the political front. She explores ways in which struggles for gender equality within the Arab community are often used as an indictment against Arab culture. She also emphasizes that Arab American feminists are in the precarious position of having to critique their culture while making sure not to fall into a politically charged stereotype.

In 2003, I crafted a proposal for a book on Arab and Arab American women's literature. I decided that I would invite several Arab women writers to contribute essays on why, where, and how they write, as well as on what obstacles they face—whether internal or external—when they write. Such a book would be the first if its kind—not a critical look at Arab American literature but a discussion by Arab American writers themselves, an opportunity for them to define their own issues and agenda. To my delight, publishers expressed interest in the project, and I soon signed a contract with one. Then the real work—and the true learning process—began.

I approached several well-known as well as up-and-coming writers and asked them to contribute an essay and sample of their creative writing to the book. Writers, including Naomi Shihab Nye, Etel Adnan, and Diana Abu-Jaber, agreed to pen essays that addressed the writing process itself: Why do we write? Are we compelled to write about Arab-related themes, and why? Who are our influences, both positive and negative? What are our obstacles? What are our thoughts and hopes for the emerging genre of Arab American literature?

The collected voices in the book addressed major themes within Arab and Arab American literature: the crisis of a dual ethnic identity, the Israeli-Palestinian conflict, discrimination against Arabs in the United States, a lack of general understanding of Islam, and related issues. Another topic that several writers addressed was the fundamental misunderstanding of the role of Arab women in the Arab world and in the Arab American community.

My publisher proved to be very supportive of the project and enthusiastic about the potential contribution the book could make to the field of ethnic American literary studies. However, the design for the book's cover nearly knocked me off my chair when I first saw it as a PDF file opening on my computer screen. The title of the book, *Scheherazade's Legacy*, had been my suggestion, a way of reclaiming the stereotype of one of literature's greatest storytellers, but I was dismayed by the image that accompanied it: toward the bottom of the cover, a woman's eyes gaze out at the viewer from between the narrow slits of her black face veil. Behind and above her, minarets loom in the dusky blue background. It was an exotic and Orientalist design, something completely anathema to the book's message.

When I expressed my concern, the publisher stated that, at such a late stage in the process of the book's publication, little could be done about the cover art. Although I understood that the marketing and design departments had already invested significant time in the cover, the blatantly stereotypical image deeply disturbed me. There was a ridiculously wide disconnect between the image on the cover and the voices within the book that struggled to articulate their disapproval of just such an image.

Yet the sad fact remains that the image on the cover of my book persists, pervading our American culture. The face behind the veil continues to be the way that the West understands Arab women. Despite recent interest in the Middle East over the past several years, following the terrorist attacks on September 11, 2001, the West has not made significant progress in its understanding of either Arab culture or the role of women in Arab society and within the Arab community in America. In fact, the image of the oppressed, silenced Arab woman is frequently used by some as *proof* of the barbarity of Arab culture, and even to justify the West's foreign policy toward the East. In the third presidential debate of 2004, President George W. Bush made much of the fact that in the recent elections in Afghanistan, the first person to vote was a nineteen-year-old woman: proof, it would seem, of the progress America's bombing and invasion of Afghanistan had caused and evidence of the goodness that can come of the Bush doctrine of "spreading liberty" around the globe. Attempts had been made to speak similarly of the status of women in Iraq under Saddam Hussein, who have allegedly fared better since the fall of the "evil" dictator. During the first and second American wars with Iraq, the few Iraqi women depicted on American television screens were heavily veiled, wearing black chadors, to show American viewers how desperately Iraq needed American liberty. Ironically, before the wars, Iraqi women were considered some of the most "liberated" in the Middle East—with some of the highest rates of women in white-collar professions—although the fundamentalist insurgency that has sprung up in reaction to the U.S. occupation will surely alter that situation dramatically.

Nevertheless, Arab and Muslim women continue to be used as a means of justifying the "spreading of liberty" across the Middle East. In a time when East and West are allegedly at odds, Arabs in America—and especially Arab women—have become key players and, too frequently, pawns.

◆   ◆   ◆

In the early 1990s, Gloria Steinem famously turned the popular feminist slogan of the seventies, "The personal is political," around on its head. "The political is personal," she declared instead, signaling that, for the new generation of feminists, political action and involvement were central to ensuring a society in which women were treated equally.[1] Her words rang true for American women, who felt that their personal lives and choices were deeply affected by legislation and government. For example, how could women become independent and pursue careers when many of the major universities barred them from enrolling? How could a woman abandon an abusive marriage or charge an attacker with rape when the courts were already biased against her? Women could achieve equality and fair treatment in the home, in the workplace, and in society only if politicians legislated that equality.

For Arab American women, feminism's core is slightly, though significantly, different. Arab American feminists must grapple with *the political and the personal*. These are two battles confronting them, and they are not the same. In American society, women of Arab descent or ethnicity find themselves portrayed in two different ways: their family and the Arab community regard them in one way (the personal), while the larger American society, and especially the American government, regards them in another way (the political). Although there is often overlap, it is more accurate to say that Arab American women face sexism in two distinct realms.

The Personal

It was a hot August day in downtown Philadelphia, as it was every year when our local chapter of the Palestine Aid Society organized its annual 10K walkathon through the city streets. As a teenager, I was involved in the New Generation of Palestine, an affiliated youth group that, in Philadelphia, had developed as an offshoot of the PAS; most of the youth in NGP had parents who were longtime PAS activists and members. Our parents had always involved us in PAS activities, encouraging our enthusiasm for Palestinian history and culture. My own parents would pack us into the car once a month and take us to their monthly meetings and on the drive home patiently explain to us what had been discussed during the meeting.

Each year the PAS parents mapped a route through downtown Philadelphia where we waved flags, American and Palestinian, handed out leaflets to the smiling, the scowling, and the bored-looking passers-by. As it was a warm day, many of us—boys and girls—were wearing cut-off pants or shorts and T-shirts. Hundreds of supporters arrived to march with us, but then an argument broke out.

A group of Palestinian men had arrived, but upon seeing several teenage girls in shorts, they refused to march. One of the organizers went to speak with them, and he was curtly told that they would not join us until *al-banaat* (the "girls") changed into more decent attire. This demand caused a heated debate, as the mothers and fathers of *al-banaat* angrily insisted there was nothing inappropriate about wearing shorts, especially on such a humid day. Others said that the parents had a point but that we should respect the feelings of those men who had arrived to march with us.

Meanwhile, *al-banaat,* including myself, stood there, holding our flags and wondering why in the world the baring of our shins and knees had caused such an uproar. Good Lord, we weren't allowed to date or have boyfriends, but now we had to worry about getting funny looks from people in our own community?

It is difficult—and actually painful—to write critically of fellow Arab Americans, especially of those individuals who obviously shared our political goals on that day. I remember telling some non-Arab friends at school the following week about the incident, and their faces registered their alarm and disgust. These friends, of course, were girls whose fathers coached their basketball teams or swim clubs, so why did I expect them to understand? I suddenly felt like a traitor, and I found myself quickly defending these men even as I criticized them, much to the confusion of my friends (and myself).

Despite the inherent difficulty of criticizing members of your community, especially when the community itself is under attack socially, culturally, and politically, the fact remains that sexism within our communities can be neither protected nor neglected. Are all Arab men so conservative as to spark a heated debate over some girls wearing shorts? No, of course not, but some are, just as there are conservative elements in every American subcultural group. Those men at the march, in the end, simply gave up and left, no doubt shaking their heads on the ride home about the lack of shame they had witnessed. In my heart, though, I was happy that they decided not to march with us on that day, because I, and some of the other girls who wore shorts, would have been uncomfortable in their presence, as if we were doing something wrong.

The problem, at the core of it all, is the erroneous notion that there is one monolithic, unchanging Arab Culture and that Arab Americans should strive not to lose it. What that Arab Culture consists of, though, differs from Arab to Arab, from generation to generation. Those men, not unlike some of the older men in my own family, were simply unaccustomed to seeing a woman bare her shins and knees in public. Yet, although I could feel sympathetic about their culture shock, I could still feel resentful that a huge fuss had not been similarly raised over the fact that several of the teenage boys, such as my brothers and cousins and friends, wore shorts and tank tops. Where was the uproar, the threat to not participate, unless *they* changed? Even if someone felt it was not right or appropriate for girls to wear shorts, why insist that they change and threaten to leave unless they did? To me, it was a blatant double standard motivated by sexism.

Many Arab American women themselves often feel a cultural shock upon realizing the enormity of this gender-based double standard. Grappling with the sometimes patriarchal attitudes and customs of the Arab culture, which are carried over and transmitted by immigrant parents and grandparents, is only one of the challenges facing Arab American women today. In *Food for Our Grandmothers: Writings by Arab-American and Arab-Canadian Feminists* (one of the earliest and most important collections of feminist writing by women of Arab descent), J. A. Khawaja writes, "My grandfather ranted at the top of his lungs for someone to bring him his food his socks his his his and my grandmother for fear for fear of for fear of being slapped at the back of the head brought him his food and his housecoat and his socks." She adds, "And when I was born my grandfather said a girl throw her in the river that's what girls are good for. In the old country we throw them in the river."[2]

Although Arab American women certainly have assertive, strong Arab women role models to emulate, it is wishful thinking to pretend that domestic abuse, emotional and physical, is completely nonexistent within the community. Like any other community, Arab Americans are impacted by sexist sociocultural factors. Nada Elia writes about the fact that, even in the absence of her father, the strong patriarchal attitudes continued. Her father, a peripatetic businessman whom she rarely saw, died when she was six years old:

When he died, everybody around me said our family was as good as dead, for he had left "only women" behind him. My mother, my three sisters, and I now made up the Elia household. I grew up surrounded by people who believed that, because none of us had a penis, we were worthless. In vain I tried to comprehend this. And I came to strongly resent the suggestion that it was my father, this occasional visitor, who had given meaning to my existence. Didn't my mother matter—who had always been there, feeding me, changing my diapers, washing me, staying up at my bedside when I was sick, rising before dawn to prepare our lunch-boxes? Later, as an adolescent, I frequently overheard discussions between my mother and some "wiser" family member—female more often than not— urging her to get my sisters and me out of school because a high-school degree would do us no good. Invariably, my mother refused. She had been denied an education and did not want her daughters helpless and dependent on husbands, as she had been.[3]

Furthermore, even in Arab American households where the paternal figure equally encourages his daughter as well as his sons to excel, girls will often feel the burden—more so than their brothers—to not become Westernized or Americanized. In my own family, where I am the only daughter (I have three wonderful brothers), I was never permitted to date, attend school dances, talk to boys on the phone, or any other staples of a teenage American girl's upbringing.

Ironically, my father pushed me to excel in school, pursue a career, and be financially independent, something most of my friends' fathers did not particularly encourage. I find this point an interesting facet of some Arab American women's upbringing. Although it may be partly related to the immigrant's instinct to see his or her children excel, there is also an element of Arab culture motivating it as well. My father, for example, loves poetry, and he used to recite to me poems from Arab women poets ranging from al-Khansaa to Fadwa Tuqan. Behind his recitations, I always sensed a pride in Arab culture, in both the male and the female Arabs who contributed to it. To mimic my father's thought process: why waste time on silly things like dating, going to the malls and the movies, when you can devote that time to your schoolwork, to reading, to building your future?

In addition, the fathers of many Arab American women emphasized the fact that the behavior of an Arab woman reflected upon the family as a whole. In her essay "Boundaries: Arab/American," also published in *Food for Our Grandmothers*, Lisa Suhair Majaj writes lovingly of her Palestinian father and American mother. She also describes the tug of war her own immigrant father experienced in wanting his daughters to adapt to his own culture:

Although he has left much of my sister's and my own upbringing to my mother, he had assumed that we would arrive at adolescence as model Arab girls: when we did not he was puzzled and annoyed. As walking became a measure of my independence, it became as well a measure of our conflict of wills. He did not like my "wandering in the streets," it was not "becoming," and it threatened his own honor. . . . [A]s my sister and I entered the "dangerous age," when our reputations were increasingly at stake and a wrong move would brand us as "loose," my father grew more and more rigid in his efforts to regulate our self-definitions.[4]

Majaj's experience with her father represents something not atypical for first-generation Arab American women, a tug-of-war between loyalty to loving fathers and an instinctive rejection of patriarchal attitudes and impositions. While we reject these patriarchal modes of thought and bristle at the limitations they try to impose, we similarly understand that our feminist self-definition is not as simple as the American model. We may be angry about being robbed of a "normal" teenager's social freedoms, but we may find support and encouragement when we decide to apply to college. So we understand, but still we bristle. No one said it was easy.

An important and groundbreaking study into the lives and needs of Arab American women is Evelyn Shakir's *Bint Arab: Arab and Arab American Women in the United States*. Published in 1997, *Bint Arab* is one of the only books to research and closely examine the lives of immigrant and first-generation Arab women. The conversations collected there, as well as the analyses and historical details provided, accurately portray the conflicts that these women face.

One particular conversation between two sets of Palestinian American sisters illustrates the pressure on young Arab American women from their families to marry at a young age. It is worth quoting at some length:

Nuha: Lately I've been rebelling against my parents.

Nawal: You have not! You got engaged. She got engaged to this dufis.

Nuha: Well, that's what my parents wanted. He was a friend of the family, he comes from the same village they do. And I was like, "Well, I should please them." At that point, my life revolved around my parents.

Nawal: No, her idea was it's an easy way to get out of the house.

Suhair: A lot of Arab girls do that . . .

Nawal (turning again to Suhair): I know you went through a lot when you married, just to go back to school.

Suhair: I know, I know. The thing is it's not him that is the problem. He actually gets mad at me sometimes if I get a C in a class. The problem, it's with his family. My father-in-law—he's my uncle—he doesn't believe in girls going to school. His first daughter, his eldest, he forced her out of school into marriage. But her husband was encouraging enough to let her go back so that she was able to finish school. When she had her kids, her mother-in-law took care of them. With me, my husband was encouraging too, but his family was very discouraging, and they lived with us at the beginning. They did everything they could to make it hard for me.[5]

The above quote illustrates the diversity within the Arab American community in that the husband of the young woman supports her educational pursuits, but his parents do not. The fact is that some young Arab American women have to deal with these sorts of restrictions on their freedom and aspirations.

Furthermore, the restrictions placed on Arab American women are often used as a method of publicly illustrating the family's conservative nature and even its honor. A "good" girl, one who has not been sexually promiscuous, can command eligible husbands from the parents' village. During the course of the above conversation, the girls also mention that, in their families, "If you marry outside the village, you're talked about." Another one adds, "Yeah, they're like, 'I wonder what happened to her.' Or, 'She must have been not a virgin.' Or 'Nobody else wanted to marry her.'"[6] Clearly, Arab American women can feel the burden of carrying their family's sense of honor and cultural responsibilities. In this way, marriage can at times become a way to escape their family's close surveillance. The fact that some girls feel marriage is the "only way out" should be cause for concern for Arab American feminists.

The Political

In her essay "The Arab Woman and I," Mona Fayad describes an experience similar to that of another famous Western feminist:

I am haunted by a constant companion called The Arab Woman. When I shut myself alone in my home, she steps out of the television screen to taunt me. In the movies, she stares down at me just as I am starting to relax. As I settle in a coffee shop to read the newspaper, she springs out at me and tries to choke me. In the classroom, when I tell my students that I grew up in Syria, she materializes suddenly as the inevitable question comes up: "Did you wear a veil?" That is when she appears in all her glory: The Faceless Veiled Woman, silent, passive, helpless, in need of rescue by the west. But there's also that other version of her, exotic and seductive, that follows me in the form of the Belly Dancer.[7]

Fayad's depiction of the Faceless Veiled Woman is the Arab American woman's version of Virginia Woolf's "the Angel in the House." The Victorian model of domestic bliss stifled the intellectual and professional ambitions of real women, like Woolf. Similarly, the ability of an Arab American woman to define herself as an individual becomes overshadowed by the Faceless Veiled Woman who, according to Fayad, prevents her "from talking about myself, pushing me to feed you what you want to hear."[8] The image of Arab women becomes a way to confirm the alleged inferiority of Arab culture and Islamic religion: the backward nature of the "other" becomes a confirmation of the dominance and superiority of the "self."

Much has been written about the creation of this image of Arab women, but little has been written about its impact on Arab American feminism. Arab American feminists today face the Faceless Veiled Woman on a number of fronts: in academia, in politics, in the social context. She signals a fundamental lack of understanding about the Middle East on the part of the West, setting up a formula by which the silenced veiled woman is the norm, and other Arab women—whether unveiled or veiled, but assertive and vocal—constitute an anomaly, a deviation.

Geraldine Brooks's *Nine Parts of Desire: The Hidden World of Islamic Women* was published in the mid-1990s and generated a substantial amount of media hype. Brooks, a longtime journalist for the *Wall Street Journal*, describes her interactions with Muslim women across the Middle East, during the several years she spent working there. It reads like the travel diary of a modern-day Lady Mary Wortley Montagu (who had good intentions but still saw "the East" through an Orientalist lens) in which Brooks notes her experiences with Muslim men and women, painting a damning portrait of modern Arab and Muslim culture.

She describes modern-day Muslims as slipping back rather than moving forward, becoming more and more fundamentalist: "I went to live among the women of Islam on a hot autumn night in 1987. I arrived as a Western reporter, living for each day's news. It took me almost a year to understand that I had arrived at a time when the events of the seventh century had begun to matter much more to the people I lived with than anything they read in the morning paper." Her opening anecdote, about not being able, as a woman, to book a hotel room in Saudi Arabia, sets the tone for the rest of the book, which essentially documents and purports to explain how women in the Middle East are suffering under Old World patriarchal customs. Chapter 2, for example, focuses on female genital mutilation while also addressing honor killings. She criticizes Arab and Muslim women who point out that FGM and honor killings are not Islamic practices, quoting at length Arab feminist Rana Kabbani's complaint that Western feminists have not "taken the trouble" to research these practices and discover they have been wrongly linked to the Islamic faith. As Brooks responds, "Could Rana Kabbani not have taken the trouble to reflect that one in five Muslim girls lives in a community where some form of clitoridectomy is sanctioned and religiously justified by local Islamic leaders? . . . Until Islam's articulate spokeswomen such as Rana Kabbani target their misguided coreligionists with the fervor they expend on outside critics, the grave mistake of conflating Islam with clitoridectomy and honor killings will continue."[9]

The "grave mistake" that has been made here, however, is Brooks's assumption that people like Rana Kabbani are *not* criticizing these practices. (In fact, Arab feminists such as Nawal el Saadawi have long written scathingly of the practice of FGM in some rural areas of Egypt and northern Africa.) Western feminists like Brooks have themselves not "taken the trouble," if I may exhaust that phrase, to investigate the activities of women's groups in the Middle East, to learn how these groups are organizing to educate and empower women. In other words, why did Brooks, a skilled journalist, not seek interviews with activists as well as the victims? She does mention one short-lived Arab women's group, Al Fanar, formed by Palestinian women to speak out against honor killings. Al Fanar fizzled out, however, when the Israeli press began highlighting their protests against honor killings in the Jewish newspapers, and "none of the West Bank Palestinian newspapers would touch the subject, steering clear of any criticism of Arab society that could be used as propaganda by Israelis."[10] However, there are many successful women's groups organizing on behalf of women's rights in the Middle East, but Brooks does not highlight them. The overall effect of her book is to portray the current state of Arab women as one of failure and victimization and to promote the notion that Arab women cannot advance their agenda in such a stifling culture and need Western feminists like Brooks to infiltrate their "hidden world" and take their story back to the rest of civilization.

The impact of books like *Nine Parts of Desire* on Arab American women's own feminist struggles is devastating. It reinforces the political message and stereotypes against which we battle. Arab American women must find a way to articulate the hypocrisy of the Western notion of Arab women and translate it back to Western culture, to uproot the deeply implanted stereotype of the Faceless Veiled Woman.

This articulation is happening, and it is most exciting to see it in the growing body of literature by Arab American women. For example, in her poem "Hijab Scene #2," from her collection *E-Mails from Scheherazad*, Mohja Kahf writes:

"You people have such restrictive dress for women,"
she said, hobbling away in three-inch heels and panty hose
to finish out another pink-collar temp pool day.

The impact of the poem slams the reader in the gut, a reminder of the blatant hypocrisy of viewing Arabs and Muslim women as victims of a backward culture while forgetting the way one's own culture often exploits women.

It is not unrealistic or paranoid to assert that the stereotypical image of the Faceless Veiled Woman is being deliberately perpetuated in American culture so that people who cannot even point out Arab countries on a world map somehow still know that Arab women are oppressed. Books like Brooks's command media attention because they are viewed as daring and insightful, helping to uncover hidden abuses, even though all they really do is confirm and perpetuate a stereotype. Furthermore, Arab American feminists feel frustrated by the fact that current U.S. policy in the Middle East is very Islamophobic and pro-Israeli, yet it is allegedly being waged in defense of "their rights." In addition, Arab American feminists have not found much help in American feminists: "Instead, [American feminists] have sometimes seemed to have a vested interest in broadcasting stories of savage Arab men and perpetuating the stereotype of the passive, pathetic Arab woman, needing to be roused from her moral, intellectual, and political stupor," writes Evelyn Shakir.[11]

However, for Arab American women, articulating feminism inadvertently becomes a political statement. Because the negative American view of and current foreign policy toward the Middle East are often justified by pointing out the oppression of Arab women, an articulation of Arab feminism becomes an attack on the government because it calls the government's policy into question. If Arab women are already so vocal and visible, Americans might realize, then why do we need to insert ourselves into their domestic affairs? And then maybe, just maybe, the current policy of neocolonialism—based on the false logic of defending American freedom by fighting Arab countries—will begin to crumble.

What has become clear is that Arab American women span a variety of countries of origin, socioeconomic classes, and religious affiliations and attitudes. They come from Lebanon, Syria, and Palestine, and, more recently, from North Africa and the Persian Gulf states. More and more are born in the United States, growing up between the Arab culture at home and the American culture at school and at work. Some are Christians, but more are Muslims; among both groups, some women are deeply religious, while others are not. Some Arab American women are doctors, lawyers, professors; some are factory workers or have retail jobs; some own their own businesses, while others work at home raising their children. Some are forbidden to work outside the home at all. Many find support from their families for pursuing careers, while some feel pressure to get married early.

In other words, the great variety one finds among women in the Arab American community mimics the diversity of other ethnic American communities: Latinas, Africans, Asians, and Southeast Asians. In terms of dealing with their community and its more patriarchal elements, Arab Americans also share the same feminist concerns as other ethnic American women: the culture clash often experienced by those Arab Americans born to immigrant parents; the burden of bearing the native culture on one's shoulders, manifested in such ways as feeling pressure to marry someone from the "homeland"; and seeking an education and establishing a career. These challenges are faced by Arab American women at all levels of intensity. Whereas some Arab American women live closely sheltered, restricted lives, others have a degree of freedom and independence that would surpass the amount of American feminists and surprise them as well.

Yet Arab American women face a universal problem: the political agenda of the United States that perpetuates a false stereotype of Arab women. The Faceless Veiled Woman, whom Mona Fayad describes and who appears on the cover of my book, continues to harass the Arab American woman and feminist. Even if she resembles nothing in our lives (and for the vast majority of Arab American women, she does not), we must still confront and re-create her. Though no less important than the struggle of battling sexism within our community, this other battle is one shared by us all. The only way to win it is to organize and begin, more intensely than before, to reconstruct our own portrait, to present not the monolithic image of Arab women that everyone seems to want—which seems convenient—but the collage of Arab American women's faces, voices, and perspectives to America and the world.

Reconstructing that portrait is, of course, a complicated process. The struggles of Arab American feminists are generally with the larger American culture, as we attempt to find ways to challenge the dominant stereotype of the Faceless Veiled Arab Woman, but also within our own communities as we seek to recognize and address elements of sexism. Furthermore, non-Arabs who vocally support us might themselves fall into the trap created by the stereotype, despite their good intentions and best efforts, forcing us to criticize our few advocates—a precarious position indeed.

Steinem's political and personal are one entity with two sides, but, for us, the political and the personal are two very different entities, each requiring a simultaneous investment of energy and effort to battle its inherent sexism. How to succeed, without exhausting our resources, will be the challenge for the Arab American feminist movement.

23

Teaching Scriptural Texts in the Classroom
The Question of Gender

MOULOUK BERRY

This chapter deals with Moulouk Berry's experience teaching a course she designed on the Quran at the University of Michigan–Dearborn. She explores the different epistemological relationship that the students have to the course than their professor and how the blurring of the line between the two can create tensions in the classroom: the professor teaching teaches about the sacred text, meaning teaching the history of the text from multiple perspectives, while the students (especially students committed to the faith of the particular sacred text under study) take the course as a course on the sacred text (which involves accepting the ahistoricity of the text and reading verses and their correspondent commentaries). She also addresses the difficulties inherited in teaching religious sacred texts in postsecondary U.S. secular institutions and the ways in which professors can navigate these difficulties and give voice to the students in the classroom. In particular, Berry looks at the students' reactions when faced with alternative liberal interpretations of key Quranic verses dealing with gender.

When we enter the classroom to teach the sacred text in the U.S. postsecondary secular academy, we teach *about the sacred text, meaning we teach the history of the text from multiple perspectives.* When students committed to the faith of the particular sacred text under study register for the class, they take a *course on the sacred text, which involves accepting the ahistoricity of the text and reading verses and their correspondent commentaries.* This blurring of the line between a course *about* and a course *on* the sacred text sometimes creates tensions in the classroom. The students have a different epistemological relationship to the course than their professor: they feel that they know their faith on one level of personal experience but are now challenged to consider it in a historical context and in relation to multiple perspectives. In this situation, it is imperative for the professor to explore ways to give voice and share authority in the classroom to avoid marginalizing and excluding student voices. This point was particularly my experience when I developed and taught a course about the Quran in the winter of 2003 at the University of Michigan–Dearborn. I constantly had to navigate tensions that were generated by way of discussions, so as not to impose my own thought and in order to encourage students to speak. It was important to think with my students *collectively* how dominant discourses—whether religious or secular—can silence, exclude, and "otherize" the other.

The Classroom

My class consisted predominantly of Muslim Arab and Muslim non-Arab Americans, one Christian Arab Chaldean American, and one Christian African American. Three of the Muslim American students were females who wore the head cover. The majority of the Muslim students were Sunnis, and a few were Shiites.[1] All of the students were brought up in the United States but traced their ancestral backgrounds to Lebanon, Syria, Egypt, Iraq, Kuwait, and Pakistan.

The course was primarily listed under modern and classical languages because it is the discipline where I am housed, but the course was also cross-listed with religious studies. The course was titled Introduction to the Quran. My syllabus consisted of two parts: The first part focused on the history of the text and the sociopolitical and cultural milieu in which the text emerged. The second part examined the content of the text. In the first half of the semester students learned the early history of Islam: the gathering, compiling, canonizing, and the transcription of the Quran; Quranic exegesis; the development of hadith literature (the collection of sayings attributed on the authority of Muhammad and his companions for Sunnis and on the authority of Muhammad and the imams in the case of Shi'is); and the development of major Islamic legal schools (Hanafi, Maliki, Shafi'i, Hanbali, and Ja'fari).

In order to demonstrate to students the heterogeneity of Islam and how different methodologies of reading the Quran (such as hermeneutics) yielded variant readings of the text, I dealt with different Quranic themes such as gender, pluralism, ethics, and science. My choice of the first two themes, gender and pluralism, was motivated by their centrality to scholarly debates dealing with Islam in the contemporary era. The second theme, ethics, is essential to Quranic exegesis in that it frames the first two themes. I chose the theme of science in order to engage students from science and engineering, as well as to explore the importance of the historical relationship that exists between Islam and scientific knowledge. In addition to the required reading texts,[2] students were assigned supplementary readings, such as chapters from various sources, for class presentations.

Most professors are familiar with the anxieties experienced in academia when teaching what is seen as controversial subjects and the concomitant methodological challenges. Frame this difficulty in the larger context of a post-9/11 U.S. campus, and the complexity of the situation begins to unfold even more. One can readily recall the controversy at the University of North Carolina (UNC) at Chapel Hill when the faculty committee decided to require all incoming undergraduates to read Michael Sells's book *Approaching the Qur'an: The Early Revelations*. The controversy provoked strong negative reactions among conservative Christian students. They objected to the teaching of such a course on campus on the grounds that it contravenes the Establishment Clause in the Constitution. The Supreme Court dismissed the case against UNC, considering the whole case nonsense.[3] In addition to the complaints by conservative Christians about being compelled to read the Quran against their Christian beliefs, the antibook campaign spurred many debates about academic freedom, diversity, and the separation between church and state.[4] The anxiety caused within institutions in dealing with such events points to how the academy has always been politically implicated in its pursuit of knowledge and drawn boundaries around what is acceptable and what is not. Censorship, not restricted to state-sponsored censorship or the silencing of marginal groups by dominant groups, implicates all of us, for we engage in self-censorship in an effort to work out the nuances, contradictions, and controversies of our own intellectual production.

My objective in teaching the Quran was to create a space where the exchange of ideas would foster better understanding through diverse perspectives as students decide for themselves what they stand for. Students' anxieties were often caused by the nature of secular education, and by extension the process of secularizing religion at its most basic core—religious sacred text. In the case of the Quran, it became almost impossible since the Quran, unlike the Bible for some Christians, is not considered a human account of God's revelation. Muslims assert repeatedly that God is the author of the book. Muslims believe that the Quran embodies divine speech, and, thus, it cannot be subjected to historicization. The transhistoricity of the text, in the Muslim view, ensures the Quran's universalism and its relevance to all times and places, not just to when and where it was revealed.[5]

How would I then teach a text in a secular institution with a class in which almost all the students believed in its sacredness and the irrelevance of historicization? The lines between the divine and the worldly were so sharply drawn that the first day of class ushered in a deafening silence—like a volcano waiting to erupt: Muslim students explicitly announced that the reason they were taking the class was to learn *The Truth*. The quest for the religious truth on the part of the students and the ever-present awareness of the institutional context, that is, the secularity of the academy, made the class one of my most attended and most intellectually challenging. Students were coming to class not only to learn but also to defend their perspectives and to ensure fair representation. In light of this situation, I announced that the class was not *on* the Quran, for such a class would be taught at the mosque. This class, I stressed, was *about* the Quran, and, therefore, it should be examined within the confines of scholarship. I asked students to think about such questions as: Who establishes the truth? Whose Islam do we study? How is the divine articulated in human medium? Whose knowledge of sacred text is authoritative, and whose is discounted? My goal was to challenge both students' preconceived notions of authority, knowledge, divinity, gender, and Islam, while at the same time refusing to exonerate secular scholars from taking responsibility for their antireligious positions by claiming objectivity. These challenges created a vibrant intellectual atmosphere in the classroom and made the course very exciting and appealing to students.

During the course of the semester, a schism along Shi'i-Sunni lines was most pronounced. Historically, Muslims divided on the question of the leadership of the community right after the Prophet Muhammad's death in the seventh century AD that resulted later in the development of two mainstream Islamic sects: the Sunni and the Shi'i. Tensions between students rose in the classroom and were kept at bay only by my intervention. Yet not even the Sunni-Shi'i tension elicited as much controversy as gender. This time, the battlefield was drawn in which my students in this particular semester and I were on opposite sides. Almost all of my Muslim students had preconceived ideas about gender in Islam. They were committed to the patriarchal interpretations of the text. Liberal Muslim interpretations were dismissed by my Muslim students and were accepted only by the two non-Muslim, that is, Christian, students. By patriarchy, I mean the interpretation of the text with a reading that privileges men as men or finds textual evidence that connect the divine with males. Liberal reading of the text involves a reading that is responsive to women's aspiration and does not favor men or women by virtue of their biological or innate functions or by divine privileging.

All students, to a varying degree, accepted women's rights to participate in political and social life with an emphasis on a woman's primary obligation to her family. When it came to debating gender equality, Muslim students (in this particular semester) invoked essentialist notions of biological differences claiming men's superiority over women and women's emotionality, resorting to such interpretations in both traditional Sunni and Shi'i traditions (specifically, those traditions that have their bases in historical developments and not necessarily tied to the Quranic text). Without realizing it, students actually treated traditional Islamic exegetical works as sacredly as they treated the Quran. In an effort to provide examples of Muslim liberal modernist interpretations, I assigned students Asma Barlas's book *"Believing Women" in Islam: Unreading Patriarchal Interpretations of the Qur'an*. Barlas puts forth an internal interrogation of the Islamic text and critiques the idea of the sacredness of the patriarchal project and interpretation of the text from a perspective that takes gender equality and women's liberation in the Quran as its point of departure. Reading a woman's interpretation of traditional exegetical works and her challenges to the different Islamic texts and the contexts in which they were codified was threatening to some of the students on a number of levels. First, it contradicted the assumption that religious knowledge of the sacred text rested with Muslim male clerics, which meant that the "true" and the "authentic" could be only that which was imparted by males. Second, the author's perceived feminist stance was seen as an attack on established traditional and patriarchal interpretations of the text: in other words, what was established as canonical in Sunni Islam and as "most reputable" (*al-mashhur*) in Shi'i Islam—*even when such interpretations contradicted the Quranic provisions.*

By virtue of not following the metanarrative of gender inequality, and by not grounding such inequality in biological gender differences, Barlas's work was rendered dubious in the eyes of the students. To assess how they related to reading the text, students had to know whether the author was following the proscribed ways of Islam. Because the author located herself within Islam and grounded her theory in the Quran, they could not attack her credibility on the premise that she was an "outsider" attacking the religion and culture. The students then resorted to the veil, always symbolizing religiosity and faithfulness vis-à-vis the not-so-good Muslim woman, which equals positioning anyone who does not fulfill the religious incumbency of covering the head as the "other." Of course, the students' inquiry had wider implications: the validity of the word of a Muslim woman had to be earned by her "proper" appearance. There was a sigh of a relief when I said that Asma Barlas might be veiled. Interestingly enough, none of my students inquired into the religiosity of Farid Esack, whose book *Introduction to the Quran* I also assigned as class reading.

I could not really gauge the full implication of the question of the veil until one of my female students, who wore a head scarf, did a presentation on the head cover, the *hijab*, in which she stated that a Muslim woman who respects herself must wear the head cover. At first, I did not take the comment personally and treated it as just the views of one student. But when the students looked at me and laughed, the point was made: I was the only Muslim woman in that class without a head cover. Her presentation was a direct attack on my own position, authority, and legitimacy as I stood to impart my knowledge *about* the Quran. "Respect is a matter of definition," I commented afterward, maintaining a "natural" posture. This situation was not about a shift in balance of power but an opportunity to educate.

Teaching the class also involved examining the history of textual and legal interpretations and the impact of legal critical thinking (*ijtihad*) in formulating Islamic laws. Having both the academic training in Islamic studies and the personal knowledge of how *ijtihad* is theorized and applied, I assisted in anticipating students' questions and problems with many issues dealt with in the class. In this case, the hardest to undo in the class was the paradigmatic thinking along the lines of right and wrong. After all, if you teach about the Quran, you are expected to narrow it to right and wrong.

In the course of the discussion and after listening to countless arguments about women's fragile nature and how women's primary duties should be to their homes, children, and husbands, Shi'i students proved more amenable to considering Muslim liberal modernist interpretations of key gender Quranic verses. This inclination is possibly owing to the different role the notion of *ijtihad* (critical thinking) plays in Shi'i jurisprudence. Because of political and historical considerations, some scholars argue that Sunnis closed the door of *ijtihad*[6] during the Abbasid period in the ninth century when the Sunni legal scholar Muhammad ibn Idris al-Shafi (d. 819), the founder of Islamic jurisprudence, curbed the diversity of legal practice and established a fixed and common methodology for all law schools. By transferring the authority for legal interpretation from individual law schools to the consensus of the scholarly community, Al-Shafi'i restricted the role of personal reasoning in the formulation of the law and, thus, closed the door of *ijtihad*.[7] Consequently, in Sunni Islam *ijtihad*, the jurist must accept the authenticity of the consensus of medieval Islamic scholars' interpretation of Islamic sources and their formulation of the law as binding and infallible and, thus, cannot attempt to read the texts in light of contemporaneous events and needs. In distinction to Sunni Islam, Shi'i Islam accepts *ijtihad* and affirms that *only the opinion of a living jurist is binding*; therefore, jurists cannot accept their predecessors' opinions as authoritative and must revisit all primary and secondary Islamic sources when deducing new rulings. According to Shi'i jurisprudence, unanimity of the Shi'i jurists' views on certain legal questions is not a source in and of itself and as such has no validity on its own. This process is dynamic and allows for the renewal of legal methodologies (*al-tajdid al-fiqhi*) to adequately assist the jurists in dealing with old, "new," and "unprecedented" issues of life and society in the contemporary era.[8] I am not claiming that Muslim Shi'i students in my classroom changed their opinion drastically, but the fact that they acceded to the notion that there could be multiple positions on this issue was in itself a hard-earned struggle.[9]

Students were generally aware of verses in the Quran that assert equality of the sexes.[10] Students could not theoretically work out the contradictions between the two divergent tendencies in the Quran: the legal but unequal gender approach and the moral-ethical but egalitarian gender tendency. Scholars such as Leila Ahmed account for this divergence and argue that Islam has always possessed these two divergent tendencies within its message. Its "ethical message" establishing the moral and spiritual equality of all human beings was undermined by the "sexual hierarchy" that privileges men. It was this message that occupied the central position in the formulation of laws and institutions, thus unarticulating Islam's message of equality of all human beings, particularly with respect to women.[11] I explained to my students the historical factors that impacted the direction of *ijtihad* in Sunni Islam that eventually led to the privileging of men and the establishment of "sexual hierarchy" in the legal sphere. I explained that the Abbasid Empire's (750–1258 CE) quest for and consolidation of political power over vast lands and diverse populations played a significant role in privileging certain readings of the Islamic textual sources over others. The Abbasids' "pluralism" and multiculturalism proved "repressive" toward Muslim women.[12] In their effort to create a unified law acceptable to their diverse populace, the Abbasids drew on diverse traditions and backgrounds. It was precisely then that many misogynist practices and traditions of diverse cultures entered Islamic sources (including Shi'i legal sources). I supplanted this historical background to my students as a prelude to discussing the importance of synthesizing the two divergent voices in the Quran and opting for a reading that is more responsive to women's aspirations. No matter what my students felt, I know that they were given the opportunity to intellectually engage in the process of rethinking old questions within a different context. These debates, students finally concluded, do not necessarily brand their author within or outside one's traditions. After meeting Asma Barlas at the 2004 Middle East Studies Association annual conference in San Francisco and discovering that she did not cover her hair, I wondered what my students' reactions would have been, had they then known!

I was aware that I was challenging my students' interpretations of dominant Islamic discourses on gender. The whole idea of having to make the scripture a subject for study and inquiry was in itself a transgression. I have since taught the class for two more terms. Although the initial blurring of the line between taking a course on the Quran versus teaching a course on the Quran persisted, I found that not all students of a particular faith under study are rigid and unwilling to question their beliefs. What is interesting to me in finding a pattern among some Muslims students—and, I think, the same pattern may apply equally to students from other faiths—is the belief that Islamic history is as sacred as Islam; therefore, any attempt at examining any particular *not-so-sacred historical events* is seen by students as an attack on the religion itself. This convergence between the sacredness of religious faith and the history of the faith is a poignant point and must be anticipated when teaching a course to students from the faith under study. Understanding of this reality makes secular education a substantial challenge. Secular institutions are not so secular (if that could ever be achieved), for they also harbor similarly rigid ideas about traditions and world religions. This rigidity makes teaching a divine text a challenge as well. We need to create spaces in which the exchange of ideas embodies the recognition of students' spiritual commitments and simultaneously engages the notions upon which their beliefs are based.

This group of students in that specific semester believed deeply in inherent differences between men and women. The persistence of Islamic essentialist discourses in certain contexts is not merely a result of the historical role of the state in codifying and controlling gender relations in the classical or modern periods, but they are part of a more complex history.

Teaching the Quran course as an Arab American feminist professor at the University of Michigan–Dearborn, in the heart of a large Arab and Muslim community in the United States (some 300,000 Arabs live in metropolitan Detroit; Dearborn with a majority of Lebanese Muslims has an Arab population of approximately 30,000), reposes universal questions of representation, the Self, the Other, and the Other Within the Self. Also, of particular importance to me as an Arab American feminist professor sharing my perspective on teaching gender and the sacred text is the interface among cultural identities, religious faith, and the wider American realities. Being simultaneously part of the ethnic Arab culture and the American subculture, Arab American feminists add to our knowledge of the complexities of women's experiences and provide an in-depth understanding of the specific role and the specific set of values and concerns that shape them and shape their communities. We not only have to educate other communities, academic and public, about the heterogeneity that exists within Islam, but also have to educate our own. Indeed, depth of knowledge about the topic at hand and familiarity with the subject matter of the class and student socialization are absolute necessities to teaching and explaining Islam; that is, not everyone who feels like it can just jump on the bandwagon and teach Islam because it has become a sexy subject today. Maintaining intellectual integrity is an absolute necessity that we must demand to hold ourselves accountable.

24

The Light in My House

IMANI YATOUMA

Imani Yatouma writes about the violence of heterosexuality, especially her experience with infertility and childhood sexual abuse. She describes how these experiences led to a paralysis in her writing and trauma-induced amnesia. She emerges from this abyss through writing and embracing a queer life. She finds herself open to queer endings; writing is still a painful discourse that creates unease and discomfort. Writing or queer sexuality do not rescue her. There is no rescue, just remainder.

To be queer and Arab is to be discreet and to protect the privacy of other Arab sisters. Sexuality is not about public face. The critics of Joseph Massad's *Desiring Arabs* want to push the agenda that Arab "queers" are not safe in the Arab environment. Racialized subjectivity is something that white queers might not see so clearly. To be white is to be a racial subject, but subjectivity is not so foregrounded. If and when I come out as Arab queer, what I say will be scrutinized and generalizations will be extrapolated even as I now mark that territory as unmarkable.

I joined a lesbian group, and as soon as I mentioned my Middle East background, an older white woman said, "You would be killed in your home country for being a lesbian, right?" I am on the defensive without giving a defensive answer. The question presumes certain rights and dignities that are inherent to the U.S. context. Rather than argue about whether the answer to this question is clearly knowable, it seems that I side with Massad in stating that it is beside the point. The imperialism is in the assumption that living in the United States is a privilege, and I should bow down before that God. It does not take into account that most rapes of women in the military inside of Iraq are by their fellow military brothers. Iraqis face many dangers, and their level of safety is worse since occupation. Iraqis, gay citizens especially, had more freedom and more mobility under

Saddam Hussein. What does this fact mean? Are we arguing semantics? Not really. The discomfort with the question comes from a discomfort with American entitlement about epistemologies. With straight friends and family, one does not accept that you are no longer straight. You are confused, or you are something other than straight. With queer friends, there is judgment about how you choose to come out. To be queer and Arab means many things, but it means a responsibility with how I present or perform myself.

Coming out as queer is not easy, and I do not really feel that it is tied to my Arab identity. I expected it to matter, and it might later when I am more visible or visually marked as such. I did not feel at home with my queerness until I joined a network of lesbian Arabs, and I met some who live in my city. What is the difference, or why did that matter? People expect you to be. The transition from straight to gay can be kind of awkward. In my (white) coming-out group, we talk about the gay uniform and how to pick up women, and what we would say or do if we like someone. Others are struggling with marriages and making the transition from straight to queer. All of us share our struggles, and it helps to get us where we need to be. I cannot believe that coming out might be a lifelong process that includes every new person I might meet. Maybe I will be read as queer and not have to say the words, or perhaps it is not the business of every person I meet. I do not want to hide. If I am coming out, when I come out, I do not want to lie or hide it from anyone in my life. I want to prepare myself for community rejection and for hardships without really thinking drama or assuming that all experiences will be arduous and impossible.

◆   ◆   ◆

Some stories read like classics, as if they transcend culture, race, and geography. Scheherazad averted rape with two and a half years of oral acrobatics. My admiration stopped when she married Shahrayar and had his children. A lesser-told version of Sleeping Beauty, the origin of the tale has the prince impregnate the princess. It is not the kiss that wakes her from her slumber but their newborn suckling at her breast that dislodges the witch's poison. The unconscious allows for sweet slumber. We sometimes do not want to wake up to our life, our history, because we might disturb the balances we think we have created.

"It is God's will." Everyone would console me when I did not get pregnant. My mother-in-law did not mean harm when she said that, without children, a couple could never have "light in their house." Again, God decided about when and how or whether one's life could be luminous. The words pained me, but, always, I fought against the truth value of the Symbolic order. It is not only Arab culture that regales the Child. Most cultures are obsessed with inheritance, one's worth tied to one's own biological prowess. Living for a future that had to include children seemed like a reign of tyranny especially if I was unable to create that baby naturally. I could have been happy without children, but self-imposed pressure and anxiety were not all that I experienced. The whole world order of gender restrictions and cultural expectations weighed down on me. I did not have to cave, but both mainstream normative American and Arab cultures colluded to force me to think about my body and mind as malfunctioning, lacking in worth and therefore not worthy of a (marital, intellectual, aesthetic) future.

To write about Arab queer sexualities is to escape a narrative of compulsory heterosexuality (the desire to create life and liberty outside of normative institutions, to negate the rules and find elasticity in culture, embracing desire that is Real and real: unruly, unintelligible, dizzying, daunting). This is an escape route that will disentangle some nets and cut knots elsewhere. I am not out yet, and I am figuring out how my new sexuality will matter or figure in my life beyond my personal decision to embrace a queer sexual identity.

How many breaks does it take? My mom said, "He must be broken." That is what the therapist said to her. He said that abusers are broken. It is an empathy tactic, and it also creates an enabler. The discursive terrain seems so accommodating. Or maybe I want words to cure, reinvent, and stop the pain. Dead spaces inside and numbness kept me on function key. Even as I really did not function or felt sexually dead and nonfunctioning.

I have not written fiction (or anything) in years because I am living in a fictional home of my own designing. In the very spacious five thousand–square-foot mansion, I never really use the basement. I only store boxes of books and papers I wrote years ago. I want my writing to be as far away as possible. I want no reminder that I could or did publish anything. If I stay silent, don't write, then nothing horrible can happen. If I stay silent, don't publish, then all shitty things are null and void. If I stay silent, protect my family secrets, then silence seeps into my core and all can be erased. I have the power to erase anything without talking. The bedrooms in this house are empty. No kids, no toys, no clutter. How many empty rooms can I create and still sleep at night? I used to sleep without waking. I used to sleep within minutes of getting into bed. What kind of bed have I made for myself these disquieting days?

In this house I created, I kept my sister in the attic, Brontë style. My house is full of spaces, empty and static, dusty and dense. Now I want to set that house on fire and to be sleeping in the room, dead asleep, like I have been for years, and to just be consumed by my own smoking rage and my own inflammatory words.

I cannot tell this story in a fictionalized version, nor can I open up very much in nonfiction. What I want to write is not memoir but a kind of textual analysis that looks at the paradoxical ways in which writing identity, sexuality, and ethnicity all collide into a space that cannot be recovered. In trying to make amends, in attempting to stabilize past and future, I want just to speak and to be silent at the same time. I have always felt like writing is my passion. If I do not write, I will die. I quit writing because I wanted to murder my creative self. I did not deserve that writing life I had started. Why can I not write about something else? Holding on is worse than letting go, and I am finding myself locked out of the house I created years ago. I do not want the key anymore.

My sister says the sex happened many times. And she recently added me to her story. I want to murder someone, mostly me; ironically, I cannot gather rage. The girl inside still maintains her right to reject any narrative that does not have an attractive veneer. No one is really broken. We have swayed and bent and kneeled and slept and whined and whispered, and then we had no more to say. I mostly do not want to tell because I want things to remain unbroken. How to escape this triangulation? What narratives are foisted upon us? We might not have the capacity to excise the story from history, but we have the prowess to invent other endings, ones that leave us intact, sexually, intellectually, ethically, and psychically. Or perhaps we do not need to think about ourselves as intact, whole. We might embrace the abject, the horror, and rather than recoiling, hiding or spending inordinate energy telling lies to cover other lies, we might just speak in languages that are unintelligible and indecipherable.

25

Guidelines

Lisa Suhair Majaj

When Lisa Suhair Majaj moved to the United States in her early twenties, she realized that although she had been born an American of Arab heritage, she had no guidelines for what it meant to be an Arab American. Everything was new territory, and she fumbled a lot as she tried to make sense of, and articulate, her identity. Majaj encountered a great deal of hostility, ignorance, and incomprehension along the way. Her poem "Guidelines" is an attempt to give voice to some of the things she wished someone had told her when she was a young Arab American just beginning to grapple with her identity. The sardonic tone is a reflection of the frustration that so many Arab Americans feel as they try to give voice to themselves.

If they ask you what you are,
say Arab. If they flinch, breathe deeply
and recall your grandmother's eyes.
If they ask you where you come from,
say Toledo. Detroit. Mission Viejo.
Fall Springs. Topeka. If they seem confused,

help them locate these places on a map.
You might inquire, Where are you from?
Have you been here long? Do you like this country?

If they ask you what you eat,
don't dissemble: if garlic is your secret friend,
admit it. Likewise, crab cakes.

If they express empathy with your cultural oppression,
smile politely and proffer a reading list.
If they ask you for belly dance lessons, keep smiling and add some titles.

If they ask you if you're white, say it depends.
Say no. Say maybe. If appropriate, inquire casually,
Have you always been white, or is it recent?

If they wave newspapers in your face and shout,
stay calm. Remember everything they never learned.
Offer to take them to the library.

If they say you're not American, don't pull out your wallet-sized flag.
Recall the Bill of Rights. Mention the Constitution.
Wear democracy like a favorite garment: comfortable, intimate.

If events drive you to the streets in protest,
link hands with whomever is beside you.
Keep your eye on the colonizer's maps,

geography's twisted strands, the many colors of struggle.
No matter how far you've come, remember:
the starting line is always closer than you think.

If they ask how long you plan to stay, say forever.
Console them if they seem upset. Say, don't worry,
you'll get used to it. Say, we live here: how about you?

26

Reflections of a Genderqueer
Palestinian American Lesbian Mother

HUDA JADALLAH

Huda Jadallah's reflection challenges how stereotypes of Arab men as terrorists and Arab women as submissive do not operate as such in cases of gender nonconformity. In addition to challenging us to rethink the intersections of racism and sexism, she also discusses the challenges of being an Arab lesbian mother and her experiences of being scrutinized as such in a racist and heterosexist society.

On Gender Nonconformity

Growing up, I was always keenly aware of being marked as dangerous, "a terrorist." I never understood as a child that this label was not simply a result of racial marking or being identified as Palestinian, but was also in part owing to being marked as genderqueer. My gender nonconformity manifested itself in being stereotyped as violent and dangerous as opposed to submissive and oppressed, as Arab women who conform to gender roles are often perceived.

One specific site where I experience the intersection of race, gender, and sexuality is public restrooms. Upon entering or exiting or actually while I am inside a public women's restroom, I am often mistaken for an Arab man. The fear in women's eyes as they recoil away from me cannot be mistaken. The stereotype of Arab men as violent and hypersexualized is, I believe, a major aspect of why these women fear me. They fear being raped. They fear being hurt. They mistrust. The fear has been so intense at times that I have felt compelled to assure women of their safety, assure them that indeed I am a woman. But, of course, I cannot assure them that I am not Palestinian. And what of those individuals who are transgender, the ones who do not have the luxury to assure others that they are indeed the "right sex in the right bathroom stall"? Do I betray them in my assurances? Do I betray myself as I seek to comfort those people who are uncomfortable with my race, gender, and sexuality?

One thing my experiences in my skin as an Arab lesbian who is a gender nonconformist informs me of is that Arab feminists writing on gender must stop essentializing gender. We must stop insisting that Arab women experience gender in specific ways that are different from Arab men. It is just simply not the case. We must begin to understand and articulate our experiences based on a more complex and nuanced comprehension of gender.

On Violence

When I think about violence I think about my five-year-old twin sons fighting in public and my interjecting myself into the scene in order to stop the fight using their names, Omar and Hady. Their names and my appearance identify us in terms of race. I am acutely aware of my discomfort with people watching my sons fight. I cannot help but imagine the racist things they are thinking about violent Arab males and bad Arab mothers. In my head I think of the misinformation put out by the U.S. media proclaiming to the public that Palestinian mothers teach their children to fight with rocks and do not care about their children's safety when they are confronted with the Israeli military, one of the strongest militaries in the world. I cringe. I do not want my Palestinian sons to fight in public. I do not want to admit it, but I am, quite frankly, ashamed. I fight against my feelings with my intellect, knowing this is how racism works.

Being a lesbian mom is somewhat like being an Arab mom in the United States in that I feel that I am held to a higher standard, that people will be closely scrutinizing my parenting and making assumptions about it based on my being a lesbian. Just as I feel people observing my parenting through a racist lens, I also feel people observe my parenting through a homophobic lens. I know that the stereotype of lesbian as sexual predator follows me even as a mother, and thus I am extracautious that no one can misconstrue anything in our family life as sexual impropriety.

On Motherhood

When I think of my experience of being a queer Arab mom I laugh to myself at how supremely perfect it all was according to cultural standards of the good woman—the virgin conception (via a syringe), the virgin birth (via C section) and twin sons (two boys, not just one!)—yet how absolutely taboo to have children without being married to a man. Being lesbian mothers posed many challenges to us. One such challenge was the economic consequences of creating family with children in a way that was either not socially acceptable or not socially recognized.

It was at the point of having children that my partner and I experienced in a very real way the political economy of being lesbian mothers. Family Student Housing at the University of California at Santa Barbara denied us housing there as a family since my partner and I could not get married and thus had no marriage license. Nor was my partner able to get legal parental status until five years later when California law changed. We paid exorbitant prices living in downtown Santa Barbara (one of the most expensive real estate markets in California), while married men and women with no children lived in Family Student Housing, which is subsidized and significantly less expensive than the general rental market. Eventually, we moved into family student housing illegally, requesting that they remove Deanna's name from the list of residents as was required for them to allow me to move in. We said it would just be our children and myself living there. We were just too deep in debt to continue living downtown. Our denial of her presence in our lives allowed us to survive economically, while we bore the impact psychically and emotionally as we lived with the long-term consequences of being unable to show any affection toward each other in public space. This experience of not being welcomed at UC Santa Barbara's Family Student Housing as a family consisting of two queer women impacted our sense of belonging and not belonging as a part of the university community. I say all this to point to the fact that we do not experience homophobia and heterosexism only as part of Arab culture. Rather, it was within the educational system, a large U.S. institution, that we experienced heterosexism that left us in deep debt and with a feeling of isolation.

On Home, Community, and Belonging

Growing up, I always felt a sense of not belonging in the communities I was a part of outside of my nuclear family. I never had words for these feelings and was not in touch with those feelings. It is only now, as an adult, in retrospect, that I can see it and put words to it.

Over the years I have participated in and been a part of several communities. The queer Arab community has been one of the most important communities to me in my adult life. This community has been an amazing source of support for my family and me. I experience kinship from close friends within the community as well as a sense of belonging to a broader network of queer Arabs who I feel are a part of my extended family.

Although I believe we are now on the brink of a baby boom in the queer Arab community, one of the challenges for me currently is that the queer Arab community that I am a part of does not have children, and our lives and worlds are radically different owing to the specifics of our daily realities. At the same time, I must acknowledge the great effort that some members of our queer Arab community have put forth in staying connected and being supportive of our children and us. The queer Arab community has been an amazing source of support for my family and myself.

Being a genderqueer Palestinian American lesbian mother is not easy. At times it feels utterly exhausting paving a road that is full of obstacles and creating a path that is mine and not someone else's. I am constantly negotiating how and where I will put my energy in this gender-controlling, racist, and heterosexist society. Two things that are essential to my well-being and survival and that I consider part of my work in helping to create a world where justice prevails are: (1) being myself, knowing who I am, and feeling good about whom I am, and (2) creating and sustaining family and community where I feel a sense of belonging. Although it may sound simple to be one's self and sustain positive communities, for me it has been a messy process that has required persistent refocusing and self-reflection.

5 HOME AND HOMELANDS

Memories, Exile, and Belonging

27

The Memory of Your Hands Is a Rainbow

AMAL HASSAN FADLALLA

Translated from the Arabic by Khaled Mattawa[1]

Amal Hassan Fadlalla conceived this poem during Sudan's two major political events: the conclusion of the peace agreement between Sudan's Northern and Southern warring parties in 2005 and the escalation of the conflict in the Darfur region in western Sudan. Globally, the war in Iraq, the Israeli-Palestinian conflict, the 9/11 attacks, and other humanitarian crises continue to generate relentless politics of fear and despair. In the poem, a woman rises to open new windows of hope and to contemplate new meanings of liberty and freedom. Fadlalla dedicates this poem to women and men in Sudan and around the globe who are fighting against the odds to make this dream come true.

ذكرى يداك قوس قزح

حبيبي طويل
طويلٌ
يلونُ النجومَ
لوّنَهُ بخضرةِ السهولِ
سوادٌ يكحلُ الغيومَ
وعندما يفيضُ حبيبي
تنطفئ حرائقُ الشمالِ والجنوب
تولدُ زهرةٌ من شفةِ المغيب
تُقبلُ هامةَ الشروق
وعندما يفيضُ حبيبي
تنحني هامةُ الذين يسرقونَ سعادةَ الأطفال
وينتهي زمنُ الحرب

والذين لا يضحكون
لا يطبخون
لا يطعِمُون
ولا يخَافونَ حينَ يقتلون
وعندما يذوبُ حبيبي في يدي
ينجبُ الكونُ ألف كتابٍ وألف إمرأةٍ جديدة
نساءُ بلونِ الأبنوسِ والقمح
حبليات
حُبلياتٍ بالتاريخ وبالسُلطةِ التي تُقسمُ النبقَ بين الفقراء
نساءٌ عاريات
عاريات كاسيات عاريات عاريات كاسيات عاريات
يرقصنَ في شوارعِ بوسطن
" اللول اللول يا لوليا، بسحروك يا لولى الحبشية"
ويحررنَ أمريكا
ويشتلنَ كربلاء
ويُغنى مُصطفى سيد أحمد
"حاتجى البنت ـ الحديقة"

حبيبي طفلٌ كبير
أنجبتهُ بفمي
فزغردتْ جدتي سبع مرات
وغرستْ في يديه تلاتة نخلات
واحدة باليمين وأثنتين باليسار
وغنت أختي الصغيرة
" الخدار خدارى من العين بضارى"
وأطلقتْ عصافيرَ كثيرة
بلون قوس قزح
وتوحد الوطن
تبعثرَ الوطن
وخرجَ الناسُ يهتفون
لبيك لك لبيك، لبيك لك لبيك؟
" البنسلين ياتمرجى نادو الحكيم ياتمرجى"
لبيك لك لبيك
ويشربونَ الماءَ صفواً صفوا

ويرقصون
"البابور جاز خلوه يشتغل، الشغل بالجاز ، خلوه يشتغل"
ويعشقونَ في الشوارع
ويصنعونَ الحبَّ في مكوار

مكوار عنوانا عداله وحرية
يانيل ياطيب وإنساني
يانيل ياطيب ومتفرع
أغسل بمويتك قسماتي
وأطلق أجنحتي وإيديا
شتتْ بمطرك تاريخي
في قلب الضفه الغربيه
كَسِّر أسورتي وأغلالى
حولني ضريره وكوفيه
لراشيل تحت الدبابه
تتحدى رصاصه ودوريه
وتفتح شارع مكسيكي
للبت الطالعه الورديه
حبيبي طويل
للبت الطالعه الورديه
ورديه
البت الماشه الورديه

أمال حسان فضل الله
جامعة ميتشجان

My beloved is tall
the color of stars
the color of plains,
and when my beloved surges
the fires of the north and south are doused
a flower is born from the sunset's mouth,
kisses the brow of sunrise,
and when my beloved floods

the heads of those who steal
children's happiness bend
and the epoch of war ends
and the time of those
who do not laugh
who do not cook
who do not feed
and who feel
no dread when they kill?
ends,
and when my beloved melts in my hand
the world gives birth to a thousand books
and a thousand new women
women the color of ebony and wheat
pregnant with history
with authority that divides lotus berries among the poor
naked women, naked clothed naked clothed naked
dancing on the streets of Boston
"al-lawl, al-lawl ya lawlia
they'll bewitch you my Ethiopian beauty"
and they liberate America
and they plant a seed of Karbala
and Mustafa Siyyid Ahmad sings
"my girl will soon come
the girl—the garden will soon come"

My love is a big child.
I birthed it with my mouth,
and my grandmother ululated
seven times
and planted in his hands
three date palms
one in the right and two in the left,
and my young sister sang
"that green one is my green
I'll hide him, not to be seen."
She released many sparrows
bearing the rainbow's colors

and the nation became one,
the nation united, then scattered
and the people stepped out,
chanting
Laubaik laka Laubaik?
We heard, here we come
"Penicillin O headnurse,
call out the doctor O headnurse"
Laubaik laka Laubaik
and they drank water purer than pure,
and they danced
"Let that diesel engine work
It's working that diesel train
Let that diesel engine work,"
and they fall in love on the street
and they make love in Maukwar,
Maukwar, its address of justice and freedom.
Sweet and generous Nile?
sweet and branched out for miles
wash my features with your water,
release my wings and my hands,
scatter my history with your rain,
in the heart of the West Bank,
break my bracelets and my chains,
turn me into a sandalwood powder rubbed in a kaffiyeh
for Rachel under the tank
facing a bullet and a platoon
and open a Mexican street
for the girl going out to her shift.

for the girl going out on her shift

28

You Are a 14-Year-Old Arab Chick Who Just Moved to Texas

RANDA JARRAR

"You Are a 14-Year-Old Arab Chick" is a second-person piece that follows a young girl as she tries to acclimate to a new life in Texas after a childhood in the Middle East.[1] Throughout the story, she is literally trying to negotiate a new place for herself in her father's home, in which he holds all the power. In a few short pages, she encounters ignorance, predatory behavior, and control from the outside male world and meets it with verve, humor, and integrity.

That fall you move with your family to America, you are diagnosed with TB, and the old white doctor points at the five-inch red rectangle on your forearm and announces, "that should be three inches smaller." He puts you on a battery of medications which worsens your acne, makes you gain thirty pounds, and gives you an overall sense of impending death. As usual, your Mama is jealous of you and wants to be the one dying instead; it is her first time without a piano, and your first time without friends to comfort you. TV is full of commercials, and your family goes to McDonald's too often; the first few times you're excited to be eating hamburgers, then a few months later you realize that it's a nasty fast food restaurant. When you go to the movies, you have to explain to your parents why the jokes are funny. Long after the credits begin to roll, the three of you still sit in the dark, you translating the movie's murder mystery into Arabic. There's nothing sadder than a fourteen-year-old explaining a movie to her middle-aged parents. In America, you think, not understanding a movie is the same as being illiterate. It could break your heart if you really think about it, so you should never think about it; you should just go to school, eat your lunch on the floor outside the library, then go into the library and spend the rest of the period reading the dictionary.

◆   ◆   ◆

Every day, Dimi wants to have lunch with you. Soon, so will Camilla and Aisha, who is black and Muslim and wants to hang out with you during Ramadan so y'all can give each other support. When these girls call the radio, they give you mad shoutouts. You don't know what a shoutout is, but you like that your name is on the radio, even if they mispronounce it. They are sixteen and drive beat-up cars and want you to hang out at the park with them when it's dark. You tell them your Baba doesn't allow it. "She said her papi don't play that," they'll translate to each other.

There are things that make it bearable: that bicycle your father bought you when you weren't looking, its handlebars shiny, nothing like the tattered, rusty bicycles you had to rent from the hashish fiend at the souk back in Ma'moura; Oreos; MTV; but mostly, the letters you get from Fakhr el-Din, your best friend who is still back in Alexandria renting bicycles from the hashish fiend at the souk in Ma'moura; letters that always begin, "I miss your face your eyes and your smile what is America like is it cold there and do you like the blonde boys better than me and my big nose?"

You write back that it's a total let down, that there aren't any cute blonde boys, and he's the best. You're lying; there are blonde twins that are straight out of a movie, and they're gorgeous, and one day you drop your box of charity choco-lates so one of them can help you pick them up. "Hey, I read about you in the newspaper," he says, and you blush. "Did you used to live in a tent, and stuff?" You lose your breath, then say, "No actually, a glass pyramid." "No kidding? Right on . . . ," and he walks away. What a fucking waste, you think to yourself.

You finally have a locker, something you've been dreaming of since you saw that 7-Up commercial when you were nine. But lockers can't make a girl happy forever. When, one weekend afternoon, your father comes into your bedroom with a letter from Fakhr in his hand, you brace yourself. There is a huge harangue. Girls should not be addressed this way, he tells you. And this boy says he misses kissing you. Did you actually kiss this boy? "No!" you say, a memory appearing in your head like a movie of yourself rolling around topless with Fakhr in an abandoned beach cabin. "Absolutely not!" you shout. The letter is torn up and discarded, and you are officially cut off from the Pride of Religion.

When Dimi and Camilla and Aisha insist that you go to a rap concert with them at Stubb's, you are met with complete resistance.

"Enough, man," Mama tells your Baba. "Let the child go, she's suffocating here."

"You, you be quiet, the girl's not going to rap concerts and getting drunk and pregnant. No, no, and no. Full stop." And to seal it, he farts three times.

"I want to have friends!" you scream, and run to your room.

"We are not here to make a friend, we are here to study and get the best out of America!" This is your Baba's mantra the entire time you are living under his roof. This is why he is in America, but not you. You want a "life," a concept you've just learned of.

You all go to the McDonald's drive-thru, and upon inspecting his cheeseburgers and finding them with pickles, your Baba backs the car up and yells into the intercom,

"I said no *bickles*, you *pitch!*"

♦   ♦   ♦

One morning, after listening to Nirvana half a dozen times, you pack a bag, kiss your brother's forehead, and sneak out of the house, balancing the bag on your bike's handlebars. You wear the bowler hat you'd bought when you first moved here, with your Mama from a street vendor by campus. Your bike flies downhill, and in your jeans' back pocket is your father's stolen credit card and around your neck every single gold pendant you've ever owned hanging from a sturdy gold chain.

Selling the gold is the first logical step, you think, starving out of your mind. So you go into a small shop and give an older man with little hair your chain. He weighs it and tells you $60. "Sixty bucks?" you yell. "Man, I know I should've gone lower," he says. No fucking way, that's all my gold, that's all I've got in the world! Only sixty bucks? You think of your mama walking around with all that gold hanging from her ears and wrists; does she know how little it's worth here in America? You snatch the necklace back and clip it around your neck, and as you turn away, the man tells you if you come home with him he'll buy you a new dress and you can have a place to stay for free.

The solution is to be a taco vendor, you decide as the day nears to a close and businessmen in their suits are flooding the avenue. You go to the place off Congress to apply for a cart, and the man asks you how old you are. Seventeen, you lie, and he asks if you've got proof. No, you say, and that's the end of that.

But I'm a taco vendor, you say, I need to sell tacos, it's part of a bigger plan to unite all people, especially Palestinians and Israelis. Oh really, he wants to know, and smiles. He's almost as old as your father, and he wants to know if you want to go home with him because he can take real good care of you and you wouldn't have to worry about a thing. You turn around and sprint to a pizza place, your mini suitcase banging against the asphalt, its wheels worn.

Quickly realizing you are prey, you walk to the nearest motel, a shit hole, and check in under a fake name, Madonna Nirvana. The man looks jaded, and wearily gives you a key. In your room, you decide that you're fucked, and call your parents.

"Goddamn you, we thought you'd been kidnapped!" your Baba yells.

"It's her, thank God!" your Mama says.

"Where are you, we're coming to get you now!" he says.

"Not so fast, buster," you say, can't believe you just called your dad buster.

"What?"

"I have conditions."

"There's no condition, you give us direction, we come get you right now, little girl."

"Bye," you say and hang up. You call back five minutes later.

"OK, OK, what is your condition?"

"Curfew extension."

"Nine p.m. is the final offer," he says.

"And resumed contact with Fakhr el-Din?"

"No, no, and no!"

You hang up again. This time you wait about an hour, strolling down to a shop on the drag and using the stolen credit card to buy a dog collar.

"OK!" he yells when he picks up the phone. "Letters allowed between you and Fakhr el-Din, but there is absolutely, positively, no dating allowed!"

"Fine," you say, "I'm in the motel on San Jacinto." In less than one year, you will regret not having negotiated more on the dating bit.

When they arrive, you are waiting on the street corner, sleepy and hungry. Your mother gets out of the car to hug you, and you see her face is pale like your Sitto's white cheese. You hug her hard and cry; you wish you hadn't hurt her. She thought she'd lost you, she says, and you tell her you're tough. She laughs and tells you to get in the car, and sits in the back with you.

That night, you hold her hand and look out of the window and at the city's lights fading away, and see for the first time how you were braver than your mother. As though she'd read your mind, she slips out a "*yikhrib baytik*," and then whispers in your ear, "I've kept all the letters for you anyway. You never asked for them!" So you'd never seen that she was an ally. It was really your fault.

Your Baba puts in a tape of Abdel Halim singing *sawah* but in the middle of it, Marky Mark and the Funky Bunch comes on, and your father says he heard it on the radio and had to tape it because he thought it gave him a good feeling. The night folds over, your head settling on your mama's shoulder, as you fall asleep and dream of a new life, an existential restart button, and a slice of pepperoni-less pizza.

29

The Long Road Home

SHERENE SEIKALY

Sherene Seikaly reflects on the search for home as a Palestinian American. Her piece ponders how identity is related to the practice of history making. As she travels across borders and through archives, she questions the possibility of belonging and the importance of the search, rather than the destination of a sense of home.

Beirut Remembered

At the lavish campus of the University of California in San Diego, on the shores of the city of La Jolla, my friend Krista told me about her creative writing class. Krista said her introduction to creative writing was to narrate her first memory. She explained—her mother showed her and her sister the patterns the sun made when you held a kiwi up to it.

A couple of years later in 1994 in my maternal family home in Beirut, working in Palestinian refugee camps and trying to come to terms with a childhood interrupted by immigration to the United States, Krista's story would resurface. The realities of the camps and the abandoned refugees who had given their lives and their children to the cause became more difficult to understand. I tried to recall my first memory.

Beirut was a treasured place in my memory; our entire extended family had settled in one place. It was perhaps the only time I felt belonging. My mother feels bad that my first memories are of war. But I am grateful. Being stuck in our building after it was hit by a bomb, seeing a man shattered to pieces fall off the balcony just above me, watching cars explode, and worrying constantly about my parents' lives were more than just formative. They instilled in me a knowledge of survival.

Sitting and writing in my latest stop, Haifa, I have come to understand that Beirut was (and in many senses continues to be) one part of Palestine for me. My aunt Lamia, who embraced me and welcomed my return, had taken me along as a child to the many visits she made to families in refugee camps. My youngest aunt,

Randa, was also active; she was the focus of most of the family's worries when fighting broke out. Together my aunts shaped my ideal of what a young woman committed to the liberation of her people should be.

These ideals were strongly called into question upon experiencing firsthand how political parties and community-based organizations competed with one another at the expense of the people they were ostensibly serving. As the long civil war in Lebanon had come to a close in the midnineties, community organizations—both in and outside the refugee camps—were shifting from service provision to what was being broadly defined as "development work." Many of the people working in nonprofit community-based organizations were certainly committed to effecting social and political change.

However, their institutions were increasingly becoming donor driven—privileging agendas ill-suited to community priorities and often compromising local needs. Although quickly adjusting to these realities in my work with local and later regional nonprofits, the realization that I was embarking on a career and not on a course for political change—however small—was a harsh one.

You were hard-pressed to enter any house in Sabra and Shatila without gaining new insight on human resilience and the various ways people struggle against injustice. I came to revile one staple part of my job—taking foreign delegations to visit the camps. Researchers and human rights workers often had good intentions and were sometimes able to give back to the people they interviewed. All too often, though, it was a perverse situation where the Palestinian refugees were an object of study and interrogation. This process became more unbearable as the "Gaza-Jericho First" phase of the Oslo negotiations rendered a narrative of defeat unavoidable. The Palestinians of the refugee camps were to be forgotten. The desire to dig one's hands in the ground and be part of something larger seemed increasingly naive. The liberation movement had given way to fierce competition over rapidly shrinking resources. The revolution that I imagined myself fighting in, like my aunts, was shattered to pieces. The collectivity Beirut had previously signified was emptied; my entire family would never again be in one place.

I found myself writing. Memory was both a burden and a gift. It was the memory of my grandmothers' homes, the grocery store at the corner of Umm Simone's house, and the school yard that had first drawn me back to Beirut. These places had been so large in my mind—they got larger as they grew to signify another life. I looked through the various images, locations, and scenes and found my first memory.

Sometime in the early seventies my father had taken my mother and I to the border of Jordan and Palestine. My parents were the world to me, a world made much more fragile by the ever-present danger of war. They parked near a look-out. There we had a clear view of a long, winding road surrounded by high walls shielding a city in the distance. I asked where we were and why. They were both sad and wistful, as if there was meaning to this place that I could not grasp. My father pointed to the city in the distance: "At the end of this road is Palestine. This is where you are from and where you should be, but you cannot go."

Haifa

I searched for a view of Haifa. The views I found were incessantly marred by bars. I could not find a house without bars, sometimes white, sometimes black. If I could find a house without bars, the view might look prettier. The sea, after all, is beautiful and crisp, its blueness breathtaking, the sun shimmering and the waves softly pouring onto the shore exhilarating. The monumental beauty brings a wave of relief that temporarily washes over me until the pain of memory returns.

Ultimately, I found a view, a spacious barless apartment owned by a young Russian couple. The building is not far from where one of our family homes still stands. When my family lived here, the street was called Shari' al Jabal (Street of the Mountain). In 1948 it was renamed United Nations Street. When the United Nations declared that Zionism parallels racism, the street was renamed Zionism Avenue. All nations are built on lies, massacres, and crimes. There is no denying that fact, but this place seemed more immediate.

I sit perched on my desk in a room converted from a balcony. I wonder what this view will offer me, what it will allow me to see. Cypress trees stand on one side, a reminder of the forestation programs all over the country. They nestle the Baha'i temple with its gardens dangling over what had been Karmel Street. Beyond the cypress trees and the Baha'i temple is the sea and the road to Jaffa. On the other side of the apartment is a full view of the city of Haifa and its coast all the way to 'Acca. Every morning over coffee I imagine my great-grandfather traveling from his clinic in 'Acca to visit his family in Haifa.

The other Palestinian American studying in Haifa had a different view. I envied her ability to adapt, to keep moving, when I was overcome so easily. One day I brought the subject up again—but isn't this place strange for you also? No, she explained, I don't live it as an occupation.

In a piercingly cold winter in Brooklyn, I spoke to my comrade Samar about the impossibility of Haifa. Even though born in Beirut, I had grown up believing myself to be from Haifa. When asked "Where are you from?" my reply was always "Haifa." That changed in 1997 when I came to Haifa for the first time and realized that I was not from this strange place. I began saying I am "originally" from Haifa.

And I believe in the right of my family and the hundreds of thousands of other Palestinian refugees to return. But I could never return to Haifa. My comrade challenged me, "Well, why not? You could actually return. You have an American passport. You can return. At least temporarily."

Samar had grown up in Haifa, originally from a village in the North, which is now an Israeli national park. Like more than five hundred other Palestinian villages, it was destroyed. Instead of being buried under trees, it lies as a site for visiting tourists to ponder a constructed national past. It was difficult to indulge my ideas with her about what was actually her city, about where she was from, even though both sides of my family had lived in historic Palestine for hundreds of years until 1948. But she had, from the beginning of our friendship, more than simply acknowledged my relationship to this place. She also understood it as being another way to think about Palestine. She challenged me with the possibility of return—the possibility of knowing Haifa.

On my first visit to Haifa in 1997, I kept insisting that my Nazarene friend Mona show me the stairs. She was perplexed. What stairs? Haifa is all staircases. My parents had said that they used to play on staircases; they remembered a staircase next to their aunt's house where they had played together. It led to the sea. We found some stairs, and I photographed the place, wondering if my parents had played there sixty years ago. Did Ramzi and Samia play here as children, running and laughing under the Haifa sun? Sixty years is not a long time. In the spread of history, how long is it really? Barely a moment. It turned out to be the right staircases, my uncle later told me. He pointed to the photograph, "Here, our aunt's house was this one."

Later, in 2001, I wrote down precise directions for all the different homes in Haifa, hoping to find them and photograph them for my aging grandmothers. My family's history was jotted down on a small white piece of paper, a map that Samar, my Haifite comrade, and I held close. People reacted in turn. One man said that the places on my paper did not exist and that the person who had told me where to go did not know what he was talking about. Fighting the urge to scream, I held my feet firmly to the ground. Was he rejecting my claims? Or was the weight of memory too heavy?

Samar was steadfast in our effort to find where my family had lived, but there was a bit of regret haunting her sentences. "I just don't know what this place is now. It is not called that anymore," but then, "We will find it, we will find it." After visiting the municipality and looking for the train station and searching different places, we retreated. On our way home we went to visit a lawyer whom Samar knew. His reaction to my story was one of delight. Many

Palestinians inside the green line reacted this way to me. Conversely, others justifiably saw that my "return"—as ephemeral as it was—was possible only because of my privileged position as an American citizen, from a middle-class urban Palestinian family. Within minutes, the lawyer had found exact directions to the houses from an older relative over the phone. He drove us around and pointed—it might be this one, or maybe that one. I photographed, numb and exhausted. Relief and sadness marked the death of something, and the birth of a new relationship to this place.

The next day, I took the city by myself. The night before, there had been a bomb scare in Haifa. It turned out to be nothing more than assumptions about an "Israeli Arab" going to a nightclub with a bag. The following morning, the streets and the beaches were empty. The inherited memories of my family accompanied me up and down the city's hilly terrain, through the Hadar, down to Wadi an-Nisnas, over to Wadi as-Salib, back down to the sea. I walked all day and took photographs of what my eye could only see as violent juxtapositions, the reflection of Palestinian homes in relentlessly tall and overbearing glass buildings.

Later, Samar said that what was most interesting to her about the search was how I had just wanted to walk around Haifa. By talking to her, I realized that the searching was much more important than the finding.

Ultimately, I found a view. I can now see the houses. They are part of my daily life. In the beginning, each memory, place, and story would inspire emotion and a desire to document. I would think, that's one house; that's another. As time passed, I preferred not knowing which houses were which. I preferred to see them as sites of what Edward Said called "a remembered presence."[1]

Being immersed in the reality of what Haifa is today offered me a lesson about the gaps between inherited memory and the lived. I still look at and tell people about my family's house down the street, now owned by the Histadrut, the Israeli Labor Federation. The initial shock has dimmed. The study of Palestinian history became the next space to search. I learned to preserve my energy for coping with those spaces of the Israeli state that any researcher must face daily.

The Archive

The archive is, in the conventional wisdom of social and hard sciences, a neutral space, the culmination of objectivity. In theory, it is a site that any interested party can access and compile whatever version of truth they seek. In any context, the archive is essential to producing a nation-state. Like the museum, it constitutes a record of any given nation's brutality. The very compilation of archives is an expression of state power. Scholars must thus attend to both the documents they find as well as how these documents are compiled and categorized. All the while, scholars must remain persistently aware and critical of the narrative in which the archive, in its inclusions and absences, is immersed.

As the very possibility of a Palestinian nation becomes increasingly tenuous, the absence of a Palestinian national archive should come as no surprise. Historians and scholars of Palestine must gather, explore, and dig for dispersed shards scattered between historic Palestine and the various localities of the Palestinian diaspora. The process requires creativity and a rigorous, critical eye. Historians of Palestine are in the position of both constructing history at the same time that they must be critical of that very process. The difficulties are further compounded when the aim is to access subaltern histories situated outside the official canon that is defined by restricted notions of the "political." Chipping away at scores of documents, newspapers, letters, and contracts in the context of Israeli institutions was intellectually challenging. My archival research began at a coexistence center named Giv'at Haviva, which was based on a kibbutz in the North and holds one of the most complete archives of Arabic-language newspapers in the country. The center had been a bastion of the Zionist Left, a vibrant place that hosted the various seminars and workshops on how the "two people of Israel," that salient and problematic ethnic-religious categorization of "Jews and Arabs," can live together in peace. This discourse, needless to say, is emptied of politics as well as any discussion of historical claims, equality, or justice. The site of Giv'at Haviva, I learned, was a British military base in the mandatory period. The British had confiscated the land of a Palestinian family, the descendant of whom is a professor who works on that site today. The knowledge of the historically loaded significance of this place was no more or less to bear than the many other places or histories in Israel/Palestine.

Yet this place was also loaded on the everyday level. During the October 2000 uprisings of the Palestinians in Israel in solidarity with their brethren in the West Bank and Gaza, the battalion that had killed thirteen Palestinian citizens boarded in Giv'at Haviva. In addition, since Giv'at Haviva was rapidly falling into financial ruin—coexistence work is apparently not what it used to be—the administration was exploring new venues. They found their solution with the Israeli army and hired the center out to soldiers in the last stretch of their service studying for matriculation exams. Most of the days I was researching there, about 230 soldiers were living on the site, fully outfitted and armed. As I searched through newspapers, inspired and intrigued by the daily events of Palestinian life, I would look up to see soldiers saunter in with their M16s to check their e-mail or read a book.

On some days, as I conducted this time travel, I could hear the Israeli army shooting in the West Bank, only a few miles to the east. The realities of Palestinians living under occupation was a world apart from Giv'at Haviva, but geographically the two places were but a short distance from one another, a powerful reminder of both the smallness of this place and the impossibility of ever living it as one contiguous territory.

The Central Zionist Archive, the National Library at the Hebrew University, and the Israel State Archives (ISA) are main stops on any archival search for Palestine. On entering the CZA in Jerusalem, I was interested to see an exhibit of posters from the mandate period. The posters were all designed in that unmistakable forties style of angular graphics and bright colors, reminiscent of that aesthetically intriguing "Rosie the Riveter" paraphernalia. It was an experience of simultaneous attraction and repulsion: close up I realized that the posters were all articulations of Zionist iconography. The archivist asked me several questions about my project, declared it unviable, and proceeded to inform me of the CZA's collection. "We have eighty million documents, four of which are digitalized." I was overwhelmed by the institutional capacity and power of the state. The place represented all that I did not have as a Palestinian, particularly in comparison to the colonial power that made that lack a reality.

The National Library at the Hebrew University was a more subdued experience. While the images and icons of the Israeli state were everywhere to be seen, the reading room was quiet and bare, and whatever book or newspaper I wanted to peruse was there to be found. Palestinian collections and documents were scattered throughout the collection. In her work on the history of the Palestinian women's movement, Ellen Fleischmann describes the journey of Hala and Dumya Sakakini, the daughters of cultural and literary figure Khalil Sakakani, to the National Library at the Hebrew University: "When Hala and Dumya Sakakini visited the Hebrew University Library after 1967, they saw their father's extensive collection of books, which had been confiscated after their family's flight to Egypt during the fighting in Jerusalem in 1948. They even recognized his handwriting on the margins of the pages but were not allowed to recover the books."[2]

One is left struggling with the desire to find these collections and to reclaim them. The Israel State Archives has turned out to be the space I spend most of my time in. It is a run-down building that is comfortably third world, the way the old Ben-Gurion Airport used to be before its renovation. The guards at the entry to the building are Mizrahim, one is Tunisian, and the other is an Iraqi Kurd. On cigarette breaks we speak in Arabic about the weather, politics, and God. Upstairs before entering the archive everyone is subject to a search and to leaving an identity card or passport. Being born in Lebanon has raised more than a few eyebrows, and once I was asked to wait while the clerk checked with his superiors. I asked him, "So being born in Beirut makes me a security threat?" He shifted his weight and looked uncomfortable. Invariably, these guards ask me who I am, why I am here, and what I am looking for. Occasionally, the hostility is difficult to miss, but usually people are just curious. Inside the archive, the staff is friendly and helpful, now well acquainted with me. On first entering the ISA, I surreptitiously photographed the foyer. On one side is an entire wall of medium-size photographs of the founding mothers and fathers of the Israeli state. On another are two laminated enlargements of the declaration of the Jewish state: "Long Live Our State" reads the headline. On lunch breaks, I took to sitting with my back to the exhibit. I knew it was there, but I preferred to save my energy for the remaining hours of the search.

Beirut

Home lives in my aging grandmothers—Umm Khalil and Umm Simone. I have spent hours at their feet listening to their memories of Palestine. Their courage and their lives are sources of history. In 1982 when the Israeli invasion of Beirut forced the evacuation of their building, my aunt Lamia urged Umm Khalil to at least retreat to the shelter. My grandmother refused. Usually a cautious woman, she decided she would not be expelled again. She preferred to die in her home. A few years ago I sat Umm Khalil down for three hours, and under the heat of a video camera cruelly drilled her for proof that we existed. She was exhausted by the end, and a bit sorrowful. At every point she repeated exasperatedly, "Look, we lived normal lives. Our families had lived there for several hundred years. We had houses, belongings. We sent our children to school. We went to market. We prayed. We buried our dead, and then we were displaced. It is really that simple."

As for my other grandmother, Umm Simone, who housed, fed, and cared for me in her aging wisdom during my four-year sojourn to Beirut, her stories were always a bit more verbose. A strong, large-framed woman, she used to boast of nursing her five children and having enough milk left to send to the neighbors. Her father, Na'im, was the first doctor in 'Acca, they had a good life, they were proud people, and they lost everything. As she made her jams that tasted like there really must be a God, she told me about her ring, the sheets, and my father's red bicycle that they took with them on their train ride across the Suez that morning in 1948. It was a Friday, and they hoped to return that Sunday.

As I was leaving Beirut that last evening in 1998, in the old house with the deep-green shutters that looked like they were shipped from a toy factory, I asked my grandmother to imagine the afterlife. She said, it is a grove, full of fruit, lemons, oranges, and, you know, a garden, a grove. She stopped and looked at me. "Palestine."

Crossing Borders

My grandmothers often told me about their trips from Haifa to Beirut. They would drive to Beirut for dinner and later return to Haifa. The distance is about three hours. One day as I looked through the newspaper *Filastin*, I found an item about the train from Haifa to Beirut. It reminded me of the train tracks that people say are still there in the North of Palestine and the road that was called *khatt al trayn* (the train line) in Beirut. On my weekly travels from Haifa to Jerusalem, I often thought if I drove the same distance in the opposite direction I could be visiting my ninety-four-year-old grandmother. In coming to Palestine I hoped to be closer to her and the rest of my family and friends in Beirut. But in reality, I was farther from them than when I was in New York. Although Beirut is only a stone's throw away from where I sit, getting there from here can take up to two days. It is only possible, of course, because of my U.S. passport, but even with that privilege there are a number of hazards one takes at each border crossing. The impossibility of traveling from Haifa to Beirut is a reminder of a large set of preposterous impossibilities, like the fact that coming here to get closer to my grandmothers has made me physically farther from them, or that on a clear day in Ramallah a West Bank resident can see Jaffa but can never visit.

Today, I travel the very long road from one home to another. Every three months I have to leave this place. Each time I leave specific instructions about my belongings with friends in case I am denied entry. I never take my computer, my camera, or my documents. If I take books, they are always in English. Despite my critical capacities and my knowledge of how authority works, I am always anxious, nervous, and afraid.

On both sides of the border, I am thoroughly searched and interrogated. The similarities in state intrusions on my life and on my body can be mind-numbing. Inevitably, on both sides of the border, my identity is in question. At the Los Angeles International Airport one September, an armed officer asked, "Where are you from?" I hesitated, "California." "No," he insisted. "Where are you really from?" On my return to Palestine, my Argentinean Israeli interrogator turned to me: "I see you are from Beirut. It is a beautiful city." I replied, "You were there in 1982?" He responded in the affirmative and added, "It is a shame what the Lebanese did to that place."

Belonging as Transience

As Rosemary Sayigh has so aptly put it, the Palestinian people are experiencing a continuous *nakba*.[3] The tools of the occupation are daily refined. Its most recent iteration is the onset of one of the largest and most expensive "separation" devices now being honed by the Israeli military apparatus. The very idea of Palestine, much less its actual landmass, is shrinking under the weight of now more than sixty years of oppression. Geography itself is assaulted, as more lives and olive trees are uprooted, displaced, and destroyed and more *dunams* of land are seized. The fragmentation of Palestine relies on a continuous process of removal and distancing, distancing people from land and history, and, perhaps most painfully, distancing people from one another.

The long road home is one I will always travel. The search for belonging is based on its very impossibility. It is the search for the sense of home that is more important and more powerful than the destination. As a daughter of refugee Palestinians, born in Beirut, and immigrating to Los Angeles, I remain on the outside of the places I travel to. Being in the margins is a position of power and privilege. It is also a position of loss of collectivity, language, family, home.

The Palestinian American experience can destabilize the hard-and-fast distinction between privilege and loss. In what is often distinguished as a "postnational" period, it is also an experience that raises difficult questions about history making and its relationship to national narratives. The historian's task is to critique the brutality of limiting identity to territory, just as she must recognize people's intimate bonds to their land, particularly as Palestinians continue their troubled but ongoing, now century-long, struggle for self-determination.

One late afternoon as I stood in Abu Dis, the suburb of Jerusalem that is being butchered and ensconced by the "separation" wall, I met an old woman, Umm Hassan. She told me that the wall, part of which was already standing in front of us, was going to eat up most of her land, which she and her family had farmed for generations. She was not going to be able to walk to Jerusalem to pray. One of her children's homes would be on the other side of the wall, and her grandchildren were going to be separated from their school. I listened, helpless and angry. "Where are you from?" she asked. I explained. My family was expelled in 1948 from Haifa. They were children. They wound up in Lebanon. I was born there. We immigrated because of the war. I grew up in the States. And now I am here doing my research. She looked at me: "All that, my dear, and you are still Palestinian?"

30

The Legacy of Exile

An Excerpt

EMANNE BAYOUMI

This story exposes the multiple layers of U.S. imperialism in the Arab world as they play out in the life of a young queer Arab woman. This piece was inspired by the strength, courage, and resilience of Arab women living with the haunting legacy of exile.

The Cast

Yara: Eleven-year-old daughter of Yasmine

Yasmine: Yara's mother. She has been living in San Francisco for the past six years. She is a janitor downtown. She has overstayed her visa, was stopped last year on the highway for speeding, and is now on parole awaiting her hearing with the Immigration and Naturalization Service.

Yasmine's mother/Yara's grandmother

Wahid

I sometimes think I see God when I look in the mirror. That sounds weird, huh? If my grandma heard me saying that, I'd probably get whooped. Mamma says she's really really strict about God and praying and things like that. Mamma always says religious stuff to her when they talk on the phone. I don't even remember what she looks like anymore. I think she must be a little ugly 'cause her voice is really mean. But actually, Mamma is pretty, so Grandma can't be that ugly, right?

Mamma says I always look sad. And then *she* gets sad. I don't like it when Mamma gets sad 'cause she locks herself up in the bathroom and I can hear her crying like she did when we first got here, through the peeling door because

This piece is inspired by and dedicated to the Iraqi families in San Francisco's Bayview district with whom I worked after September 11th.

there's no windows in the bathroom so the humidity from the shower makes it peel all the time. I can always hear Mamma hitting her head against the wall like that wooden thing she pounds the garlic in, and at first I got kind of scared, but now it happens all the time and she doesn't do it really hard, so I sorta got used to it. Like the loud ugly man's voice upstairs when he's really angry at something which is—oh my god—ALL the time. But I get a little uncomfortable 'cause I'm not sure what I should do, and I think she thinks I can't hear it but I can. I'm not that dumb.

Itnayn

"You make us miss you, Yasmine. Why don't you come visit us anymore? We all wish to see your daughter, Yara. She must be so big now, *mash'allah*."

"Mama, you know that I would if I could—it's complicated. I've told you over and ov—"

"I'm getting old, my daughter. I can't walk to the market anymore. Your poor sister has to take me everywhere in the Peugeot. Everything is so expensive here now, you won't believe it. A kilo of potatoes is three guineas now—can you imagine? And the cost of a loaf of bread is different every day. Your brother, Khaled, doesn't ask about me anymore. I always knew that boy was going to be difficult. From the minute he came out wrong at his birth I knew it . . ."

"Mama, why don't you come visit me here? I can work extra hours at the company—you know how they always need an extra engineer in San Jose and—"

"Yeeeee, no, no, my daughter! That's impossible. No, I like my feet firmly planted on the earth. I will go when God wishes to take me. I will be buried here in the place I was born, *insha'allah*. What if I die in Amreeka? Yeeeeeeeeee!"

Talata

The clicking of Yasmine's heels against the cement always brings with it the waves of loss more profoundly. The mundane can be dangerous that way. It is days like this Yasmine misses her mother most. She crosses the street to catch the 9:00 bus. As always, it is late. She finds a seat near the middle and rests her head against the cool pane of the window. Her makeup leaves a smudged mark where she rests her face, and somehow this fills her with satisfaction—proof that she has really been there. It is sometimes difficult to have a sense of presence when people pretend they do not see you. Nobody has ever smiled at her on this bus, and Yasmine thinks that she must remind them of the hysterical Iraqi women on CNN, as if she is about to start screaming "Allahu akbar!" suddenly and pull out a Kalashnikov. Usually she looks out the window, following the golden hilltops with her gaze. She always thinks of that Joni Mitchell song as she watches the hills pass across the horizon.

Her uncle Gamal had first introduced her to Joni Mitchell years ago. They were sitting together on the steps of the apartment a few meters away from the shore of the Mediterranean, enjoying the jasmine entangled through the metal gate of the garden, smoking cigarettes and swatting at flies. They were alike in so many ways, but it was not something they talked about. Yasmine had always known that Gamal was gay, but there was not a language to talk about those things with family. The silence between them was more fluent than any language when it came to those matters. He never said a word about her either, but it was as if their secret instinct about one another strengthened their friendship. It was a silent pact with one another, and words would only complicate things. Spending time with him, although rare, was always good. Her guard would come down a little, and they would talk for hours about their favorite music, his painting career, her hopes and dreams. He was the one who had first encouraged her to leave for America. If only she could sit with him now by the shore of the Mediterranean. She wanted to tell him that America was not the sanctuary they had thought it would be. That here, in this country, there was nothing left unspoken. That queers had created a language for themselves, but it was being used against her. That last night she had found a letter on her doorstep: *ayrab dyke go back to the desert where you came from you whore. P.S. This note is written in pig's blood.*

A wash of loneliness hits hard between her breasts, and she holds her breath as it passes. She hopes that her daughter, Yara, can somehow leave this cruel solitude behind, that it is not a legacy of exile.

Arba'aa

Her lightly calloused hands caress my belly, border crossings along the boundaries of my breasts. When we lay together as we lay now, facing each other, tracing the edges of our desires with dark fingers, the solace is within reach. Her kisses are like the visa that I need to escape the grind of this country that traps me here like an animal. My tears trickle down the hollow of my neck, and the sadness soon grows indistinguishable from the desire that races as she licks the salt droplets from my neck. Her arms soften the anger that we hoard like mementos from back home; her kisses erase for a short time the powerlessness, the fear, and the flashes of dead bodies from Al Jazeera that swim in my head, that follow me like daily companions, keeping me awake at night. Palestinian mothers, fathers, Iraqi babies, the young men, the little girls—all who have lost the privilege to choose whether to live or die. Sex blurs the boundaries of sadness, quenching for a moment the thirsty grief of bringing up a young child alone in this unforgiving place. Her tongue is relentless. She calls my name, Yasmine. Nothing has ever sounded sweeter, and I live. For a few fleeting moments, curled against each other, I rest in the solace of the way things were before I left, the vastness and the brine of the Mediterranean, of what was left behind. The sound of our hearts beating sometimes in time, sometimes not, tunes out the sound of the bombs. As we lay, the borders come down, and we are free. For a moment, the war stops. For a time, I safely return home.

Nassim alayna'l hawa
Bil mafra'a il wadi
Ya hawa, ya lil hawa
Khudni ala'a bladi[1]

Khamsa

"Mamma, when are we going to do anything fun?" Yara looks through her mother's dresses and pulls out her favorite—a red cotton gauze gypsy dress that is hidden in the very back of the closet. "My counselor at school says that I need to do more fun things because she thinks something is wrong with my head."

"What are you talking about, baby? What do you mean she thinks something is wrong with your head?"

"Well, she said that my teacher gave her some of my writing to look at, and I overheard them talking in the hallway and they said my writing borders on the macabre. I looked that word up in the dictionary, and it means that I like to write about death and bad things like that. She thinks I need help."

"Yara habibti, who is this counselor? She has no right to say things like that to you. What's her name? First thing tomorrow I'm going straight to her office—how dare she say things like this to you!"

"Mamma, don't get mad. I knew you'd get mad. It's not that bad. I'll bring you my stories." Yara rushes to her backpack and pulls out a pink Hello Kitty folder. "Here, this one is my favorite. It's a choose-your-own-adventure story that I wrote all by myself! It's about this girl who is the last girl on the face of the planet, and she has to save the world from destruction."

"Baby, go to bed. I'm going to school with you tomorrow morning."

"Don't you have work, Mamma?"

"Yes, baby, but it's okay. This is more important."

"Okay, we'll ride the bus together, yeah! Goodnight, Mamma."

"Goodnight, baby."

That night, Yasmine cries herself to sleep over her daughter's stories. The bed shakes gently as she whimpers, the pillow soaking up the grief.

Sitta

Those stupid kids at school—they don't know anything. Mamma doesn't know that I can swear in English. Don't tell her, okay? She wouldn't be very happy with me. My mamma is almost never happy with me 'cause I cause a lot of trouble around the house. Yesterday she got really mad at me 'cause I wouldn't talk to her in Arabic. It's not like I don't like my language. I love my language so much. I like the way it bounces in my head so soft like sugar or my hair after Mamma puts olive oil in it. The stupid kids at school don't think so, but who cares about them? Sometimes I forget the word in English, and it comes out accidentally in Arabic, but I swear sometimes I can't control it. And boy, do I get whooped after school. They call me things like sand nigger—I have no idea what that means, and I even looked it up in the dictionary in my class. And they call me Osama's wife. I really, really hate it when they do that. Osama's fucking ugly—who'd want to marry him anyways? Oh, don't tell my mamma I said the F word. I don't want her to be mad at me. I love my mamma very much. I don't want nothing to happen to her. I usually go home as fast as I can, and I try to hide the scratches on my arm. I really hate those days 'cause I really, really try hard, but I just can't see God in the mirror. But I put on my favorite tape that my mamma said she used to play for me when I was still in her belly, and I feel better:

Summertime and the livin' is easy
Fish are jumpin' and the cotton is fine
Oh, your daddy's rich and your ma is good-lookin'
So hush little baby, don't you cry.[2]

31

Stealth Muslim

EVELYN ALSULTANY

Evelyn Alsultany reflects on her experiences as a "stealth Muslim" who is not visually identifiable at a time of heightened anti-Arab and anti-Muslim racism. She describes the ways in which various Muslims and non-Muslims react upon discovering her Muslim identity, often perpetuating essentialist notions of Islam. She remarks on the contradictions in government officials, media pundits, and citizens declaring a "color-blind" era.

Stealth Racial, Ethnic, and Religious Identities

> *Stealth:* the attribute or characteristic of acting in secrecy, or in such a way that the actions are unnoticed or difficult to detect by others.

In her course Introduction to Latino/a Studies, my colleague Maria Cotera asks "stealth Latinos/as" to stand and identify themselves. Students who appear to be "white," "black," "South Asian," "Arab," "Latino," "Filipino," "Native American," and "racially ambiguous" stand up. Cotera makes the point that many Latinos move through the world unidentifiable as Latino/a since Latino/a appearance is diverse and does not necessarily conform to a particular "look" or "racial type." Latinos are not the only group of people whose appearance does not conform to a "racial type."

I had invited some Arab American artists as special guests to class. After their presentation, students were excited to meet them and discuss their work, and the Arab American students who were visually identifiable as such easily participated in coethnic camaraderie with these artists. Later, a stealth Arab American student came to my office, distressed. She felt excluded by the coethnic camaraderie, as the artists ignored her efforts to connect with them. A stealth Latina student

I would like to thank Nadine Naber, Rabab Abdulhadi, Mona El-Ghobashy, Randa Jarrar, and Dahlia Petrus for their generous feedback on earlier versions of this piece.

307

told me that while in high school, a group of Latinas questioned her for speaking Spanish: "How come you speak Spanish?" When she explained that she is Latina and speaks Spanish at home, they responded: "But you're white." Both of these students' appearances betrayed them in an ideological social system that assumes that one's racial or ethnic identity is visible and easily facilitates categorization and belonging.

How does the notion that everyone can be racially or ethnically visually identified operate in the case of religion, particularly religions that have come to be racialized in the United States, such as Islam? The ways in which religion is structured in the United States are wrought with contradictions. On the one hand, religion is figured as private—the presumed separation of "church and state" and the practice of religion in the private sphere. This idea is not unique to the United States, as controversies over Muslim women wearing the *hijab* in public institutions in France and Turkey have revealed how some societies consider visible markers of Islam inappropriate in the public sphere. On the other hand, religion—Judeo-Christianity in particular—is a public affair when citizens must swear on the Bible before testifying at court hearings and presidents are sworn into office on the Bible. When priests and rabbis visualize their religion, there is a general sentiment in the United States that it is socially acceptable because their "uniform" signals not only their religious affiliation but also their status as religious leaders. The same acceptance does not apply to Hassidic Jews, Hare Krishna, Sikhs, and Muslim women who wear the *hijab* when they are practicing their right to freedom of religion. Although it is commonly understood that not all Jewish men wear yarmulkes, not all Christians wear crosses, not all Muslim women wear a *hijab*, there are historical moments in which religion becomes racialized and, in this process, presumably visualized. Different standards of "tolerance" operate for different religious groups and forms of religious expression and shift depending on the historical moment.

Consider these three cases. First, during World War II, *Time* magazine included an article on how to tell the difference between Chinese and Japanese people to make clear that the enemy was Japanese, not Chinese, people.[1] Second, in Nazi Germany, it was presumed that Jews were visually distinct by their large noses. Third, the slew of hate crimes after 9/11 revealed that Islam is visually associated with non-Muslim Sikh turbans and Muslim head scarves. The first case is an example of visualizing race, the second is an example of visualizing religion, and the third is a case of conflating Arabs and Muslims and mistakenly visualizing both onto Sikhs. The process of racializing presumes visual identification that often proves to be arbitrary and inaccurate.

To what extent is Islam believed to be detectable post-9/11? After 9/11, it was widely assumed that Muslims could be identified and "racially profiled." But religion, including Islam, is not always visually identifiable through a head scarf, religious clothing, or being Arab- or South Asian–"looking." What have become the other identifiable markers of Islam? Arabic names became one way to identify a potential terrorist. Watch lists were created based on Arabic-sounding names, and extra searches at airports were conducted based on these names. At airports, Arabs and Muslims were spotted if they read Arabic newspapers or books or if they spoke English with an accent that marked them as a foreigner. Other "evidence" of being a potential Muslim included whether someone had visited or lived in an Arab or Muslim country, attended a Muslim school, or donated to a Muslim charity. Detecting who was potentially a Muslim became synonymous with detecting who was potentially a terrorist.

September 11, 2001, does not mark the beginning of the conflation and racialization of Arabs and Muslims, but it does mark a significant shift.[2] Arab and Muslim racialization not only became more intensified and overt after 9/11 but also importantly came with a public discourse on race and racial profiling that was previously unavailable. In the post-9/11 political climate, some Muslims chose to become stealth to protect themselves. Some Muslim leaders in the United States and United Kingdom encouraged women to remove their *hijabs* to avoid being the targets of hate crimes.[3] Other Muslim women in the United States who formerly did not cover their hair as an expression of their religious faith chose to start wearing the *hijab* as a political act. These women chose to no longer fly under the radar undetectable as Muslim and to visualize their identities. Wearing the *hijab* became an expression of solidarity with other Muslims under siege, as a mark of identity as opposed to an expression of religious piety. Some Muslims changed their names—for example, from Muhammad to Mike or, the reverse, from Mike to Muhammad. Some Muslims stopped reading Arabic in public. Some Muslims took precautions to become stealth, while others refused to become stealth and took measures to make themselves more visible as an act of resistance—to counteract the increased anti-Arab and anti-Muslim racism.

Stealth Muslim

After 9/11, I was scared to leave my apartment. I had never felt so Arab and Muslim in my life—never so aware of how my identity was being perceived: terrorist, fanatic, violent, crazy, backward. For the first time, the fact that I am part Latina seemed irrelevant as I became an Arab Muslim woman scared to leave her apartment, reading e-mail after e-mail and news report after news report announcing another instance of an Arab or Muslim—or someone mistakenly perceived to be Arab or Muslim—attacked, harassed, or even murdered. Signs in my neighborhood read "Hate Free Zone." It made me feel good to know that my neighbors were against hate crimes, but it freaked me out that these signs referred to me and my safety.

I looked at the Quranic calligraphy on my wall. My parents sent it to me days before 9/11, and it arrived with a cracked glass frame. I had set it aside to take to the frame shop. After 9/11, I would look at the frame and postpone taking it for repair, afraid of how the store clerk might react. I waited for months, hoping the intense hatred and potential violence would subside. When I finally took it to the shop, I was relieved that the white woman working there was unfazed by the Islamic calligraphy, telling me to pick it up in two days. I returned two days later, and it proceeded like any normal transaction, except that I was filled with trepidation. I wondered if she was simply being professional and whether she mentioned to someone that she received something Muslim in her shop. Regardless, I was grateful that there were decent people in the world. I was grateful that my fears were not confirmed. She was nothing like the white woman sitting next to me on the plane who told me that had she lost someone on 9/11 and that she would never be able to forgive *me* for being Arab.

I am a stealth Latina. I am also a stealth Arab and a stealth Muslim. My ambiguous appearance often provokes people to inquire into my ethnic background. More than a decade ago, I wrote a short reflective essay about how people tended to react to my mixed race identity—usually highlighting or erasing parts of my identity to facilitate relating or not relating through categorizing.[4] I return to this question at a historical moment in which identity politics have changed, a moment in which I have come to inhabit a criminalized identity—Muslim—in stealth mode. Nothing about my appearance provokes people to ask about my religious background, beliefs, practices, or identifications. I do not wear a *hijab*, and my beliefs are deeply personal and not part of my outward appearance or expression. The revelation that I am Muslim is usually met with a range of reactions.

Essentializing Muslims

My parents' white American friends are perplexed: "How is it possible that your daughter is both a Muslim and a feminist? How could that be?" Islam and feminism are positioned as antithetical by dominant U.S. discourses. Consistent with this logic, one cannot be a Muslim and a feminist because it is assumed that Islam is inherently oppressive to women, and therefore if one accepts Islam, one accepts being subservient to men.[5] Islam takes on a monolithic form, one in which the only possibility for a Muslim woman is oppression. The way, then, to free oneself from oppression is to denounce and renounce Islam.

The best-selling book *Infidel*, by Ayaan Hirsi Ali, is invoked by my parents' friends as a model of how to free oneself by renouncing Islam and embracing atheism and Western values. They want to know if I saw this brave woman's horror story on *60 Minutes*: how this Somali Muslim woman was genitally mutilated at age five, wore the *hijab* as a youth, and was forced into an arranged marriage that she escaped from by seeking asylum and salvation in the Netherlands, where she became a member of Parliament. They want to know how I could continue to identify as a Muslim, given her story of oppression and the death threats she received from Muslims after she publicized her experiences and criticized Islam. Other possible experiences remain beyond imagination. Yet is it a contradiction to be a feminist and a Christian? A feminist and a Jew? To believe in the equality of men and women and also to believe in God? It is as if the body of scholarship on feminist interpretations of the Quran and feminist social movements in Muslim countries never happened.[6]

As a graduate student at Stanford University, a professor marveled at how delighted she was to meet a Muslim woman (me) who does not wear a head scarf and is therefore not oppressed. In this case the head scarf was equated with oppression, and the fact that I do not wear one signified my liberation as a Muslim woman. When I told them, my parents were stunned. They believe that I am part of a highly educated elite circle of professors where everyone is well informed and brilliant. They cannot believe that any of my former professors or current colleagues could be misinformed about Islam and base their knowledge on the corporate media. They think that they are stuck dealing with imperceptive friends because they are not part of academia. They wish they were armed with well-formulated academic arguments to assist them through these interactions.

However, as Edward Said put it, Orientalism is constructed not by "Bavarian Beer drinkers" but by people in positions of authority—government, journalists, scholars, Hollywood films, and the like.[7] In other words, monolithically representing the experiences of 1.2 billion Muslims worldwide is not the result of ignorance or a lack of education. Rather, what gives this "ignorance" power is the fact that meanings about Islam as violent and barbaric are produced through a confluence of forces, through the "knitted-togetherness" of how political events and cultural texts produce meanings for each other.[8] As for my colleagues, whether they are informed about Islam or not, many of them assume that none of us is particularly religious or observant because, as Karl Marx stated, "religion is the opiate of the masses." As intellectuals, we are presumably above societal illusions and therefore "secular." I put the term "secular" in quotation marks because I feel deeply uncomfortable with the way in which "religious" and "secular" operate as binary terms, neither of which I find particularly useful in describing my experiences.

As for me, in this situation with the professor at Stanford, I thought to myself, "Are you kidding me?" and "Here we go again," having to explain: we do not support violence; the *hijab* does not symbolize oppression, it all depends on the context; Islam is not inherently oppressive to women, patriarchal structures are; and yes, "Allah" really is the Arabic word for "God" and really does refer to the same God as in Christianity and Judaism—there are actually many similarities among these three monotheistic faiths. How many times do I have to repeat this mantra?

Yet responding is no easy task when Bin Laden is planning violent attacks and saying that it is in the name of Islam and when Muslims protest the cartoons published in a Danish newspaper that depict the Prophet Muhammad as a terrorist by calling for the beheading of those individuals who disrespect Islam. As my Muslim friend Shahid put it, it is as if some Muslims are saying, "Apologize for saying my religion is violent or I'll kill you." The consequence of these acts of violence and calls for violence are exponential and come to represent the religion of Islam, overshadowing other possible perspectives. Christians who bomb abortion clinics, priests who molest children, and Jews who bulldoze homes in Palestine, killing the family living within it on behalf of the Israeli military, do not become representative of people who believe in Christianity and Judaism. But in the case of Islam, the violent examples come to stand in for the entire religion, and all the Muslim organizations that make statements against the use of violence do not receive a fraction of the media attention as do the calls for violence.

Such instances have been mobilized and used by the U.S. government and corporate media as evidence that "Islam" condones violence. The continual representation of Islam-as-monolithic, unchanging, violent, fanatical, the enemy, and in need of being contained and controlled has not only served to legitimate abuses of U.S. power but also effectively defined the rhetorical parameters around acceptable and unacceptable discourse about Muslims. It becomes nearly impossible to have a nuanced discussion that accounts for Muslims who denounce violence or viewpoints that distinguish between terrorism and resistance to colonialism or occupation—violence deemed legitimate by international law. The blanket labeling of violence perpetrated by Arabs and Muslims as terrorism and violence perpetrated by the United States and Israel as justice limits the extent to which the logics and justifications for all forms of violence can be interrogated. Those individuals who question how certain forms of violence (that is, perpetrated by the United States and Israel) come to be framed as legitimate, necessary, and in the service of peace, regardless of how many civilians are killed, and how other forms of violence (that is, Hezbollah and Hamas) come to be framed as illegitimate, unnecessary, and in the service of conflict, regardless of the conditions under which Palestinians are living, suffering, surviving, and dying, are charged with supporting terrorism. In other words, these rhetorical parameters not only obscure both nonviolent Muslims and nonviolent forms of resistance to occupation by Arabs and Muslims but also obscure the ways in which violence itself is framed by government and media discourses to legitimate the enactment of violence only by particular perpetrators—in this case, the United States and Israel.

Although I find myself trying to explain to some non-Muslims that Islam is not inherently violent, oppressive, static, or unchanging, with some Muslims I find that I am expected to perform my Muslim identity in specific ways. While teaching a class of Muslim students at the University of Michigan–Dearborn, a student was sure to inform me that I am not a "real" Muslim because I do not cover my hair. Those Muslims who are committed to particularly rigid notions of "Muslim tradition" define authenticity through the idea of choosing to wear the *hijab* and policing other Muslims' devoutness. Alternately, some Muslim friends marvel in amazement that I fast during Ramadan. As nonpracticing Muslims, they assume that since I share their politics and live a "secular" lifestyle, I do not observe religious practices and simply identify as "culturally Muslim." Among Muslims, it seems that internal community discourses have produced different "religious types" according to religious beliefs, devoutness, politics, and appearance.

Being a stealth Muslim seems to imply that I am working in secrecy. It also seems to imply that my actions are difficult to detect. I am not intentionally "working in secrecy," but the reactions I receive from Muslims and non-Muslims alike encourage me to embrace a stealth Muslim identity to circumvent such rigid notions of how I am supposed to perform my identity and practice my faith. At the same time, I am able to pass as non-Muslim, and by passing I do not have to directly deal with anti-Muslim sentiment on a daily basis. Passing is a privilege at a time when Islam has been ascribed with negative and threatening meanings.

Stealth Racism

During the 2009 presidential campaigns, Barack Obama was accused of being a stealth Muslim. Some bloggers suggested that he was a closet Muslim, secret Muslim, and sleeper agent, and a poll revealed that one-third of voters believed that Obama is a Muslim.[9] The Republican Party attempted to discredit Obama during the presidential campaign by accusing him of being Muslim. Obama's middle name, "Hussein"; that he spent some of his childhood in Indonesia, allegedly attending a Muslim school; and that his father was Muslim were used as proof that "once a Muslim, always a Muslim." E-mails circulated accusing Obama of not wearing the flag pin and refusing to stand for the national anthem. Other e-mails stated that he took his oath for political office on the Quran, would side with Muslims over Americans, and is anti-Israel.[10] Obama had to "go stealth" with whatever associations he had with Islam or risk his chance at the U.S. presidency. Obama asserted his commitment to Christianity and assured the American public that he is not nor has he ever been a Muslim.[11] He distanced himself from his father's Islam, his Muslim relatives in Kenya, and his childhood in Indonesia, and did not visit mosques despite invitations, revealing that as long as he was not Muslim, he was acceptable as an American presidential candidate.[12] Eight years after 9/11, "American" and "Muslim" remain signified as irreconcilable and opposed identities. The irony is that after the various accusations of being a Muslim and therefore un-American failed, the "radical" religion used to criminalize Obama was Christianity—the black Christianity of Jeremiah Wright, leading to Obama's resignation from that church. Writing for the *New York Times*, Nicholas D. Kristof observed that religious prejudice had become a proxy for racial prejudice.[13]

Government officials, media pundits, and U.S. citizens have declared that by electing the first African American U.S. president we have entered a postracial era of color blindness where race no longer matters. However, the fact that color blindness is being declared while Muslims go stealth reveals a contradiction in the assertion of color blindness. It seems to me that this notion of color blindness is racism in stealth mode. Declaring a postracial era enables the ability to enact racist policies and practices while denying them at the same time. In other words, declaring color blindness is racism acting in secrecy and in ways that are unnoticed or difficult to detect by others. It allows for denial and "blindness" to its persistence and different forms, only enabling it further.

32

Where Is Home?

Fragmented Lives, Borders Crossings, and the Politics of Exile

Rabab Abdulhadi

The meaning of home and homeland—two concepts that seem to be self-evident or readily understood for most people—is fraught with complex emotions and contradictory memories for exilic and diasporic communities. In this essay, Abdulhadi reflects on her awareness that Arabs and Muslims were seen as dangerous and as suspect in the United States exactly as Palestinians have been by Israel and its military, police, and intelligence services. Writing an eclectic mix of diary notes, commentary, and spoken word, the only way she felt she could express the anger and pain she experienced after September 11, 2001, Abdulhadi draws on her recollections from three sites: her journeys to Palestine to visit family and conduct dissertation field research in 1998, her trips to Lebanon to interview Palestinian survivors of the 1982 Sabra and Shatila massacre, and her experiences in New York during the month of September 2001 after her return from Egypt. Her object is to problematize the concepts used to reflect on where, to whom, and to what we belong, such as visit, return, journey, home, and homeland.

For the politically exiled, "going home" means more than taking a journey to the place where one was born. The ability to go, the decision to embark on such a trip, and the experience of crossing borders to one's "native" land involve an examination of the makeup of the individual and the collective self, a definition and a redefinition of the meaning and the location of *home*, and a reexamination of one's current and former political commitments. In the Palestinian case, *going home* assumes further complications, especially in view of the Israeli Law of Return that bestows automatic citizenship on Jews arriving in Israel while

An earlier version of this essay was published in *Radical History Review* 68 (2003): 89–101. Copyright 2003, MARHO: Radical Historians Collective. Reprinted by permission of the publisher, Duke University Press.

denying the indigenous Palestinian population the right to return to Palestine and to the homes from which they have been uprooted since 1948. For the Palestinian exiled, then, *going home* brings back memories of one's worst nightmares at international borders: interrogation and harassment, suspicion of malintent, and rejection of one's chosen self-identification. *Going home* ceases to be just about traveling to where one was born; instead, going home is transformed into a politically charged project in which the struggle for self-identification, self-determination, freedom, and dignity becomes as salient as one's physical and mental safety.

Do We Belong? Home Is a Safe Space

When life under Israeli occupation became worse in Palestine, my siblings and I began a campaign to convince our parents to leave. We felt that they should relocate either to the United States, where I lived, or to England, where my sister, Reem, is based. My parents would refuse again and again. Whenever pressed, they would invariably say, "Illi waqe' 'ala nass waqe' aleina" (Our fate is not different from others), or "Who ihna ahsan min ennas?" (Do you think that we are better than others?). When we persisted, they would respond by invoking Palestinian dispossession, "Ma hada be-3eid illi sar fil '48!" (No one will ever think of repeating what happened in 1948!).

My brother and sister-in-law shared my parents' sentiments. They were nonetheless contemplating a relocation to give their daughters a better education, a safe environment, and an innocent childhood. Nasser and Lana felt that they had to make the sacrifice and risk their residence in Jerusalem. The "situation on the ground," as Palestinians refer to their daily reality, was becoming unbearable: Israeli tanks were holding Palestinian towns under siege. Violence was on the rise, and Palestinians were criminalized for being Palestinians or just for being.

Nasser, Lana, and the girls never left Israeli-annexed Jerusalem. With the closure of U.S. borders to Arab and Muslim immigrants, it did not look like they would make it to New York anytime soon. But I did. On August 27, 2001, I came back from a year in Egypt where I taught at the American University in Cairo. I returned "home" to this anonymous city to take in its cultures, to thrive in its rhythms, to disappear and reappear in a sea of accents, tongues, cultures, and lifestyles. Two weeks later, my life came to a standstill, and so did the lives of hundreds of thousands of Arabs, Arab Americans, Muslim Americans, and central and South Asians.

Besides the fear for our loved ones whom we could not locate for several hours on that infamous day, we no longer feel safe: no longer could we draw on New York City's rich, vibrant, and diverse cultural scene, and no longer could we enjoy the anonymity of this city in the manner in which we enjoyed before. We rationalize things to make ourselves feel better. We are alive! Our loved ones are alive! It is more than what many other New Yorkers could say. We should be grateful. My mother's words ring in my ear, "Illi waqe' 'ala nass waqe' aleina" (Whatever happens to other people will happen to us—we are not *alone* in this!).

True, we are not alone. Along with thousands of New Yorkers, we felt miserable, sad, hurt, and wounded. But in more profound ways than one, it was not so: my mother's assurances do not apply here—we were alone, very much so!

The experience of diasporic and fragmented lives in which our souls and concerns are split between here and there sets us apart: we who have a particular skin shade, a particular accent, a certain last or first name, or markings on the body that betray some affiliation with the enemy.

Be careful if you happen to be named Osama, or even if you own a restaurant named "Osama's Place!"

You should worry if your last name is Abdul, Ahmad, Mohammad, or Masoud!

Change your name if you can, from Mohammad to Mike!

If you're Jamal, Jimmy might be a safer bet! Americanize!

Be thankful for winter: Wear a heavy long coat and a big hat. It allows you to hide your beliefs from the public space that is supposed to accommodate all beliefs: If you are a Sikh man or a devout Muslim woman, do not parade your convictions in public—the public is too narrow for you.

Do not speak up. Save your words. Try not to use words with a "P" if you are an Arab. If you may mix it up with a "B," someone will ask, "Where are you from?" Do you really want to answer?

Try to avoid situations in which you have to present an ID: do not drive a car, do not use a credit card, pay in cash. Money laundering is not a priority for law and order now. No one will check if you present big bills.

Avoid as much as you can Being You

Pass if you can

Melt in this melting pot!

Do not cry multi-culturalism and diversity! This is not the time . . . better save your life!

Better yet: "Go home," foreigner!¹

What if you have no home to go back to? What if this is your home?

Divided loyalty? Not a real American? But what do you mean when you say real American? Are you speaking of those to whom these lands belonged before anyone else? How many "real" Americans are left after the civilized European arrived?

Crossing Borders: Passing and Passing Through

September 11, 2001

I am stuck on Ninety-sixth Street and Lexington Avenue. I cannot get home. No trains are running. I desperately need to hear Jaime's voice, to know that he is alive. I cannot reach him. A long line is getting longer at the phone booth. I begin walking aimlessly, hoping to find an available phone to call my mother-in-law. Right in front of me, a woman pushing a baby carriage starts to cross the street. Her head is covered. I am debating whether to say something. Finally, I decide to approach her: "Go home!" Immediately I realize how awful I must have sounded. She looks at me with a mix of fear and resentment, too polite to ask me to mind my own business and probably too afraid to fight back. I come closer and declare a part of me I thought I would never claim: "I am a Muslim like you! Go home now. You cannot run with a baby. When they realize what has happened, they will attack." I am already bracing myself for "their" attacks against "us."

My hand instinctively goes to my neck to hide the chain with the Quranic inscription my students Ghalia and Hedayat gave me before I left Cairo. Luckily, I had forgotten to put it on today. My split lives are on a collision course again: I feel like such a traitor for *passing*. But wouldn't it be better to *pass* today? Do I want to identify with "them," though? Do I want to escape the collective guilt by association, the fate of my fellow Arabs, Palestinians, and Muslims? Should I renege on my roots? There is this nagging feeling that I need some sort of a symbol to shout to the world who I am. I want so much to defy this monolithic image.

Better tread lightly, I conclude! "Don't be foolish. Today is not the time for bravado!" I tell myself. The thought of what will happen to women with the *hijab* sends shivers down my back. "But we all make choices," one part of me says. "Not always as we please," the radical in me shouts back.

Passing is a survival mechanism.
Lay low until the storm has passed and hope for the best.

I find a Caribbean taxi driver who agrees to take me home. Four white businessmen jump in on 125th street. They do not ask if they could join me; I would not have said no had they asked. Everyone needs to get home. It is becoming very dangerous to be out in the streets. As the only passenger who knows the back roads around blockaded bridges,[2] I begin to give him directions. Then I begin to worry that someone may notice my accent and ask where I came from. I am not sure I want to declare my activist credentials as I usually do and take advantage of the opening to explain the plight of the Palestinian people. A passenger next to me says, "So this is how it feels to live with terrorist bombings." I am certain that he is referring to Palestinian suicide bombings in Israel. There is no way he could be relating to how Palestinian towns are being bombarded all the time, most recently in Gaza. I almost say something about the value of Palestinian life. I want to share what I have personally experienced this past year alone, but I am not sure that it is such a good idea. I keep my mouth shut and try to *pass* for a professional "American" woman. Another passenger, I realize from his accent, is Iranian. But we somehow bond in survival, making a silent pact not to out each other. We both pretend not to notice each other's accents.

Police cars are stationed at the bridges and on different checkpoints along the highway. I should be calm. I have seen this situation before. But West Bank memories add to, rather than alleviate, my anxiety: what if they stop us now to check our IDs? They *will* surely notice my last name. Would I be safe? What if a cop became trigger happy, as happens to Palestinians at Israeli checkpoints? Would it do me any good if they were to apologize to my family afterward?

I shudder to remember Nasser and Lana telling me about a "road incident" they experienced. A few months before Yasmeen's first birthday, they were driving from Israeli-annexed Jerusalem to our parents' home in Nablus with the baby in the backseat. At an Israeli checkpoint, a large rock flew at them out of nowhere, shattering the windshield and almost killing them. Twice privileged for having a Jerusalem ID and for being employed for a UN agency, Lana got out of the car full of rage and lashed out at the Israeli soldiers who controlled the human traffic in and out of Palestinian Authority areas. "It is not our fault!" yelled an eighteen-year-old soldier. "It was the settlers. What am I supposed to do?" was all he could say, shrugging away Lana's fears and contributing to her sense of helplessness.

For Nasser and Lana and the three million Palestinians living in the West Bank and Gaza, "road incidents" are a daily routine. There is no ordinary travel. If you live under Israeli control, you are never sure whether you will make it to your destination alive. "You were given a new life," Palestinians say to each other whenever one succeeds in making it home safely across the never-ending checkpoints.

It was what happened on a recent drive to Nablus that finally convinced Lana and Nasser that it was time to make the move to the United States.[3] During my visit to Nablus in July 2001, Lana was bringing the girls over to see me. As they were about to get out of their Jerusalem apartment, then four-year-old

Yasmeen asked her mother if she could bring along their kitten, Nadia, named for her youngest sister. It was not the request, but rather the way Yasmeen asked that broke Lana's heart: "Do you think the army will let her pass through, Mama?"

September 13, 2001

I am working at home. No one is allowed below Fourteenth Street in Manhattan unless she or he can prove a legitimate reason, the mayor of New York City declares. I am so grateful that I cannot get to work. I still do not have a valid ID. September 11 was the day on which my New York University paperwork was to be completed and the date of my first lecture in Introduction to Women's Studies. I am spared the trouble of having to go through checkpoints or to reveal my identity.

A police car stops in front of the house. Almost automatically I begin to suspect that they have come for me. Rationally, I am aware that I should not be concerned since I have done nothing wrong. But deep down I am worried. I start thinking of the reasons: Maybe a neighbor called and said that a Palestinian lives here. Maybe because our house has no flags while the neighborhood is full of them—flags are everywhere, on the cars, doors, windows, poles . . . Our next-door neighbor has two flags on the front of her house, two on the back porch, one on a planter, and two on her car; her husband has three flags on his van.

The only public symbol of Palestine we could speak of is a sticker my dad had given us with the phrase, "Falasteen fil qalb" (Palestine in my heart).[4] Palestinians made it in 1994 when they thought they would soon have a state. Better remove it immediately. The next day, Jaime says after he came back from work, "I am glad we removed the sticker. There were so many roadblocks. The car was searched twice. They even asked me to open the trunk." Any sense of security I might have had is wiped out. This *home* is becoming so similar to what happens *back home*.

I share this experience with non-Arab friends, but I sense skepticism in their eyes, at least a flicker of disappointment. I should not be jumping to conclusions, they seem to be cautioning. My loneliness deepens.

Another Road—"Back Home"—May 14, 1998

I am leaving Ramallah on the eve of the fiftieth anniversary of Nakbah, or Palestinian dispossession. My cousin's children ask if I want to hoist a Palestinian flag with the slogan of the occasion, "So we will not forget," on the car. "Sure, why not?" I say, not really thinking things through. I exit Palestinian Authority "Area A" and drive through "Area B" with joint Israeli-Palestinian patrol (Palestinians control the population, and Israel controls everything else, according to Oslo

Accords) to catch the highway to Nablus. It is a beautiful summer day. I should make it home in thirty minutes or so. So far, so good! At the fork, one direction leads to Ofra, a Jewish settlement built on a sparsely olive tree–dotted hilltop. The other road, to which I am allowed passage, because of my U.S. citizenship, leads to "Area C" (part of the West Bank 1967 borders but under total Israeli control) and 'Aber Samera. 'Aber Samera, or the Samaria Bypass, is a modern highway carved out of West Bank mountains by then Israeli minister of infrastructure Ariel Sharon to shorten the commute to West Jerusalem and Tel Aviv and thus attract "ordinary" and "secular" Israelis who are not "ideologically" drawn to the settlements to make their homes there.[5] Winding through Palestinian towns and villages whose residents are not allowed to use it, the Samaria Bypass also links the network of Israeli Jewish settlements, sparing the almost two hundred thousand settlers from the constant reminders of the Palestinians whose land was seized to construct these privileged gated colonies with their lush gardens, children's playgrounds, and Palestinian-style red rooftops.

Along the highway, electric poles are covered with Israeli flags. It is Israel's sixtieth birthday as a state and as a haven, we are told, for diasporic refugees escaping discrimination, intolerance, and the Holocaust. But there is no space in this celebration of Jewish diversity for the indigenous inhabitants of these lands. Neither I nor my lonely flag is welcomed. Cars with Israeli license plates packed with settlers honk in annoyance and make obscene gestures at me. Palestinian drivers steer away from my provocative car.

Passing is a survival strategy.

September 24, 2001

A day before traveling from New York to Washington, D.C., to speak at an anti-globalization teach-in, a scholar of a certain descent reserves the train ticket over the phone and begins to suspect that the agent placed her on hold while the FBI checked her name.

She begins packing, going through her wallet, cleaning it up, a product of her familiarity with the ritual of trying to pass under the radar. She finds a Home Depot receipt that she sets aside lest an unexpected search raise questions as to why certain tools were bought! She takes out her U.S. passport. With a name like hers, a driver's license and a faculty ID from a major university might not be enough to prove her legality or "Americanness." After all, equality does not mean total equality; it only means that some of us are more equal than others!

She goes through her briefcase. Should she take her laptop along? Would it be searched, causing a delay and humiliation in front of other passengers? It is a short trip. She has a lot of work to do. Take the laptop, but better leave early to avoid embarrassment. Better ask someone to go with her to the station: what if she is held? Someone needs to notify the organizers of the teach-in—someone needs to call a lawyer!

She arrives at the station one hour early. She approaches the window to pick up her ticket. She slips in the credit card and driver's license under the glass ever so discretely, hoping that the clerk would not address her by her last name. It is taking a while to print the ticket. All the while, she is wondering whether a camera above the window is taking her photo. She picks up the ticket with no incident and goes to the tracks. Five policemen are standing on the platform. She is convinced that they are looking directly at her. She begins rehearsing what to say when approached—not *if* but *when* approached: what she is doing here, why she is going to D.C. "Did I bring the formal invitation on the official letterhead?" she wonders. She treads ever so lightly, moving away from the eyes of the cops burning her back to the center of the station. She gets more nervous and starts babbling away. Her companion warns, "You are attracting attention. Relax!" to no avail.

The train pulls into the station. She gets on and finds a seat. Now it is the turn of the conductor to check her ticket. What is he going to do when he sees her name? She opens the briefcase to take out a paper to read. *Al-Hayat?* You cannot read *Al-Hayat* here! She puts it away before anyone notices the Arabic script. She turns on the laptop. "Can the passenger behind me see what I am working on?" Like a little third grader who guards her work from cheaters, she wraps her arms around her laptop before she gives up and puts it away.

The train arrives. The D.C. station is full of military and police personnel; she cannot tell what units, rank, or specialty. Will someone pull her aside for questioning? Nothing happens! She is free to go where she wants. Why does she feel so choked? Is this paranoia? She has not done anything wrong!

Her mind travels to another time, another place, and another continent a few months earlier.

June 10, 2001

The plane is approaching the airport. Butterflies in the stomach: excited to arrive, soon to be "home," soon to see parents and the sixteen nieces and nephews. She disembarks and gets on the bus. A short distance and they are at border control, standing in a line marked "Foreign Passports."

Butterflies in the stomach: fear and anxiety: "Did I clean up my wallet? Did I remove all business cards from the briefcase? Is my calendar clean? Did I erase suspect dates? What should I say if they ask about the letters from the kids in Shatila to their friends in Dheisheh?" She rehearses her story and reminds herself to limit her answer to yes or no. No need to elaborate: this is where they try to trick you; it only prolongs the interrogation. Do I smile or keep a straight face, be rude or docile? Which image should I present to the world here today? What do I do when asked again and again the same question?

Here it comes, here we go again . . .

King Hussein Bridge: July 1994, Going
in Ben-Gurion Airport; July 2001, Getting Out

"Rabab, what is the purpose of your visit to Israel?" a young Israeli woman behind the counter asks. I am a bit annoyed for being addressed by my first name, almost wanting to say, "Do I know you?" but I bite my tongue and maintain my calm. I respond that I am visiting the Palestinian areas to see my family. She asks again: "You have family in Israel? Where do they live?" I answer, "In Nablus." She retorts, "Shekhem?" (the Hebrew name Israel assigned to my hometown). I calmly say, "Nablus, yes." Now, I am directed to step aside so that my luggage will be searched. I remember, a bit too late, that I should have said that I was staying in Jerusalem or Tel Aviv to prevent the hassle of luggage search. I am taken, along with my luggage, aside.

An undercover intelligence officer approaches me, declaring that he is from Israeli security and wants to ask me a few questions, and that it is for my safety. I do not bother to question his concern for my safety; I have been through enough Israeli border crossings to know not to waste my time. I am too tired; I just want to get *home*. He and a young female soldier search my bags, taking everything out and spreading my clothes on the table. My underwear is there for everyone to see. An elderly Palestinian man is being searched at the next table. We pretend not to notice each other's intimate belongings, but my face is getting very hot with embarrassment. They wave an electrical device over all my stuff. Having as usual found nothing dangerous, they attempt to put my things back as they found them, but it is not possible either to replicate the manner in which I packed my stuff or to restore my dignity.

Exile and Exclusion: Home—October 5, 2001

> News Bulletin: "*reconstruction of the downtown area is being discussed*"
> Who moves back?
> Who goes home?
> Who returns?
> And who is left behind?

Homelands—June 2001

Beirut is a city reconstructed—with a beautiful, fashionable downtown. The "Paris of the Orient" is resurrected!

Shatila is a sad place. It is a crowded area of one square kilometer on which seventeen thousand people live and where expanding the livable space is not an option. People in Shatila, though, are resourceful. To make space, "they buy air," says Nohad Hamad, director of the Shatila Center for Social Development. I first dismiss what she said, thinking that she was making a joke. "Do not dwell on it!" I think to myself. But then she repeats the same statement. So, I ask. "It is very simple," she says. "There are more [Palestinian] people than land" to the extent that "the only choice left for camp residents is to expand vertically," buying the roof of a house and building another house on top of it—the towers of Babel without the glory! The geography of dispossession in action!

The streets of Shatila—alleys would be more accurate—are narrow. Sewage is open to the eye to see, and the garbage is piling up. In the winter, rain and cesspools flood the alleys. In the summer, the acrid smell of the garbage threatens to suffocate you. Residents do what they can to take care of their camp, but there are barely any services. UNRWA, the only body responsible for Palestinian refugee camps, does not have the resources or the human power to clean up or to maintain the camp. It was supposed to be a temporary solution until the people could return to their homes anyway. If you lived here, you might want to move too!

The people of Shatila have nowhere to go. The only place to which they want to return is a home:

Rabie's Saffouriah is erased from the map
But you hold it tenderly in your heart
Your memories embrace it, refusing to let go
You'd like to go home
BUT the Borders are closed today!

Home—September 21, 2001

> News Bulletin: "Artists, developers and families discuss how to memorialize 9/11 victims."

Back Home—July 2001

We are walking toward the mass grave. This grave is where most of the victims of the massacre are buried. A sign at the gate announces: "Here lie the martyrs of the Sabra and Shatila Massacre." We enter through the gate. A lone man is watering the plants: Adnan, the custodian, is not a Palestinian; he came with his family from the South of Lebanon to escape Israeli incursions. With little access to resources, Adnan's family could only afford to live in the Palestinian neighborhood, viewed as a ghetto in dominant Lebanese discourse. Their fate was not much better than the fate of their Palestinian neighbors. The Miqdadis, thirty-eight members of Adnan's family, were slaughtered during the 1982 massacre. To honor them and other victims, Adnan planted flowers and greeneries but "not the tomatoes," he said. "I did not plant the tomatoes; they grew out all on their own."

Home—October 20, 2001

A mobile phone message with the last words is saved. Cellular companies offer it to families free of charge.

Back Home—July 2001

We are sitting in the living room of Maher Srour as he remembers what happened to him and his family nineteen years ago. He speaks in matter-of-fact tones, and a ghost of a smile comes across and slowly disappears on his face as he tells us how fifteen-month-old Shadia, his youngest sister, was ordered to stand and put her hands up in surrender, like the rest of her family members. "'But she cannot walk! She is still crawling!' we told them. Their leader said, 'Yes, she can.' Sure enough, she walked. It was her first time walking . . . Shadia walked just like the rest of us. She stood in line with her hands up and walked. They shot her, and she fell right there between the bodies of my mother and my father. You see? Right there on the floor. That is Shadia." Maher points out to the television and the homemade video he assembled from newspaper cuttings and fading copies of family photos he collected from exhibits organized to remember Palestinian refugees killed in the 1982 massacre at Sabra and Shatila camps on the outskirts of Beirut.

Tears are flowing down our cheeks; none of us can stop. Each one is trying very hard to stop, but it is impossible as Maher re-members, or tries to reassemble the memories of his family that was broken forever; the only remaining memories are faded photos and a broken heart. As Maher remembers, my mind drifts to another setting. Ciraj Rassoul, a cofounder of the District 6 Museum in Cape Town, recounts how this community was completely razed to the ground by apartheid's Group Area Act, save for a mosque and a church. "Remembering," Ciraj says, "is re-membering, putting together. District 6 Museum is all about re-membering our community, putting it together."

A video of faded pictures here, a Museum there: People do remember. And
people do memorialize.
The question is
Whose memories are considered valid?
For whom memorials are built?
Does your life, as a Palestinian, count if you are dispossessed?

Home—October 25, 2001

"478 people are confirmed dead at the World Trade Center."
New York grieves for people with a mix of names, cultures, professions, lifestyles,
religious beliefs and family arrangements.

Grieve New York, Grieve!
Can you grieve for the Pakistani man who died in INS detention center of
a heart attack while awaiting deportation: Prisoners are not entitled to
adequate healthcare! What does his family say or feel? Do we get to know?

Grieve for the Egyptian who moved to New York in search of a safer life but
found no peace of mind. Does he count?

Grieve for the West African who used to pray in the Bronx. Where does he hide?

Grieve for all those anonymous beings whose labor no one credits, names no
one remembers, and bodies no one dares to claim . . .

Grieve for the mothers and fathers, the daughters and the sons, the lovers and
the beloved, the friends and the coworkers . . .

Grieve for shuttered dreams, for lives lost, for closed possibilities

Grieve for a loss of human life and Remember!

Remember, New York!
If I tell you about them, would you remember?
Would you remember Iman Hajou, the 15-month-old baby girl whose brains were
splattered on the back seat of her father's car as he went looking for help?
No hospital for Iman
No passing through checkpoints . . .
The "road situation" is bad today!

Grieve for Mohamed el-Dura
A boy with a father who could not protect his son from death

The way fathers ought to do
Bullet after bullet after bullet
Ribbed the boy
The father watches
Crying like a baby
A Palestinian Amadou Diallo?
Grieve, New York
Search your heart
Is there a small spot there to grieve for all?
Then, grieve, if you will, for the Afghans whose screams of pain no one seems to
    hear . . .
Grieve . . .

Where Is Home?

I once believed that the restoration of my dignity was possible in New York. In theory at least, people are supposed to be equal before the law. I am not naive: I am fully aware of subtle and not so subtle systems of domination and discrimination. But no longer can we pretend that equality before the law applies to us as well.

As we continue to be ethnically and racially profiled, thousands of Arabs, Arab Americans, Muslims, and Muslim Americans are feeling foreign at home: we do not feel welcomed, nor do we feel safe. Call it what you want, but the melting-pot theory fails as "America" insists on grinding the coarse kernels of our foods, refusing to name them what they are and accept them on their own terms: garlicky, oniony, spicy, strong, and fulfilling. Beneath the facade of liberal multiculturalism lies an ethnocentric New York that continues to deny our existence except as bloodthirsty and suspect male villains, helpless female victims, and exoticized alien others. Our cultures are erased, our lives flattened to fit neatly in the folds of "Americanness." No longer can we draw on New York City's rich, vibrant, and diverse cultural scene: red, white and blue may be a safety blanket to some, but to the rest of us, they symbolize exclusion. Safety in this anonymous city is a precious commodity reserved for some, achieved only by those persons who *pass* for something other than the multiplicities and complexities in which we are embedded.

Rationalizing exclusion is a Band-Aid solution to dull the pain. But when thousands are detained and thousands more are "voluntarily" coerced into interviews, New York and indeed the United States feel suspiciously like occupied Palestine. But it is not Palestine, though, where most Palestinians are subject to misery and terror. As my mother would say: "Illi waqe' 'ala nass waqe' aleina."

We are very alone here
Our diasporic lives—fragmented!
Our souls bleed!
It is perhaps time to go home
To where?
Homeland erased, nowhere to go!
Yet
"falasteen fil qlab"/"Palestine in the heart"
My father's sticker insists
Memories of him, of Amer and of the land
Green, dry, barren, and mountainous
Locked, loved, guarded
A secret, cheapened if shared
"falasteen fil qalb"
My father's sticker reminds me
Of a homeland erased
Return to sender?
No such address exists?
But we insist
"falasteen fil qalb"

Notes

Bibliography

Index

Notes

Arab and Arab American Feminisms: An Introduction

1. Tamer El-Ghobashy, "Palestinian Flag Flap," *New York Daily News*, Nov. 22, 2002, http://www.nydailynews.com/news/local/story/37234p-35169c.html.

2. Sarah Wheaton, "Obama Camp Apologizes to Muslim Women," and "Obama Calls Muslim Women Barred from Stage," *Caucus*, June 18, 2008.

3. Wheaton, "Obama Calls Muslim Women."

4. For more on the effort to make Muslims compatible with U.S. multiculturalism, see Evelyn Alsultany, "Selling American Diversity and Muslim American Identity Through Non-profit Advertising Post-9/11/2001," *American Quarterly* 59, no. 3 (2007): 593–622.

5. Rabab Abdulhadi, "'White' or Not? Displacement and the Construction of (Racialized and Gendered) Palestinianness in the U.S.," paper presented at the MESA annual meeting, Washington, D.C., Nov. 2002.

6. For a copy of the statement, see http://electronicintifada.net/v2/article10111.shtml. For an analysis of the multiple logics of racism, see Andrea Smith, "Heteropatriarchy and the Three Pillars of White Supremacy: Rethinking Women of Color Organizing," in *Color of Violence: The INCITE! Anthology*, ed. Incite! Women of Color Against Violence (Boston: South End Press, 2006), 66–73.

7. A. Smith, "Three Pillars of White Supremacy."

8. Edward W. Said, *Orientalism* (New York: Vintage Books, 1978), 2–3. See also Minoo Moallem, *Between Warrior Brother and Veiled Sister: Islamic Fundamentalism and Patriarchy in Iran* (Berkeley and Los Angeles: Univ. of California Press, 2005), 10.

9. The top six countries with the largest Muslim populations are Indonesia, Pakistan, Bangladesh, India, Turkey, and Iran. None of these countries is Arab.

10. C. Wright Mills, *The Power Elite* (Oxford: Oxford Univ. Press, 1956).

11. Lisa Suheir Majaj currently lives in Cyprus.

12. Joan W. Scott, "Gender: A Useful Category of Historical Analysis," *American Historical Review* 91, no. 5 (1986): 1053–75.

13. Kimberlé Williams Crenshaw, "Demarginalizing the Intersection of Race and Sex: A Black Feminist Critique of Antidiscrimination Doctrine, Feminist Theory and Antiracist Politics," *University of Chicago Legal Forum* (1989): 139–67. See also Cathy J. Cohen, "Punks, Bulldaggers, and Welfare Queens: The Radical Potential of Queer Politics?" *GLQ: A Journal of Lesbian and Gay Studies* 3, no. 4 (1997): 437–65; and Emi Koyama, "Whose Feminism Is It Anyway? The Unspoken Racism of the Trans-inclusion Debate," in *The Transgender Studies Reader*, ed. Susan Stryker and Stephen Whittle (London: Routledge, 2006), 698–705.

14. Chandra Talpade Mohanty, *Feminism Without Borders: Decolonizing Theory, Practicing Solidarity* (Durham, N.C.: Duke Univ. Press, 2003).

15. Rabab Abdulhadi would like to clarify that the topic of the lecture she gave on March 24, 2002, "A Female Suicide Bomber? Revisiting Feminist Thinking on Gender, War, and Peace," was in fact initiated by her and that it was not suggested by either the Humanities Council or the Gender and Women's Studies Program at Yale University.

16. The panelists included Rabab Abdulhadi, Evelyn Alsultany, Lara Deeb, Rosina Hassoun, Mervat Hatem, Huda Jadallah, Nadine Naber, Ella Shohat, and Zeina Zaatari (Nathalie Handal, Sherene Seikaly, and Lisa Majaj were unable to make it to the conference).

17. Shari Stone-Mediatore, *Reading Across Borders: Storytelling and Knowledges of Resistance* (New York: Palgrave Macmillan, 2003), 126.

18. As this book went to press, we sadly mourn the loss of Evelyn Shakir, as well as Michael Suleiman, a pioneer of Arab American studies.

19. Cherríe Moraga and Gloria Anzaldúa, eds., *This Bridge Called My Back: Writings by Radical Women of Color* (New York: Kitchen Table Women of Color Press, 1983), 23.

20. Stone-Mediatore, 159.

21. Moraga and Gloria Anzaldúa, 23; Sandra G. Harding, *Feminism and Methodology: Social Science Issues* (Bloomington: Indiana Univ. Press, 1987).

22. Conversation with Andrea Smith.

23. For more on anti-Arab political racism, see Nabeel Abraham, "Anti-Arab Racism and Violence in the United States," in *The Development of Arab-American Identity*, ed. Ernest McCarus (Ann Arbor: Univ. of Michigan Press, 1994); Therese Saliba, "Resisting Invisibility: Arab Americans in Academia and Activism," and Helen Hatab Samhan, "Not Quite White: Race Classification and the Arab-American Experience," in *Arabs in America: Building a New Future*, ed. Michael W. Suleiman (Philadelphia: Temple Univ. Press, 1999); Nadine Naber, Eman Desouky, and Lina Baroudi, "The Forgotten '-Ism': An Arab American Women's Perspective on Zionism, Racism, and Sexism," http://www.awsa.net/forgottenism.pdf; and Steve Salaita, *Anti-Arab Racism in the USA: Where It Comes from and What It Means for Politics Today* (Ann Arbor, Mich.: Pluto Press, 2006). For a discussion of how Zionist activists have historically subverted the inclusion of Palestinian rights in U.S. peace movement mobilizations, see Rabab Abdulhadi, "Activism and Exile: Palestinianness and the Politics of Solidarity," in *Local Actions: Cultural Activism, Power, and Public Life in America*, ed. Melissa Checker and Maggie Fishman (New York: Columbia Univ. Press, 2004).

24. On Arab Americans vis-à-vis whiteness, see Samhan, 209–26; Sarah Gualtieri, *Between Arab and White: Race and Ethnicity in the Early Syrian Diaspora* (Berkeley: Univ. of California Press, 2009); Nada Elia, "The 'White' Sheep of the Family: But Bleaching Is Like Starvation," in *This Bridge We Call Home: Radical Visions for Transformation*, ed. Gloria Anzaldúa and AnaLouise Keating (New York: Routledge, 2002), 223–31; and Evelyn Alsultany, "From Ambiguity to Abjection: Iraqi-Americans Negotiating Race in the United States," in *The Arab Diaspora: Voices of an Anguished Scream*, ed. Zahia Smail Salhi and Ian Richard Netton (London: Routledge, 2006).

25. Our use of the term "transphobia" follows customary usages. Yet it is important to note that antiqueer sentiments and violence do not always result from fear/phobia but also result from ideological oppositions.

2. The Political and Cultural Representations of Arabs, Arab Americans, and Arab American Feminisms after September 11, 2001

1. Zahid Bukhari, "Demography, Identity, Space: Defining American Muslim," in *Muslims in the United States*, ed. Philippa Strum and Daniel Tarantolo (Washington, D.C.: Woodrow Wilson International Center for Scholars, 2003), 9. It is worth noting here that some of the estimates offered of African American Muslims are much higher than the ones offered by this author.

2. Mervat F. Hatem, "Racial Profiling in the Pursuit of Arabs and Muslims in the U.S.," in *It's a Free Country: Personal Freedom in America after September 11*, ed. Danny Goldberg, Victor Goldberg, and Robert Greenwald (New York: Nation Books, 2003).

3. Mervat F. Hatem, "Discourses on the 'War on Terrorism' in the U.S. and Its Views on the Arab, Muslim, and Gendered 'Other,'" *Arab Studies Journal* 11–12 (Fall 2003–Spring 2004): 77–103.

4. Mervat F. Hatem, "In the Eye of the Storm: Islamic Societies and Muslim Women in Globalization Discourses," in *Beyond the Boundaries of the Old Geographies*, ed. Ali Mirsepassi (forthcoming).

5. Frantz Fanon, *The Wretched of the Earth* (New York: Grove Press, 1963).

6. Mervat F. Hatem, "Homeland Security in a Global World" (e-book), *Democracy and Homeland Security: Strategies, Controversies, and Impact*, ed. Nawwal Ammar (Kent, Ohio: Kent State Univ. Press, 2004).

7. Brian Urquhart, *Ralph Bunche: An American Life* (New York: W. W. Norton, 1993), chap. 11.

8. Ralph Bunche, introduction to *The Near East and the Great Powers*, ed. Richard Frye (Port Washington, N.Y.: Kennikat Press, 1953), 5.

9. Ralph Bunche, "Appendix I: Discussions," in *The Near East and the Great Powers*, ed. Richard Frye (Port Washington, N.Y.: Kennikat Press, 1953), 203.

10. Bunche, introduction, 4, 116.

11. Melani McAlister, *Epic Encounters: Culture, Media, and U.S. Interests in the Middle East since 1945* (Berkeley and Los Angeles: Univ. of California Press, 2005), 32–33.

12. Ralph Bunche, "Man, Democracy, and Peace-Foundations for Peace: Human Rights and Fundamental Freedoms," in *Ralph Bunche: Selected Speeches and Writings*, ed. Charles P. Henry (Ann Arbor: Univ. of Michigan Press, 1995), 174.

13. Bunche, introduction, 5.

14. McAlister, 34.

15. McAlister, 84–90.

16. McAlister, 93.

17. McAlister, chap. 3.

18. Michael Suleiman and Baha Abu Louban, introduction to *Arab Americans: Continuity and Change*, ed. Michael Suleiman and Baha Abu Louban (Belmont, Mass.: AAUG, 1989), 6.

19. Interview with Elaine Hagopian in Boston on March 7, 2002.

20. McAlister, chap. 3.

21. Suleiman and Abu Louban, 6.

22. Helen Hatab Samhan, "Arab Americans and the Elections of 1988: A Constituency Come of Age" in *Arab Americans*, 245.

23. Mervat H. Hatem, "How the Gulf War Changed the AAUG's Discourse on Arab Nationalism and Gender Politics?" *Middle East Journal* 2 (Spring 2001): 290–96.

24. Interviews with former students who were active in the Arab Student Organizations on the University of Michigan campus in the 1970s and those who were active in Muslim Student Associations in the 1990s in April 2002. Both groups preferred to remain anonymous.

25. Aminah Beverly McCloud, "A Challenging Intellectual Heritage: A Look at the Social and Political Space of African American Muslims," in *Muslims in the United States,* ed. Philippa Strum and Daniel Tarantolo (Washington, D.C.: Woodrow Wilson International Center for Scholars, 2003), 91–92.

26. Conversations with Rosina Hassoun and comments made by Nadine Naber during the discussion section of the panel "Arab/Arab American Feminists and American Studies," American Studies Association meetings, Oct. 18, 2003, Hartford, Conn.

27. I am grateful to Amaney Jamal for pointing out this important development.

28. Interview with a participant in the University of Michigan's *Hijab* Days who preferred to remain anonymous (Mar. 24, 2002).

29. According to one of the participants in *Hijab* Days in Ann Arbor, the Universities of Chicago and Wisconsin also organized several days to express solidarity with Muslim women. In contrast, the Universities of Texas and New Mexico joined this solidarity movement by organizing a single *Hijab* Day on their campuses.

30. Personal e-mail communication with Zareena Grewal, one of the organizers of *Hijab* Days at the University of Michigan campus (Oct. 6, 2002).

31. Omaima Abou-Bakr, "Islamic Feminism: What's in a Name? Preliminary Reflections," *Middle East Women's Studies Review* 15–16 (Winter–Spring 2001): 1–4.

32. John Berger, *Ways of Seeing* (London: Hamondsworth, Penguin, 1972).

3. Palestinian Women's Disappearing Act:
The Suicide Bomber Through Western Feminist Eyes

1. miriam cooke, "Women's Jihad Before and After 9/11," in *Women and Gender in the Middle East and the Islamic World Today,* UCIAS Edited Volumes, vol. 4 (2003): Article 1063, http:// repositories.cdlib.org/uciaspubs/editedvolumes/4/1063, 195.

2. Barbara Victor, *Army of Roses: Inside the World of Palestinian Suicide Bombers* (New York: Rodale, 2003), 20.

3. cooke, "Women's Jihad Before and After 9/11," 195.

4. For works on gender and nationalism, see Cynthia Enloe, *Bananas, Beaches, and Bases: Making Feminist Sense of International Politics* (Berkeley and Los Angeles: Univ. of California Press, 1990); Caren Kaplan, Norma Alarcón, and Minoo Moallem, *Between Woman and Nation: Nationalism, Transnational Feminism, and the State* (Durham, N.C.: Duke Univ. Press, 1990); Valentine M. Moghadam, *Gender and National Identity: Women and Politics in Muslim Societies* (London: Zed Books, 1994); Andrew Parker, Mary Russo, Doris Sommer, and Patricia Yaeger, *Nationalisms and Sexualities* (New York: Routledge, 1992); Nira Yuval-Davis, *Gender and Nationalism* (London: Sage, 1998). For works that address gender and Palestinian nationalism, see Nahla Abdo, "Nationalism and Feminism in the Palestinian Women's Movement," in *Gender and National Identity: Women and Politics in Muslim Societies,* ed. Valentine Moghadam (London: Zed Press, 1994); Rita Giacaman, Islah Jad, and Penny Johnson, "For the Public Good? Gender and Social Citizenship in Palestine," *Middle East Report* 198 (1996): 11–16; Frances S. Hasso, "The 'Women's Front': Nationalism, Feminism, and Modernity in Palestine," *Gender and Society* 12, no. 4 (1998): 441–86; Tami

Amanda Jacoby, "Feminism, Nationalism, and Difference: Reflections on the Palestinian Women's Movement," *Women's Studies International Forum* 22, no. 5 (1999): 511–23; Rhoda Ann Kanaaneh, *Rebirthing the Nation: Strategies of Palestinian Women in Israel* (Berkeley and Los Angeles: Univ. of California Press, 2002); Rajeswari Mohan, "Loving Palestine: Nationalist Activism and Feminist Agency in Leila Khaled's *Subversive Bodily Acts*," *Interventions* 1, no. 1 (1998): 52–80; and Julie Peteet, *Gender in Crisis: Women and the Palestinian Resistance Movement* (New York: Columbia Univ. Press, 1992).

5. For examples of works on suicide bombing, see Lori Allen, "There Are Many Reasons Why: Suicide Bombers and Martyrs in Palestine," *GSC Quarterly* (Summer 2002); John Borneman, "Genital Anxiety," *Anthropological Quarterly* 75, no. 1 (2002): 129–37; Joyce M. Davis, *Martyrs: Innocence, Vengeance, and Despair in the Middle East* (New York: Palgrave Macmillan, 2003); Ghassan Hage, "'Comes a Time We Are All Enthusiasm': Understanding Palestinian Suicide Bombers in Times of Exighophobia," *Public Culture* 15, no. 1 (2003): 65–89; Hilal Khashan, "Collective Palestinian Frustration and Suicide Bombings," *Third World Quarterly* 24, no. 6 (2003): 1049–67; Assaf Moghadam, "Palestinian Suicide Terrorism in the Second Intifada: Motivations and Organizational Aspects," *Studies in Conflict and Terrorism* 26 (2003): 65–92; Sylvain Perdigon, "Life of an Infamous Woman: The Funerals of Wafa Idris, Palestine's First Female Suicide-Bomber" (unpublished paper, 2004); and Leonard Weinberg, Ami Pedahzur, and Daphna Canetti-Nisim, "The Social and Religious Characteristics of Suicide Bombers and Their Victims," *Terrorism and Political Violence* 15, no. 3 (2003): 139–53.

6. According to this "theory," young Muslim men become suicide bombers because they are promised sex with seventy-two virgins in the afterlife. This "theory" joins two Orientalist views of Muslim societies by casting sexual repression as a marker of their present and sexual excess as a marker of their future. For a refutation of this explanation of suicide bombing, see As'ad Abukhalil, "Sex and the Suicide Bomber," 2001, http://archive.salon.com/sex/feature/2001/11/07/islam/index_np.html.

7. *Sati* refers to the practice of widow burning in India. The word also refers to the woman who engages in such an act. For insightful work on *sati*, see Lata Mani, *Contentious Traditions: The Debate on Sati in Colonial India* (Berkeley and Los Angeles: Univ. of California Press, 1998).

8. In this context, culture is equivalent to "nature" in the nature-culture dichotomy that second-wave feminists have engaged with much passion.

9. This is the favorite propaganda argument of Israeli security. See, for instance, "The Role of Palestinian Women in Suicide Terrorism,"
http://www.mfa.gov.il/MFA/MFAArchive/2000_2009/2003/1/The%20Role%20of%20
Palestinian%20Women%20in%20Suicide%20Terrorism.

10. In fact, Phyllis Chesler, a Zionist radical feminist, declares that suicide bombing by women is "another form of Arab honor killing."

11. Palestinian women's organizations have been largely silent on the issue of the women suicide bombers and have developed no feminist discourse to either support or oppose them. As for the women themselves, if one is to judge by the statements they left behind, nationalism is emphasized as their motive, not women's rights. In the Arab and Islamist context, which I analyze in detail elsewhere, the *istishhadeya* are presented as models of Muslim womanhood to shame the secular feminists.

12. Earlier, Angela Dworkin wrote: "As for the Palestinians, I can only imagine the humiliation of losing to, being conquered by, the weakest, most despised, most castrated people on the face of

the earth. This is a feminist point about manhood" ("Israel: Whose Country Is It Anyway?" *Ms.*, Sept.–Oct. 1990, http://www.nostatusquo.com/ACLU/dworkin/IsraelI.html). The problem with this description is that it excludes Palestinian women. Israeli conquest of the Palestinians is seen as an affair between men, as if women did not suffer loss, displacement, death, and injury.

13. During her encounters with Palestinian women in 1990, Dworkin was better able to hear their grievances against the Israeli occupation. She wrote: "Palestinian women came out of the audience to give first-person testimony about what the Occupation was doing to them. They especially spoke about the brutality of the Israeli soldiers. They talked about being humiliated, being forcibly detained, being trespassed on, being threatened. They spoke about themselves and about women. For Palestinian women, the Occupation is a police state and the Israeli secret police are a constant danger; there is no 'safe space'" (n.p.).

14. miriam cooke makes a similar argument in "Women's Jihad Before and After 9/11." Moreover, in her discussion of Wafa Idris, cooke refers to her as a Muslim woman participating in jihad, even though Idris was dispatched and claimed by a secular group. Without any justification, she places her in the history of Muslim women fighters, not Palestinian women nationalists, thus undermining the latter and privileging a distant history over the more immediate lived one.

15. Robin Morgan, *The Demon Lover: The Roots of Terrorism* (New York: Washington Square Press, 2001), 252.

16. Victor, 7, 8, 18.

17. Victor, 9, 10. This notion is inaccurate: women's dress code changed during the first intifada into a more conservative one and not the other way around, when women's bodies were targeted by Islamic political groups as a way to exert political control. See Rima Hammami, "Women, the Hijab, and the Intifada," *Middle East Report* 20, nos. 3–4 (1990): 24–28.

18. Victor, 23, 34, 46, 32.

19. Victor, 102, 103, 261, 265, 247, 265.

20. Victor, 49.

21. Victor, 105.

22. Victor, 17, 16, 165, 97.

23. Karen Valby, who calls Victor "mean spirited," writes: "The journalist has great affection for unnamed sources. Much of the dredged-up dirt here has already been revealed in gossip columns, so don't expect much in the way of revelation" (book review of *Goddess: Inside Madonna*, by Barbara Victor, *Entertainment Weekly*, Nov. 23, 2001, 74, http://mutex.gmu.edu:2079/pqdweb?index=1&did=0 00000092322114&SrchMode=1&sid=2&Fmt=3&VInst=PROD&VType=PQD&RQT=309&VName =PQD&TS=1101145767&clientId=31810).

24. Jacqueline Rose, writing for the *London Review of Books*, is the only exception; she questions Victor's unnamed sources, her fictional narratives, and her prejudice. Baruch Kimmerling, on the other hand, in his review of the book for the *Nation*, fails to questions Victor's discourse.

25. Victor, 4–5.

26. Victor seems particularly sensitive to Palestinian women nationalists' charms. She describes Leila Khaled as "a stunning young woman in her twenties" (62).

27. Sarah Pollack, "Lipstick Martyrs: A New Breed of Palestinian Terrorist," CBN, May 28, 2003, http://www.cbn.com/CBNNews/News/030523d.asp; Kevin Toolis, "Walls of Death," *Observer*, November 23, 2003, http://www.aljazeera.info/Opinion%20editorials/2003%20Opinion%20 Editorials/November/24%20o/Walls%20of%20death%20Kevin%20Toolis.htm; Kevin Toolis, "Why

Women Turn to Suicide Bombing," *Observer*, Oct. 12, 2003, http://www.countercurrents.org/pa-toolis121003.htm.

28. Victor, 2.

4. Arab Jews, Diasporas, and Multicultural Feminism: An Interview with Ella Shohat

1. See, for example, Ella Shohat, "Rupture and Return: Zionist Discourse and the Study of Arab-Jews," *Social Text* 21, no. 2 (2003). Also included in Ella Shohat, *Taboo Memories, Diasporic Voices* (Durham, N.C.: Duke Univ. Press, 2006).

2. See, for example, Ella Shohat, "The Invention of the Mizrahim," *Journal of Palestine Studies* 29, no. 1 (1999): 5–20; "The Narrative of the Nation and the Discourse of Modernization: The Case of the Mizrahim," *Critique* 10 (Spring 1997): 3–18; "Mizrahi Feminism: The Politics of Gender, Race, and Multiculturalism," *News from Within* 12, no. 4 (1996): 17–26; "Rethinking Jews and Muslims: Quincentennial Reflections," *Middle East Report* (Sept.–Oct. 1992): 25–29; "Dislocated Identities: Reflections of an Arab-Jew," *Movement Research: Performance Journal*, no. 5 (Fall–Winter 1992): 8; and "Master Narrative/Counter Readings," *Resisting Images: Essays on Cinema and History*, ed. Robert Sklar and Charles Musser (Philadelphia: Temple Univ. Press, 1990), 251–78.

3. Edward W. Said, "Zionism from the Standpoint of Its Victims," *Social Text* 1 (Winter 1979): 7–58; Ella Shohat, "Zionism from the Standpoint of Its Jewish Victims," *Social Text* 19–20 (Fall 1988): 1–35. Both essays were published originally in *Social Text* and reprinted in *Dangerous Liaisons: Gender, Nation, and Postcolonial Perspectives*, ed. Ella Shohat, Aamir Mufti, and Anne McClintock (Minneapolis: Univ. of Minnesota Press, 1997).

4. On such analogies, see Ella Shohat, "Staging the Quincentenary: The Middle East and the Americas," *Third Text* 21 (Winter 1992–93): 95–105; and "Taboo Memories, Diasporic Visions: Columbus, Palestine, and Arab-Jews," in *Performing Hybridity*, ed. May Joseph and Jennifer Fink (Minneapolis: Univ. of Minnesota Press, 1999), 131–56. Also included in Shohat, *Taboo Memories, Diasporic Voices*.

5. For more on this topic, see Ella Shohat, "The 'Postcolonial' in Translation: Reading Said in Hebrew," *Journal of Palestine Studies* 33, no. 3 (2004): 55–75. Also included in Shohat, *Taboo Memories, Diasporic Voices*.

6. Ella Shohat, "Gender and the Culture of Empire: Toward a Feminist Ethnography of the Cinema," *Quarterly Review of Film and Video* 131, nos. 1–2 (1991): 45–84; and "Imaging Terra Incognita: The Disciplinary Gaze of Empire," *Public Culture* 3, no. 2 (1991): 41–70.

7. Ella Shohat and Robert Stam, "Traveling Multiculturalism: A Trinational Debate in Translation," in *Postcolonial Studies and Beyond*, ed. Ania Loomba et al. (Durham, N.C.: Duke Univ. Press, 2005), 293–316; and *The Culture Wars in Translation* (New York: New York Univ. Press, forthcoming).

5. In the Belly of the Beast: Struggling for Nonviolent Belonging

1. bell hooks and T. McKinnon, "Sisterhood: Beyond Public and Private," *Signs: Journal of Women in Culture and Society* 21, no. 41 (1996): 814–29.

2. Michel Foucault, *The History of Sexuality: An Introduction*, vol. 1 (New York: Vintage Books, 1990), 74, and *Discipline and Punish: The Birth of the Prison*, trans. A. Sheridan (New York: Vintage Books, 1977).

3. There are numerous examples from the nomination of Gonzales to H.R. 10 to the thousands of detainees since 9/11 in U.S. detention prisons and in Guantánamo Bay, Patriot Acts I and II,

and numerous other legislations. In addition, the prowar position of both presidential candidates is an indication of the desire for elimination. For an assessment of the candidate's positions on the war, two articles present alternative viewpoints: http://www.isreview.org/issues/39/right_wing_repub .shtml and http://www.isreview.org/issues/39/antiwar_movement.shtml.

4. The incessant display of affection toward Israel on behalf of both the Democratic and the Republican presidential candidates in the 2004 campaigns is available in newspaper articles and on Web sites. For more information, check Haaretz, especially between July and December 2004, as well as http://www.aipac.org.

5. There are several articles about two Muslim women who were barred from the Obama rally because of their head scarves in June 2008: http://www.politico.com/news/stories/0608/11168.html; http://latimesblogs.latimes.com/washington/2008/06/obama-muslim.html; and http://www.cbsnews .com/stories/2008/06/18/politics/politico/main4191084.shtml?source=mostpop_story. For information on critiques of Obama's positions on Israel and the Arab world, see the following sources: Ralph Nader, open letter to Senator Barak Obama, Nov. 3, 2008, http://www.votenader.org/media/2008/11/03/letter toobama/; and Ali Abunimah on the topic, http://electronicintifada.net/v2/article9427.shtml.

Transcripts of Obama's speech in front of AIPAC in June 2008 can be found on NPR's Web site, http://www.npr.org/templates/story/story.php?storyId=91150432. For commentary in Haartez on Obama's earlier speech to AIPAC in February 2008, see http://www.haaretz.com/hasen/spages/832668 .html.

6. Regarding Muslim supporters of Obama in the United States on the complexities of the positions they find themselves in, see http://www.nhregister.com/articles/2008/11/16/life/doc492001 3831207710106350.txt. For more about religion and how the media covered it in the campaign, see http://www.journalism.org/node/13790.

7. Obama chose a strong pro-Israel hard-liner for chief of staff, Rahm Emanuel (http://electronic intifada.net/v2/article9939.shtml).

Hillary Clinton's support of Israel and Israeli policy has been very strong over the years. See http://www.jewishaz.com/issues/story.mv?080201+clinton; http://clinton.senate.gov/issues/national security/israel/index.cfm; and, in 2005, http://www.villagevoice.com/2005-12-06/news/hillary-calls-israel-a-beacon-of-democracy/.

8. Rasha Ghappour put it very succinctly in her poems titled "Colors," *Mizna* 4, no. 1 (2001): 7–8. Here is an excerpt:

> I am tired of explaining that Allah is God
> and not a three headed creation.
> That we believe in Noah and Moses and Jesus, too.
> But sometimes that's expected.
> I just never thought
> I would have to explain
> the struggles of color
> to you.

9. Saida, or Sidon, is the largest city in South Lebanon and an ancient biblical port.

10. Antonio Gramsci, *Selections from the Prison Notebooks*, trans. and ed. Q. Hoare and G. Nowell Smitth (New York: International Publishers, 1971); Joanna Kadi, *Thinking Class: Sketches from a Cultural Worker* (Boston: South End Press, 1996), 46.

11. Pierre Bourdieu, *Outline of a Theory of Practice*, trans. R. Nice (1972; reprint, New York: Cambridge Univ. Press, 1977).

12. bell hooks, "Out of the Academy and into the Streets," Ms., July–Aug. 1992, 80–82; Henrietta Moore, *A Passion for Difference: Essays in Anthropology and Gender* (London: Polity Press, 1994), 81.

13. The limited space does not allow me to engage in a lengthy explanation of these major moments in the past one hundred years of Arab history.

14. "This book is more than the story of Wilma Mankiller. It is also the extraordinary story of the Cherokee people and their indomitable courage. The chapters of this book weave together the story of one Cherokee woman with the history of all the people of the Cherokee Nation, much as traditional Cherokee stories weave together the unbroken threads of tribal history, wisdom, and culture preserved by each generation" (Wilma Mankiller and M. Wallis, *Mankiller: A Chief and Her People* [New York: St. Martin's Press, 1993], xiii).

15. Maya Angelou's *Gather Together in My Name* (New York: Bantam, 1974) and *The Heart of a Woman* (New York: Bantam, 1981) are but two examples.

16. June Jordan, "Waking Up in the Middle of Some American Dreams," in *Technical Difficulties: African American Notes on the State of the Union* (New York: Vintage Books, 1992), 15, 17.

17. Personal correspondence, 2003.

18. Evelyn Alsultany, "The Prime-Time Plight of the Arab Muslim American After 9/11: Configurations of Race and Nation in TV Dramas," in *Race and Arab Americans Before and After 9/11: From Invisible Citizens to Visible Subjects*, ed. Amaney Jamal and Nadine Naber (Syracuse: Syracuse Univ. Press, 2008), 204–28.

19. Nadine Naber, "White but Not Quiet: Arab American Invisibility," *Ethnic and Racial Studies* 23, no. 1 (2000): 37–62.

20. June Jordan, "Of Those So Close Beside Me, Which Are You?" in *Technical Difficulties: African American Notes on the State of the Union* (New York: Vintage Books, 1992), 27.

21. I would argue anthropology also has a colonial present, though perhaps it does not permeate the discipline as a whole.

22. Said, *Orientalism*, 42.

23. Kadi, *Thinking Class*, 11.

24. Several researchers have written about Orientalism in its various forms after Said's landmark book in 1978, *Orientalism*, as well as critiques of Western feminism. See Mohja Kahf, *Western Representations of the Muslim Woman: From Termagant to Odalisque* (Austin: Univ. of Texas Press, 1999); Malika Mehdid, "A Western Invention of Arab Womanhood: The 'Oriental' Female," in *Women in the Middle East: Perceptions, Realities, and Struggles for Liberation*, ed. H. Afshar (London: Macmillan, 1996), 18–58; Chandra Talpade Mohanty, "Under Western Eyes: Feminist Scholarship and Colonial Discourses," *Boundary 2* 12, no. 3 (1984): 333–58; Lila Abu-Lughod, introduction to *Remaking Women: Feminism and Modernity in the Middle East*, ed. Lila Abu-Lughod (Princeton: Princeton Univ. Press, 1998), 3–31; and Shohat and Stam, introduction to *Unthinking Eurocentrism*, 1–12.

25. Gayatri Chakravorty Spivak, "Can the Subaltern Speak?" in *Marxism and the Interpretation of Culture*, ed. C. Nelson and L. Grossberg (Basingstoke: Macmillan Education, 1988), 271–313.

26. During my years of graduate school, I placed Ruth Foreman's poem "I Will Speak Genius to Myself" (from her book *We Are the Young Magicians* [Boston: Beacon Press, 1993]) on my desk and often read it to myself. I quote here but a piece of it:

So Tired of trying to prove myself
analyticalphilosophicalintellectually
know what I mean?
Those epistemologicaterminal terms dammit
clutter my mind. Styrofoam words.
What happened to
using your own words
as long as you made yourself understood?
Now
I must recite flawlessly
another's vocabulary
before I can make sense in my own.
When I was a child
people understood me by watching my bright eyes and butterfly hands.
In the academy I suppose
some white man taught everyone
to go blind—
to memorize terminology
to clap for words
seen as academic
to refuse one whose words are not. (47)

27. Arundhati Roy, *Power Politics* (Boston: South End Press, 2001), 24.

28. Nadine Naber, "Ambiguous Insiders: An Investigation of Arab American Invisibility," *Ethnic and Racial Studies* 23, no. 1 (2000): 38–50.

29. A statistics teaching assistant at the University of California, Davis, displayed a manufactured picture of a plane crashing into Mecca during the pilgrimage season.

30. For more information on Handala and the artist who created him, Naji el Ali, see http://www.handala.org/ and http://www.najialali.com/. On the Right of Return Legally and in the UN Resolutions, see http://www.al-awda.org/facts.html.

31. There is even a Web site that guides you through ways to host such a week on campus: http://www.terrorismawareness.org/islamo-fascism/49/a-students-guide-to-hosting-islamo-fascism-awareness-week/.

32. Irshad Manji and Ayan Hirshi Ali are but two examples of this recent trend.

33. See http://www.incite-national.org/index.php?s=135.

34. Zeina Zaatari, "On Silencing Arab Feminists: An Open Letter to the Editors and Staff of Critical Half (a Publication of Women for Women International) on Silencing Their 'Sisters'" (2007), http://www.arab-american.net, available at http://wewillreturn.blogspot.com/2007/11/letter-to-critical-half-on-silencing.html; http://www.arab-american.net/Community/Community%20Pages/onsilencingarabfeminists.html. For more information on the Forgotten -Ism, please see http://www.incite-national.org/index.php?s=135.

35. MADRE's press statement: http://www.commondreams.org/news2007/0711-02.htm. The press statement titled "Defining Terms in the Age of Imperialism: Challenging Alleged 'Strategic Solidarity'" was published in *Left Turn* in August 2007 (http://www.leftturn.org/?q=node/728).

36. Those others include institutions with a one-track agenda like MADRE, Islamophobic organizations, institutions, and researchers like the U.S. administration's claim of saving Afghan or Iraqi women from the prey of patriarchy, and the new emergent class of well-trained, well-funded superstars like Fouad Ajami, Irshad Manji, and others.

37. On the Call to Boycott World Pride from QUIT and other organizations, see http://www.boycottworldpride.org/.

38. Gramsci.

39. Frantz Fanon, *The Wretched of the Earth* (New York: Grove Press, 1963), 35.

40. Roy, *Power Politics*, 28.

41. For statistics on rape and violence against women and its prevalence on college campuses, see the following organizations: Rape, Abuse, and Incest National Network (http://www.rainn.org/get-information/statistics/sexual-assault-victims), Feminist.com (http://www.feminist.com/antiviolence/facts.html), and V-Day (http://newsite.vday.org/).

6. Decolonizing Culture: Beyond Orientalist and Anti-Orientalist Feminisms

1. I draw upon Gayatri Gopinath's analysis of how the "woman" and "compulsory heterosexuality" as figures of the nation take on new form in the diaspora (*Impossible Desires: Queer Diasporas and South Asian Public Cultures* [Durham: Duke Univ. Press, 2005]).

2. To some extent, working-class Arab kids we knew from church or school faced similar struggles. Yet the stakes seemed to be different among middle-class immigrant families, as the reputation of one's father's family name was very much tied up in socioeconomic class status. Working-class families had less to lose—less at stake, at least in terms of maintaining their socioeconomic status—when their children transgressed their parents' demands.

3. Anouar Majid, *Unveiling Traditions: Postcolonial Islam in a Polycentric World* (Durham: Duke Univ. Press, 2000), 7; Minoo Moallem, *Between Warrior Brother and Veiled Sister: Islamic Fundamentalism and the Politics of Patriarchy in Iran* (Berkeley and Los Angeles: Univ. of California Press, 2005); Ella Shohat and Robert Stam, *Unthinking Eurocentrism: Multiculturalism and the Media* (New York: Routledge, 1994).

4. Rabab Abdulhadi, "Sexualities and the Social Order in Arab and Muslim Communities," in *Islam and Homosexuality*, ed. Samar Habib (Santa Barbara: Praeger, 2010), 470.

5. This also includes South Asians and others perceived to be any of these categories (Sunaina Maira, *Missing: Youth, Citizenship, and Empire after 9/11* [Durham: Duke Univ. Press, 2009]).

6. Jasbir K. Puar, *Terrorist Assemblages: Homonationalism in Queer Times*, Next Wave (Durham: Duke Univ. Press, 2007); Lila Abu-Lughod, "Do Muslim Women Really Need Saving? Anthropological Reflections on Cultural Relativism and Its Others," *American Anthropologist* 104, no. 3 (2002). Feminist scholars like Robin L. Riley, Chandra Talpade Mohanty, and Minnie Bruce Pratt ("Feminism and U.S. Wars: Mapping the Ground," introduction to *Feminism and War: Confronting U.S. Imperialism* [London: Zed, 2008], 1–19), Andrea Smith ("Heteropatriarchy and the Three Pillars of White Supremacy: Rethinking Women of Color Organizing," in *Color of Violence: The INCITE! Anthology*, ed. Incite! Women of Color Against Violence [Boston: South End Press, 2006], 66–73), Sherene H. Razack (*Casting Out: The Eviction of Muslims from Western Law and Politics* [Toronto: Univ. of Toronto Press, 2008]), and Chandra Talpade Mohanty ("U.S. Empire and the Project of Women's Studies: Stories of Citizenship, Complicity, and Dissent," *Gender, Place, and Culture* 13,

no. 1 [2006]: 7–20) have contributed an invaluable assessment of how the new Orientalism operates in relationship to imperial feminisms. Queer-studies scholars like Jasbir Puar have theorized the logic of homonationalism, thus contributing an analysis of how the idea of a "failed heterosexuality" serves as a crucial justification for violence and war (see Puar; and Puar and Amit S. Rai, "Monster, Terrorist, Fag: The War on Terrorism and the Production of Docile Patriots," *Social Text* 20, no. 3 [2002]: 117–48).

7. For analyses of intensified xenophobia and racism in California, see Jewelle Taylor Gibbs and Teiahsha Bankhead, *Preserving Privilege: California Politics, Propositions, and People of Color* (Westport, Conn.: Praeger, 2001); and Tomas Almaguer, *Racial Fault Lines: The Historical Origins of White Supremacy in California* (Berkeley and Los Angeles: Univ. of California Press, 1994). Engseng Ho ("Empire Through Diasporic Eyes: A View from the Other Boat," *Comparative Studies in Society and History* 46, no. 2 [2004]: 210–46) provides a useful analysis of the United States as an empire. He argues that U.S. empire is a mode of imperial domination that has global reach and disavows administration on the ground. He argues that the logic of U.S. empire purports that nations are free to choose their destinies and friends and that the United States epitomizes religious, political, social, and sexual liberation. Yet at the same time, the United States has a devastating mode of domination that forces local governments to make appalling choices. Generally, the theorization of U.S. empire contends that U.S. empire works through covert and overt mechanisms and through economic, military, and cultural hegemony, which continue to take on new forms in different historical contexts inside and outside the United States. See Andrea Smith and J. Kehaulani Kauanui, "Native Feminisms Engage American Studies," *American Quarterly* 60, no. 2 (2008): 241–49; George Steinmetz, "Return to Empire: The New U.S. Imperialism in Comparative Historical Perspective," *Sociological Theory* 23, no. 4 (2005): 339–67; Ann Stoler, *Haunted by Empire: Geographies of Intimacy in North American History* (Durham: Duke Univ. Press, 2006); Amy Kaplan, *The Anarchy of Empire in the Making of U.S. Culture* (Cambridge: Harvard Univ. Press, 2005); Nadia Kim, *Imperial Citizens: Koreans and Race from Seoul to LA* (Stanford: Stanford Univ. Press, 2008); Jodi Kim, *Ends of Empire: Asian American Critique and the Cold War* (Minneapolis: Univ. of Minnesota Press, 2010); Vicente M. Diaz and J. Kehaulani Kauanui, "Native Pacific Cultural Studies on the Edge," *Contemporary Pacific* 13, no. 2 (2001): 315–41; David Harvey, *The New Imperialism*, Clarendon Lectures in Geography and Environmental Studies (Oxford: Oxford Univ. Press, 2003); Reza Hammami and Martina Rieker, "Feminist Orientalism and Orientalist Marxism," *New Left Review* 1, no. 170 (1988); and Michael Mann, *Incoherent Empire* (London: Verso, 2003). See the following discussions about how the central aspects of U.S. empire in the Middle East have been the U.S. relationship to Israel and the U.S. support of repressive regimes: Mahmood Mamdani, *Good Muslim, Bad Muslim: America, the Cold War, and the Roots of Terror* (New York: Pantheon Books, 2004); Maira; Rashid Khalidi, *Resurrecting Empire: Western Footprints and America's Perilous Path in the Middle East* (Boston: Beacon Press, 2004); and Melani McAlister, *Epic Encounters: Culture, Media, and U.S. Interests in the Middle East since 1945* (Berkeley and Los Angeles: Univ. of California Press, 2005).

8. Vijay Prashad, *The Karma of Brown Folk* (Minneapolis: Univ. of Minnesota Press, 2000); Yen Le Espiritu, *Home Bound: Filipino American Lives Across Cultures, Communities, and Countries* (Berkeley and Los Angeles: Univ. of California Press, 2003); Cathy J. Cohen, *The Boundaries of Blackness: AIDS and the Breakdown of Black Politics* (Chicago: Univ. of Chicago Press, 1999); Kevin Gaines, *Uplifting the Race: Black Leadership, Politics, and Culture in the Twentieth Century* (Chapel Hill: Univ. of North Carolina Press, 1996).

9. Prashad, 150.

10. Lila Abu-Lughod, "The Marriage of Feminism and Islamism in Egypt: Selective Repudiation as a Dynamic of Postcolonial Cultural Politics," in *Remaking Women: Feminism and Modernity in the Middle East*, ed. Lila Abu-Lughod (Princeton: Princeton Univ. Press, 1998), 243–69; Homa Hoodfar, *Between Marriage and the Market: Intimate Politics and Survival in Cairo*, Comparative Studies on Muslim Societies, vol. 24 (Berkeley and Los Angeles: Univ. of California Press, 1997).

11. Afsaneh Najmabadi, *Women with Mustaches and Men Without Beards: Gender and Sexual Anxieties of Iranian Modernity* (Berkeley and Los Angeles: Univ. of California Press, 2005); Abdulhadi, "Sexualities and Social Order"; Leila Ahmed, *Women and Gender in Islam: Historical Roots of a Modern Debate* (New Haven: Yale Univ. Press, 1992).

12. Abdulhadi, "Sexualities and Social Order"; Joseph Andoni Massad, *Desiring Arabs* (Chicago: Univ. of Chicago Press, 2007); Najmabadi; Samar Habib, ed., *Islam and Homosexuality* (Santa Barbara: Praeger, 2010).

13. Elizabeth A. Povinelli, *The Cunning of Recognition: Indigenous Alterities and the Making of Australian Multiculturalism* (Durham: Duke Univ. Press, 2002); Minoo Moallem and Iain A. Boal, "Multicultural Nationalism and the Poetics of Inauguration," in *Between Woman and Nation: Nationalism, Transnationalism Feminism, and the State*, ed. Caren Kaplan, Norma Alarcon, and Minoo Moallem (Durham: Duke Univ. Press, 1999), 243–64; Lisa Lowe, *Immigrant Acts: On Asian American Cultural Politics* (Durham: Duke Univ. Press, 1996); Prashad.

14. Prashad, 112.

15. Cohen, *Boundaries of Blackness*.

16. I use the term "official movement logic" to refer to an ideology that reflected the views of particular leaders and came to dominate the movement. The movement's leadership included a range of identities and perspectives on these issues—including women, queer people, and men who supported an antisexist agenda. Yet the official movement logic became the normative pattern of functioning and subordinated other points of view.

17. For further analysis of the deployment of images of women in discourses of war, see Amira Jarmakani, *Imagining Arab Womanhood: The Cultural Mythology of Veils, Harems, and Belly Dancers in the U.S.* (New York: Palgrave Macmillan, 2008); Abu-Lughod, "Do Muslim Women Really Need Saving?"; and Sherene H. Razack, "Geopolitics, Culture Clash, and Gender after September 11," *Social Justice* 32, no. 4 (2005).

18. Various chapters of the Arab Women's Solidarity Association organized these conference delegations and presentations. See, for example, Nadine Naber, Eman Desouky, and Lina Baroudi, "The Forgotten '-Ism': Arab American Perspectives on Zionism, Racism, and Sexism" (http://www.awsa.net/forgottenism.pdf), published in the book *Time to Rise* by the Women of Color Resource Center. This essay was presented and distributed at the United Nations World Conference Against Racism in Durban, South Africa.

19. Puar.

7. Inanna

1. Elizabeth Winslow is a fiction writer and a graduate of the Iowa Writers' Workshop. Her translation of Dunya Mikhail's *The War Works Hard* won the PEN prize for translation in 2004 and was published by New Directions in 2005. She has had other translated poems published in *Modern Poetry in Translation*, *Poetry International*, *Words Without Borders*, *Circumference*, and *World*

Literature Today and short stories or nonfiction published in *Phoebe, Blue Mesa Review, Louisville Review,* and *Variety.*

2. Inanna is the Sumerian goddess of love, fertility, procreation, and war, the first goddess of recorded history.

9. Quandaries of Representation

1. I am thinking of such recent fictional and nonfictional confessional works as Ayaan Hirsi Ali, *The Caged Virgin: An Emancipation Proclamation for Women and Islam* (New York: Free Press, 2006); Asra Nomani, *Standing Alone in Mecca: An American Woman's Struggle for the Soul of Islam* (New York: HarperCollins, 2005); Nedjma and C. Jane Hunter, *The Almond: The Sexual Awakening of a Muslim Woman* (New York: Grove Press, 2005); and Irshad Manji, *The Trouble with Islam: A Muslim's Call for Reform in Her Faith* (New York: St. Martin's Press, 2004).

2. Virginia Woolf, *Three Guineas* (New York: Harcourt, 1938), 94.

3. Edward W. Said, *Out of Place* (New York: Vintage, 2000), 295.

11. The Pity Committee and the Careful Reader:
How Not to Buy Stereotypes about Muslim Women

1. Many Pakistani feminist and human rights groups have also worked on reforming the misogynistic rape law enshrined in the Zina Ordinance since the mid-1980s, supposedly shariah based but in fact in violation of shariah principles. See Asifa Quraishi, "Her Honor: An Islamic Critique of the Rape Laws of Pakistan from a Woman-Sensitive Position," in *Windows of Faith: Muslim Women's Scholar-Activists,* ed. Gisela Webb (Syracuse: Syracuse Univ. Press, 2000), 102–35. However, the specific problems with the rape law did not hinder prosecution in the *Mai* case. The Zina Ordinance was reformed in 2004 and is under challenge for further reform.

2. Here is the link to the interview, so that the reader can refer to it in the following discussion: http://www.Islamicamagazine.com/issue-15/interview-with-mukhtaran-mai.html.

3. Here is a link to the Kristof piece: http://query.nytimes.com/gst/fullpage.html?res=980DE1D C1438F93AA1575AC0A9629C8B63&scp=2&sq=mukhtaran%20bibi%20osama&st=cse.

4. For a fuller discussion, see Mohja Kahf, "Packaging Huda: Sha'rawi's Memoirs in the U.S. Reading Environment," in *The Politics of Reception: Globalizing Third World Women's Literature,* ed. Amal Amireh and Lisa Suhair Majaj (New York: Garland, 2000), 148–72.

5. However, sometimes the stereotyped image is forced on authors who do not want it. Susan Muaddi Darraj wrote a book, *Scheherazad's Legacy: Arab and Arab American Women on Writing,* collecting essays by sixteen Arab and Arab American women writers, none of them having to do with the stereotype in the slightest, many of them in any case not Muslim but Christian, and her publisher imposed the exotic veiled Muslim woman image on the book cover, against her will, as she disclosed to this author. Similarly, the profaith Islamic feminist Amina Wadud was forced to accept such a cliché on the cover of her book, *Inside the Gender Jihad,* as this author knows from personal communication and being consulted by Dr. Wadud during the publication process.

6. See Hadia Mubarak, "The Politicization of Gender Reform: The Islamists' Discourse on Repealing Article 340 of the Jordanian Penal Code" (master's thesis, Georgetown Univ., 2005).

7. In her International Women's Day lecture at Evergreen State College, Olympia, Wash., Mar. 9, 2007. LaDuke was speaking about her struggles to regain land and rights belonging to her Ojibwe Tribe through the White Earth Land Recovery Project.

8. See http://www.nbcactionnews.com/news/local/story.aspx?content_id=C6C407E2-D5F8-46AA-BA9E-40.

9. Martin Buber, *I and Thou: A New Translation with a Prologue*, trans. Walter Arnold Kaufman (New York: Scribner, 1970), 103.

12. History's Traces: Personal Narrative, Diaspora, and the Arab Jewish Experience

1. E-mail communication, Dec. 30, 31, 2005.

2. Chandra Talpade Mohanty, "Cartographies of Struggle: Third World Women and the Politics of Feminism," in *Third World Women and the Politics of Feminism*, ed. Chandra Mohanty, Ann Russo, and Lourdes Torres (Bloomington: Indiana Univ. Press, 1991), 33, 34.

3. Mary Louise Pratt, *Imperial Eyes: Travel Writing and Transculturation* (London: Routledge, 1992), 7.

4. Christine Stansell, "Sisterly Sentimentalism: Feminism and the Politics of Empathy," presentation at Sense and Sentiment Conference, Pomona College, Feb. 11, 2006. See Lauren Berlant, "Poor Eliza," *American Literature* 70, no. 3 (1998); and Saidiya Hartman's *Scenes of Subjection: Terror, Slavery, and Self-Making in Nineteenth-Century America* (Oxford: Oxford Univ. Press, 1997) for critiques of suffering and empathy, what Berlant acidly refers to as "pain alliances," as affective tropes around which both progressive and reactionary politics are organized.

5. See Berlant again but also Wendy Brown's *States of Injury: Power and Freedom in Late Modernity* (Princeton: Princeton Univ. Press, 1995), in which she argues that contemporary liberal politics not only encourages the formation of identities around narratives of suffering but also encourages groups to remain invested in their injured status instead of pursuing collective transformation.

6. bell hooks, "Postmodern Blackness," in *Yearning: Race, Gender and Cultural Politics* (Boston: South End Press, 1990), 23–32.

7. This recalls Frantz Fanon's famous example of being interpellated into blackness when a child looks at him and says, "Look, a Negro!" Of the experience of being a black Antillean in France he writes, "I came into the world imbued with the will to find a meaning in things, my spirit filled with the desire to attain to the source of the world, and then I found that I was an object in the midst of other objects. Sealed into that crushing objecthood" (*Black Skin, White Masks: The Experiences of a Black Man in a White World* [New York: Grove Press, 1952], 109). I might add that my mother was more than happy to explode the fantasy as well: walking out of customs and into the greeting area in Casablanca, she squinted at me and said: "*What* are you wearing?" Not much gets past my mother.

8. Caren Kaplan, "Beyond the Pale: Rearticulating U.S. Jewish Whiteness," in *Talking Visions: Multicultural Feminism in a Transnational Age*, ed. Ella Shohat (New York: New Museum of Contemporary Art, 1998), 456.

9. Daniel J. Elazar, "Can Sephardic Judaism Be Reconstructed?" Jerusalem Center for Public Affairs, http://www.jcpa.org/dje/articles3/sephardic.htm.

10. Edward Said, *Orientalism* (New York: Vintage, 1979), 25. Palestinian intellectual and activist Edward Said quotes Gramsci in his introduction to Orientalism in which he explains, "Much of my personal investment in this stuff derives from my awareness of being an 'Oriental' as a child growing up in two British colonies. . . . In many ways my study of Orientalism has been an attempt to inventory the traces upon me, the Oriental subject of the culture whose domination has been so powerful a factor in the life of all Orientals" (25).

11. M. Jacqui Alexander and Chandra Talpade Mohanty, "Introduction: Genealogies, Legacies, Movements," in *Feminist Genealogies, Colonial Legacies, Democratic Futures*, ed. M. Jacqui Alexander and Chandra Talpade Mohanty (New York: Routledge, 1997), xxi.

12. Sami Chetrit, "Mizrachi Politics in Israel: Between Integration and Alternative," *Journal of Palestine Studies* 29, no. 4 (2000): 52. See also http://www.jimena.org/forgotten/Jewish_Exodus_MiddleEast.htm. Chetrit argues that this campaign effectively set the pattern for Mizrahi political activity in Israel and that those Mizrahi leaders who worked to facilitate emigration ultimately found employment in the Mossad and the Israeli government.

13. I am not making a claim here that anti-Zionism is the same thing as anti-Semitism. I am making the claim, however, that in the history of Jewish experience in the Arab world since 1948, these two sentiments build off of, and support, each other, resulting, at times, in particularly violence against Jews in Arab countries.

14. This point was brought home to me most wrenchingly a few years ago when I realized that I had no language in common with one of my own aunts.

15. See Beverly Mizrachi, "Non-mainstream Education, Limited Mobility, and the Second Generation of Moroccan Immigrant Women: The Case of the Kindergarten Teacher's Assistant," *NASHIM: A Journal of Women's Studies and Gender Issues* 8 (Fall 5765/2004): 50–72.

16. I understand exceptionalism here in conversation with definitions of U.S. exceptionalism, in which national history is organized, both within the academy and in popular discourse, in terms of the inevitability of the specific nation-state. See also Henriette Dahan-Kalev, "You're So Pretty—You Don't Look Moroccan," *Israel Studies* 6, no. 1 (2001): 3. In this foundational paper of Mizrahi-Israeli feminism, Dahan-Kalev discusses the damaging psychological effects of Israeli education on her identity.

17. Chetrit, 1. According to the ADVA center (for information on equality and social justice in Israel), Mizrahi Jews earn, on average, 36 percent less than Ashkenazim (http://www.adva.org/pearim.htm). For more information on the history of Mizrahi radicalism in Israel, see Sami Chetrit's important film, *The Black Panthers Speak*.

18. Generally known by the problematic appellation "Berber," Imazighen is the correct name for indigenous peoples of North Africa. The singular of "Imazighen" is "Amazigh."

19. Judith Butler, "Contingent Foundations: Feminism and the Question of 'Postmodernism,'" in *Feminists Theorize the Political*, ed. Judith Butler and Joan W. Scott (New York and London: Routledge, 1992), 3–21.

20. Todd Samuel Presner writes, "These intersecting Zionist discourses extended from the aesthetic and the therapeutic to the eugenic and the colonial. . . . [I]n medicine and eugenics, the muscle Jew represents a radically hygienic and racially charged counterimage to the 'degeneracy' of the Ostjude; and in Zionist colonial discourses, the strength of the muscle Jew is the prerequisite for successfully building a nation in Palestine" ("'Clear Heads, Solid Stomachs, and Hard Muscles': Max Nordau and the Aesthetics of Jewish Regeneration," *Modernism/Modernity* 10, no. 2 [2003]: 270).

21. Ella Shohat, "Rupture and Return: Zionist Discourse and the Study of Arab Jews," *Social Text* 21, no. 2 (2003): 50.

22. Shohat, "Rupture and Return," 50; Sami Chetrit, talk given at Pomona College, Mar. 7, 2006.

23. For a reworking of this myth, see Mark Cohen, *Under Crescent and Cross: The Jews in the Middle Ages* (Princeton: Princeton Univ. Press, 1995).

24. Marrano Jews are those Jews who escaped the Spanish Inquisition or hid out in Spain by concealing their identities as Jews. In recent years many of these communities have been rediscovered; community members may still practice certain Jewish customs, either in secret or simply because they are "traditional," without knowing their Jewish roots.

25. See my article "Towards a Sephardic Jewish Renaissance," *Tikkun* (Mar.–Apr. 2002).

26. An orthodox Ashkenazic organization that is very well organized globally and seeks to return Jews to what it sees as correct religious practice.

27. Nadine Naber, "Muslim First, Arab Second: A Strategic Politics of Race and Gender," *Muslim World* 95, no. 4 (2005): 479–95.

28. Chetrit, talk given at Pomona College, Mar. 7, 2006.

29. See Henriette Dahan-Kalev, "Tensions in Israeli Feminism: The Mizrahi-Ashkenazi Rift," *Women's Studies International Forum* 24, no. 6 (2001): 669–84; and Smadar Lavie, "Academic Apartheid in Israel and the Lily White Feminism of the Upper Middle Class," *Anthropology News* (2003).

13. The Burden of Representation: When Palestinians Speak Out

1. At the time of this writing (February 2009), the number of dead keeps growing, as Gazans are still dying as a result of injuries suffered during the Israeli attack, particularly from white phosphorous–related burns.

2. See, for example, Muhammad Idries Ahmad, "BBC's 'Impartiality' Anything But," *Electronic Intifada*, http://electronicintifada.net/v2/article10275.shtml.

3. Hugh Samson, "Letter to *New York Times* Editor," *Electronic Intifada*, http://www.electronic intifada.net/v2/article3315.shtml. I would contend that numerous oppressed peoples are actually more underrepresented than the Palestinians, but that none are as misrepresented, because while underrepresented cultures rarely make the news, Palestinians do so very regularly, but in an overwhelmingly negative light—as aggressors, terrorists, and so on.

4. See http://www.nawalsaadawi.net/articlesby/racialdiscrimination.htm.

5. "There is no such thing as a Palestinian people. . . . It is not as if we came and threw them out and took their country. They didn't exist," Meir told a reporter of the *Sunday Times* (London) (June 15, 1969).

6. The complete text of the 1948 United Nations General Assembly Convention on Genocide is available at http://www.hrweb.org/legal/genocide.html. Article 1 states that "genocide, whether committed in time of peace or in time of war, is a crime under international law," while Article 2 explains, "In the present Convention, genocide means any of the following acts committed with intent to destroy, in whole or in part, a national, ethnical, racial or religious group, as such:

(a) Killing members of the group; (b) Causing serious bodily or mental harm to members of the group; (c) Deliberately inflicting on the group conditions of life calculated to bring about its physical destruction in whole or in part; (d) Imposing measures intended to prevent births within the group; (e) Forcibly transferring children of the group to another group." One could argue that the forced removal of the Palestinians from their towns and villages immediately prior to the creation of the state of Israel constituted "ethnic cleansing" rather than genocide. Nevertheless, the ongoing treatment of and official policy toward Palestinians outside of "Israel proper" constitute genocidal practices.

7. http://www.commondreams.org/news2001/0903-04.htm; Colin Powell, "World Conference Against Racism," U.S. Department of State, Sept. 3, 2001.

8. http://www.forusa.org/fellowship/nov-dec_01/ramey_elephant.html.

9. Audre Lorde, "The Transformation of Silence into Language and Action," in *Sister Outsider: Essays and Speeches* (Ithaca, N.Y.: Crossing Press, 1984), 42.

10. I have refrained from identifying the conference itself to safeguard the privacy of some of the speakers and participants who have since communicated with me via e-mail, saying that they, too, felt that the format had been problematic and thanking me for speaking out, even as they expressed reservations about being openly associated with "my" point of view.

11. Audre Lorde, "The Master's Tools Will Never Dismantle the Master's House," in *Sister Outsider: Essays and Speeches* (Ithaca, N.Y.: Crossing Press, 1984), 112.

12. Lorde, "Master's Tools," 113.

13. Since this anthology is now in print, with the editors actually mentioning, in the preface, the conflict I am discussing here, I feel that I can identify the book itself. However, since there were more than seventy contributors to the anthology, not all of whom signed up on the Listserv, and many of whom used nicknames, I cannot identify specific individuals who participated in the heated discussions that ensued. See Gloria Anzaldúa and AnaLouise Keating, eds., *This Bridge We Call Home: Radical Visions for Transformation* (New York: Routledge, 2002).

14. Gloria Anzaldúa and Cherríe Moraga, eds., *This Bridge Called My Back: Writings by Radical Women of Color* (New York: Kitchen Table Women of Color Press, 1981).

15. Anzaldúa and Keating, 11. This is the actual text of the call for submissions for the collection that became *This Bridge We Call Home:*

This Bridge Called My Back, 20 Years Later—Call for Submissions
From: AnaLouise Keating

Gloria Anzaldúa and I are co-editing an anthology, THIS BRIDGE CALLED MY BACK, 20 YEARS LATER. We'd welcome contributions (essays, poems, personal narratives, fiction, stories, artwork, etc.) that addressed the impact of recent technology (the Internet, etc.) on BRIDGE-related issues, such as the following (#1 & #2 seem especially appropriate):

1. New Issues which have arisen since THIS BRIDGE's publication. What new issues confront us today, almost twenty years after THIS BRIDGE's publication? (Environmental issues? Issues related to aging & healthcare?)

2. Envisioning Change. Where do we go from here? What can the political visions, the calls for revolutionary change, and the desire to create new forms of coalition articulated in THIS BRIDGE teach us as we enter the 21st century? How might THIS BRIDGE help us to envision change?

3. Influence. What impact has THIS BRIDGE made on individual women, on feminist/womanist theorizing, on ethnic studies, on queer theory, on the academy, on US feminisms, on feminism in other countries, on the development of an international feminism?

4. The current status of issues raised in THIS BRIDGE. To what extent have the challenges BRIDGE contributors made in this groundbreaking anthology been met? To what extent do the challenges remain unfulfilled? How much progress have we made?

We welcome contributions from people of all colors and genders. Papers (approximately 10 to 30 double-spaced pages for essays by August 31, 1999. Send two copies of all submissions, a short bio, & disk versions of both (wordperfect or microsoft word).

16. Max Wolf Valerio, "Now That You're a White Man: Changing Sex in a Postmodern World—Being, Becoming, and Borders," in *This Bridge We Call Home: Radical Visions for Transformation*, ed. Gloria Anzaldúa and AnaLouise Keating (New York: Routledge, 2002), 247. It is easy to dismiss criticism of Valerio's essay as transphobic, hence I think it important to explain that my discomfort with the inclusion of this essay stems from Valerio's celebration of the power of privilege, whereas the reader may have wished to see an articulation of the difficulties and challenges of being transgender, a conscious wrestling with the complexities of becoming "the colonizer," after having been colonized. Max had first appeared as Anita Valerio, a Native American woman, in *This Bridge Called My Back*, and Anita's essay seems to be the only reason Max is included in *This Bridge We Call Home*, for there is nothing "radical" about his essay.

17. Anzaldúa and Keating, 4.

18. Lorde, "Transformation of Silence," 42.

19. http://www.johnkerry.com.

20. See, for example, Stephen Zunes, "Is Kerry Really More Open than Bush to Alternative Foreign Policy Perspectives?" *Common Dreams*, http://www.commondreams.org/views2004/0915-13.htm.

16. *Arabiya* Made Invisible: Between Marginalization of Agency and Silencing of Dissent

1. See Nikki Craft, "A Call on Feminists to Protest the War Against Afghanistan," Nov. 8, 2001, Available at http://www.nostatusquo.com/ACLU/terrorism/terrorism1.html. (Feminist Majority representatives testify before Congress in support of war.)

2. In 1948, 100,000 of the 800,000 indigenous Arab-Palestinian population did not flee, and those who remained have now grown to a population of 1.2 million, constituting 20 percent of the Israeli population. According to a study done by Salman Abu-Sitta, that population will outnumber the Israeli population by 2025. What does that mean for Israel?

3. "Between ourselves it must be clear that there is no room for both peoples together in this country. We shall not achieve our goal if the Arabs are in this small country. There is no other way than to transfer the Arabs from here to neighboring countries—all of them. Not one village, not one tribe should be left" (Joseph Weitz, head of the Jewish Agency's Colonization Department in 1940, from "A Solution to the Refugee Problem," Joseph Weitz, Davar, September 29, 1967, cited in Uri Davis and Norton Mevinsky, eds., *Documents from Israel, 1967–1973*, 21).

4. E-mail from "Oly" to Boalt Hall Women's Association Listserv, "Women in Black Rally on Friday," Mar. 2005.

5. Cynthia Enloe, *Bananas, Beaches, and Bases: Making Feminist Sense of International Politics* (Berkeley and Los Angeles: University of California Press, 1990), 56.

6. Campus Watch is a watchdog organization that monitors universities for professors and students who express criticism of U.S. foreign policy vis-à-vis the Middle East, particularly anti-Israel sentiments.

7. Abraham Miller, *Revising History at Berkeley: Israeli "Occupation 101*," Feb. 16, 2005, http://www.campus-watch.org/article/id/1656.

17. On Rachel Corrie, Palestine, and Feminist Solidarity

1. Susan Sontag, "On Courage and Resistance," *Nation*, May 5, 2003, 11.

2. June Jordan, "Moving Towards Home," in *Living Room: New Poems by June Jordan* (New York: Thunders Mouth Press, 1985), 132. Special thanks to Suheir Hammad for pointing out to me

Jordan's verb emphasis, "I am become a Palestinian." I interpret this to mean that the process of "becoming other" is a process of identification that is never completed. Certainly, as Rachel Corrie consistently reminds us in her writings, her white, international, U.S. privilege set her apart from the Palestinians; it also in many ways accounts for her emergence as an international figure of justice and the widespread popularity of her story. Nevertheless, the criticism, censorship, and vilification of Rachel resonate with charges projected onto the Palestinian people in their struggle for self-determination.

3. Arundhati Roy, *An Ordinary Person's Guide to Empire* (Cambridge, Mass.: South End Press, 2004), 41.

4. Zillah Eisenstein, *Against Empire: Feminisms, Racism, and the West* (London: Zed Books, 2004), xix; Lisa Suhair Majaj, "Arab-American Ethnicity: Locations, Coalitions, and Cultural Negotiations," in *Arabs in America: Building a New Future*, ed. Michael Suleiman (Philadelphia: Temple Univ. Press, 1999), 332.

5. Rachel Corrie, "Rachel's War," *Guardian*, Mar. 17, 2003.

6. Corrie, "Rachel's War."

7. Edward W. Said, "The Meaning of Rachel Corrie: Of Dignity and Solidarity," in *Peace under Fire: Israel/Palestine and the International Solidarity Movement*, ed. Josie Sandercock et al. (London: Verso, 2004), xxii.

8. See Nadine Naber, "So Our History Doesn't Become Your Future: The Local and Global Politics of Coalition Building Post–September 11th," *Journal of Asian and African Studies* (Oct. 2002): 223.

9. Sontag, 11; Imad Jadaa, "The Beautiful Face of the United States," *Juventud Rebelde*, Mar. 18, 2003; Ahmed El Khameesy, "Rachel Corrie: The Conscience of a Rose," trans. Somaya Ramadan, *Akhbar El Adab* (Cairo), Mar. 2004; Rebecca Gould, "Rachel Corrie: A Witness for Our Times," in *To Kill, to Die: Feminist Contestations on Gender and Political Violence*, newsletter (New York: New School for Social Research, Mar. 2004), 3; June Jordan, "Life after Lebanon," in *On Call: Political Essays* (Boston: South End Press, 1985), 84; Corrie, "Rachel's War."

10. Corrie, "Rachel's War"; Rabab Abdulhadi and Reem Abdelhadi, "Nomadic Existence: Exile, Gender, and Palestine (an E-mail Conversation Between Sisters)," in *This Bridge We Call Home: Radical Visions for Transformation*, ed. Gloria Anzaldúa and AnaLouise Keating (New York: Routledge, 2002), 168; Edward W. Said, *The Question of Palestine* (1979; reprint, New York: Vintage Books, 1992), 112, 65.

11. Therese Saliba, "Resisting Invisibility: Arab Americans in Academia and Activism," in *Arabs in America: Building a New Future*, ed. Michael W. Suleiman (Philadelphia: Temple Univ. Press, 1999), 305.

12. As of this writing, more than five years after her death, a permanent memorial to Rachel has yet to be established on the Evergreen campus or in the Olympia community.

13. Seth Goldstein and Mohammed Abu-Nimer, *The Search for Peace: The Palestinian-Israeli Conflict; Difficult Dialogues*, video recording (Olympia, Wash.: TVW, 2004).

14. Joel Beinin, "The New American McCarthyism: Policing Thought about the Middle East," *Race and Class* 46, no. 1 (2004): 112; Judith Butler, "The Charge of Anti-Semitism: Jews, Israel, and the Risks of Public Critique," in *Precarious Life: The Powers of Mourning and Violence* (London: Verso, 2004), 103, 115–16.

15. Jordan, "Life after Lebanon," 82–83.

16. This bill later became H.R. 509. See "A Sample of Opinions on Title VI, H.R. 509 (formerly H.R. 3077) and Middle East Studies" (http://programs.ssrc.org/mena/MES_Opinions).

17. Beinin, 104.

18. Salah D. Hassan, "Arabs, Race, and the Post–September 11 National Security State," *Middle East Report* 224 (2002): 18; Jordan, "Life after Lebanon," 81 (emphasis added).

19. In Rachel's e-mails to her mother, she defends her use of the term "genocide," enumerating Israeli house demolitions; the destruction of orchards, greenhouses, farmland, and livelihoods; the chronic malnutrition; ongoing military violence; enclosure of the population; and so on, as the "destruction of the ability of a particular group of people to survive" (*Let Me Stand Alone: The Journals of Rachel Corrie* [New York: W. W. Norton, 2008], 271–74).

20. Human Rights Watch, "Razing Rafah: Mass Home Demolitions in the Gaza Strip," Oct. 18, 2004 (http://www.hrw.org/reports/2004/rafah1004/); Mona El Farra, "Diary of the Dispossessed: Women's Misery and Suffering under Israeli Occupation," in *Women and the Politics of Military Confrontation: Palestinian and Israeli Gendered Narratives of Dislocation*, ed. Nahla Abdo and Ronit Lentin (New York: Bergham Books, 2002), 159.

21. I use the term "ethnic cleansing" here to characterize a clearing process that is taking place in parts of the Palestinian territories, particularly along the border areas with the Separation Wall, as well as in East Jerusalem. Home demolitions along the Rafah-Egypt border, as well as the destruction of homes and farmlands in the path of the Wall (which was declared illegal by the International Court of Justice in 2004), effectively "cleanse" the borderlands of Palestinians, while taking more land for Israeli settlements and for access to water resources, purportedly for Israeli security concerns. This activity is not the same as the "ethnic cleansing" or expulsion of 750,000 Palestinians in 1948, which included the destruction of more than four hundred Palestinian villages; rather, it is a process of clearing Palestinians from areas deemed desirable to Israel as it moves to unilaterally declare its borders. In East Jerusalem, this process is even more bureaucratic and systematically limits Palestinian presence in the occupied city. Throughout the territories, it is a process that combines removing Palestinians from desirable land and containing them in smaller and smaller spaces, marked by checkpoints and the Separation Wall. In this sense, the apartheid analogy may be more accurate, but it is not possible without clearing Palestinians from considerable areas of land, as Rachel witnessed in Rafah. Israeli activist Michel Warschawski uses the term "ethnic cleansing" to also describe the process by which Israel was emptied of Palestinian workers and the territories were "sealed off" in the 1990s (*On the Border*, trans. Levi Laub [Cambridge, Mass.: South End Press, 2005], 150).

22. Thalif Deen, "Palestinian Women Hard Hit by Israeli Occupation," United Nations, Feb. 2004 (http://www.palestinemonitor.org/Reports/palestinian_women_hit_hard_by_occupation); James Bennet, "In Palestinian Children, Signs of Increasing Malnutrition," *New York Times*, July 26, 2002; World Bank, "West Bank and Gaza: Economic Development and Prospects, March 2008" (http://go.worldbank.org/A6Y2KDMCJ0); Deen.

23. For statistics on Palestinian deaths, see "UN Press Conference on Gaza Humanitarian Crisis," http://www.un.org/News/briefings/docs/2009/090120_Gaza. Also, more recent statistics can be found at the Web site of the Palestinian Centre for Human Rights: http://www.pchrgaza.org/portal/en/. In the same period, thirteen Israelis were killed, ten of them soldiers.

24. For more detailed accounts of these violations, see Al-Haq, "Legal Brief on Gaza" (http://www.alhaq.org/pdfs/Legal_Brief_Gaza_Cast_Lead_Jan.pdf); "UN Press Conference on Gaza

Humanitarian Situation" (un.org/News/briefings/docs/2009/090120_Gaza); Amnesty International, *The Conflict in Gaza: A Briefing on Applicable Law, Investigation, and Accountability* (London: Amnesty International, 2009); and International Committee of the Red Cross, "Gaza: Emergency Aid Alone Is Not Enough" (http://icrc.org/web.eng/siteeng0.nsf/html/Palestine-update-220109?opendocument), as a few examples.

25. See, for example, Fida Qishta and Peter Beaumont, "Israel Accused of War Crimes over Assault on Gaza Village," *Observer*, Jan. 18, 2009; and Al-Haq, "Re: Gross Human Rights Violations and War Crimes in the Gaza Strip," Jan. 7, 2009 (http://alhaq.or/etemplate.php?id=140).

26. Gould, 3; *Congressional Record*, "Support for Israel in Its Battle with Hamas and the Israeli-Palestinian Peace Process," S.R. 10, Jan. 8, 2009; *Congressional Record*, "Recognizing Israel's Right to Defend Itself Against Attacks from Gaza," H.R. 34, Jan. 9, 2009.

27. See Naomi Klein, "On Rescuing Private Lynch and Forgetting Rachel Corrie," *Guardian*, May 22, 2003. Tom Hurndall and James Miller (United Kingdom) were killed by the IDF, and Brian Avery (United States) was severely wounded in the weeks following Rachel's death.

28. For more details on this case, see Tom Wright and Therese Saliba, "Rachel Corrie's Case for Justice," Counterpunch.org, Mar. 15–16, 2008 (http://counterpunch.org/wright03152008/html).

29. For information on the Olympia-Rafah Sister City Project, see http://orscp.org.

30. Fida Qishta, personal conversation, Apr. 20, 2006.

31. "Israeli Attacks Kill over 310 in Gaza in One of Israel's Bloodiest Attacks on Palestinians since 1948," *Democracy Now!* Dec. 29, 2008 (http://www.democracynow.org/2008/12/29/israeli_attacks_kill_over_310_in).

32. *Washington Post*, Mar. 16, 2004.

33. See http://rachelswords.org.

34. Philip Weiss, "Why These Tickets Are Too Hot for New York," *Nation*, Apr. 3, 2006, 14, 13.

35. Wright and Saliba, "Rachel Corrie's Case for Justice"; Corrie, *Let Me Stand Alone*, 290;

36. Said, "Meaning of Rachel Corrie," xxii; Nada Elia, "The 'White' Sheep of the Family: But Bleaching Is Like Starvation," in *This Bridge We Call Home: Radical Visions for Transformation*, ed. Gloria Anzaldúa and AnaLouise Keating (New York: Routledge, 2002), 230; Chandra Talpade Mohanty, *Feminism Without Borders: Decolonizing Theory, Practicing Solidarity* (Durham, N.C.: Duke Univ. Press, 2003), 124.

37. See Eleanor Adbella Doumato, *Women and Globalization in the Arab Middle East: Gender, Economy, and Society* (Boulder, Colo.: Lynne Rienner, 2003).

38. See Hammad's Web site: http://suheirhammad.org.

39. Suheir Hammad, "On the Brink of . . . ," in *Russell Simmons Def Poetry Jam on Broadway . . . and More*, ed. Danny Simmons (New York: Atria Books, 2004), 197.

40. Gila Svirsky, "Feminist Peace Activism During the al-Aqsa Intifada," in *Women and the Politics of Military Confrontation: Palestinian and Israeli Gendered Narratives of Dislocation*, ed. Nahla Abdo and Ronit Lentin (New York: Bergham Books, 2002), 244; Corrie, "Rachel's War."

41. See Mohanty, *Feminism Without Borders*; and Tom Wright and Therese Saliba, *Checkpoint: The Palestinians after Oslo* (Arab Film Distribution, 1997).

19. Dissidents, Displacements, and Diasporas: An Interview with Dena Al-Adeeb

1. Before the emergence of the state of Iraq, citizens of Iraq had either an Ottoman *taba'iyya* (affiliation) or Iranian *taba'iyya*. Some Iraqis chose the Iranian *taba'iyya* even though they were not

of Iranian descent because it could lead to avoiding the Ottoman draft. Some members of my family adopted the Iranian *taba'iyya* to avoid the Ottoman draft, and some were actually of Iranian descent. Saddam Hussein's deportation campaigns were an attempt to ethnically cleanse Iraq of Iraqis of Iranian descent (especially those persons in opposition, ruling elites, and any who had economic wealth and power).

2. The Mukhabarat are the Iraqi secret police that operated in countries around the world as well as in Iraq.

3. Karbala is a city in Iraq, situated approximately fifty-five miles southwest of Baghdad, on the western bank of the Euphrates and at the right side of Husainiya Creek. It witnessed the bloody battle that took place in AD 680 between the army of the Umayyad Caliph Yazid Bin Mu'awiya and Imam Husayn—the son of Ali and the grandson of Prophet Mohammed—and his followers, who were on route to claim leadership over Kufa. This battle resulted in the brutal massacre of all male members of *ahl-al-bayt*—the house of the Prophet—while women were taken as *sabaya* (captives). The city has become a sacred place of pilgrimage—both physical and spiritual—for the redemption of suffering by Shiite Muslims.

4. The 'Ashura rituals commemorating the martyrdom of Imam Husayn by Shiites take place every year on the tenth of Muharram of the Muslim Hijri Lunar month and last for forty days. The ritual commemoration may involve the physical or spiritual pilgrimage of Shiites to Karbala, where the battle of Karbala took place in AD 680. The massacre of Husayn and his seventy-two followers in Karbala is the central point of the Shia narrative.

20. Arab American Feminisms: Mobilizing the Politics of Invisibility

1. miriam cooke and Margot Badran, *Opening the Gates: A Century of Arab Feminist Writing* (Bloomington: Indiana Univ. Press, 1990).

2. Lila Abu-Lughod, "Do Muslim Women Really Need Saving? Anthropological Reflections on Cultural Relativism and Its Others," *American Anthropologist* 104, no. 3 (2002): 783–90; Charles Hirschkind and Saba Mahmood, "Feminism, the Taliban, and the Politics of Counter-Insurgency," *Anthropological Quarterly* 72, no. 2 (2002): 339–54.

3. Leila Ahmed, *Women and Gender in Islam: Historical Roots of a Modern Debate* (New Haven, Conn.: Yale Univ. Press, 1992).

4. Marnia Lazreg, *The Eloquence of Silence: Algerian Women in Question* (New York: Routledge, 1994); Frantz Fanon, *A Dying Colonialism*, trans. Haakon Chevalier (New York: Grove Press, 1965).

5. Nilufer Gole, *The Forbidden Modern* (Ann Arbor: Univ. of Michigan Press, 1996); Qasim Amin, "The Liberation of Women," "The New Woman": Two Documents in the History of Egyptian Feminism, trans. Samiha Peterson (Cairo: American Univ. in Cairo Press, 1992); Abu-Lughod, *Remaking Women*; Joan Wallach Scott, *The Politics of the Veil* (Princeton: Princeton Univ. Press, 2007).

6. For exceptions, see Lara Deeb, *An Enchanted Modern: Gender and Public Piety in Shi'i Lebanon* (Princeton: Princeton Univ. Press, 2006); Homa Hoodfar, "The Veil in Their Minds and on Our Heads: Veiling Practices and Muslim Women," in *The Politics of Culture in the Shadow of Capital*, ed. Lisa Lowe and David Lloyd (Durham, N.C.: Duke Univ. Press, 1997), 248–79; Fadwa el Guindi, *Veil: Modesty, Privacy, Resistance* (Oxford: Berg, 1999); and Saba Mahmood, *The Politics of Piety: The Islamic Revival and the Feminist Subject* (Princeton: Princeton Univ. Press, 2005).

7. Minoo Moallem, *Between Warrior Brother and Veiled Sister: Islamic Fundamentalism and Patriarchy in Iran* (Berkeley and Los Angeles: Univ. of California Press, 2005), 2.

8. Alisa Bierria, Mayaba Liebenthal, and Incite! Women of Color Against Violence, "To Render Ourselves Visible: Women of Color Organizing and Hurricane Katrina," in *What Lies Beneath: Katrina, Race, and the State of the Nation*, ed. South End Press Collective (Cambridge, Mass.: South End Press, 2007), 32.

9. Phyllis Chesler, *The Death of Feminism: What's Next in the Struggle for Women's Freedom* (New York: Palgrave Macmillan, 2005).

10. Christina Hoff Sommers, "The Subjection of Islamic Women," *Weekly Standard*, May 21, 2007.

11. For further critique of these "native testimonials," see Saba Mahmood, "Feminism, Democracy, and Empire: Islam and the War of Terror," in *Women's Studies on the Edge*, ed. Joan Wallach Scott (Durham, N.C.: Duke University Press, 2008), 81–114.

12. Leila Ahmed, "Western Ethnocentrism and Perceptions of the Harem," *Feminist Studies* 8, no. 3 (1982): 521, 522.

13. David Horowitz, "Islamo-Fascism Awareness Week," *Front Page*, Sept. 21, 2007 (http://www.frontpagemag.com/Articles).

14. Robert Spencer, "Islamic Misogyny," *Front Page*, Jan. 4, 2008 (http://www.frontpagemag.com/Articles); Horowitz, "Islamo-Fascism Awareness Week."

15. David Horowitz, "A Response to Feminists on the Violent Oppression of Women in Islam," *Front Page*, Jan. 24, 2008 (http://www.frontpagemag.com/Articles).

16. Katha Pollitt, "Sign the Open Letter from American Feminists," *Blog: And Another Thing* (http://www.thenation.com/blogs/anotherthing?pid=273005).

17. Amira Jarmakani, *Imagining Arab Womanhood: The Cultural Mythology of Veils, Harems, and Belly Dancers in the U.S.* (New York: Palgrave Macmillan, 2008).

18. Amal Amireh, "Framing Nawal el Saadawi: Arab Feminism in a Transnational World," *Signs: Journal of Women in Culture and Society* 26, no. 1 (2000): 224.

19. See also Susan Muaddi Darraj in this volume.

20. Amira Jarmakani, "Belly Dancing for Liberation," in *Arabs in the Americas: Interdisciplinary Essays on the Arab Diaspora*, ed. Darcy Zabel (New York: Peter Lang Press, 2006), 145–68.

21. Mitsuye Yamada, "Asian Pacific American Women and Feminism," in *This Bridge Called My Back: Writings By Radical Women of Color*, ed. Cherríe Moraga and Gloria Anzaldúa (New York: Kitchen Table Women of Color Press, 1981), 71; Mitsuye Yamada, "Invisibility Is an Unnatural Disaster: Reflections of an Asian American Woman," in *This Bridge Called My Back: Writings by Radical Women of Color*, ed. Cherríe Moraga and Gloria Anzaldúa (New York: Kitchen Table Women of Color Press, 1981), 37.

22. Beshara Doumani, "Between Coercion and Privatization," in *Academic Freedom after September 11* (New York: Zone Books, 2006), 11; Horowitz, "Islamo-Fascism Awareness Week."

23. Chela Sandoval, "Feminism and Racism: A Report on the 1981 National Women's Studies Association Conference," in *Making Face, Making Soul/Haciendo Caras*, ed. Gloria Anzaldúa (San Francisco: Aunt Lute, 1990), 66.

24. Sandoval, 66, 67.

22. Personal and Political: The Dynamics of Arab American Feminism

1. See, for example, Gloria Steinem, *Revolution from Within: A Book of Self-Esteem* (New York: Little, Brown, 1993).

2. J. A. Khawaja, "The Queen, Carcasses, and Other Things," in *Food for Our Grandmothers: Writings by Arab-American and Arab-Canadian Feminists*, ed. Joanna Kadi (Cambridge, Mass.: South End Press, 1994), 43.

3. Nada Elia, "A Woman's Place Is in the Struggle," in *Food for Our Grandmothers: Writings by Arab-American and Arab-Canadian Feminists*, ed. Joanna Kadi (Cambridge, Mass.: South End Press, 1994), 118.

4. Lisa Suhair Majaj, "Boundaries: Arab/American," in *Food for Our Grandmothers: Writings by Arab-American and Arab-Canadian Feminists*, ed. Joanna Kadi (Cambridge, Mass.: South End Press, 1994), 77–78.

5. Evelyn Shakir, *Bint Arab: Arab and Arab American Women in the United States* (Westport, Conn.: Praeger, 1997), 146.

6. Shakir, 146.

7. Mona Fayad, "The Arab Woman and I," in *Food for Our Grandmothers: Writings by Arab-American and Arab-Canadian Feminists*, ed. Joanna Kadi (Cambridge, Mass.: South End Press, 1994), 170.

8. Fayad, 171.

9. Geraldine Brooks, *Nine Parts of Desire: The Hidden World of Islamic Women* (New York: Anchor Books, 1995), 5–6, 54.

10. Brooks, 52.

11. Shakir, 3.

23. Teaching Scriptural Texts in the Classroom: The Question of Gender

1. Historically, the split in Islam along Sunni-Shi'i lines occurred after the death of Prophet Muhammad in AD 632. The Muslim community differed on the question of succession to Muhammad. As a result, two distinct doctrines developed, the Sunni caliphate and the Shi'i imamate. For Sunnis, the caliph is the elected successor to the Prophet in matters political and military but not religious. In contrast, for the Shi'i, the leadership of the community is vested in the imam, who is divinely ordained and occupies a religio-political post. For more, see John L. Esposito, *Islam: The Straight Path*, expanded ed. (Oxford: Oxford Univ. Press, 1988), 45–47.

2. Such as Farid Esack, *The Qur'an: A Short Introduction*, (Oxford: Oneworld, 2002); and Asma Barlas, *"Believing Women" in Islam: Unreading Patriarchal Interpretations of the Qur'an* (Austin: Univ. of Texas Press, 2002).

3. Thomas L. Friedman, "Cukoo in Carolina," *New York Times*, Aug. 28, 2002.

4. For instance, UNC's home Web site refers to the incident under "Summer Reading Controversy."

5. Asma Barlas, "Texts and Textualities: The Qur'an, *Tafsir*, and *Ahadith*," in *"Believing Women" in Islam: Unreading Patriarchal Interpretations of the Qur'an* (Austin: Univ. of Texas Press, 2002), 50.

6. This topic is a hotly debated issue among scholars of Islam. Regardless of whether the door of *ijtihad* has been actually closed, the consensus of the community established by al-Shafi'i is a block in the way of any serious rereading and challenging the textual interpretations established during the doctrinal development of Islam. Any novel reinterpretation of texts is only possible and only if the opinions of the Muslim scholars and jurists are stripped of the sacredness that is usually accorded to the Quran.

7. John L. Esposito, "Religious Life: Belief and Practice," in *Islam: The Straight Path* (Oxford: Oxford Univ. Press, 1988), 78.

8. Moulouk Berry, "Radical Transitions: Shifting Gender Discourses in Lebanese Muslim Shi'i Jurisprudence and Ideology, 1960–1999" (Ph.D. diss., University of Michigan, 2002), 77–78.

9. A considerable number of class sessions were spent in dealing with cases of interpretations of Quranic verses and the new emerging legal rulings on gender, particularly those rulings dealing with personal status laws. Many of my students believed in the universal applicability of the key words "to excel" and "a degree above" (*faddala* and *darajah*) in the controversial Quranic verses 4:34 and 2:28, though restricted by some contemporary legal scholars to marital life and the financial obligation of the husband. The verses read as follows: "Men have authority (*qawwamuna*) over women on account of the qualities with which God hath caused the one of them to excel (*faddala*) over the other and for what they spent of their property" and "and for the woman shall be similar rights (over men) in fairness, and for men (their rights) on women, is a degree above (*wa-lil-rijali 'alayhinna darajah*); and God is Mighty, Wise." The two key Quranic terms *qawwam* and *fadl* in this context, for instance, have been interpreted by some Shi'i scholars to indicate that men are intrinsically superior to women; therefore, in the general affairs of life, men have dominion over women. This interpretation is owing to the interpreter's already preconceived patriarchal notions of gender inequality—despite the fact that other verses in the Quran establish gender equality. For example, one of the students, Adel, whose parents came from Lebanon but who was born in the United States and lived all his life in Dearborn, Michigan, insisted that women were emotional and thus could not be trusted with political, legal, and military posts. Adel's insistence to uphold such interpretations was the result of the transpositions between the Quran and its exegesis. As Barlas argues in this context, "*Tafsir* [exegesis] became confused with the Qur'an and was thus given a suprahistorical status" ("Texts and Textualities," 38).

10. "So their Lord did respond to them (saying) 'I will not suffer the work of any of you that worketh to be lost, be he male or female, the one of you being from the other'" (3:195); "And covet not that by which God hath raised some of you above others; for men shall have of what they earn; and for women shall have of what they earn; and ask God of His Grace; Verily, God is (very well) in the Know of all things" (4:32); "O' (Our) Prophet (Muhammad!) when come unto thee believer women pledging that they will associate not aught with God, and they will steal not, and they will commit not adultery and kill not their children, and they will utter not slander, nor utter any falsehood which they had forged themselves between their hands and their feet and they will not disobey thee in what is fair, then accept thou their pledge, and ask forgiveness for them from God is Oft-Forgiving, the Most Merciful" (60:12); and "Whosoever did good, whether male or female, and he be a believer, then We will certainly make him live a life good and pure, and certainly We will give them their return with the best of what they were doing." Quoted from the *Holy Qur'an*, trans. Ahmed Ali, s.v. "Mir."

11. Leila Ahmed, *Women and Gender in Islam: Historical Roots of a Modern Debate* (New Haven, Conn.: Yale Univ. Press, 1992), 238.

12. C. Belesey quoted in Barlas, "Text and Textualities," 44.

27. The Memory of Your Hands Is a Rainbow

1. Khaled Mattawa is the author of four books of poetry: *Tocqueville* (Kalamazoo, Mich.: New Issues Press, 2010), *Amorisco* (Keene, N.Y.: Ausable Press, 2008), *Zodiac of Echoes* (Keene, N.Y.: Ausable Press, 2003), and *Ismailia Eclipse* (Riverdale, N.Y.: Sheep Meadow Press, 1996). He has translated six books of contemporary Arab poetry by Joumana Haddad, Saadi Youssef, Fadhil Al-Azzawi, Hatif

Janabi, and Maram Al-Massri and coedited two anthologies of Arab American literature. Mattawa was born in Libya and came to the United States in his teens. Mattawa is an assistant professor in the Department of English at the University of Michigan.

28. You Are a 14-Year-Old Arab Chick Who Just Moved to Texas

1. Excerpted from Randa Jarrar, *A Map of Home* (New York: Other Press, 2008).

29. The Long Road Home

1. Edward W. Said, "Invention, Memory, and Place," *Critical Inquiry* 26, no. 2 (2000): 184.

2. Ellen Fleischmann, *The Nation and Its New Women: The Palestinian Women's Movement, 1920–1948* (Berkeley and Los Angeles: University of California Press, 2003), 51, 225–26.

3. Rosemary quoted from a talk delivered at a conference called "Between the Archival Forest and the Anecdotal Trees: A Multi Disciplinary Approach to Palestinian Social History?" Institute of Law, Birzeit University, Nov. 21–22, 2003.

30. The Legacy of Exile: An Excerpt

1. Rahbani Brothers, "Nassam Alayna al-Hawa," on *Safarbarlek/Bint el-Haress* (Digital Press Hellas, 2000).

2. Billie Holiday, "Summertime," on *The Best of Billie Holiday* (Intersound, 2000).

31. Stealth Muslim

1. "How to Tell Your Friends from the Japs," *Time*, Dec. 22, 1941, 33.

2. See Nadine Naber, introduction to *Race and Arab Americans Before and After September 11th: From Invisible Citizens to Visible Subjects*, ed. Nadine Naber and Amaney Jamal (Syracuse: Syracuse Univ. Press, 2008).

3. Vikram Dodd, "Muslim Women Advised to Abandon *Hijab* to Avoid Attack," *Guardian*, Aug. 4, 2005 (http://www.guardian.co.uk/uk/2005/aug/04/race.july7).

4. Evelyn Alsultany, "*Los Intersticios*: Recasting Moving Selves," in *This Bridge We Call Home: Radical Visions for Transformation*, ed. Gloria Anzaldúa and AnaLouise Keating (New York: Routledge, 2002).

5. See Rabab Abdulhadi, "Tread Lightly: Teaching Gender and Sexuality in the Time of War," *Journal of Women's History* 17, no. 4 (2005): 154–58.

6. For scholarship, see, for example, Leila Ahmed, *Women and Gender in Islam: Historical Roots of a Modern Debate* (New Haven, Conn.: Yale Univ. Press, 1992); Yvonne Yazbeck Haddad and John L. Esposito, eds., *Islam, Gender, and Social Change* (New York: Oxford Univ. Press, 1998); Suad Joseph and Susan Slyomovics, *Women and Power in the Middle East* (Philadelphia: Univ. of Pennsylvania Press, 2000); Deniz Kandiyoti, ed., *Gendering the Middle East: Emerging Perspectives* (Syracuse: Syracuse Univ. Press, 1996); Fatima Mernissi, *The Veil and the Male Elite: A Feminist Interpretation of Women's Rights in Islam* (Reading, Mass.: Addison-Wesley, 1991); Barbara Stowasser, *Women in the Qur'an, Traditions, and Interpretations* (New York: Oxford Univ. Press, 1994); Amina Waddud, *Qur'an and Woman: Rereading the Sacred Text from a Woman's Perspective* (New York: Oxford Univ. Press, 1999); and Asma Barlas, *"Believing Women" in Islam: Unreading Patriarchal Interpretations of the Qur'an* (Austin: Univ. of Texas Press, 2002); and Qadreya Hussein, *Famous Women of the Islamic World (Shahirat al nissaa fil alam al Islamy)*, trans. Abdel-Aziz El-Khanki (Cairo: Women and Memory Forum, 2004).

7. Edward W. Said, "Arabs, Islam, and the Dogmas of the West," *New York Times Book Review*, Oct. 31, 1976, republished in *Orientalism: A Reader*, ed. A. L. Macfie (New York: New York Univ. Press, 2001), 104–5.

8. See Said, *Orientalism*, 6. See also Melani McAlister, *Epic Encounters: Culture, Media, and U.S. Interests in the Middle East since 1945* (Berkeley and Los Angeles: Univ. of California Press, 2005), 82.

9. Nicholas D. Kristof, "The Push to 'Otherize' Obama," *New York Times*, Sept. 21, 2008 (http://www.nytimes.com/2008/09/21/opinion/21kristof.html); Charles A. Radin, "False Alarms," *Jewish Advocate*, Sept. 19, 2008, 13 (http://jadvocate.tclhosting.co.uk/this_weeks_issue/columnists/radin/?content_id=5567); Fraser Sherman, "Beware! The Islamofascists Walk among Us!" *McClatchy-Tribune Business News*, May 31, 2008 (http://www.thedestinlog.com/opinion/among_4840_article.html/beware_islamofascists.html).

10. Debbie Schlussel, "Barack Hussein Obama: Once a Muslim, Always a Muslim," Debbieschlussel.com, Dec. 18, 2006 (http://www.debbieschlussel.com/archives/2006/12/barack_hussein.html); Ben Smith and Jonathan Martin, "Untraceable E-mails Spread Obama Rumor," Politico.com, Oct. 13, 2007, http://www.politico.com/news/stories/1007/6314.html; Michael Barbaro, "Bloomberg, in Florida, Blasts Rumor about Obama," *New York Times*, June 21, 2008 (http://www.nytimes.com/2008/06/21/nyregion/21jewish.html).

11. Amy Chozick, "Campaign '08: Obama Walks a Fine Line with Muslims; Campaign's Efforts to Dispel Rumors Risk Offending a Base of Support," *Wall Street Journal*, June 23, 2008, A10 (http://online.wsj.com/article/SB121417738005395419.html?mod=googlenews_wsj).

12. Andrea Elliott, "Muslim Voters Detect a Snub from Obama," *New York Times*, June 24, 2008 (http://www.nytimes.com/2008/06/24/us/politics/24muslim.html).

13. Ed Griffin-Nolan, "Pulpit Bullied," *Syracuse New Times*, June 18, 2008, 4 (http://www.syracusenewtimes.com/index.php?option=com_content&task=view&id=2008&Itemid=147); Kristof.

32. Where Is Home? Fragmented Lives, Borders Crossings, and the Politics of Exile

1. It is interesting to note that more than nine years since September 11, 2001, Arabs and Muslims are being told to "go home" or "get the . . . out of the USA," as an e-mail told me after my name appeared on a press release by the California Scholars for Academic Freedoms condemning the Israeli war on Gaza (http://electronicintifada.net/v2/article10111.shtml).

2. During the 2002 Israeli invasion of West Bank cities, my youngest brother, Amer, used to broadcast a "road situation bulletin," on his radio station, Tariq Al Mahabbeh, TMFM, 97.7 FM, in Nablus. Each "Road Situation Bulletin" would inform Palestinian drivers where the Israeli military checkpoints were for that day and time, which roads were easier to take, how to avoid areas of Israeli artillery bombardment, and what the closest way to hospitals were. See Amer Abdelhadi, "Surviving Siege, Closure, and Curfew: The Story of a Radio Station," in *Journal of Palestine Studies* 34, no. 1 (2004): 51–67. Amer used to write a daily diary of life under curfew that he would sign with, "The whole world is watching, yet little is being done." Having survived the Israeli invasion and the three Israeli bombings of the radio station and its transmitters, Amer had run out of options to support his family, his wife, Khawlah, and his children, Omar, Qamar, and Ameed, and decided to relocate outside Palestine in search of a decent job. He was killed at the young age of forty-three in a car accident in Dubai. For more information on Amer and the station, see Amer Abdelhadi, "Do You Hear

Me?" in *Live from Palestine: International and Palestinian Direct Action Against Israeli Occupation,* ed. Nancy Stohlman and Laurieann Aladin (Boston: South End Press, 2003); http://www.southend press.org/2004/items/LivePalestine; and http://www.thecornerreport.com/index.php?p=968&more =1&c=1&tb=1&pb=1#more968.

3. Nasser, Lana, and the girls never left for the United States. A few months after the 2002 Israeli invasion of a West Bank city, a jeep stopped in front of the house of Lana's parents. An Israeli soldier came out of the jeep, took out his machine gun, and sprayed Lana's parents as her mother, Auntie Shaden, sat down on the steps to the garden embroidering and Lana's father, Dr. Jamal, was picking oregano from a planted pot. See http://www.remembershaden.org/published_articles.htm for a full account of the murder of Shaden Abu Hijleh.

4. A little more than a year after September 11, 2001, my father passed away, having spent the last months of his life under almost twenty-four-hour-per-day curfew. The immediate cause was an extreme drop in the sugar level in his blood. He was diagnosed with prostate cancer, which, I have come to learn, does not usually kill if discovered early and treated properly. My father neither neglected his health nor surrendered to the disease. He fought it with a strong will and all the resources available to him. However, he and the rest of us were defeated by the power of the Israeli occupation and the blanket curfews that were imposed on Nablus for most of the time of his illness and death. Our biggest concern on the day he passed was not whether it would rain but whether there would be a curfew that would prevent us from giving him the proper funeral he deserved and whether my cousins and other relatives would be allowed by the Israeli military to enter Nablus. For more, see "Lucky in Death," http://www.jerusalemites.org/articles/english/jan2003/23.htm.

5. Samaria is the name Israel assigned to the West Bank.

Bibliography

Abdelhadi, Amer. "Do You Hear Me?" In *Live from Palestine: International and Palestinian Direct Action Against Israeli Occupation*, ed. Nancy Stohlman and Laurieann Aladin. Boston: South End Press, 2003.

———. "Surviving Siege, Closure, and Curfew: The Story of a Radio Station." *Journal of Palestine Studies* 34, no. 1 (2004): 51–67.

Abdo, Nahla. "Gender, Civil Society, and Politics under the PA." *Journal of Palestine Studies* (Fall 2002): 20–47.

———. "Nationalism and Feminism in the Palestinian Women's Movement." In *Gender and National Identity: Women and Politics in Muslim Societies*, ed. Valentine Moghadam. London: Zed Press, 1994.

———. "Women of the *Intifada*: Gender, Class, and National Liberation." *Race and Class* 32, no. 4 (1991): 19–34.

Abdulhadi, Rabab. "Activism and Exile: Palestinianness and the Politics of Solidarity." In *Local Actions: Cultural Activism, Power, and Public Life in America*, ed. Melissa Checker and Maggie Fishman. New York: Columbia Univ. Press, 2004.

———. "Lucky in Death." *Jerusalemites*, Jan. 23, 2003. http://www.jerusalemites.org/articles/english/jan2003/23.htm.

———. "Sexualities and the Social Order in Arab and Muslim Communities." In *Islam and Homosexuality*, ed. Samar Habib. 2:463–88. Santa Barbara: Praeger, 2010.

———. "Tread Lightly: Teaching Gender and Sexuality in the Time of War." *Journal of Women's History* 17, no. 4 (2005): 154–58.

———. "'White' or Not? Displacement and the Construction of (Racialized and Gendered) Palestinianness in the U.S." Paper presented at the MESA annual meeting, Washington, D.C., Nov. 2002.

Abdulhadi, Rabab, and Reem Abdelhadi. "Nomadic Existence: Exile, Gender, and Palestine (an E-mail Conversation Between Sisters)." In *This Bridge We Call Home: Radical Visions for Transformation*, ed. Gloria Anzaldúa and AnaLouise Keating, 165–75. New York: Routledge, 2002.

Abou-Bakr, Omaima. "Islamic Feminism: What's in a Name? Preliminary Reflections." *Middle East Women's Studies Review* 15–16 (Winter–Spring 2001): 1–4.

Abraham, Nabeel. "Anti-Arab Racism and Violence in the United States." In *The Development of Arab-American Identity*, ed. Ernest McCarus. Ann Arbor: Univ. of Michigan Press, 1994.

Abukhalil, As'ad. "Sex and the Suicide Bomber." 2001. http://archive.salon.com/sex/feature/2001/11/07/islam/index_np.html.

Abu-Lughod, Lila. "Do Muslim Women Really Need Saving? Anthropological Reflections on Cultural Relativism and Its Others." *American Anthropologist* 104, no. 3 (2002): 783–90.

———. "Feminist Longings and Postcolonial Conditions." In *Remaking Women: Feminism and Modernity in the Middle East*, ed. Lila Abu-Lughod, 3–32. Princeton: Princeton Univ. Press, 1998.

———. "The Marriage of Feminism and Islamism in Egypt: Selective Repudiation as a Dynamic of Postcolonial Cultural Politics." In *Remaking Women: Feminism and Modernity in the Middle East*, ed. Lila Abu-Lughod, 243–69. Princeton: Princeton Univ. Press, 1998.

———, ed. *Remaking Women: Feminism and Modernity in the Middle East*. Princeton: Princeton Univ. Press, 1998.

Abunimah, Ali. "Obama Picks Pro-Israel Hardliner for Top Post." *Electronic Intifada*, Nov. 5, 2008. http://electronicintifada.net/v2/article9939.shtml.

———. "The Senator, His Pastor, and the Israel Lobby." *Electronic Intifada*, Mar. 31, 2008. http://electronicintifada.net/v2/article9427.shtml.

Ahmad, Muhammad Idries. "BBC's 'Impartiality' Anything But." *Electronic Intifada*. http://electronicintifada.net/v2/article10275.shtml.

Ahmed, Leila. *Women and Gender in Islam: Historical Roots of a Modern Debate*. New Haven, Conn.: Yale Univ. Press, 1992.

———. "Western Ethnocentrism and Perceptions of the Harem." *Feminist Studies* 8, no. 3 (1982): 521–34.

Alexander, M. Jacqui, and Chandra Talpade Mohanty. "Introduction: Genealogies, Legacies, Movements." In *Feminist Genealogies, Colonial Legacies, Democratic Futures*, ed. M. Jacqui Alexander and Chandra Talpade Mohanty. New York: Routledge, 1997.

Ali, Ayaan Hirsi. *The Caged Virgin: An Emancipation Proclamation for Women and Islam*. New York: Free Press, 2006.

Allen, Lori. "There Are Many Reasons Why: Suicide Bombers and Martyrs in Palestine." *GSC Quarterly* (Summer 2002). http://www.ssrc.org/programs/gsc/gsc_quarterly/newsletter5/content/allen.page.

Almaguer, Tomas. *Racial Fault Lines: The Historical Origins of White Supremacy in California*. Berkeley and Los Angeles: Univ. of California Press, 1994.

Alsultany, Evelyn. "From Ambiguity to Abjection: Iraqi-Americans Negotiating Race in the United States." In *The Arab Diaspora: Voices of an Anguished Scream*, ed. Zahia Smail Salhi and Ian Richard Netton. London: Routledge, 2006.

————. "*Los Intersticios:* Recasting Moving Selves." In *This Bridge We Call Home: Radical Visions for Transformation,* ed. Gloria Anzaldúa and AnaLouise Keating. New York: Routledge, 2002.

————. "The Prime-Time Plight of the Arab Muslim American after 9/11: Configurations of Race and Nation in TV Dramas." In *Race and Arab Americans Before and After 9/11: From Invisible Citizens to Visible Subjects,* ed. Amaney Jamal and Nadine Naber, 204–28. Syracuse: Syracuse Univ. Press, 2008.

————. "Selling American Diversity and Muslim American Identity Through Non-profit Advertising Post-9/11/2001." *American Quarterly* 59, no. 3 (2007): 593–622.

Amin, Qasim. *The Liberation of Women, the New Woman: Two Documents in the History of Egyptian Feminism.* Trans. Samiha Peterson. Cairo: American Univ. in Cairo Press, 1992.

Amireh, Amal. "Between Complicity and Subversion: Body Politics in Palestinian National Narrative." *South Atlantic Quarterly* 102, no. 4 (2003): 747–72.

————. "Framing Nawal el Saadawi: Arab Feminism in a Transnational World." *Signs: Journal of Women in Culture and Society* 26, no. 1 (2000): 215–43.

Amnesty International. *The Conflict in Gaza: A Briefing on Applicable Law, Investigation, and Accountability.* London: Amnesty International, 2009.

Angelou, Maya. *Gather Together in My Name.* New York: Bantam, 1974.

————. *The Heart of a Woman.* New York: Bantam, 1981.

Anzaldúa, Gloria, and AnaLouise Keating, eds. *This Bridge We Call Home: Radical Visions for Transformation.* New York: Routledge, 2002.

Barbaro, Michael. "Bloomberg, in Florida, Blasts Rumor about Obama." *New York Times,* June 21, 2008. http://www.nytimes.com/2008/06/21/nyregion/21jewish.html.

Barlas, Asma. *"Believing Women" in Islam: Unreading Patriarchal Interpretations of the Qur'an.* Austin: Univ. of Texas Press, 2002.

————. "Texts and Textualities: The Qur'an, *Tafsir,* and *Ahadith.*" In *"Believing Women" in Islam: Unreading Patriarchal Interpretations of the Qur'an,* 50. Austin: Univ. of Texas Press, 2002.

Beinin, Joel. "The New American McCarthyism: Policing Thought about the Middle East." *Race and Class* 46, no. 1 (2004): 101–15.

Bennet, James. "In Palestinian Children, Signs of Increasing Malnutrition." *New York Times,* July 26, 2002.

Berger, John. *Ways of Seeing.* London: Hamondsworth, Penguin, 1972.

Berlant, Lauren. "Poor Eliza." *American Literature* 70, no. 3 (1998).

Berry, Moulouk. "Radical Transitions: Shifting Gender Discourses in Lebanese Muslim Shi'i Jurisprudence and Ideology, 1960–1999." Ph.D. diss., Univ. of Michigan, 2002.

Bierria, Alisa, Mayaba Liebenthal, and Incite! Women of Color Against Violence. "To Render Ourselves Visible: Women of Color Organizing and Hurricane Katrina." In *What Lies Beneath: Katrina, Race, and the State of the Nation,* ed. the South End Press Collective, 31–47. Cambridge, Mass.: South End Press, 2007.

Borneman, John. "Genital Anxiety." *Anthropological Quarterly* 75, no. 1 (2002): 129–37.

Bourdieu, Pierre. *Outline of a Theory of Practice.* Trans. R. Nice. 1972. Reprint, New York: Cambridge Univ. Press, 1977.

Brooks, Geraldine. *Nine Parts of Desire: The Hidden World of Islamic Women.* New York: Anchor Books, 1995.

Brown, Wendy. *States of Injury: Power and Freedom in Late Modernity.* Princeton: Princeton Univ. Press, 1995.

Buber, Martin. *I and Thou: A New Translation with a Prologue.* Trans. Walter Arnold Kaufman. New York: Scribner, 1970.

Bukhari, Zahid. "Demography, Identity, Space: Defining American Muslim." In *Muslims in the United States,* ed. Philippa Strum and Daniel Tarantolo. Washington, D.C.: Woodrow Wilson International Center for Scholars, 2003.

Bunche, Ralph. "Appendix I: Discussions." In *The Near East and the Great Powers,* ed. Richard Frye. Port Washington, N.Y.: Kennikat Press, 1953.

———. Introduction to *The Near East and the Great Powers,* ed. Richard Frye. Port Washington, N.Y.: Kennikat Press, 1953.

———. "Man, Democracy, and Peace-Foundations for Peace: Human Rights and Fundamental Freedoms." In *Ralph Bunche: Selected Speeches and Writings,* ed. Charles P. Henry. Ann Arbor: Univ. of Michigan Press, 1995.

Butler, Judith. "The Charge of Anti-Semitism: Jews, Israel, and the Risks of Public Critique." In *Precarious Life: The Powers of Mourning and Violence.* London: Verso, 2004.

———. "Contingent Foundations: Feminism and the Question of 'Postmodernism.'" In *Feminists Theorize the Political,* ed. Judith Butler and Joan W. Scott, 3–21. New York and London: Routledge, 1992.

California Scholars for Academic Freedom. "U.S. Academic Group Decries the Targeting of Schools in Gaza." *Electronic Intifada,* Jan. 4, 2009. http://electronicintifada.net/v2/article10111.shtml.

Chesler, Phyllis. *The Death of Feminism: What's Next in the Struggle for Women's Freedom.* New York: Palgrave Macmillan, 2005.

———. "Forced Female Suicide." *FrontPageMagazine.com,* Jan. 22, 2004.

Chetrit, Sami. "Mizrahi Politics in Israel: Between Integration and Alternative." *Journal of Palestine Studies* 29, no. 4 (2000): 51–65.

Chozick, Amy. "Campaign '08: Obama Walks a Fine Line with Muslims; Campaign's Efforts to Dispel Rumors Risk Offending a Base of Support." *Wall Street Journal,* June 23, 2008, A10. http://online.wsj.com/article/SB121417738005395419.html?mod=googlenews_wsj.

Cockburn, Alexander, and Jeffrey St. Clair, eds. *The Politics of Anti-Semitism.* Petrolia, Calif.: Counterpunch, 2003.

Cohen, Cathy J. *The Boundaries of Blackness: AIDS and the Breakdown of Black Politics.* Chicago: Univ. of Chicago Press, 1999.

———. "Punks, Bulldaggers, and Welfare Queens: The Radical Potential of Queer Politics?" *GLQ: A Journal of Lesbian and Gay Studies* 3, no. 4 (1997): 437–65.

Cohen, Mark. *Under Crescent and Cross: The Jews in the Middle Ages.* Princeton: Princeton Univ. Press, 1995.

Congressional Record. "Recognizing Israel's Right to Defend Itself Against Attacks from Gaza." H.R. 34, Jan. 9, 2009.

———. "Support for Israel in Its Battle with Hamas and the Israeli-Palestinian Peace Process." S.R. 10, Jan. 8, 2009.

cooke, miriam. "WO-man, Retelling the War Myth." In *Gendering War Talk*, ed. miriam cooke and Angela Woollacott. Princeton: Princeton Univ. Press, 1993.

———. "Women's Jihad Before and After 9/11." In *Women and Gender in the Middle East and the Islamic World Today.* UCIAS Edited Volumes, vol. 4 (2003): Article 1063. http://repositories.cdlib.org/uciaspubs/editedvolumes/4/1063.

cooke, miriam, and Margot Badran, eds. *Opening the Gates: A Century of Arab Feminist Writing.* Bloomington: Indiana Univ. Press, 1990.

Corrie, Rachel. *Let Me Stand Alone: The Journals of Rachel Corrie.* New York: W. W. Norton, 2008.

———. *My Name Is Rachel Corrie.* Ed. Alan Rickman and Katharine Viner. New York : Theatre Communications Group, 2006.

———. "Rachel's War." *Guardian*, Mar. 17, 2003.

Craft, Nikki. "A Call on Feminists to Protest the War Against Afghanistan." Nov. 8, 2001. http://www.nostatusquo.com/ACLU/terrorism/terrorism1.html.

Crenshaw Williams, Kimberlé. "Demarginalizing the Intersection of Race and Sex: A Black Feminist Critique of Antidiscrimination Doctrine, Feminist Theory, and Antiracist Politics." *University of Chicago Legal Forum* (1989): 139–67.

Dahan-Kalev, Henriette. "On the Logic of Feminism and the Implications of African American Feminist Thought for Israeli Mizrahi Feminism." *American Philosophical Association Newsletter on Feminism and Philosophy* 3 (2003).

———. "Tensions in Israeli Feminism: The Mizrahi-Ashkenazi Rift." *Women's Studies International Forum* 24, no. 6 (2001): 669–84.

———. "You're So Pretty—You Don't Look Moroccan." *Israel Studies* 6, no. 1 (2001): 1–14.

Davis, Joyce M. *Martyrs: Innocence, Vengeance, and Despair in the Middle East.* New York: Palgrave Macmillan, 2003.

Deeb, Lara. *An Enchanted Modern: Gender and Public Piety in Shi'i Lebanon.* Princeton: Princeton Univ. Press, 2006.

Deen, Thalif. "Palestinian Women Hard Hit by Israeli Occupation." United Nations, Feb. 2004. http://www.palestinemonitor.org/Reports/palestinian_women_hit_hard_by_occupation.

"Defining Terms in the Age of Imperialism: Challenging Alleged 'Strategic Solidarity.'" *Left Turn*, Aug. 2007. http://www.leftturn.org/?q=node/728.

Diaz, Vicente M., and J. Kehaulani Kauanui. "Native Pacific Cultural Studies on the Edge." *Contemporary Pacific* 13, no. 2 (2001): 315–41.

Dodd, Vikram. "Muslim Women Advised to Abandon *Hijab* to Avoid Attack." *Guardian*, Aug. 4, 2005. http://www.guardian.co.uk/uk/2005/aug/04/race.july7.

Doumani, Beshara, ed. *Academic Freedom after September 11*. New York: Zone Books, 2006.

Doumato, Eleanor Adbella. *Women and Globalization in the Arab Middle East: Gender, Economy, and Society*. Boulder, Colo.: Lynne Rienner, 2003.

Dworkin, Andrea. "Israel: Whose Country Is It Anyway?" *Ms.*, Sept.–Oct. 1990. http://www.nostatusquo.com/ACLU/dworkin/IsraelI.html.

———. "The Women Suicide Bombers." *Feminista!* 5, no. 1 (2002). http://www.feminista.com/archives/v5n1/dworkin.html.

Eisenstein, Zillah. *Against Empire: Feminisms, Racism, and the West*. London: Zed Books, 2004.

Elazar, Daniel J. "Can Sephardic Judaism Be Reconstructed?" Jerusalem Center for Public Affairs. http://www.jcpa.org/dje/articles3/sephardic.htm.

El Farra, Mona. "Diary of the Dispossessed: Women's Misery and Suffering under Israeli Occupation." In *Women and the Politics of Military Confrontation: Palestinian and Israeli Gendered Narratives of Dislocation*, ed. Nahla Abdo and Ronit Lentin, 159–63. New York: Bergham Books.

El-Ghobashy, Tamer. "Palestinian Flag Flap." *New York Daily News*, Nov. 22, 2002. http://www.nydailynews.com/news/local/story/37234p-35169c.html.

el Guindi, Fadwa. *Veil: Modesty, Privacy, Resistance*. Oxford: Berg, 1999.

Elia, Nada. "The 'White' Sheep of the Family: But Bleaching Is Like Starvation." In *This Bridge We Call Home: Radical Visions for Transformation*, ed. Gloria Anzaldúa and AnaLouise Keating, 223–31. New York: Routledge, 2002.

———. "A Woman's Place Is in the Struggle." In *Food for Our Grandmothers: Writings by Arab-American and Arab-Canadian Feminists*, ed. Joanna Kadi, 114–19. Cambridge, Mass.: South End Press, 1994.

El Khameesy, Ahmed. "Rachel Corrie: The Conscience of a Rose." Trans. Somaya Ramadan. *Akhbar El Adab* (Cairo), Mar. 2004.

Elliott, Andrea. "Muslim Voters Detect a Snub from Obama." *New York Times*, June 24, 2008. http://www.nytimes.com/2008/06/24/us/politics/24muslim.html.

Enloe, Cynthia. *Bananas, Beaches, and Bases: Making Feminist Sense of International Politics*. Berkeley and Los Angeles: Univ. of California Press, 1990.

———. *Maneuvers: The International Politics of Militarizing Women's Lives*. Berkeley and Los Angeles: Univ, of California Press, 2000.

Esack, Farid. *The Qur'an: A Short Introduction*. Oxford: Oneworld, 2002.

Espiritu, Yen Lee. *Home Bound: Filipino American Lives Across Cultures, Communities, and Countries*. Berkeley and Los Angeles: Univ. of California Press, 2003.

Esposito, John L. *Islam: The Straight Path*. Expanded ed. Oxford: Oxford Univ. Press, 1988.

———. "Religious Life: Belief and Practice." In *Islam: The Straight Path*, 78. Oxford: Oxford Univ. Press, 1988.

"Facts About Violence." Feminist.com. http://www.feminist.com/antiviolence/facts.html.

"Factsheet: The Right to Return, a Basic Right Still Denied." *Al-Awda: The Palestine Right to Return Coalition,* Sept. 12, 2006. http://www.al-awda.org/facts.html.

"False Rumors That Obama Is a Muslim." Pew Research Center's Project for Excellence in Journalism, Nov. 20, 2008. http://www.journalism.org/node/13790.

Fanon, Frantz. *Black Skin, White Masks: The Experiences of a Black Man in a White World.* New York: Grove Press, 1952.

———. *A Dying Colonialism.* Trans. Haakon Chevalier. New York: Grove Press, 1965.

———. *The Wretched of the Earth.* New York: Grove Press, 1963.

Fayad, Mona. "The Arab Woman and I." In *Food for Our Grandmothers: Writings by Arab-American and Arab-Canadian Feminists,* ed. Joanna Kadi, 170–72. Cambridge, Mass.: South End Press, 1994.

Fleischmann, Ellen. *The Nation and Its New Women: The Palestinian Women's Movement, 1920–1948.* Berkeley and Los Angeles: Univ. of California Press, 2003.

Foreman, Ruth. "I Will Speak Genius to Myself." In *We Are the Young Magicians.* Boston: Beacon Press, 1993.

Foucault, Michel. *Discipline and Punish: The Birth of the Prison.* New York: Vintage Books, 1977.

———. *The History of Sexuality: An Introduction.* Vol. 1. New York: Vintage Books, 1990.

Friedman, Thomas L. "Cukoo in Carolina." *New York Times,* Aug. 28, 2002.

Gaines, Kevin. *Uplifting the Race: Black Leadership, Politics, and Culture in the Twentieth Century.* Chapel Hill: Univ. of North Carolina Press, 1996.

Ghappour, Rasha. "Colors." *Mizna* 4, no. 1 (2001): 7–8.

Giacaman, Rita, Islah Jad, and Penny Johnson. "For the Public Good? Gender and Social Citizenship in Palestine." *Middle East Report* 198 (1996): 11–16.

Gibbs, Jewelle Taylor, and Teiahsha Bankhead. *Preserving Privilege: California Politics, Propositions, and People of Color.* Westport, Conn.: Praeger, 2001.

Goldstein, Seth, and Mohammed Abu-Nimer. *The Search for Peace: The Palestinian-Israeli Conflict; Difficult Dialogues.* Video recording. Olympia, Wash.: TVW, 2004.

Gole, Nilufer. *The Forbidden Modern.* Ann Arbor: Univ. of Michigan Press, 1996.

Gopinath, Gayatri. *Impossible Desires: Queer Diasporas and South Asian Public Cultures.* Durham: Duke Univ. Press, 2005.

Gould, Rebecca. "Rachel Corrie: A Witness for Our Times." In *To Kill, to Die: Feminist Contestations on Gender and Political Violence.* Newsletter. New York: New School for Social Research, Mar. 3–4, 2004.

Gramsci, Antonio. *Selections from the Prison Notebooks.* Translated and ed. Q. Hoare and G. Nowell Smith. New York: International Publishers, 1971.

Griffin-Nolan, Ed. "Pulpit Bullied." *Syracuse New Times,* June 18, 2008, 4. http://www.syracusenewtimes.com/index.php?option=com_content&task=view&id=2008&Itemid=147.

Gualtieri, Sarah. "Becoming 'White': Race, Religion, and the Foundations of Syrian/Lebanese Ethnicity in the United States." *Journal of American Ethnic History* (Summer 2001): 29–53.

———. *Between Arab and White: Race and Ethnicity in the Early Syrian Diaspora.* Berkeley and Los Angeles: Univ. of California Press, 2009.

Habib, Samar, ed. *Islam and Homosexuality.* Santa Barbara: Praeger, 2010.

Haddad, Yvonne Yazbeck, and John L. Esposito, eds. *Islam, Gender, and Social Change.* New York: Oxford Univ. Press, 1998.

Hage, Ghassan. "'Comes a Time We Are All Enthusiasm': Understanding Palestinian Suicide Bombers in Times of Exighophobia." *Public Culture* 15, no. 1 (2003): 65–89.

Hall, Stuart. "Cultural Identity and Diaspora." In *Colonial Discourse and Postcolonial Theory: A Reader,* ed. Patrick Williams and Laura Chrisman. New York: Columbia Univ. Press, 1994.

Hammad, Suheir. "On the Brink of . . ." In *Russell Simmons Def Poetry Jam on Broadway . . . and More,* ed. Danny Simmons. New York: Atria Books, 2004.

Hammami, Rima. "Women, the Hijab, and the Intifada." *Middle East Report* 20, nos. 3–4 (1990): 24–28.

Hammami, Reza, and Martina Rieker. "Feminist Orientalism and Orientalist Marxism." *New Left Review* 1, no. 170 (1988).

Al-Haq. "Legal Brief on Gaza." http://www.alhaq.org/pdfs/Legal_Brief_Gaza_Cast_Lead_Jan.pdf.

———. "Re: Gross Human Rights Violations and War Crimes in the Gaza Strip." Jan. 7, 2009. http://alhaq.or/etemplate.php?id=140.

Harding, Sandra G. *Feminism and Methodology: Social Science Issues.* Bloomington: Indiana Univ. Press, 1987.

Hartman, Saidiya. *Scenes of Subjection: Terror, Slavery, and Self-Making in Nineteenth-Century America.* Oxford: Oxford Univ. Press, 1997.

Harvey, David. *The New Imperialism.* Clarendon Lectures in Geography and Environmental Studies. Oxford: Oxford Univ. Press, 2003.

Hassan, Salah D. "Arabs, Race, and the Post–September 11 National Security State." *Middle East Report* 224 (2002): 16–21.

Hasso, Frances S. "Feminist Generations? The Long-Term Impact of Social Movement Involvement on Palestinian Women's Lives." *American Journal of Sociology* 107, no. 3 (2001): 586–613.

———. "The 'Women's Front': Nationalism, Feminism, and Modernity in Palestine." *Gender and Society* 12, no. 4 (1998): 441–86.

Hatem, Mervat F. "Discourses on the 'War on Terrorism' in the U.S. and Its Views on the Arab, Muslim, and Gendered 'Other.'" *Arab Studies Journal* 11–12 (Fall 2003–Spring 2004): 77–103.

———. "Homeland Security in a Global World." In *Democracy and Homeland Security: Strategies, Controversies, and Impact,* ed. Nawwal Ammar. Kent, Ohio: Kent State Univ. Press, forthcoming.

———. "How the Gulf War Changed the AAUG's Discourse on Arab Nationalism and Gender Politics." *Middle East Journal* 2 (Spring 2001): 290–96.

————. "In the Eye of the Storm: Islamic Societies and Muslim Women in Globalization Discourses." In *Beyond the Boundaries of the Old Geographies*, ed. Ali Mirsepassi. Forthcoming.

————. "Racial Profiling in the Pursuit of Arabs and Muslims in the U.S." In *It's a Free Country: Personal Freedom in America after September 11*, ed. Danny Goldberg, Victor Goldberg, and Robert Greenwald. New York: Nation Books, 2003.

Hirschkind, Charles, and Saba Mahmood. "Feminism, the Taliban, and the Politics of Counter-Insurgency." *Anthropological Quarterly* 72, no. 2 (2002): 339–54.

Ho, Engseng. "Empire Through Diasporic Eyes: A View from the Other Boat." *Comparative Studies in Society and History* 46, no. 2 (2004): 210–46.

Holliday, Billie. "Summertime." On *The Best of Billie Holiday*. Intersound, 2000.

Hoodfar, Homa. *Between Marriage and the Market: Intimate Politics and Survival in Cairo*. Comparative Studies on Muslim Societies. Vol. 24. Berkeley and Los Angeles: Univ. of California Press, 1997.

————. "The Veil in Their Minds and on Our Heads: Veiling Practices and Muslim Women." In *The Politics of Culture in the Shadow of Capital*, ed. Lisa Lowe and David Lloyd, 248–79. Durham, N.C.: Duke Univ. Press, 1997.

hooks, bell. "Out of the Academy and into the Streets." *Ms.*, July–Aug. 1992, 80–82.

————. "Postmodern Blackness." In *Yearning: Race, Gender, and Cultural Politics*. Boston: South End Press, 1990.

hooks, bell, and T. McKinnon. "Sisterhood: Beyond Public and Private." *Signs: Journal of Women in Culture and Society* 21, no. 41 (1996): 814–29.

Horowitz, David. "Islamo-Fascism Awareness Week." *Front Page*, Sept. 21, 2007. http://www.frontpagemag.com/Articles.

————. "A Response to Feminists on the Violent Oppression of Women in Islam." *Front Page*, Jan. 24, 2008. http://www.frontpagemag.com/Articles.

"How to Tell Your Friends from the Japs." *Time*, Dec. 22, 1941, 33.

Human Rights Watch. "Disappointment as U.S. Bolts Race Conference." Common Dreams Progressive Newswire. http://www.commondreams.org/news2001/0903-04.htm.

————. "Razing Rafah: Mass Home Demolitions in the Gaza Strip." Oct. 18, 2004. http://www.hrw.org/reports/2004/rafah1004/.

Hunter, Nedjma, and C. Jane Hunter. *The Almond: The Sexual Awakening of a Muslim Woman*. New York: Grove Press, 2005.

Hussein, Qadreya. *Famous Women of the Islamic World (Shahirat al nissaa fil alam al Islamy)*. Trans. Abdel-Aziz El-Khanki. Cairo: Women and Memory Forum, 2004.

International Committee of the Red Cross. "Gaza: Emergency Aid Alone Is Not Enough." http://www.icrc.org/web.eng/siteeng0.nsf/html/Palestine-update-220109?open document.

"Israeli Attacks Kill over 310 in Gaza in One of Israel's Bloodiest Attacks on Palestinians since 1948." *Democracy Now!* Dec. 29, 2008. http://www.democracynow.org/2008/12/29/israeli_attacks_kill_over_310_in.

Jacoby, Tami Amanda. "Feminism, Nationalism, and Difference: Reflections on the Palestinian Women's Movement." *Women's Studies International Forum* 22, no. 5 (1999): 511–23.

Jadaa, Imad. "The Beautiful Face of the United States." *Juventud Rebelde*, Mar. 18, 2003.

Jarmakani, Amira. "Belly Dancing for Liberation." In *Arabs in the Americas: Interdisciplinary Essays on the Arab Diaspora*, ed. Darcy Zabel, 145–68. New York: Peter Lang Press, 2006.

———. *Imagining Arab Womanhood: The Cultural Mythology of Veils, Harems, and Belly Dancers in the U.S.* New York: Palgrave Macmillan, 2008.

Jarrar, Randa. *A Map of Home*. New York: Other Press, 2008.

Jordan, June. "Life after Lebanon." In *On Call: Political Essays*. Boston: South End Press, 1985.

———. "Moving Towards Home." In *Living Room: New Poems by June Jordan*. New York: Thunders Mouth Press, 1985.

———. "Of Those So Close Beside Me, Which Are You?" In *Technical Difficulties: African American Notes on the State of the Union*, 25–31. New York: Vintage Books, 1992.

———. "Waking Up in the Middle of Some American Dreams." In *Technical Difficulties: African American Notes on the State of the Union*, 11–24. New York: Vintage Books, 1992.

Joseph, Suad, and Susan Slyomovics. *Women and Power in the Middle East*. Philadelphia: Univ. of Pennsylvania Press, 2000.

Kadi, Joanna, ed. *Food for Our Grandmothers: Writings by Arab-American and Arab-Canadian Feminists*. Boston: South End Press, 1994.

———. "Speaking (about) Silence." In *Sing, Whisper, Shout, Pray: Feminist Visions for a Just World*, ed. M. Jacqui Alexander et al., 539–45. Fort Bragg, Calif.: EdgeWork Books, 2003.

———. *Thinking Class: Sketches from a Cultural Worker*. Boston: South End Press, 1996.

Kahf, Mohja. *E-Mails from Scheherazad*. Gainesville: Univ. Press of Florida, 2003.

———. "Packaging Huda: Sha'rawi's Memoirs in the U.S. Reading Environment." In *The Politics of Reception: Globalizing Third World Women's Literature*, ed. Amal Amireh and Lisa Suhair Majaj, 148–72. New York: Garland, 2000.

———. *Western Representations of the Muslim Woman: From Termagant to Odalisque*. Austin: Univ. of Texas Press, 1999.

Kanaaneh, Rhoda Ann. *Rebirthing the Nation: Strategies of Palestinian Women in Israel*. Berkeley and Los Angeles: Univ. of California Press, 2002.

Kandiyoti, Deniz, ed. *Gendering the Middle East: Emerging Perspectives*. Syracuse: Syracuse Univ. Press, 1996.

Kaplan, Amy. *The Anarchy of Empire in the Making of U.S. Culture*. Cambridge: Harvard Univ. Press, 2005.

Kaplan, Caren. "Beyond the Pale: Rearticulating U.S. Jewish Whiteness." In *Talking Visions: Multicultural Feminism in a Transnational Age*, ed. Ella Shohat. New York: New Museum of Contemporary Art, 1998.

Kaplan, Caren, Norma Alarcón, and Minoo Moallem. *Between Woman and Nation: Nationalism, Transnational Feminism, and the State*. Durham, N.C.: Duke Univ. Press, 1990.

Khalidi, Rashid. *Resurrecting Empire: Western Footprints and America's Perilous Path in the Middle East*. Boston: Beacon Press, 2004.

Khashan, Hilal. "Collective Palestinian Frustration and Suicide Bombings." *Third World Quarterly* 24, no. 6 (2003): 1049–67.

Khawaja, J. A. "The Queen, Carcasses, and Other Things." In *Food for Our Grandmothers: Writings by Arab-American and Arab-Canadian Feminists*, ed. Joanna Kadi, 39–47. Cambridge, Mass.: South End Press, 1994.

Kim, Jodi. *Ends of Empire: Asian American Critique and the Cold War*. Minneapolis: Univ. of Minnesota Press, 2010.

Kim, Nadia. *Imperial Citizens: Koreans and Race from Seoul to LA*. Stanford: Stanford Univ. Press, 2008.

Kimmerling, Baruch. "Sacred Rage." *Nation*, Nov. 26, 2003. http://www.thenation.com/doc.mhtml?i=20031215&c=1&s=kimmerling.

Klein, Naomi. "On Rescuing Private Lynch and Forgetting Rachel Corrie." *Guardian*, May 22, 2003.

Kolodner, Meredith. "The Future of the Antiwar Movement." *International Socialist Review* 39 (Jan.–Feb. 2005).

Koyama, Emi. "Whose Feminism Is It Anyway? The Unspoken Racism of the Trans-inclusion Debate." In *The Transgender Studies Reader*, ed. Susan Stryker and Stephen Whittle, 698–705. London: Routledge, 2006.

Kristof, Nicholas D. "The Push to 'Otherize' Obama." *New York Times*, Sept. 21, 2008. http://www.nytimes.com/2008/09/21/opinion/21kristof.html.

Lavie, Smadar. "Academic Apartheid in Israel and the Lily White Feminism of the Upper Middle Class." *Anthropology News* (2003).

Lazreg, Marnia. *The Eloquence of Silence: Algerian Women in Question*. New York: Routledge, 1994.

Lombardi, Kristen. "Hillary Calls Israel a 'Beacon' of Democracy." *Village Voice*, Dec. 5, 2005. http://www.villagevoice.com/2005-12-06/news/hillary-calls-israel-a-beacon-of-democracy.

Lorde, Audre. "The Master's Tools Will Never Dismantle the Master's House." In *Sister Outsider: Essays and Speeches*. Ithaca, N.Y.: Crossing Press, 1984.

———. "The Transformation of Silence into Language and Action." In *Sister Outsider: Essays and Speeches*. Ithaca, N.Y.: Crossing Press, 1984.

Lowe, Lisa. *Immigrant Acts: On Asian American Cultural Politics*. Durham, N.C.: Duke Univ. Press, 1996.

MADRE. "Palestine in the Age of Hamas: The Challenge of Progressive Solidarity." CommonDreams.org, July 11, 2007. http://www.commondreams.org/news2007/0711-02.htm.

Mahalingam, Ramaswami, and Janxin Leu. "Culture, Essentialism, Immigration, and Representations of Gender." *Theory and Psychology* 15, no. 6 (2005): 839–60.

Mahmood, Saba. "Feminism, Democracy, and Empire: Islam and the War of Terror." In *Women's Studies on the Edge*, ed. Joan Wallach Scott, 81–114. Durham, N.C.: Duke Univ. Press, 2008.

———. *The Politics of Piety: The Islamic Revival and the Feminist Subject.* Princeton: Princeton Univ. Press, 2005.

Maira, Sunaina. *Missing: Youth, Citizenship, and Empire after 9/11.* Durham: Duke Univ. Press, 2009.

Majaj, Lisa Suhair. "Arab-American Ethnicity: Locations, Coalitions, and Cultural Negotiations." In *Arabs in America: Building a New Future*, ed. Michael Suleiman, 320–36. Philadelphia: Temple Univ. Press, 1996.

———. "Boundaries: Arab/American." In *Food for Our Grandmothers: Writings by Arab-American and Arab-Canadian Feminists*, ed. Joanna Kadi, 65–86. Cambridge, Mass.: South End Press, 1994.

Majid, Anouar. *Unveiling Traditions: Postcolonial Islam in a Polycentric World.* Durham: Duke Univ. Press, 2000.

Malcolm, Andrew. "Obama Rally Inclusive—Except for Two Muslim Women in Scarves." *Los Angeles Times*, June 2008. http://latimesblogs.latimes.com/washington/2008/06/obama-muslim.html.

Mamdani, Mahmood. *Good Muslim, Bad Muslim: America, the Cold War, and the Roots of Terror.* New York: Pantheon Books, 2004.

Mani, Lata. *Contentious Traditions: The Debate on Sati in Colonial India.* Berkeley and Los Angeles: Univ. of California Press, 1998.

Manji, Irshad. *The Trouble with Islam: A Muslim's Call for Reform in Her Faith.* New York: St. Martin's Press, 2004.

Mankiller, Wilma, and M. Wallis. *Mankiller: A Chief and Her People.* New York: St. Martin's Press, 1993.

Mann, Michael. *Incoherent Empire.* London: Verso, 2003.

Massad, Joseph Andoni. *Desiring Arabs.* Chicago: Univ. of Chicago Press, 2007.

Mattawa, Khaled. *Amorisco.* Keene, N.Y.: Ausable Press, 2008.

———. *Ismailia Eclipse.* Riverdale, N.Y.: Sheep Meadow Press, 1996.

———. *Tocqueville.* Kalamazoo, Mich.: New Issues Press, 2010.

———. *Zodiac of Echoes.* Keene, N.Y.: Ausable Press, 2003.

McAlister, Melani. *Epic Encounters: Culture, Media, and U.S. Interests in the Middle East since 1945.* Berkeley and Los Angeles: Univ. of California Press, 2005.

McCloud, Aminah Beverly. "A Challenging Intellectual Heritage: A Look at the Social and Political Space of African American Muslims." In *Muslims in the United States*, ed. Philippa Strum and Daniel Tarantola. Washington, D.C.: Woodrow Wilson International Center for Scholars, 2003.

Mehdid, Malika. "A Western Invention of Arab Womanhood: The 'Oriental' Female." In *Women in the Middle East: Perceptions, Realities, and Struggles for Liberation*, ed. H. Afshar, 18–58. London: Macmillan, 1996.

Mernissi, Fatima. *The Veil and the Male Elite: A Feminist Interpretation of Women's Rights in Islam*. Reading, Mass.: Addison-Wesley, 1991.

Miller, Abraham. "Revising History at Berkeley: Israeli 'Occupation 101.'" *Campus Watch*. http://www.campus-watch.org/article/id/1656.

Mills, C. Wright. *The Power Elite*. Oxford: Oxford Univ. Press, 1956.

Mizrachi, Beverly. "Non-mainstream Education, Limited Mobility, and the Second Generation of Moroccan Immigrant Women: The Case of the Kindergarten Teacher's Assistant." *NASHIM: A Journal of Women's Studies and Gender Issues* 8 (Fall 5765/2004): 50–72.

Moallem, Minoo. *Between Warrior Brother and Veiled Sister: Islamic Fundamentalism and Patriarchy in Iran*. Berkeley and Los Angeles: Univ. of California Press, 2005.

Moallem, Minoo, and Iain A. Boal. "Multicultural Nationalism and the Poetics of Inauguration." In *Between Woman and Nation: Nationalism, Transnationalism Feminism, and the State*, ed. Caren Kaplan, Norma Alarcon, and Minoo Moallem, 243–64. Durham: Duke Univ. Press, 1999.

Moghadam, Assaf. "Palestinian Suicide Terrorism in the Second Intifada: Motivations and Organizational Aspects." *Studies in Conflict and Terrorism* 26 (2003): 65–92.

Moghadam, Valentine M. *Gender and National Identity: Women and Politics in Muslim Societies*. London: Zed Books, 1994.

Mohan, Rajeswari. "Loving Palestine: Nationalist Activism and Feminist Agency in Leila Khaled's Subversive Bodily Acts." *Interventions* 1, no. 1 (1998): 52–80.

Mohanty, Chandra Talpade. "Cartographies of Struggle: Third World Women and the Politics of Feminism." In *Third World Women and the Politics of Feminism*, ed. Chandra Talpade Mohanty, Ann Russo, and Lourdes Torres. Bloomington: Indiana Univ. Press, 1991.

———. *Feminism Without Borders: Decolonizing Theory, Practicing Solidarity*. Durham, N.C.: Duke Univ. Press, 2003.

———. "Under Western Eyes: Feminist Scholarship and Colonial Discourses." *Boundary 2* 12, no. 3 (1984): 333–58.

———. "U.S. Empire and the Project of Women's Studies: Stories of Citizenship, Complicity, and Dissent." *Gender, Place, and Culture* 13, no. 1 (2006): 7–20.

Moore, Henrietta. *A Passion for Difference: Essays in Anthropology and Gender*. London: Polity Press, 1994.

Moraga, Cherríe, and Gloria Anzaldúa, eds. *This Bridge Called My Back: Writings by Radical Women of Color*. New York: Kitchen Table Women of Color Press, 1981.

Morgan, Robin. "The Demon Lover Syndrome." *Ms.*, 2002, 17.

———. *The Demon Lover: The Roots of Terrorism*. New York: Washington Square Press, 2001.

Motzafi-Haller, Pnina. "Scholarship, Identity, Power: Mizrahi Women in Israel." *Signs* 26, no. 3 (2001): 697–734.

Mubarak, Hadia. "The Politicization of Gender Reform: The Islamists' Discourse on Repealing Article 340 of the Jordanian Penal Code." Master's thesis, Georgetown Univ., 2005.

Naber, Nadine. "Ambiguous Insiders: An Investigation of Arab American Invisibility." *Ethnic and Racial Studies* 23, no. 1 (2000): 38–50.

———. Introduction to *Race and Arab Americans Before and After September 11th: From Invisible Citizens to Visible Subjects*, ed. Nadine Naber and Amaney Jamal. Syracuse: Syracuse Univ. Press, 2008.

———. "Look, Mohammed the Terrorist Is Coming." In *Race and Arab Americans Before and After September 11th: From Invisible Citizens to Visible Subjects*, ed. Nadine Naber and Amaney Jamal, 276–304. Syracuse: Syracuse Univ. Press, 2008.

———. "Muslim First, Arab Second: A Strategic Politics of Race and Gender." *Muslim World* 95, no. 4 (2005): 479–95.

———. "So Our History Doesn't Become Your Future: The Local and Global Politics of Coalition Building Post–September 11th." *Journal of Asian and African Studies* (Oct. 2002): 217–42.

———. "White but Not Quiet: Arab American Invisibility." *Ethnic and Racial Studies* 23, no. 1 (2000): 37–62.

Naber, Nadine, Eman Desouky, and Lina Baroudi. "The Forgotten '-Ism': An Arab American Women's Perspective on Zionism, Racism, and Sexism." Arab Women's Solidarity Association, San Francisco Chapter, 2001. http://www.awsa.net/forgottenism.pdf.

Najmabadi, Afsaneh. *Women with Mustaches and Men Without Beards: Gender and Sexual Anxieties of Iranian Modernity*. Berkeley and Los Angeles: Univ. of California Press, 2005.

Narayan, Uma. *Dislocating Cultures: Identities, Traditions, and Third World Feminism*. New York: Routledge, 1997.

Ngai, Mae. *Impossible Subjects: Illegal Aliens and the Making of Modern America*. Princeton: Princeton Univ. Press, 2005.

Nomani, Asra. *Standing Alone in Mecca: An American Woman's Struggle for the Soul of Islam*. New York: HarperCollins, 2005.

Ono, Kent, and John Sloop. *Shifting Borders: Rhetoric, Immigration, and California's Proposition 187*. Philadelphia: Temple Univ. Press, 2002.

Parker, Andrew, Mary Russo, Doris Sommer, and Patricia Yaeger. *Nationalisms and Sexualities*. New York: Routledge, 1992.

Perdigon, Sylvain. "Life of an Infamous Woman: The Funerals of Wafa Idris, Palestine's First Female Suicide-Bomber." Unpublished paper, 2004.

Peteet, Julie. *Gender in Crisis: Women and the Palestinian Resistance Movement*. New York: Columbia Univ. Press, 1992.

———. "Icons and Militants: Mothering in the Danger Zone." *Signs* 23, no. 1 (1994): 103–29.

Pollack, Sarah. "Lipstick Martyrs: A New Breed of Palestinian Terrorist." *CBN*, May 28, 2003.

Pollitt, Katha. "Sign the Open Letter from American Feminists." *Blog: And Another Thing.* http://www.thenation.com/blogs/anotherthing?pid=273005.

Povinelli, Elizabeth A. *The Cunning of Recognition: Indigenous Alterities and the Making of Australian Multiculturalism.* Durham: Duke Univ. Press, 2002.

Powell, Colin. "World Conference Against Racism." U.S. Department of State, Sept. 3, 2001.

Prashad, Vijay. *The Karma of Brown Folk.* Minneapolis: Univ. of Minnesota Press, 2000.

Pratt, Mary Louise. *Imperial Eyes: Travel Writing and Transculturation.* London: Routledge, 1992.

Presner, Todd Samuel. "'Clear Heads, Solid Stomachs, and Hard Muscles': Max Nordau and the Aesthetics of Jewish Regeneration." *Modernism/Modernity* 10, no. 2 (2003): 269–96.

Puar, Jasbir K. *Terrorist Assemblages: Homonationalism in Queer Times.* Next Wave. Durham: Duke Univ. Press, 2007.

Puar, Jasbir K., and Amit S. Rai. "Monster, Terrorist, Fag: The War on Terrorism and the Production of Docile Patriots." *Social Text* 20, no. 3 (2002): 117–48.

Qishta, Fida, and Peter Beaumont. "Israel Accused of War Crimes over Assault on Gaza Village." *Observer*, Jan. 18, 2009.

Quraishi, Asifa. "Her Honor: An Islamic Critique of the Rape Laws of Pakistan from a Woman-Sensitive Position." In *Windows of Faith: Muslim Women's Scholar-Activists*, ed. Gisela Webb, 102–35. Syracuse: Syracuse Univ. Press, 2000.

Radin, Charles A. "False Alarms." *Jewish Advocate*, Sept. 19, 2008, 13. http://jadvocate.tclhosting.co.uk/this_weeks_issue/columnists/radin/?content_id=5567.

Rahbani Brothers. "Nassam Alayna al-Hawa." On *Safarbarlek/Bint el-Haress.* Digital Press Hellas, 2000.

Ramey, Ibrahim Abdil-Mu'id. "Deconstructing the Elephant: The Durban UN Conference Against Racism, and Beyond." *Fellowship.* http://www.forusa.org/fellowship/nov-dec_01/ramey_elephant.html.

Rape, Abuse, and Incest National Network. "Who Are the Victims?" http://www.rainn.org/get-information/statistics/sexual-assault-victims.

Razack, Sherene H. *Casting Out: The Eviction of Muslims from Western Law and Politics.* Toronto: Univ. of Toronto Press, 2008.

———. *Dark Threats and White Knights: The Somalia Affair, Peacekeeping and the New Imperialism.* Toronto: Univ. of Toronto Press, 2004.

———. "Geopolitics, Culture Clash, and Gender after September 11." *Social Justice* 32, no. 4 (2005).

————. "Imperilled Muslim Women, Dangerous Muslim Men and Civilised Europeans: Legal and Social Responses to Forced Marriage." *Feminist Legal Studies* 12 (2004): 129–74.

Reuter, Christoph. *My Life as a Weapon: A Modern History of Suicide Bombing.* Princeton: Princeton Univ. Press, 2004.

Riley, Robin L., Chandra Talpade Mohanty, and Minnie Bruce Pratt. "Feminism and U.S. Wars: Mapping the Ground." Introduction to *Feminism and War: Confronting U.S. Imperialism*, 1–19. London: Zed, 2008.

Rose, Jacqueline. "Deadly Embrace." *London Review of Books* 26, no. 21 (2004). http://www.lrb.co.uk/v26/n21/rose01_.html.

Rosner, Shmuel. "In AIPAC Speech, Obama Repeats Support for Israel, Peace Talks." *Haaretz*, Mar. 3, 2008. http://www.haaretz.com/hasen/spages/832668.html.

Roy, Arundhati. *An Ordinary Person's Guide to Empire.* Cambridge, Mass.: South End Press, 2004.

————. *Power Politics.* Boston: South End Press, 2001.

Said, Edward W. "Arabs, Islam, and the Dogmas of the West." *New York Times Book Review*, Oct. 31, 1976.

————. "Invention, Memory, and Place." *Critical Inquiry* 26, no. 2 (2000): 175–92.

————. "The Meaning of Rachel Corrie: Of Dignity and Solidarity." In *Peace under Fire: Israel/Palestine and the International Solidarity Movement*, ed. Josie Sandercock, Radhika Sainath, Marissa McLaughlin, Hussein Khalili, Nicholas Blincoe, Huwaida Arraf, and Ghassan Andoni. London: Verso, 2004.

————. *Orientalism.* New York: Vintage, 1979.

————. *Orientalism: A Reader.* Ed. A. L. Macfie. New York: New York Univ. Press, 2001.

————. *Out of Place.* New York: Vintage, 2000.

————. *The Question of Palestine.* 1979. Reprint, New York: Vintage Books, 1992.

————. "Zionism from the Standpoint of Its Victims." *Social Text* 1 (Winter 1979): 7–58.

Salaita, Steve. *Anti-Arab Racism in the USA: Where It Comes from and What It Means for Politics Today.* Ann Arbor, Mich.: Pluto Press, 2006.

Saliba, Therese. "Resisting Invisibility: Arab Americans in Academia and Activism." In *Arabs in America: Building a New Future*, ed. Michael W. Suleiman. Philadelphia: Temple Univ. Press, 1999.

Samhan, Helen Hatab. "Not Quite White: Race Classification and the Arab-American Experience." In *Arabs in America: Building a New Future*, ed. Michael W. Suleiman. Philadelphia: Temple Univ. Press, 1999.

Samson, Hugh. "Letter to *New York Times* Editor." *Electronic Intifada.* http://www.electronicintifada.net/v2/article3315.shtml.

Sandoval, Chela. "Feminism and Racism: A Report on the 1981 National Women's Studies Association Conference." In *Making Face, Making Soul/Haciendo Caras*, ed. Gloria Anzaldúa, 55–71. San Francisco: Aunt Lute, 1990.

Schlussel, Debbie. "Barack Hussein Obama: Once a Muslim, Always a Muslim." Debbieschlussel.com, Dec. 18, 2006. http://www.debbieschlussel.com/archives/2006/12/barack_hussein.html.

Scott, Joan W. "Gender: A Useful Category of Historical Analysis." *The American Historical Review* 91, no. 5 (1986): 1053–75.

———. *The Politics of the Veil*. Princeton: Princeton Univ. Press, 2007.

Selfa, Lance. "Right-Wing Republic? Bush's Victory, the Collapse of Liberalism, and the Future of U.S. Politics." *International Socialist Review* 39 (Jan.–Feb. 2005).

Sells, Michael. *Approaching the Qur'an: The Early Revelations*. Ashland, Ore.: White Cloud Press, 2001.

Shadmi, Erella. "Gendering and Racializing Israeli Jewish Ashkenazi Whiteness." *Women's Studies International Forum* 26, no. 3 (2003): 205–19.

Shakir, Evelyn. *Bint Arab: Arab and Arab American Women in the United States*. Westport, Conn.: Praeger, 1997.

Shelton, Jim. "Left Out of Obama Fest." *New Haven Register*, Nov. 16, 2008. http://www.nhregister.com/articles/2008/11/16/life/doc4920013831207710106350.txt.

Sherman, Fraser. "Beware! The Islamofascists Walk among Us!" *McClatchy-Tribune Business News*, May 31, 2008. http://www.thedestinlog.com/opinion/among_4840_article.html/beware_islamofascists.html.

Shohat, Ella. "Dislocated Identities: Reflections of an Arab-Jew." *Movement Research: Performance Journal*, no. 5 (Fall–Winter 1992): 8.

———. "Gender and the Culture of Empire: Toward a Feminist Ethnography of the Cinema." *Quarterly Review of Film and Video* 131, nos. 1–2 (1991): 45–84.

———. "Imaging Terra Incognita: The Disciplinary Gaze of Empire." *Public Culture* 3, no. 2 (1991): 41–70.

———. "The Invention of the Mizrahim." *Journal of Palestine Studies* 29, no. 1 (1999): 5–20.

———. *Israeli Cinema: East/West and the Politics of Representation*. Austin: Univ. of Texas Press, 1989.

———. "Master Narrative/Counter Readings." In *Resisting Images: Essays on Cinema and History*, ed. Robert Sklar and Charles Musser, 251–78. Philadelphia: Temple Univ. Press, 1990.

———. "Mizrahi Feminism: The Politics of Gender, Race, and Multiculturalism." *News from Within* 12, no. 4 (1996): 17–26.

———. "The Narrative of the Nation and the Discourse of Modernization: The Case of the Mizrahim." *Critique* 10 (Spring 1997): 3–18.

———. "The 'Postcolonial' in Translation: Reading Said in Hebrew." *Journal of Palestine Studies* 33, no. 3 (2004): 55–75.

———. "Rethinking Jews and Muslims: Quincentennial Reflections." *Middle East Report* (Sept.–Oct. 1992): 25–29.

———. "Rupture and Return: Zionist Discourse and the Study of Arab Jews." *Social Text* 21, no. 2 (2003): 49–74.

———. "Sephardim in Israel: Zionism from the Standpoint of Its Jewish Victims." *Social Text* 19–20 (1988): 1–35.

———. "Staging the Quincentenary: The Middle East and the Americas." *Third Text* 21 (Winter 1992–93): 95–105.

———. "Taboo Memories, Diasporic Visions: Columbus, Palestine, and Arab-Jews." In *Performing Hybridity*, ed. May Joseph and Jennifer Fink, 131–56. Minneapolis: Univ. of Minnesota Press, 1999.

———. *Taboo Memories, Diasporic Voices*. Durham, N.C.: Duke Univ. Press, 2006.

———, ed. *Talking Visions: Multicultural Feminism in a Transnational Age*. Cambridge, Mass., and New York: MIT Press and the New Museum, 1997.

———. "Zionism from the Standpoint of Its Jewish Victims." *Social Text* 19–20 (Fall 1988): 1–35.

Shohat, Ella, Aamir Mufti, and Anne McClintock, eds. *Dangerous Liaisons: Gender, Nation, and Postcolonial Perspectives*. Minneapolis: Univ. of Minnesota Press, 1997.

Shohat, Ella, and Robert Stam. *Culture Wars in Translation*. New York: New York Univ. Press, forthcoming.

———. "Traveling Multiculturalism: A Trinational Debate in Translation." In *Postcolonial Studies and Beyond*, ed. Ania Loomba, Suvir Kaul, Matti Bunzel, Antoinette Burton, and Jed Esty, 293–316. Durham, N.C.: Duke Univ. Press, 2005.

———. *Unthinking Eurocentrism: Multiculturalism and the Media*. New York: Routledge, 1994.

Smith, Andrea. *Conquest: Sexual Violence and American Indian Genocide*. Boston: South End Press, 2005.

———. "Heteropatriarchy and the Three Pillars of White Supremacy: Rethinking Women of Color Organizing." In *Color of Violence: The INCITE! Anthology*, ed. Incite! Women of Color Against Violence, 66–73. Boston: South End Press, 2006.

Smith, Andrea, and J. Kehaulani Kauanui. "Native Feminisms Engage American Studies." *American Quarterly* 60, no. 2 (2008): 241–49.

Smith, Ben. "Muslims Barred from Picture at Obama Event." Politico.com, June 18, 2008. http://www.politico.com/news/stories/0608/11168.html.

———. "Muslim Women Moved from Obama TV Spot." CBS News, June 18, 2008. http://www.cbsnews.com/stories/2008/06/18/politics/politico/main4191084.shtml ?source=mostpop_story.

Smith, Ben, and Jonathan Martin. "Untraceable E-mails Spread Obama Rumor." Politico .com, Oct. 13, 2007. http://www.politico.com/news/stories/1007/6314.html.

Sommers, Christina Hoff. "The Subjection of Islamic Women." *Weekly Standard*, May 21, 2007.

Sontag, Susan. "On Courage and Resistance." *Nation*, May 5, 2003, 11–14.

Spencer, Robert. "Islamic Misogyny." *Front Page*, Jan. 4, 2008. http://www.frontpagemag.com/Articles.

Spivak, Gayatri Chakravorty. "Can the Subaltern Speak?" In *Marxism and the Interpretation of Culture*, ed. C. Nelson and L. Grossberg, 271–313. Basingstoke: Macmillan Education, 1988.

Sprinker, Michael, ed. *Edward Said: A Critical Reader*. London and New York: Blackwell, 1992.

Stansell, Christine. "Sisterly Sentimentalism: Feminism and the Politics of Empathy." Presentation at the Sense and Sentiment Conference, Pomona College, Feb. 11, 2006.

Steinem, Gloria. *Revolution from Within: A Book of Self-Esteem*. New York: Little, Brown, 1993.

Steinmetz, George. "Return to Empire: The New U.S. Imperialism in Comparative Historical Perspective." *Sociological Theory* 23, no. 4 (2005): 339–67.

Stern, Susie, and Steve Grossman. "Hillary Clinton: Israel Connection." Jewish News of Greater Phoenix Online, Feb. 1, 2008. http://www.jewishaz.com/issues/story.mv?080201+clinton.

Stoler, Ann. *Haunted by Empire: Geographies of Intimacy in North American History*. Durham: Duke Univ. Press, 2006.

Stone-Mediatore, Shari. *Reading Across Borders: Storytelling and Knowledges of Resistance*. New York: Palgrave Macmillan, 2003.

Stowasser, Barbara. *Women in the Qur'an, Traditions, and Interpretations*. New York: Oxford Univ. Press, 1994.

"A Student's Guide to Hosting Islamo-Fascism Awareness Week." Terrorism Awareness Network. http://www.terrorismawareness.org/islamo-fascism/49/a-students-guide-to-hosting-islamo-fascism-awareness-week.

Suleiman, Michael, and Baha Abu Louban. Introduction to *Arab Americans: Continuity and Change*, ed. Michael Suleiman and Baha Abu Louban. Belmont, Mass.: AAUG, 1989.

Svirsky, Gila. "Feminist Peace Activism During the al-Aqsa Intifada." In *Women and the Politics of Military Confrontation: Palestinian and Israeli Gendered Narratives of Dislocation*, ed. Nahla Abdo and Ronit Lentin, 234–48. New York: Bergham Books, 2002.

Toensing, Gale Courey. "Journalist Amer Abdelhadi Has Died." Corner Report, Nov. 13, 2006. http://www.thecornerreport.com/index.php?p=968&more=1&c=1&tb=1&pb=1#more968.

Tompkins, Kyla Wazana. "Towards a Sephardic Jewish Renaissance." *Tikkun* (Mar.–Apr. 2002).

Toolis, Kevin. "Walls of Death." *Observer*, Nov. 23, 2003. http://www.aljazeerah.info/Opinion%20editorials/2003%20Opinion%20Editorials/November/24%20o/Walls%20of%20death%20Kevin%20Toolis.htm.

———. "Why Women Turn to Suicide Bombing." *Observer*, Oct. 12, 2003. http://www.countercurrents.org/pa-toolis121003.htm.

"Transcript: Obama's Speech at AIPAC." National Public Radio, June 4, 2008. http://www.npr.org/templates/story/story.php?storyId=91150432.

United Nations General Assembly Convention on Genocide. http://www.hrweb.org/legal/genocide.html.

"UN Press Conference on Gaza Humanitarian Crisis." http://www.un.org/News/briefings/docs/2009/090120_Gaza.

Urquhart, Brian. *Ralph Bunche: An American Life*. New York: W. W. Norton, 1993.

Valby, Karen. Book review of *Goddess: Inside Madonna*, by Barbara Victor. *Entertainment Weekly*, Nov. 23, 2001, 74. http://mutex.gmu.edu:2079/pqdweb?index=1&did=000000092322114&SrchMode=1&sid=2&Fmt=3&VInst=PROD&VType=PQD&RQT=309&VName=PQD&TS=1101145767&clientId=31810.

Valerio, Max Wolf. "Now That You're a White Man: Changing Sex in a Postmodern World—Being, Becoming, and Borders." In *This Bridge We Call Home: Radical Visions for Transformation*, ed. Gloria Anzaldúa and AnaLouise Keating. New York: Routledge, 2002.

Victor, Barbara. *Army of Roses: Inside the World of Palestinian Suicide Bombers*. New York: Rodale, 2003.

Visweswaran, Kamala. "Race and the Culture of Anthropology." *American Anthropologist* 100, no. 1 (1998): 70–83.

Waddud, Amina. *Qur'an and Woman: Rereading the Sacred Text from a Woman's Perspective*. New York: Oxford Univ. Press, 1999.

Warschawski, Michel. *On the Border*. Trans. Levi Laub. Cambridge, Mass.: South End Press, 2005.

Weinberg, Leonard, Ami Pedahzur, and Daphna Canetti-Nisim. "The Social and Religious Characteristics of Suicide Bombers and Their Victims." *Terrorism and Political Violence* 15, no. 3 (2003): 139–53.

Weiss, Philip. "Why These Tickets Are Too Hot for New York." *Nation*, Apr. 3, 2006, 13–18.

Weitz, Joseph. "A Solution to the Refugee Problem." *Davar*, Sept. 29, 1967.

Wheaton, Sarah. "Obama Calls Muslim Women Barred from Stage." *Caucus*, June 18, 2008.

———. "Obama Camp Apologizes to Muslim Women." *Caucus*, June 18, 2008.

Woolf, Virginia. *Three Guineas*. New York: Harcourt, 1938.

World Bank. "West Bank and Gaza: Economic Development and Prospects, March 2008." http://go.worldbank.org/A6Y2KDMCJ0.

Wright, Tom, and Therese Saliba. *Checkpoint: The Palestinians after Oslo*. Arab Film Distribution, 1997.

———. *Checkpoint: The Palestinians after Oslo*. Arab Film Distribution, 2007.

———. "Rachel Corrie's Case for Justice." Counterpunch.org, Mar. 15–16, 2008. http://counterpunch.org/wright03152008/html.

Yamada, Mitsuye. "Asian Pacific American Women and Feminism." In *This Bridge Called My Back: Writings by Radical Women of Color*, ed. Cherríe Moraga and Gloria Anzaldúa, 71–75. New York: Kitchen Table Women of Color Press, 1981.

———. "Invisibility Is an Unnatural Disaster: Reflections of an Asian American Woman." In *This Bridge Called My Back: Writings by Radical Women of Color*, ed. Cherríe Moraga and Gloria Anzaldúa, 35–40. New York: Kitchen Table Women of Color Press, 1981.

Yuval-Davis, Nira. *Gender and Nationalism*. London: Sage, 1998.

Zaatari, Zeina. "On Silencing Arab Feminists." Nov. 2007. http://www.arab-american.net/Community/Community%20Pages/onsilencingarabfeminists.html.

Zunes, Stephen. "Is Kerry Really More Open than Bush to Alternative Foreign Policy Perspectives?" Common Dreams. http://www.commondreams.org/views2004/0915-13.htm.

Index

383